THE OTTOMAN CANON AND THE CONSTRUCTION OF ARABIC AND TURKISH LITERATURES

Edinburgh Studies on the Ottoman Empire
Series Editor: Kent F. Schull

Published and forthcoming titles

The Ottoman Canon and the Construction of Arabic and Turkish Literatures
C. Ceyhun Arslan

Migrating Texts: Circulating Translations around the Ottoman Mediterranean
Edited by Marilyn Booth

Death and Life in the Ottoman Palace: Revelations of the Sultan Abdülhamid I Tomb
Douglas Brookes

Ottoman Sunnism: New Perspectives
Edited by Vefa Erginbaş

Jews and Palestinians in the Late Ottoman Era, 1908–1914: Claiming the Homeland
Louis A. Fishman

Spiritual Vernacular of the Early Ottoman Frontier: The Yazıcıoğlu Family
Carlos Grenier

The Politics of Armenian Migration to North America, 1885–1915: Sojourners, Smugglers and Dubious Citizens
David Gutman

The Kizilbash-Alevis in Ottoman Anatolia: Sufism, Politics and Community
Ayfer Karakaya-Stump

Çemberlitaş Hamamı in Istanbul: The Biographical Memoir of a Turkish Bath
Nina Macaraig

Hagia Sophia in the Long Nineteenth Century
Edited by Emily Neumeier and Benjamin Anderson

The Kurdish Nobility in the Ottoman Empire: Loyalty, Autonomy and Privilege
Nilay Özok-Gündoğan

Nineteenth-century Local Governance in Ottoman Bulgaria: Politics in Provincial Councils
M. Safa Saraçoğlu

Prisons in the Late Ottoman Empire: Microcosms of Modernity
Kent F. Schull

Ruler Visibility and Popular Belonging in the Ottoman Empire, 1808–1908
Darin N. Stephanov

The North Caucasus Borderland: Between Muscovy and the Ottoman Empire, 1555–1605
Murat Yasar

Children and Childhood in the Ottoman Empire: From the 15th to the 20th Century
Edited by Gülay Yilmaz and Fruma Zachs

euppublishing.com/series/esoe

THE OTTOMAN CANON AND THE CONSTRUCTION OF ARABIC AND TURKISH LITERATURES

C. Ceyhun Arslan

EDINBURGH
University Press

To my parents, Melahat Arslan and Fikri Arslan

Edinburgh University Press is one of the leading university presses in the UK. We publish academic books and journals in our selected subject areas across the humanities and social sciences, combining cutting-edge scholarship with high editorial and production values to produce academic works of lasting importance. For more information visit our website: edinburghuniversitypress.com

Edinburgh University Press Ltd
13 Infirmary Street
Edinburgh EH1 1LT

First published in hardback by Edinburgh University Press 2024

Typeset in Jaghbuni by
Cheshire Typesetting Ltd, Cuddington, Cheshire

A CIP record for this book is available from the British Library

ISBN 978 1 3995 2582 4 (hardback)
ISBN 978 1 3995 2583 1 (paperback)
ISBN 978 1 3995 2584 8 (webready PDF)
ISBN 978 1 3995 2585 5 (epub)

Contents

Acknowledgements vi
Note on Translation and Transliteration x

Introduction: Beyond the Influence Paradigm 1
1. A Multilingual Ottoman Ocean: Taverns, Exclusions and Ziya Pasha's *Harabat* 29
2. Jurjī Zaydān, Literary Comparisons and the Formation of Arabic and Turkish Literatures 56
3. The Ottoman Tarboosh: Disguise and the Novel Genre in Ahmet Midhat's *Hasan Mellah* and Muḥammad al-Muwayliḥī's *What ᶜĪsā ibn Hishām Told Us* 83
4. Kaᶜb ibn Zuhayr Weeps for Sultan Murad IV: Baghdad, Translation and the Turkish Language in Maᶜrūf al-Ruṣāfī's Works 118
5. From 'Ottoman Literature is Arabic Literature' to 'Arabs Possess a Literature': Hacı İbrahim, Ahmet Rasim and the Fetters of Influence 145
6. Family Matters: Oedipus, Tawfīq al-Ḥakīm and Ahmet Hamdi Tanpınar 170
Conclusion: Modernity, Ottoman Saᶜdī and Ottoman al-Mutanabbī 196

References 205
Index 224

Acknowledgements

Acknowledgments are one the most difficult sections to write in an academic monograph. I profusely apologise in advance to people who supported me emotionally and academically throughout the many years I worked on *The Ottoman Canon and the Construction of Arabic and Turkish Literatures* yet who I did not address in this section. I promise to express my gratitude to them in other ways.

My parents, Melahat Arslan and Fikri Arslan, have unconditionally supported my career, even if they may have no idea about both the joys and difficulties of life in academia. They have made many sacrifices for my education, without which this book would not have come into existence. They taught me that hard work eventually pays off, even if disappointments abound in the process.

My PhD advisor, William Granara, steered my life towards new and exciting pathways that I could not have fathomed. He envisioned the core idea of *The Ottoman Canon* and has given me invaluable suggestions, both during my doctoral studies and after graduation. As an Ottoman historian who also supports literary critics, Cemal Kafadar has given me the courage to write a book that ultimately appeared in the Edinburgh Studies on the Ottoman Empire series. Karen L. Thornber's unfaltering commitment to opening up the discipline of Comparative Literature beyond its Eurocentric boundaries has inspired my teaching and scholarship. Afsaneh Najmabadi has taught me lessons on friendship and made me feel at home on Thanksgiving days when the streets of Cambridge were empty. I also thank Sami Alkyam, Ali Asani, David Damrosch, Justine Landau, Himmet Taşkömür, Gülru Necipoğlu and Malika Zeghal, who all enrichened my PhD experience at Harvard. Greg Halaby and Han Hsien Liew, my special friends, witnessed me transforming into the person and scholar I have now become.

Acknowledgements

If I achieve anything in my academic career, it is mainly thanks to the support I received from Aylin Küntay, who was the Dean of the College of Social Sciences and Humanities during my first years at Koç University. Sooyong Kim's commitment to my department has motivated me to do better, as he also provided valuable suggestions on my book proposal. My department colleagues – Nazmi Ağıl, Meliz Ergin, Şima İmşir, Sooyong Kim and Mehmet Fatih Uslu – have helped me thrive in a collegial and peaceful environment. Alexis Wick and Dahlia Gubara, my colleagues from the history department, have supported me with their warm hospitality and firm belief in my project. Mustafa Ergül and Rana Otur from Koç University's Suna Kıraç Library searched for and shared with me numerous issues from the Ottoman newspapers that I quote in Chapter 5. I finished the final stretches of this book in the 'writing marathons' I shared with Burcu Gürsel, Burcu Kayışçı Akkoyun, Gordon Marsh and Mehmet Fatih Uslu, who saved me from the social isolation that scholarly life often entails. I will never forget the heartfelt joy that Melih Levi expressed when he learned that I had signed a book contract. Charles D. Sabatos's wisdom and exemplary friendship has sustained me during joyful and difficult times.

I laid out the basic tenets and ideas for Chapter 3 during my postdoctoral fellowship at the Research Center for Anatolian Civilizations at Koç University in Fall 2017. I thank Bilal Orfali, who invited me to the American University of Beirut (AUB) in order to spend a productive summer in 2019, and the Koç Visiting Scholar Program, which provided financial support for this stay. I consulted in AUB's library many Arabic books I could not have found anywhere else. Selim Kuru sent me a supportive email with constructive feedback after my article in *Comparative Literature Studies* (2017) had been published, and I incorporated his suggestions into Chapter 1. I am grateful to Adam Talib, who patiently went over earlier versions of the article that appeared in the *Journal of Arabic Literature* (2019). That article was difficult to write since it attempted to generate a new conceptual framework; however, Adam Talib's support helped me finish that essay, which then inspired me to write this book. Suzanne Pinckney Stetkevych and Huda J. Fakhreddine provided me with key suggestions for my chapter in *The Routledge Handbook of Arabic Poetry*, which I incorporated into Chapter 4. Matthew L. Keegan meticulously read Chapter 5 and gave very helpful comments. Özen Nergis Dolcerocca showed invaluable support when she read Chapter 6.

I presented earlier versions of this book's chapters at the University of Texas at Austin (2023), EUME's (Europe in the Middle East-The Middle East in Europe) Berliner Seminar (2023), the American Comparative Literature Association Annual Meeting (2021 and 2023), Harvard

University (2018 and 2022), the Swedish Research Institute in Istanbul (2022), Mimar Sinan University (2022), Columbia University (2017 and 2022), the Middle East Studies Association Annual Meeting (2017 and 2019), Ibn Haldun University (2018) and Bilkent University (2018). My colleagues who listened to these presentations pushed my thinking in new directions.

A portion of Chapter 1 has been published as 'Canons as Reservoirs: The Ottoman Ocean in Ziya Pasha's *Harabat* and Reframing the History of Comparative Literature', *Comparative Literature Studies* 54, no. 1 (2017): 731–48, https://doi.org/10.5325/complitstudies.54.4.0731 (Copyright © 2017 by the Penn State University Press. Used with permission from the Penn State University Press). While the article in *Comparative Literature Studies* focused on *Harabat*'s introduction only, Chapter 1 also provides an extensive analysis of Arabic, Persian and Turkish poems in *Harabat*. An earlier and shorter iteration of Chapter 2 appeared in the *Journal of Arabic Literature*: 'Entanglements between *the Tanzimat* and *al-Nahḍah*: Jurjī Zaydān between *Tārīkh ādāb al-lughah al-turkiyyah* and *Tārīkh ādāb al-lughah al-^{c}arabiyyah*', *Journal of Arabic Literature* 50, no. 3/4 (2019): 258–84, https://doi.org/10.1163/1570064x-12341389 (Copyright © 2019 by C. Ceyhun Arslan. Used with permission from Brill). A small portion of Chapter 4 and Conclusion has been published as 'Ka^{c}b ibn Zuhayr Weeps for Sultan Murad IV: Baghdad, Heritage and the Ottoman Empire in Ma^{c}rūf al-Ruṣāfī's Poetry', in *The Routledge Handbook of Arabic Poetry*, ed. Suzanne Pinckney Stetkevych and Huda J. Fakhreddine (London: Routledge, 2024), 201–18 (Copyright © 2024 by C. Ceyhun Arslan. Used with permission from Taylor & Francis Group). Unlike this chapter, *The Ottoman Canon* examines al-Ruṣāfī's prose writings. The chapter in Stetkevych and Fakhreddine's edited volume also gives a more comprehensive analysis of al-Ruṣāfī's poetry.

The Ottoman Canon was subsidised in part by Harvard Studies in Comparative Literature. Harvard's Schofield Publication Subsidy provided generous support for various costs related to the book's production.

Finally, I want to express my sincere gratitude to Edinburgh University Press. Thanks to its high level of professionalism, the publication process turned into a true source of joy. Rachel Bridgewater, Emma House and Kent F. Schull immediately understood the vision I had for this book. Isobel Birks and Eddie Clark promptly answered every single enquiry I had. The book has significantly improved in quality thanks to Nina Macaraig's superb editing. *The Ottoman Canon* underwent numerous rounds of reviews and revisions. The feedback I received from the Series Advisory Board of the Edinburgh Studies on the Ottoman Empire helped me re-envision the book's main subject and overall structure. Two anonymous reviewers carefully read my book proposal and sample chapters and provided comprehensive and constructive feedback. Later, the book's final typescript received highly supportive comments. I implemented almost all the suggestions from these reviewers, who helped *The Ottoman Canon* get into its best possible shape. Of course, all errors and omissions remain my own.

Note on Translation and Transliteration

Whenever available, I have used published English translations; otherwise, translations from Arabic, Persian, French, Ottoman Turkish and modern Turkish into English are mine. Where I have used a published translation, I have also indicated the page number of the source text in which the original quote appears. I am grateful to the copy-editors who made the necessary grammatical corrections in some of my English translations and occasionally provided stylistic suggestions for them.

Generally, I have followed the transliteration system of the *International Journal of Middle Eastern Studies* (IJMES) for the sake of consistency. As per IJMES guidelines, I have employed modern Turkish orthography for Ottoman Turkish words since *The Ottoman Canon* uses both Ottoman and modern Turkish sources. If a word of Arabic origin appeared in a Turkish source text, I have usually used the Turkish orthography. Similarly, if a word of Turkish origin appeared in an Arabic source text, I have usually used the Arabic transliteration. However, I have preferred Turkish orthography for those authors who have been studied almost exclusively within the field of Turkish literature (for example, Namık Kemal), even when their name appeared in Arabic works, much like I have used Arabic transliteration for authors who have been studied almost exclusively within the field of Arabic literature (for example, Jurjī Zaydān), even when their name appeared in Turkish works. I have provided both Arabic transliteration and Turkish orthography when referring to several authors or historical figures who have been studied in the fields of both Turkish literature and Arabic literature (for example, Mehmed Ali/Muḥammad ʿAlī Pasha).

For Arabic and Turkish words that are also used in English (for example, tarboosh), I have employed the English spelling. My transliteration of Arabic poetry excerpts has included accents in word endings (for example, *sayfu*), while I have not indicated accents in word endings when transliterating Arabic prose texts. Headline-style capitalisation appears in Turkish titles and sentence-style capitalisation in Arabic titles. I have often followed the Turkish Language Association guidelines for the use of the circumflex accent (*düzeltme işareti*) in Turkish words. I have also used circumflex accents if they were already used in the titles of published works.

If the publication dates of my sources are given in the Hijri calendar, I have retained these dates and also provided their equivalents in the Gregorian calendar. For the few sources with their publication dates given in the Rumi calendar, I have only provided the equivalent of these dates in the Gregorian calendar.

Ottoman and Turkish Studies often refer to the full name of all writers who were born before 1935, even after the first time the writer is mentioned, since the surname law in Turkey entered into force only in 1935. This is why, for instance, I have referred to Süleyman Nazif as 'Süleyman Nazif' and not as 'Nazif' throughout the book. For authors who acquired a new surname after the 1935 law, I have often put a squared parenthesis around their surnames. I have not used squared parenthesis for a few authors whose surnames are widely known (for example, Ahmet Hamdi Tanpınar).

Introduction: Beyond the Influence Paradigm

The Meccan scholar Quṭb al-Dīn al-Nahrawālī (1511/12–82) travelled to Istanbul because he wanted the Ottoman administration to dismiss a military commander in Medina, Piri. During his stay in Istanbul in 1558, al-Nahrawālī met many prominent people of the Ottoman court. One of these was Ahmed Çelebi (d. 1563), who was the son of the famous grand mufti Ebussuud Efendi (d. 1574) and served as instructor at the Sahn-ı Seman Medrese in Istanbul. Al-Nahrawālī was impressed with Ahmed Çelebi's great erudition and wrote: 'In his magnificent expressions, his purity of speech and his Arab-like qualities, he was similar to his father, inasmuch as he recited to me from memory and with the utmost mastery, chasteness of speech and harmony of sense, a number of al-Ḥarīrī's *Maqāmāt* as well as some verses from his own Arabic, Persian and Turkish poetry'.[1] Later, Ahmed Çelebi recited to al-Nahrawālī the following Arabic lines from his quintain or *takhmīs*:[2]

> The pearls of my necklaces o'er the horizons have I strewn
> And my instructive thoughts have I set to verse in the path of poetry,
> Who, then, would my equal be, when such are my singular gems of poesy?
>
> Time is but one of my odes' reciters;
> Whenever I a poem utter, Time becomes a reciter.[3]

While Ahmed Çelebi had composed the first three lines, the last two lines belonged to al-Mutanabbī (d. 965). Highly impressed with this *takhmīs*, al-Nahrawālī indicated that even the most eloquent Arabs could not create such a work.[4]

Al-Nahrawālī witnessed an imperialist practice of the Ottoman Empire that incorporated works by poets such as al-Mutanabbī into a multilingual repertoire of authors and works that, for poets like Ahmed Çelebi, constituted the Ottoman canon. Earlier scholarship has adopted an 'influence paradigm' and argued that Ottoman literature developed under the strong influence of Arabic and Persian literatures before it modernised under the influence of French literature in the nineteenth century. As Victoria Rowe Holbrook has put it, this paradigm resulted from the significant emphasis that Orientalist philology put on a culture's origins, hence its valorisation of Arabic and Persian over Turkish:

> Among the organizing principles basic to Orientalist philology – following one trajectory of Muslim scholarly practice – was the positing of Islamic culture as a continuity beginning in the seventh century with the advent of the prophet Mohammed's mission. It proceeded narratively from the study of the Arabic Koran and 'classic Islamic' golden age, institutionally producing scholars of Arabic, Persian, Turkish, and periods designated by the successive political ascendance of users of each language. The culture of each period was evaluated as an instance of Islamic history to be traced back along a text-chain to its original (=more Islamic) source.[5]

As a result, 'by virtue of the essentialist value philology assigned to origin, Turkish, being most distant from it, would be least worthy of study'.[6]

Arabic works like al-Mutanabbī's poems are today often designated as a source of influence under which Ottoman identity took shape, since, as Saliha Paker has noted, 'the "influence" studies established by [Fuad] Köprülü's methodology became a major research paradigm for future generations of Turkish scholars'.[7] This paradigm overlooks many Ottoman Turkish writings that considered these poems a key constituent of Ottoman culture, rather than works of 'Arab ancestors' who had a clear cultural superiority over Ottoman writers. These writings did not express a sense of submission and anxiety as they engaged with the Arabic and Persian traditions. Nor did their authors necessarily identify themselves as part of an Arabised or Persianate cultural community due to this engagement. In fact, some of these authors even categorised Arabic and Persian writings as Ottoman. *The Ottoman Canon and the Construction of Arabic and Turkish Literatures* moves beyond this 'influence paradigm' to undermine what Christopher Markiewicz has called 'a twentieth-century concern with nationally circumscribed historiographical fields that privileges the linear evolution of distinct monolingual literary traditions, whether Turkish, Persian, or Arabic'.[8] Hence, it challenges the tendency to study Ottoman literature as Turkish literature and to overlook what I call the 'new life' that al-Mutanabbī's poems attained in the Ottoman context.

Literary Modernity and the Canon

Arabic and Turkish literary modernities have been defined by a wide range of stylistic and thematic shifts that emerged when writers began adopting Western styles and forms in the nineteenth century.[9] To provide a reassessment of this definition, my book examines the hitherto neglected engagement of late Ottoman Arabic and Turkish writings with the Ottoman canon. Alexander Jabbari has studied Persian literary histories of the nineteenth and early twentieth centuries in order to demonstrate that refashionings of the Persianate past have played a fundamental role for Persian literary modernity in both Indian and Iranian contexts. According to Jabbari, these refashionings also caused Persian literature to be 'structured by a sense of time that is particular to European capitalist modernity'.[10] In other words, modern Persian literary histories have compiled Persian texts in a linear, chronological order and reinforced a stark division between classical and modern Persian literatures. As a result, these histories not only erased the 'cosmopolitan connections' that the Persianate texts had with other milieus, but also 'present[ed] an image of national heritage that appeared to be sui generis, independent, self-contained'.[11]

In a similar vein, *The Ottoman Canon* will examine how Ottoman texts refashioned Arabic, Turkish and Persian textual traditions during the late nineteenth and early twentieth centuries. Contrary to the typical assumption, not all Ottoman writings defined Ottoman literature as the compilation of Turkish works produced within the Ottoman Empire (1299–1922). Instead, they envisioned an Ottoman canon that included a reservoir of works from diverse periods and cultures, such as al-Mutanabbī's poems. My book pays attention to the reconfiguration of the relationships among the different linguistic traditions of the multilingual Ottoman canon during the late nineteenth and early twentieth centuries. Many late Ottoman Turkish writings classified pre-modern Arabic texts as works of distant ancestors rather than as integral constituents of this canon. Authors of late Ottoman Arabic works categorised the same pre-modern Arabic texts as the classics of their heritage, while they also translated or wrote about late Ottoman Turkish writings. My book will present historically contextualised close readings of late Ottoman and post-Ottoman Arabic and Turkish works from authors such as Ziya Pasha (1829–80), Ahmet Midhat (1844–1912) and Tawfīq al-Ḥakīm (1898–1987). Thus, it challenges the prevalent view that classical Arabic heritage served as the root from which modern Arabic literature naturally grew.

While *The Ottoman Canon* calls for moving beyond what it calls the 'influence paradigm', it does not claim that Ottoman poets never engaged with Arabic and Persian works. Orit Bashkin and Sooyong Kim have described the features of what they call 'an Ottoman literati' in discussing Evliya Çelebi (1611–c. 1682), author of the famous seventeenth-century travelogue *Seyahatname* (*Book of Travels*): 'Evliya himself was a Muslim and an Ottoman literati, Turkophone in speech and received an education appropriate to his religious affiliation and social rank, which entailed a training in Arabic and Persian to the extent that he could give instruction at least in their elevated varieties. In addition, he was expected to engage with the respective literatures and as a testament to that, the *Seyahatname* is replete with Arabic and particularly Persian literary references'.[12] According to Kim, members of the Ottoman literati needed to have certain qualifications. They had to be Muslim, work for the Ottoman administration in upper-level positions and become familiar with the Arabic, Persian and Turkish literary traditions.[13] These members generally did not feel a sense of anxiety when they drew on Arabic and Persian works. In fact, the Ottoman poet Nefi (d. 1635) claimed that his Persian verses were so advanced that they '[s]pread tremor in the realms of India and Persia'.[14] While poets such as Nefi wrote in Persian or even drew on the Persian canon, they did not necessarily consider themselves part of a Persianate community.

In contrast, Halide Edib [Adıvar] (1884–1964) captured 'the influence paradigm' as she described the impact of Persian literature on Ottoman authors:

> The philosophical and mystical beauty of Persian literature with its exquisite delicacy of form made me feel that there is a spirituality and significance in form when it achieves the heights which it undoubtedly has in Persian literature. But its very perfection is a danger to any other literature and art which fall under its sway. It acts on them very powerfully and always in the direction of destroying originality. The admirers and imitators of the Persian culture were entirely enslaved and chained by its form as well as its spirit, and any slavery to form creates rigid and conventional artists. Once caught in such a formal school, any new and freer personal expression of beauty is stifled and killed. And this was what happened to the old Turkish literature.[15]

Here, Halide Edib's writings posit Persian literature as a source of influence the perfection of which enslaved Turkish literature. Like many other authors of her time, Halide Edib reflected on issues of sovereignty: Turkish literature never could have declared independence because it remained under the influence of Persian literature. Halide Edib also generated a distinction between what she called an 'old Turkish literature' and a 'new Turkish literature'. Therefore, as I argue throughout this book, attempts to reinforce a strong boundary between 'old literature' and 'new literature' have habituated critics to study Turkish literature as a category that has always existed throughout the centuries.

Halide Edib's observations capture the epistemological shifts that shaped the late Ottoman period. Both the interviewer and authors who feature in *Diyorlar ki* (They are Saying So, 1918) – a set of interviews that Ruşen Eşref [Ünaydın] (1892–1959) conducted with various authors such as Nigar Hanım (1862–1918), Sami Paşazade Sezai (1860–1936), Halid Ziya [Uşaklıgil] (1865–1945), Rıza Tevfik (1869–1949) and Cenab Şahabeddin (1871–1934) – frequently used the terms 'old literature' (*eski edebiyat, edebiyat-ı kadime*) and 'new literature' (*edebiyat-ı cedide*).[16] Here, 'old literature' refers to the classical Ottoman poetry that had developed under the Arabic and Persian influence, while the 'new literature' refers to the literature that started to 'modernise and rejuvenate' in the nineteenth century due to its engagement with the West. The prevalent assumption that the nineteenth century witnessed a transition from 'old literature' to 'new literature' has caused critics to think that 'Arabic literature' and 'Turkish literature' had existed throughout the centuries; they merely 'modernised' and 'renewed' themselves during the late Ottoman period. Nevertheless, *The Ottoman Canon* will demonstrate that there were not necessarily two distinct monolingual literary traditions of Arabic and Turkish that awaited rejuvenation as 'pioneers' such as Namık Kemal (1840–88) or Muḥammad al-Muwayliḥī (1858–1930) solely 'modernised' their respective national heritages.

As critics have maintained a stark boundary between 'classical literature' and 'new' or 'modern literature', they overlooked many pre-Ottoman poets's 'afterlives' in the Ottoman context. 'Afterlife' has become one of the most widely used concepts in Comparative Literature over the past few decades.[17] The discipline has thus steered attention to the new receptions, or 'new lives', that a text attains in a new context and moved beyond an almost exclusive focus on a text's original context, or its 'source culture', as the sole milieu in which it should be studied. In a similar vein, my book pays attention to the 'new life' that pre-Ottoman Arabic and Persian works adopted in the Ottoman context. Ultimately, *The Ottoman Canon* argues that, as Ottoman writers incorporated poets from pre-Ottoman times, such as al-Mutanabbī, into the Ottoman canon, they generated an 'Ottoman al-Mutanabbī' in their works.

The institutional divisions that Holbrook has identified as the impact of Orientalist philology has also caused critics to overlook al-Mutanabbī's Ottoman afterlife and instead study al-Mutanabbī within the context of the classical Arabic canon only. Instead, my work studies pre-Ottoman poets such as Kaᶜb ibn Zuhayr (d. c. 646/47) as part of the multilingual Ottoman canon. Samuel Hodgkin has analysed how Soviet writers contributed to 'the replacement of a Persianate canon, a set of literary practices and model texts, with *the* Persian canon, a pantheon of heroic writers and a discursive "heritage" defined in relation to the broader field of world literature'.[18] I observe a similar dynamic in late Ottoman Arabic and Turkish works that conceptualise Arabic and Turkish literatures as national literatures which are comparable with and translatable to other national literatures of the world. This conceptualisation could not have taken place without the reassessments of the Ottoman canon during the late and post-Ottoman periods.

To draw attention to the new afterlives that pre-Ottoman works attained in the Ottoman context, I depict the Ottoman canon as a 'reservoir' in order to emphasise that texts can have multiple affiliations which are not solely circumscribed by the time and place of their production. The Ottoman reservoir includes Islamicate texts circulating from different source cultures and time-periods, such as the pre-Islamic poems of *al-Muᶜallaqāt* and works by Firdavsī (c. 940–c. 1020–26). Saliha Paker has built on Anthony Pym's concept of 'interculture' – 'beliefs and practices found in intersections or overlaps of cultures, where people combine something of two or more cultures at once' – and argued that '[Ottoman interculture] would have to be conceptualized in the intersection of three cultures (Persian, Arabic and Turkish), as the trilingual, tricultural site of operation of Ottoman poet-translators'.[19] Paker has also emphasised that Ottoman interculture 'should be distinguished from the generally held notion of a "common Islamic culture"'.[20]

The Ottoman Canon builds on and extends Paker's work. As my book will examine what Paker has called 'Ottoman poet-translators's' engagement with Arabic and Persian sources, it moves beyond the tendency to study the works of these poet-translators only. The earlier scholarship has examined the Arabic and Persian works that 'Ottoman-era authors' produced; for example, it has studied Köprülüzade Abdullah Pasha's (d. AH 1148 [1735/36]) Arabic works,[21] or Nefi's Persian poems.[22] *The Ottoman Canon* emphasises that critics should not only study the Arabic and Persian works that these writers composed; they should also examine the new 'meanings' or 'afterlives' that pre-Ottoman and/or non-Ottoman Arabic and Persian texts accrued in the Ottoman context. Furthermore, my book emphasises that many members of the Ottoman literati did not engage with Arabic, Persian and Turkish *languages* only. They also engaged with specific *poets and texts* from the Arabic and Persian linguistic traditions that earlier scholarship has categorised as a source of influence rather than as a stream feeding the Ottoman reservoir.

This shift of emphasis from an almost exclusive focus on languages to specific poets and texts brings attention to a rather obvious and yet sometimes neglected key point: Ottoman interculture does not encompass all Arabic and Persian texts. Yet, the prevalent view that Ottoman literature drew on the Arabic and Persian traditions has sometimes reinforced the assumption that the Ottoman literati merely accepted the Arabic and Persian canons as givens. However, they selectively appropriated works from the Arabic and Persian traditions and excluded many others as they forged the Ottoman canon.

The canon, often defined as 'a pantheon of high-cultural works from the past',[23] has received significant attention in literary studies, because scholarship on canons has demonstrated that a text's value significantly depends on extrinsic factors rather than on its innate high quality. These extrinstic factors include audiences and institutions such as universities that consume, disseminate and make value judgments on these texts. Ottoman Studies has also witnessed a rising interest in canonisation over the past few years. For example, Sooyong Kim has analysed Zati's (1471–1546) poetry to reveal the 'fundamentally contingent and constructed process of Ottoman canon-making'.[24] Likewise, Tahera Qutbuddin has analysed the 'Ottoman canon of Arabic philology and literature at the turn of the [sixteenth] century'.[25] In her analysis of Mihri Hatun's (c. 1460–c. 1506) works, Didem Havlioğlu has observed that the sixteenth century witnessed 'the self-construction of the early modern Ottoman literati through many textual maneuvers'.[26]

Like any canon, the Ottoman canon is an imaginary construct. As John Guillory has noted, 'the canon is never other than an imaginary list; it never appears as a complete and uncontested list in any particular time and place, not even in the form of the omnibus anthology, which remains a selection from a larger list which does not itself appear anywhere in the anthology's table of contents'.[27] The canon may have an imaginary character; in other words, no single work captures 'the Ottoman canon'. However, its imaginary character does not mean that the canon has no tangible impact or that the canon simply does not exist. The canon shapes the discussions and literary biographies (*tezkire*) of the early modern Ottoman period; anthologies shape the decisions, selections and exclusions that Ottoman authors exerted in their writings. Conversely, these authors 'imagined' the canon as they discussed and quoted the authors and texts they deemed of high value. Although no work can provide a list of texts that constitutes the Ottoman canon, one can have 'access to the canon',[28] as Guillory has also put it, since one gives a close reading of anthologies and debates in Ottoman texts to identify texts that authors deem valuable.

The sense of imaginary unity that a canon upholds necessitates the 'deracination' of its components from their immediate historical context. For example, in order for al-Mutanabbī to become an 'Ottoman poet', he needed to be taken out of his original 'classical Arabic context' and instead become transplanted into an Ottoman context in which his verses bolstered Ahmed Çelebi's reputation. Here, al-Mutanabbī became a part of what Trevor Ross calls an 'imaginary packaging', since canons as 'imaginary packagings' link texts from highly disparate milieus.[29] Only when late Ottoman authors no longer saw Arabic and Persian texts as part of the Ottoman 'imaginary packaging' could Ottoman literature start to be envisioned as the precursor of modern Turkish literature.

Throughout this book, I use the term 'Ottoman literati' rather than 'Ottoman authors' when I refer to the circumscribed community that Paker, Havlioğlu, Kim and Bashkin have described: Turkophone people (almost always men) who engaged with Arabic, Persian and Turkish poetic traditions and often held high administrative positions in the empire. Therefore, while Muḥammad al-Muwayliḥī may be classified as an Ottoman author, he does not belong to the Ottoman literati. 'The Ottoman canon' which I will discuss throughout the present work refers to the 'imaginary packaging' of authors and texts to which the members of the Ottoman literati alluded in their writings. The Ottoman canon, like the community that upholds it, is far from stable, and shifting socioeconomic contexts have always generated vast changes in what this canon constitutes. At the same time, many of the texts that I will examine bestow a sense of permanence and unity upon what they call the 'Ottoman language' or 'Ottoman literature'. Therefore, I use the term 'the Ottoman canon' to refer to an imaginary textual tradition that, according to many members of the Ottoman literati, seems to have little, if ever, changed throughout the centuries and achieved to consolidate an elite and exclusionist community of letters.

As it points to the key distinction between the Ottoman literati and Ottoman authors, *The Ottoman Canon* contributes to recent works that have paid attention to 'Ottoman Arabic texts' – that is, Arabic works produced in the Ottoman era. These works make up for the earlier neglect of the Ottoman period in Arabic Studies, which has examined the Ottoman era as an age of decadence. Recent works have undertaken the highly fundamental task of examining Ottoman Arabic texts. For example, Esther-Miriam Wagner's edited volume *A Handbook and Reader of Ottoman Arabic* came out in 2021.[30] Similarly, in 2022 Ghayde Ghraowi and Hacı Osman Gündüz (Ozzy) have edited an issue of *Philological Encounters*, titled 'The Ascendent Field: Critical Engagements with Ottoman Arabic Literature'.[31] As my book builds on the burgeoning field of 'Ottoman Arabic literature', it also pays attention to the Ottoman canon in order to study 'non-Ottoman Arabic texts' as part of the Ottoman cultural landscape. I will show diverse instances in which these texts attained a 'new life' in Ottoman Turkish writings, such as Ziya Pasha's *Harabat* (AH 1291–92 [1874/75–75/76]) and Süleyman Nazif's (1869–1927) *Firak-ı Irak* (1918). I will compare these works with Arabic texts such as Maᶜrūf al-Ruṣāfī's (1875–1945) and Tawfīq al-Ḥakīm's writings that refashioned pre-modern Arabic texts as pedestals on which modern Arab identity stood. As recent work on Ottoman Arabic literature has shown, authors such as al-Ḥakīm often overlooked this literature because they believed that Arabs suffered from a cultural decline during the Ottoman period. At the same time, *The Ottoman Canon* points to a key point that recent scholarship on the Ottoman-era Arabic texts has overlooked: although the Ottoman 'imaginary packaging' in the works of the Ottoman literati includes many Arabic texts, it excludes almost all works of 'Ottoman Arabic literature'.

As it points out various forms of exclusions, *The Ottoman Canon* builds on Arif Camoglu, who has called for '[u]nearthening the imperial epistemology that permeates nineteenth-century Ottoman writing'.[32] As the earlier scholarship has focused almost exclusively on how Ottoman Turkish authors engaged with Western European imperialism, it has tended to overlook the imperialistic and expansionist discourse that also characterises their works. Camoglu, instead, has steered attention to this expansionist discourse in order to 'activat[e] Ottoman literature as a zone of interrogation for the critique of imperialism in literary studies'.[33]

The Ottoman Canon will also discuss the exclusion of women from the canons, both Ottoman and national. For example, as Boutheina Khaldi has demonstrated, Mayy Ziyāda (1886–1941) faced numerous misogynistic remarks. Many people assumed that only a man could have written what Ziyāda wrote and sometimes 'went so far as to believe that she might be hiring a male writer to write for her or be plagiarizing'.[34] Yet, Ziyāda also received immense praise for her work during her lifetime.[35] Women writers such as Ziyāda did not necessarily remain marginalised within literary circles, even if they frequently encountered misogynistic attitudes. However, *The Ottoman Canon* will show that it was often the male authors who either saw themselves or were described by others as 'pioneers' who modernised their national literatures. They also thought that their national community needed to have or even 'possess' a literature so that it could become like other advanced nations. The writers I will examine in this book rarely expressed a strong skepticism towards the very notion of literature itself, like the notion one finds in the following words from another woman writer, Halide Edib: 'Whenever I see or read of a great military hero performing his deeds and of history or literature recording them, I wonder in the same way, not about the children only, but about the simple grown-up people as well. If only history would refuse to record martial glories and literature and art to immortalize them, there might be some semblance of peace and relative human happiness in the world'.[36] Women authors played key roles in the literary circles of the late Ottoman and post-Ottoman periods. At the same time, *The Ottoman Canon* will focus mostly on male writers, since, as Chapter 2 will examine more in depth, it was often male authors who put forth the current paradigms and assumptions that solidified the institutional divisions that Holbrook has also observed in Middle Eastern Studies.

Some recent works that have emphasised the need to do away with the question of the canon and move beyond an analysis of people who have been studied as figures who 'pioneered' modernity movements have redirected attention to the numerous linguistic traditions that circulated widely within the late Ottoman Empire, such as Greek, Armenian, Karamanlıca (Turkish written in Greek letters) and Judeo-Spanish (Ladino).[37] They have thus studied texts by women and/or non-Muslim writers, such as Fatma Fahrünnisa (1876–1969) and Evangelinos Misailidis (1820–90), and examined the issues of multilingualism and boundary transgressions that characterised the period. While acknowledging the crucial need for more similar works, this book focuses on canonised Ottoman intellectuals who have been studied as 'pioneers' and generated a rather exclusionist understanding of Ottoman literature and identity. The exclusionist Ottoman reservoir that shaped the cultural vision of authors such as Ziya Pasha does not capture the linguistically and culturally rich literary landscape of the empire that the recent scholarship has laid out. Much like this scholarship that has overcome the nationalistic frameworks which shaped Ottoman Studies by mapping out the diverse linguistic traditions circulating within the empire, my work serves the same aim through another approach. It demonstrates that the Ottoman literary reservoir includes works written outside the Ottoman territories and even before the establishment of the empire.

Instead of merely mapping out the literary networks of the Ottoman Empire or listing similarities between the Arabic and Turkish literatures, my book calls for examining how the terms 'Arabic literature' and 'Turkish literature' have emerged and eventually shifted in meaning. I here build on recent works that reveal nineteenth-century epistemological transformations which have shaped how we think of the terms '*adab*' and

'Arabic literature' today. For example, although the term '*adab*' initially referred to the compilation of all works from diverse genres that made a person educated and moral, it began to refer only to fictional works such as poems and novels starting in the nineteenth century.[38] Furthermore, as Chapter 2 will discuss in depth, recent scholarship by critics such as Karim Mattar, Yaseen Noorani, Shaden M. Tageldin and Michael Allan has demonstrated how Western frameworks transformed the ways in which critics have studied Arabic literature.[39] Likewise, M. Kaya Bilgegil has demonstrated that, although the terms '*edeb*' or '*edebiyat*' corresponded to a wide range of knowledge areas, they started to be used as literature in the modern sense only in the nineteenth century.[40] My book reveals another kind of epistemological shift: it proposes that the conceptualisation of the histories of Arabic and Turkish literature as two linear trajectories in the nineteenth century could not have taken place without reassessments of the Ottoman canon.

A canon as an imaginary list provides a sense of imaginary unity for the community that affiliates with this canon. Therefore, debates on the canon ultimately shape debates on the communal selves whose boundaries become reinforced as they affiliate with the 'imaginary packagings' that canons constitute. Walter Feldman has noted that the moments in which new canons were consolidated in the Ottoman Empire corresponded to those time-periods in which a sense of self emerged: '[A] consciousness of "self" coincided with the need to create standards and canons that were more amenable to centralization, whether toward the state in the seventeenth century, or towad a nationalistically oriented academia at the begininng of the twentieth'.[41] Therefore, the construction of Arabic and Turkish literatures that involved reassessments of the multilingual Ottoman canon took shape in conjunction with the construction of a new sense of communal self – a bounded, modern national subject.

For example, Mervat F. Hatem has observed that a key marker of the transition 'from an Ottoman centered community into an increasingly narrow national one in nineteenth-century Egypt' was 'a change in the power relations between Turkish and Arabic (and to a lesser extent Persian) as literary and official languages'.[42] Turkish still presented an important cultural capital in Egypt in the nineteenth century, because many school textbooks were published in Turkish and Turkish was a language of literary expression.[43] At the same time, many members of the Arabic-speaking intelligentsia obtained important positions in the Ottoman government. Since most people in Egypt spoke Arabic, the Arabic language generated a sense of social solidarity among Egyptians and ultimately laid the basis for Arab cultural nationalism.[44]

A study of these linguistic and cultural shifts will also lead to a reassessment of how scholars study classical Arabic and Ottoman literatures. *The Ottoman Canon* undermines the current scholarship's tendency to study Ottoman literature as a precursor of modern Turkish literature or to examine the history of Arabic and Turkish literature as two parallel trajectories that did not flow together within the Ottoman literary reservoir. The re-assignment of the literary traditions that fill up the Ottoman reservoir to distinct cultural and political communities constitute a shared feature of what has been studied separately as Arabic and Turkish literary modernities. Veli N. Yashin has noted that the late Ottoman period witnessed philological practices that aimed to organise the scattered works of different languages within a linear historical trajectory, hence reinforcing the division between classical and modern literatures.[45] As Arabic and Turkish writings of the late Ottoman period organised their respective linguistic tradition in a strictly historical order, they had to reflect on an Ottoman canon in which their tradition became intertwined with other Islamicate traditions.

By fleshing out characteristics of the Ottoman literary reservoir, my book provides new perspectives on the study of the *Tanzimat*, a period of statewide reforms and cultural transformations in the late Ottoman Empire, and *al-nahḍa*, a period of Arab cultural 'awakening'. Many historians of the Ottoman Empire often use the term '*Tanzimat*' (literally reorganisation) to refer to the period between 1839 and 1876 when the empire undertook many political and cultural reforms due to the growing Western influence.[46] While critics have often used the term '*al-nahḍa*' to refer to political, cultural and literary transformations throughout the Arab world that emerged in the nineteenth century under increasing Western influence,[47] Tarek El-Ariss has examined the *nahḍa* as a speech act and performance.[48] He has demonstrated that many intellectuals across the Arab world have actually used the term '*nahḍa*' to refer to a series of interconnected issues such as change, modernisation and civilisation, rather than to a delimited time-period or a set of texts. By foregrounding the numerous trials and contradictions within *nahḍa* texts, El-Ariss's work has undermined the typical perception of the *nahḍa* as a 'unified and homogeneous project'.[49]

Recent scholarship on the *Tanzimat* has amplified the linguistic diversity of the empire's literary landscape for providing new perspectives on the *Tanzimat*; however, most scholars still tend to view the *Tanzimat* as a homogenous modernisation project within a delimited time-period. Yet, the term '*Tanzimat*' has also been used as a speech act in those Turkish writings that employed the term to evoke a series of interconnected themes and ideas. For example, Ahmet Hamdi Tanpınar (1901–62), one of the most influential figures in the field of Turkish literature, personified the *Tanzimat* and depicted it as a subject. After noting that the 'Turkish subject' transformed in the late Ottoman period, he wrote: 'This is what the *Tanzimat* did'.[50] *The Ottoman Canon* will thus examine the *Tanzimat* and *al-nahḍa* also as speech acts that contributed to the consolidation of autonomous, national selves, such as 'the Turkish subject' that Tanpınar discussed.

Methodology and the Historical Context

To undermine attempts to assign texts to a single period and culture, *The Ottoman Canon* will often follow the methodology of 'literary thinking and a practice of close reading', which, as Selim Kuru has pointed out, can also serve as a possible future direction for Ottoman Studies, which has largely shunned these approaches:

> Literature defies periodization because it will never belong to any given period – no matter how carefully crafted by literary historians. Literature belongs to, if not overflows from, the grand arc of a language. Consequently, literary thinking and practice of close reading of documentary and literary sources, which are largely absent in current Ottoman history-writing, may be an antidote to the pitfalls of strict periodization – pitfalls such as the use of the fraught term 'early modern'.[51]

I thus use the methodology of close reading to undermine the tendency to assign texts to one historical context only and to overcome the strict periodisations that have characterised the fields of Arabic literature and Ottoman Studies.

Concerning the distinction between history and literature in terms of their methodological approaches, Sharon Marcus has noted: 'If one can identify the core method of any discipline, then the method of theory is the critique of existing assumptions; the method of history is generalization based on immersion in the largest and widest range of sources possible; and the method of literary and visual criticism is interpretation based on close reading'.[52] The discipline of history has shaped the main methodological approaches in Ottoman Studies. As Alexis Wick has put it, '[t]he disciplines of history and Orientalism have shared from the outset a distrust of theory and philosophy, a legacy that Ottoman studies, perhaps more than any other field, has inherited'.[53] Due to this legacy, Ottomanists do not engage much in self-reflection, as they become largely preoccupied with 'the immense treasure trove that are the Ottoman archives, containing a wealth of continuous documentary that remains across time and space probably unequaled in the world'.[54] Perhaps due to the impact of the discipline of history and its methodological inclinations on Ottoman Studies, Ottomanists have often studied events and texts of the Ottoman period and overlooked the new life that pre-Ottoman works took on in the Ottoman context.

At the same time, the past few years have witnessed a rise in works in Ottoman Studies that emphasise the need for more collaborations between historians and literary critics, suggesting that the future direction of Ottoman Studies for which Kuru has called will likely take place. For example, Monica M. Ringer and Etienne E. Charrière, the editors of *Ottoman Culture and the Project of Modernity*, have noted that they asked for contributions from both historians and literary critics for their project: 'Historians often use novels as illustrations – as textual "images" that accompany analysis of historical context. [. . .] Literary scholars, on the other hand, are much more concerned with examining literary technique and applying literary analysis'.[55]

All methodological choices come with a cost. As *The Ottoman Canon* gives historically contextualised close readings of late Ottoman and post-Ottoman literary works, it does not provide a comprehensive historical overview of the institutions that contributed to the consolidation of the imperial and national canons.[56] Nor does it pinpoint the 'exact' historical moment when these canons came into existence. While my book touches on various institutions such as medreses (Introduction), the Rüşdiye schools (Chapter 4) and Istanbul University (Chapter 6), which all played a major role in the consolidations of canons, further research in history and sociology can shed light on the sociological and historical factors that culminated in the solidification of these canons.

At the same time, literary analysis provides significant advantages in order to observe how a canon links works from highly disparate times and locations – that is, its 'imaginary' character. I thus 'have access to the canon', as my book points out how late Ottoman and post-Ottoman texts discuss poets and works from pre-modern times while they also respond to the shifting dynamics of their times. Close readings provide in-depth case-studies that demonstrate how authors who have been studied as 'pioneers' of their respective national traditions generated diverse 'imaginary packagings' as they made literary comparisons and wrote about literature. Furthermore, rather than assigning the authors whom I study to a single historical and literary movement, a close reading fleshes out the contradictions and paradoxes that characterise the works under study. I point to these contradictions without feeling a need to resolve them, to show that it is not possible to pinpoint the 'exact' moment when the Ottoman canon disappeared and national literatures emerged. As I observe certain cultural shifts, such as the tendency of late Ottoman works to categorise pre-modern texts as 'classics', *The Ottoman Canon* also uses close reading as a methodology to lay out the complexity of the texts it examines.

At first, it may seem an unlikely choice for a work on the Ottoman canon to perform close readings of late rather than early modern Ottoman works. As Kuru, Kim and Havlioğlu have demonstrated, the sixteenth century witnessed the consolidation of the Ottoman literati and the multilingual Ottoman canon that they 'imagined'. However, I focus on the late Ottoman period, as this canon becomes visible especially when more authors criticised what they called the 'old literature' and the canon that this 'old literature' stood for, because '[l]ike everything that passes, the canon is easier to see in its twilight'.[57] Late Ottoman and post-Ottoman works that often called for a 'new literature' allow critics many opportunities 'to have access' to the Ottoman canon as they can observe the languages, texts and authors that this canon brought together.

The close readings that *The Ottoman Canon* conducts also pay significant attention to historical and socioeconomic contexts. As a result, *The Ottoman Canon* elaborates on important similarities between modern Arabic and Turkish literatures, because many authors of late Ottoman Arabic and Turkish literatures also responded to a common set of economic, cultural and political transformations that shaped the entire empire.[58] While the Ottoman Empire had conquered much of the Arab world by 1517, political and cultural reforms in the empire during the nineteenth century resulted in a state centralisation that intensified interactions between the Arabic and Turkish cultures. The imperial administration also had a growing presence in the Arab lands, due to various factors such as the pan-Islamist policies of Sultan Abdülhamid II (r. 1876–1909), vast territorial losses on the Balkans and an expanding network of railways and telegraphs. Authors of both Arabic and Turkish literatures during the late Ottoman period confronted similar socioeconomic changes, including the rise of a merchant class and the privatisation of state land.[59] These authors also confronted the rise of Western imperialism and sometimes claimed that the West had political, military, scientific and even cultural superiority over the Islamic world in their writings. This confrontation with Western European hegemony led many writers to develop a nostalgia for medieval and early modern times, as they believed that Islamic civilisation had been superior to Western civilisation during these periods.

Furthermore, *The Ottoman Canon* directs attention to travels and textual circulations as key factors contributing to the formation of national subjects and the literatures to which they seek claim. As *nahḍa* authors wrote about their Arabic heritage (*al-turāth*), they met in person or wrote about Ottoman Turkish writers. Numerous *nahḍa* authors also spent a portion of their lives in Istanbul. In a similar vein, many late Ottoman Turkish authors lived and worked in administrative positions in Alexandria, Baghdad, Damascus, or Beirut. These authors also wrote about the history of the Arabs, as they travelled to the Ottoman Arab provinces and read Orientalist works. During their travels, they may have become more aware of the discrepancy between the Arabic that they used and the Arabic that the people who lived in these provinces spoke. Even though these authors may have had a solid reading knowledge of Arabic, this does not necessarily mean that they could easily communicate in Arabic. For example, Halide Edib noted that '[t]he Arabic [she] had learned from books did not help [her] much'[60] when she was in Alexandria. Likewise, when she was in Syria, she talked 'to [an Arab] in broken Arabic'.[61] Cenab Şahabeddin also noted that the Arabic he had learned did not help him much during his travels in Alexandria.[62] The diverse encounters that travels and textual circulations generated contributed to the consolidation of national subjects. As Mary Louise Pratt has put it, '[a] "contact" perspective emphasizes how subjects are constituted in and by their relations to each other'.[63] Although the Ottoman Empire had significant differences from the colonial contexts that Pratt's work examines, my study will also demonstrate that it is useful and even necessary to conduct a comparative study of Arabic and Turkish literary modernities, because both modernities were shaped by the contacts and encounters that late Ottoman travels and textual circulations generated.

Since many Ottoman writings substantially engaged with classical Persian works, there is a clear need for more studies that reassess Persian and Turkish literary modernities by studying their engagement with the Ottoman reservoir.[64] Still, *The Ottoman Canon* mainly focuses on late Ottoman Arabic and Turkish works, due to their similar historical and socioeconomic contexts, to put emphasis on the entangled processes that led to the formation of Arab and Turkish national subjects. Furthermore, as Chapters 1 and 5 will discuss in greater depth, late Ottoman authors showed a substantial engagement with Orientalist works, which posited Arabic culture and literature as the 'origin' that later 'Oriental' civilisations copied. Even authors who complained about the Persian influence on Ottoman literature ultimately viewed Arabic literature as the ultimate 'source' that had influenced Persian literature and Arabic texts as works that 'Arabised' Ottoman writers. Therefore, even though Persian literature has been claimed to have had a substantial influence on Ottoman literature, many debates on what it means to be an Ottoman revolved around discussions on Arabic literature and Arab identity during the nineteenth and early twentieth centuries.

Although recent scholarship in *Nahḍa* Studies has undermined the typical assumption that modernity was simply borrowed from the West, it often did not elaborate on the diverse manners in which *nahḍa* intellectuals engaged with Ottoman Turkish literature. Intellectuals who have been studied as pioneers of Arab cultural nationalism often expressed discontent with the Turkish or Ottoman political hegemony; however, this discontentment did not deter them from engaging with the Ottoman literary reservoir in various ways. As *The Ottoman Canon* will show, authors such as Ibrāhīm al-Muwayliḥī (1846–1906), in fact, considered themselves pioneers who would give a new direction to the Ottoman Empire in their writings that included important advice about how the empire should modernise.

Late Ottoman and post-Ottoman Arabic writings often complained about the Ottoman political hegemony over Arab lands. Ulrich W. Haarmann and Şükran Fazlıoğlu have revealed that many Arabic writings of the late Ottoman Empire depicted Turks as despots.[65] Ussama Makdisi and Selim Deringil have demonstrated that the central Istanbul administration infringed on diverse parts of the empire, such as Beirut and Baghdad, more than ever in the late nineteenth and early twentieth centuries.[66] Yet, these political shifts do not necessarily suggest that an Istanbul centre generated a full cultural hegemony over the Arab world. In other words, political power hierarchies among different linguistic and ethnic communities in the Ottoman Empire did not neatly map onto the power hierarchies that shaped the empire's literary and cultural domains. Therefore, *The Ottoman Canon* also examines those Arabic writings that translated or discussed Ottoman Turkish works in order to further nuance our understanding of the power dynamics that shaped the Ottoman cultural and literary landscape. At this point, it is important to emphasise that *The Ottoman Canon* will not provide a comprehensive overview of 'the Arab image' in late Ottoman Turkish writings since it will focus on Turkish works from a relatively circumscribed community. While, as my book will show, members of the circle of Ottoman literati often made discriminatory remarks about the empire's ethnic and religious groups, including Arabs, further research may point to diverse representations from different communities on which my book does not dwell much.

Outline of the Book

Apart from the introduction and the conclusion, *The Ottoman Canon* consists of six chapters. The first two chapters will examine the reassessment of the relationships among the linguistic heritages that constituted the Ottoman reservoir. Chapters 3, 4 and 5 will demonstrate that the increasing mobility of people and texts in the late Ottoman Empire led to new interpretations of Ottoman culture and identity. Chapter 6 will show that the Ottoman reservoir could find new embodiments in Arabic and Turkish novels after the empire's demise.

Chapter 1 will examine Ziya Pasha's (1829–80) famous anthology of Arabic, Persian and Turkish poetry, *Harabat* (Tavern, AH 1291–92 [1874/75–75/76]) and the anthology's introduction that provides a comparative history of these traditions. I pay attention to two metaphors – ocean and spring – that stand for different kinds of canon formation circumscribing the texts that literary communities choose to preserve and remember. *Harabat* asserts that Arabic, Persian and Turkish traditions mix so perfectly that they form, in Ziya Pasha's words, an 'ocean'. I use the term 'reservoir' to designate what Ziya Pasha called an ocean, because this ocean encompasses works from various 'streams' – that is, languages – while it also has strict boundaries, as it excludes works such as folk poems or Greek texts that also circulated in the Ottoman Empire. Later, the chapter will demonstrate that many literary histories written after *Harabat* claim that Ottoman literature could not surpass and merely imitated the Arabic and Persian literatures which had set the standard for eloquence and poetics. They also describe Arabic and Persian literatures as springs (*menba*) that ultimately nourished Ottoman literature. Despite key differences between *Harabat* and later literary histories, Chapter 1 will also undermine the typical scholarly view that *Harabat* presents one of the last examples of the classical Ottoman tradition. Although Ziya Pasha's praise for classical Ottoman poetry may be interpreted as a reaction against modernity, *Harabat* provides new perspectives on the relationships among linguistic traditions that constituted the Ottoman literary reservoir. To demonstrate how *Harabat* refashions the poetic heritage, the chapter will present a close reading of the Arabic poems that *Harabat* quotes and an excerpt from its introduction that provides a history of Arabic literature.

Chapter 2 will examine literary histories from the late Ottoman period. In particular, I focus on the literary histories by Jurjī Zaydān (1861–1914), whose writings have played a formative role for the field of Arabic literature. This chapter will argue that late Ottoman literary histories often depicted the histories of Arabic and Turkish literatures as two parallel trajectories that did not intersect with each other, contributing to the current conceptualisation of the classical Arabic heritage as the root from which modern Arabic literature grew. I will offer a close reading of an article in the famous journal that Zaydān edited, *al-Hilāl*, on Namık Kemal

(1840–88), who is often studied as a pioneer of modern Turkish literature. The article describes Namık Kemal as the pioneer of a modern 'Turkish *nahḍa*'. By describing Namık Kemal as a pioneer, the article renders the Ottoman cultural landscape familiar for Arabic readers and overlooks Namık Kemal's vision for a new Ottoman literature in which Arabic works played a key role. I will then focus on another article in which Zaydān writes about 'the history of Turkish language arts' (*tārīkh ādāb al-lugha al-turkiyya*) and point out the similarities between this article and one of the most canonised works in the field of Arabic literature, *Tārīkh ādāb al-lugha al-ᶜarabiyya* (The History of Arabic Language Arts, first serialised in *al-Hilāl* in 1894–1895 and eventually published as a multi-volume work in 1911–14). These similarities reinforce the depiction of Arabic and Turkish literatures as akin to mirror-images that look alike but never intersect in the Ottoman cultural reservoir. To lay out his vision of modern Arab identity, Jurjī Zaydān had to reassess not only the history of Arabic literature, but also the multilingual Ottoman reservoir. The second section will examine the use of the term 'classics' or 'classical' in the literary histories by Jurjī Zaydān, Rūḥī al-Khālidī (1864–1913) and İsmail Hakkı [Eldem] (1871–1944). It will demonstrate that these works established a linear historical trajectory for both Arabic and Turkish literatures. In particular, they depicted Arabic literature as a source of influence the origin of which predated the emergence of Turkish literature, rather than as an integral influx into the Ottoman reservoir.

Chapter 3 will pay attention to the dissolution of old economic, ethnic, religious and cultural hierarchies during the late Ottoman period. In particular, it examines the reception of two key markers of modernisation that became prevalent in late Ottoman society because of this dissolution: the tarboosh headgear and the novel genre. As some of these markers such as the tarboosh signified a more egalitarian vision of Ottoman identity, various late Ottoman writings depicted both tarboosh and novel as a means of disguise. For example, they feature characters who wander in disguise after they put on a tarboosh and describe the novel as a piece of clothing that old texts, such as *The Thousand and One Nights*, can put on. Therefore, they reinforce the impression that the new markers of modernity signified shifts in appearance rather than in essence. As a case-study, I will perform a close reading of *Hasan Mellah* (AH 1291 [1874/75]) by Ahmet Midhat (1844–1912) and *What ᶜĪsā ibn Hishām Told Us* (*Ḥadīth ᶜĪsā ibn Hishām*, 1898–1902) by Muḥammad al-Muwayliḥī (1858–1930). This chapter will point out a paradox: while late Ottoman writers claimed that new markers of modernity, such as the novel genre, did not signify the dissolution of the cultural and political order that the Ottoman reservoir served, the material conditions of their societies prepared the ground for the social displacements that generated a reassessment of this reservoir. I will ultimately examine what late Ottoman works 'camouflage', which helps me focus attention on the shared socioeconomic context that renders a comparative study of the construction of Arabic and Turkish literatures fruitful. The chapter's conclusion will emphasise that those works which seek to identify 'the first novel' in both Arabic and Turkish contexts often study the novel as a visible marker of rupture between classical and modern literatures; they have thus habituated critics to view Arabic and Turkish literatures as national literatures that have existed since time immemorial.

Chapter 4 will examine translations between Arabic and Turkish in the late Ottoman Empire. Earlier scholarship has analysed the increasing number of translations from Western languages, French in particular, as a key marker of literary modernity. However, this period also witnessed an increase in the number of translations between Arabic and Turkish. Chapter 4 will argue that translations between these two languages during the late Ottoman period generated a common repertoire of themes and concepts in Arabic and Turkish writings, while largely impeding linguistic exchanges. As a case-study, I will analyse *Dafᶜ al-hujna fī irtiḍākh al-lukna* (Overcoming the Flaws of Speech Defects, AH 1331 [1912/13]) by Maᶜrūf al-Ruṣāfī (1875–1945) and then examine al-Ruṣāfī's engagement with Ottoman Turkish writings. *Dafᶜ al-hujna* provides a list of Arabic words that were borrowed from Turkish. Al-Ruṣāfī claimed that these words had become more popular among Arabic speakers because 'unskilled translators' had popularised them through their translations from Turkish to Arabic. The chapter will then investigate *al-Ruʾyā fī baḥth al-ḥurriya*, which is al-Ruṣāfī's Arabic translation of *Rüya* (Dream, published posthumously in 1908) by Namık Kemal (1840–88). In particular, I compare the source text *Rüya* with its Arabic translation *al-Ruʾyā* to understand the choices that al-Ruṣāfī made as translator. While al-Ruṣāfī's translation remains 'faithful' to the source text in terms of content, it replaces expressions that he would later list in *Dafᶜ al-hujna* as corrupt borrowings from Turkish with what al-Ruṣāfī considered their 'true' Arabic equivalents. Finally, I will present a close reading of al-Ruṣāfī's poem 'Nuwāḥ Dijla' (The Lamentation of the Tigris) and Süleyman Nazif's (1869–1927) *Firak-ı Irak* (The Separation from Iraq, 1918), a compilation of works on the Ottoman defeat in Iraq during World War I. Although the Ottoman defeat in Iraq becomes a shared source of suffering for al-Ruṣāfī and Süleyman Nazif, both writers provided different interpretations of the same event. While Süleyman Nazif associated the Ottoman defeat with the dissolution of an Ottoman reservoir that included works by poets such as Imruʾ al-Qays (d. c. 550), al-Mutanabbī (d. 965) and Nefi (d. 1635), al-Ruṣāfī lamented the loss of Ottoman military and political power. At the same time, his work does not openly advocate a cultural vision in which Arabic works belong to an Ottoman reservoir.

Chapter 5 will demonstrate that proponents of both 'old literature' and 'new literature' in the late Ottoman Empire contributed to the conceptualisation of Arabic works as a source of influence that Arabised Ottoman culture. First, my chapter will analyse Hacı İbrahim's (1826–88) articles on Arabic language and literature. Hacı İbrahim has been studied as a 'conservative' author who criticised *Tanzimat* modernisation because he constantly praised Arabic language and literature. At the same time, as a proponent of 'old literature', he advocated 'modern' views. For example, he emphasised that Ottomans should not merely understand Arabic works; they should also translate them into Turkish. Furthermore, Hacı İbrahim believed that there was no difference between Arabic and Ottoman literatures; in fact, an anonymous author who shared his key beliefs also claimed in the 162nd issue of the newspaper *Malumat* that 'Ottoman literature means Arabic literature'. Finally, while Hacı İbrahim claimed to resist the empire's Westernisation efforts, his articles draw on the Orientalist discourse to substantiate his points about Arabic and Ottoman literatures. The second section of this chapter will study a key juxtaposition in the newspaper *Malumat*: its issues feature photos from late Ottoman Syria, likely taken during Ahmet Rasim's (1864–1932) expedition to Syria, and pre-Ottoman Arabic poems with their Turkish explanations on the same pages. One may first interpret these pages as juxtaposition between tradition, signified by classical Arabic works, and modernity, signified by the photos of Ottoman Arab provinces. At the same time, I interpret both photos and poems as signs of Ottoman modernisation. As the photos reveal how Ottoman provinces became an object of the gaze, the section on the poems will pinpoint the increasing tendency to view Arabic and Turkish works as translatable between each other. I will then present a close reading of Ahmet Rasim's *Arapların Terakkiyat-ı Medeniyyesi* (The Civilisational Development of Arabs, AH 1304 [1886/87]), which translates excerpts from Gustave Le Bon's (1841–1931) *La Civilisation des Arabes* (The Arab Civilisation, 1884). While Ahmet Rasim chose not to translate many sections in Le Bon's works, he, like Le Bon, emphasised that each community *possessed* a literature. After pointing out the similarities between Hacı İbrahim and Ahmet Rasim, the chapter's conclusion will discuss Ahmet Rasim's post-Ottoman biography of Şinasi (1826–71) to demonstrate that a pre-Ottoman element of the Ottoman literary reservoir, an excerpt from al-Ḥarīrī's (d. 1122) *Maqāmāt*, appears even in a post-Ottoman work that claims to have left behind the classical tradition.

Chapter 6 will examine how the critical and fictional works of Ahmet Hamdi Tanpınar (1901–62) and Tawfīq al-Ḥakīm (1898–1987), who have been studied as pioneering figures of modern Turkish and Arabic literature, respectively, described the relationship between the Ottoman past and their national communities. In particular, it will discuss both authors' shared engagement with *Oedipus Rex* (c. 429–25 BC) by Sophocles (d. 406/5 BC) to provide new perspectives on their reception of the Ottoman past. This chapter will argue that both Tanpınar and al-Ḥakīm depicted the Ottoman past as a source of psychological complexes that undermined the spiritual health of their national communities. *Oedipus Rex* constituted a rich source of reflection for Tanpınar who wrote about what it meant to be a Turk and for al-Ḥakīm who wrote about what it meant to be an Egyptian and an Arab. Tanpınar claimed that all Turkish people suffered from an Oedipal complex, while al-Ḥakīm wrote an Arabic adaptation of the play and claimed that the play was appealing to the Egyptian mind. Furthermore, Tanpınar's *On Dokuzuncu Asır Türk Edebiyatı Tarihi* (History of Nineteenth-Century Turkish Literature, 1949), claims that works of classical Arabic literature, such as *al-Muᶜallaqāt* and al-Ḥarīrī's *Maqāmāt*, deprived the Turkish subject of authenticity. While al-Ḥakīm did not write about Turkish literature in his critical works, the main character in his novel *Return of the Spirit* (*ᶜAwdat al-rūḥ*, 1933), Muḥsin, struggles against his Turkish mother who sabotages Muḥsin's dream to become a writer who expresses the 'eloquent tongue of his nation'. Similarly, the main character in Tanpınar's *The Time Regulation Institute* (*Saatleri Ayarlama Enstitüsü*, 1954), Hayri İrdal, can never break free from Abdüsselam Efendi, a Tunisian who is described as Hayri İrdal's father-figure by Hayri İrdal's psychoanalyst doctor. Both Muḥsin and Hayri İrdal want to transform the dynamics of the families that carry the traces of the cosmopolitan Ottoman past so as to be able to produce a new culture that generates a sense of emancipation; however, they realise that this aspiration to emancipation and authenticity is difficult and even impossible to achieve. Through an analysis of the characters who received little attention in earlier scholarship – the Turkish mother in al-Ḥakīm's novel and the Tunisian father-figure in Tanpınar's novel – this chapter will undermine the most typical readings of the *Return of the Spirit* as the realisation of a nationalist vision and *The Time Regulation Institute* as a satire of Turkish modernisation. It will also conclude that, although the Ottoman Empire's demise generated political and linguistic divisions, Tanpınar and al-Ḥakīm had similar visions of identity, culture and literature.

The conclusion will discuss my book's contributions to the most recent scholarship on multilingualism and modernities in the Ottoman Empire. More works today study translations and textual circulations to reassess different modernities, such as the *nahḍa* and the *haskala* (Jewish modernity), within a shared Ottoman context. Instead of merely mapping out translations and textual circulations, literary critics can also study the epistemological and material shifts that led to the formation of new canons and the reassessment of old ones. Likewise, while recent works have studied 'Arabic literature as world literature' and 'Turkish literature as world literature' to overcome earlier nationalistic approaches to literature, my work reveals another way to achieve the same goal: it studies how the concepts of 'Arabic literature' and 'Turkish literature' emerged within a transnational context. As my work focuses on how Arabic texts took on 'new lives' in the Ottoman context, it also suggests that recent studies examining late Ottoman Armenian, Greek and Judeo-Spanish works sometimes risks generating a one-to-one correspondence between texts and people; for example, it risks projecting Judeo-Spanish literary works as the possession of a Judeo-Spanish community. Such an assumption can sometimes overlook the 'new lives' or 'afterlives' that these works could have experienced and the diverse communities they could have cultivated. Finally, the conclusion posits that poets such as Ka^c^b ibn Zuhayr or Sa^c^dī (c. 1213–91/92) inhabited 'multiple worlds', hence emphasising the need for more works that study the 'Ottoman Ka^c^b ibn Zuhayr' or the 'Ottoman Sa^c^dī'.

Notes

1. Qutb al-Din al-Nahrawali, *Journey to the Sublime Porte: The Arabic Memoir of a Sharifian Agent's Diplomatic Mission to the Ottoman Imperial Court in the Era of Süleyman the Magnificent*, trans. Richard Blackburn (Beirut: Ergon Verlag Würzburg in Kommission, 2005), 181. Blackburn's translation is accompanied by a CD-ROM that contains the Arabic manuscript.
2. *Takhmīs* is a poetic form in which a poet adds three hemistiches to each *bayt* (two hemistiches) of an existing poem.
3. al-Nahrawali, *Journey to the Sublime Porte*, 182. For al-Mutanabbī's verse which Ahmed Çelebi quotes, see Abū al-Ṭayyib al-Mutanabbī, *Dīwān al-Mutanabbī* (Beirut: Dār Bayrūt, 1983), 373. Ziya Pasha's *Harabat*, which Chapter 1 will analyse, also quotes the same verse. Ziya Paşa, *Harabat* (Istanbul: Matbaa-i Amire, AH 1291–92 [1874/75–75/76]), 2: 493.
4. al-Nahrawali, *Journey to the Sublime Porte*, 182.
5. Victoria Rowe Holbrook, *The Unreadable Shores of Love: Turkish Modernity and Mystic Romance* (Austin: University of Texas Press, 1994), 15–16.

6. Holbrook, *The Unreadable Shores of Love*, 16.
7. Saliha Paker, 'On the Poetic Practices of "a Singularly Uninventive People" and the Anxiety of Imitation: A Critical Re-Appraisal in Terms of Translation, Creative Mediation and "Originality"', in *Tradition, Tension and Translation in Turkey*, ed. John Milton, Saliha Paker and Şehnaz Tahir Gürçağlar (Amsterdam: John Benjamins Publishing Company, 2015), 30.
8. Christopher Markiewicz, 'Books on the Secretarial Arts and Literary Prose', in *Treasures of Knowledge: An Inventory of the Ottoman Palace Library (1502/3–1503/4)*, ed. Gülru Necipoğlu, Cemal Kafadar and Cornell H. Fleischer (Leiden: Brill, 2019), 1: 658.
9. As I will show throughout this book, many late Ottoman writings declared that they started to produce a 'new literature' which draws on Western forms and themes. Much of the earlier scholarship has thus defined both Arabic and Turkish literary modernities as thematic and stylistic shifts that occurred in the nineteenth century due to their authors's engagement with the West. However, more recent works have challenged the notion that modernity resulted from the simple imitation of Western ideas in Middle Eastern contexts. For some recent examples, see Marilyn Booth and Claire Savina (eds), *Ottoman Translations: Circulating Texts from Bombay to Paris* (Edinburgh: Edinburgh University Press, 2023); Rebecca C. Johnson, *Stranger Fictions: A History of the Novel in Arabic Translation* (Ithaca: Cornell University Press, 2021); Monica M. Ringer and Etienne E. Charrière (eds), *Ottoman Culture and the Project of Modernity: Reform and Translation in the Tanzimat Novel* (New York: I. B. Tauris, 2020); Elizabeth M. Holt, *Fictitious Capital: Silk, Cotton and the Rise of the Arabic Novel* (New York: Fordham University Press, 2017); Karim Mattar, *Specters of World Literature: Orientalism, Modernity and the Novel in the Middle East* (Edinburgh: Edinburgh University Press, 2020); and Marilyn Booth (ed.), *Migrating Texts: Circulating Translations around the Ottoman Mediterranean* (Edinburgh: Edinburgh University Press, 2019).
10. Alexander Jabbari, 'The Making of Modernity in Persianate Literary History', *Comparative Studies of South Asia, Africa and the Middle East* 36, no. 3 (2016): 420.
11. Alexander Jabbari, 'From Persianate Cosmopolis to Persianate Modernity: Translating from Urdu to Persian in Twentieth-Century Iran and Afghanistan', *Iranian Studies* 55, no. 3 (2022): 613. Here, Jabbari notes that Urdu scholarly works, such as Shiblī Nu^{c}mānī's (1857–1914) *Shi^{c}r al-^{c}Ajam* (Poetry of the Persians, 1908–18), played a fundamental role in the 'emergence of national literature and literary history in Iran and Afghanistan' (612).
12. Sooyong Kim and Orit Bashkin, 'Revisiting Multilingualism in the Ottoman Empire', *Review of Middle East Studies* 55, no. 1 (2021): 130–31.
13. Sooyong Kim, *The Last of an Age: The Making and Unmaking of a Sixteenth-Century Ottoman Poet* (London: Routledge, 2018), 13.
14. Sooyong Kim, 'The Poet Nef^{c}ī, Fresh Persian Verse and Ottoman Freshness', *Iranian Studies* 55, no. 2 (2022): 551.

15. Halide Edib Adıvar, *Memoirs of Halidé Edib. 1926. New Introduction by Hülya Adak.* (Piscataway: Gorgias Press, 2004), 183.
16. Ruşen Eşref, *Diyorlar ki* (Istanbul: Kanaat Matbaası, 1918), 25, 28, 36, 39, 40, 43, 57, 62, 64, 135, 144, 249.
17. See Patricia Novillo-Corvalán, 'Joyce's and Borges's Afterlives of Shakespeare', *Comparative Literature* 60, no. 3 (2008): 207–27; Darrah Lustig, 'The Task of the Survivor in Ruth Klüger's "weiter leben" (1992) and "Still Alive" (2001)', *Studia austriaca* 21 (2013): 29–50; Vilashini Cooppan, 'The Ethics of World Literature: Reading Others, Reading Otherwise', in *Teaching World Literature*, ed. David Damrosch (New York: The Modern Language Association of America, 2009), 34–43.
18. Samuel Hodgkin, 'Classical Persian Canons of the Revolutionary Press: Abū al-Qāsim Lāhūtī's Circles in Istanbul and Moscow', in *Persian Literature and Modernity: Production and Reception*, ed. Hamid Rezaei Yazdi and Arshavez Mozafari (London: Routledge, 2019), 187.
19. Saliha Paker, 'Translation as *Terceme* and *Nazire*: Culture-bound Concepts and Their Implications for a Conceptual Framework for Research on Ottoman Translational History', in *Crosscultural Transgressions: Research Models in Translation Studies II: Historical and Ideological Issues*, ed. Theo Hermans (Manchester: St. Jerome Publishing, 2002), 137.
20. Paker, 'Translation as *Terceme* and *Nazire*', 121.
21. Orhan İyişenyürek, 'Köprülüzâde Abdullah Paşa ve El Yazısı Divanının Muhtevası', *Cumhuriyet İlahiyat Dergisi* 26, no. 1 (2022): 23–44.
22. Kim, 'The Poet Nefʿī'.
23. Jonathan Brody Kramnick, *Making the English Canon: Print-Capitalism and the Cultural Past, 1700–1770* (Cambridge: Cambridge University Press, 1998), 1.
24. Kim, *The Last of an Age*, 139.
25. Tahera Qutbuddin, 'Books on Arabic Philology and Literature: A Teaching Collection Focused on Religious Learning and the State Chancery', in *Treasures of Knowledge: An Inventory of the Ottoman Palace Library (1502/3–1503/4)*, ed. Gülru Necipoğlu, Cemal Kafadar and Cornell H. Fleischer (Leiden: Brill, 2019), 1: 609.
26. Didem Havlioğlu, *Mihrî Hatun: Performance, Gender-Bending and Subversion in Ottoman Intellectual History* (New York: Syracuse University Press, 2017), 43. Although late Ottoman authors did not specifically use the term 'canon' (*kanon*), Chapter 2 shows that they employed the term 'classics' (*klasikler*) in their writings as they identified works which had a high cultural value for them.
27. John Guillory, *Cultural Capital: The Problem of Literary Canon Formation* (Chicago: University of Chicago Press, 1993), 30.
28. Guillory, *Cultural Capital*, 30.
29. Trevor Ross, *The Making of the English Literary Canon: From the Middle Ages to the Late Eighteenth Century* (Montreal and Kingston: McGill-Queen's University Press, 1998), 24.

30. Esther-Miriam Wagner (ed.), *A Handbook and Reader of Ottoman Arabic* (Cambridge: Open Book Publishers, 2021).
31. Ghayde Ghraowi and Hacı Osman Gündüz (Ozzy) (eds), 'The Ascendant Field: Critical Engagements with Ottoman Arabic Literature', *Philological Encounters* 7, no. 3–4 (2022).
32. Arif Camoglu, 'Inter-imperial Dimensions of Turkish Literary Modernity', *MFS: Modern Fiction Studies* 64, no. 3 (2018): 449.
33. Camoglu, 'Inter-imperial Dimensions', 449.
34. Boutheina Khaldi, *Egypt Awakening in the Early Twentieth Century: Mayy Ziyādah's Intellectual Circles* (New York: Palgrave Macmillan, 2012), 142.
35. Khaldi, *Egypt Awakening*, 155.
36. Adıvar, *Memoirs of Halidé Edib*, 118–19.
37. For works that study the diverse languages of the empire, see Booth and Savina (eds), *Ottoman Translations*; Ringer and Charrière (eds), *Ottoman Culture and the Project Of Modernity*; Booth (ed.), *Migrating Texts*; and Mehmet Fatih Uslu and Fatih Altuğ (eds), *Tanzimat ve Edebiyat: Osmanlı İstanbulu'nda Modern Edebi Kültür* (Istanbul: Türkiye İş Bankası Kültür Yayınları, 2014).
38. Michael Allan, *In the Shadow of World Literature: Sites of Reading in Colonial Egypt* (Princeton: Princeton University Press, 2016), 76.
39. Allan, *In the Shadow of World Literature*; Karim Mattar, *Specters of World Literature*; Yaseen Noorani, 'Translating World Literature into Arabic and Arabic into World Literature: Sulayman al-Bustani's *al-Ilyadha* and Ruhi al-Khalidi's Arabic Rendition of Victor Hugo', in *Migrating Texts: Circulating Translations around the Ottoman Mediterranean*, ed. Marilyn Booth (Edinburgh: Edinburgh University Press, 2019), 236–65; and Shaden M. Tageldin, *Disarming Words: Empire and the Seductions of Translation in Egypt* (Berkeley: University of California Press, 2011).
40. M. Kaya Bilgegil, *M. Kaya Bilgegil'in Makaleleri*, ed. Zöhre Bilgegil (Ankara: Kültür Bakanlığı, 1993), 256.
41. Walter Feldman, 'The Indian Style and the Ottoman Literary Canon', *International Journal of Persian Literature* 3 (2018): 33.
42. Mervat F. Hatem, *Literature, Gender and Nation-Building in Nineteenth-Century Egypt: The Life and Works of ʿAʾisha Taymur* (New York: Palgrave Macmillan, 2011), 8.
43. Hatem indicates that Persian literary works also circulated in Egypt. At the same time, because schools in Egypt started to have a technocratic bent in the nineteenth century, there was a decrease in the use of Persian in the late Ottoman Egypt. See Hatem, *Literature, Gender and Nation-Building*, 50–52.
44. Ibid., 54.
45. Veli N. Yashin, '"The True Face of the Work": Sovereignty and Literary Form in Literary Historiography', *Middle Eastern Literatures* 20, no. 2 (2017): 166.
46. Etienne E. Charrière and Monica M. Ringer have recently called for a more comprehensive definition of the term '*Tanzimat*' and used it to refer to the

last years of the Ottoman Empire starting from 1839. Etienne E. Charrière and Monica M. Ringer, 'Introduction', in *Ottoman Culture and The Project of Modernity: Reform and Translation in the Tanzimat Novel*, ed. Monica M. Ringer and Etienne E. Charrière (New York: I. B. Tauris, 2020), 2–3. Literary critics have also used the term '*Tanzimat* literature' (*Tanzimat edebiyatı*) for categorising literary works from the late Ottoman Empire. Like in the *Nahḍa* Studies, more works among the *Tanzimat* Studies of the past few years have challenged these typical definitions of the *Tanzimat*. See M. Kayahan Özgül, *Dîvan Yolu'ndan Pera'ya Selâmetle: Modern Türk Şiirine Doğru* (Ankara: Hece Yayınları, 2006).

47. This book will draw on recent scholarly works that have undermined an understanding of the *nahḍa* as a stark rupture from an authentic classical tradition that initiated modernity. For a compilation of representative *nahḍa* texts, see Tarek El-Ariss, ed., *The Arab Renaissance: A Bilingual Anthology of the* Nahda (New York: The Modern Language Association of America, 2018).
48. Tarek El-Ariss, 'Let There be *Nahdah*!' *Cambridge Journal of Postcolonial Literary Inquiry* 2, no. 2 (2015): 260–66.
49. El-Ariss, 'Let There be *Nahdah*!', 263.
50. Ahmet Hamdi Tanpınar, *On Dokuzuncu Asır Türk Edebiyatı Tarihi* (Istanbul: Dergâh Yayınları, 2018), 52.
51. Selim Kuru, 'Early, Yet Already Late: Literary Musings on Historical Questions', *Journal of the Ottoman and Turkish Studies Association* 7, no. 1 (2020): 57.
52. Sharon Marcus, *Between Women: Friendship, Desire and Marriage in Victorian England* (Princeton: Princeton University Press, 2007), 7.
53. Alexis Wick, *The Red Sea: In Search of Lost Space* (Oakland: University of California Press, 2016), 54.
54. Wick, *The Red Sea*, 54.
55. Ringer and Charrière, 'Introduction', 11.
56. For a comprehensive overview of shifts in the meaning of the term '*edebiyat*' during the late Ottoman Empire and institutional transformations that contributed to the construction of a national literary canon in early republican Turkey, see Kani İrfan Karakoç, 'Ulus-devletleşme Süreci ve "'Türk' Edebiyatı"nın İnşası (1923–1950)' (Unpubl. PhD dissertation, İhsan Doğramacı Bilkent University, 2012).
57. Kramnick, *Making the English Canon*, 9.
58. Although *The Ottoman Canon* goes beyond the earlier scholarship that often compared Arabic or Turkish literature with only Western literatures, it is clearly not the first work that compares Turkish literature with Arabic literature. Critics such as Ḥusayn Mujīb al-Mıṣrī and Stephan Guth have compared the two literary traditions in a comprehensive manner. See Ḥusayn Mujīb al-Miṣrī, *Bayna al-adab al-ʿarabī wa-l-turkī: dirāsa fī al-adab al-islāmī al-muqāran* (Cairo: al-Dār al-Thaqāfiyya li-l-Nashr, 2003), and Stephan Guth, *Brückenschläge: eine integrierte 'turkoarabische' Romangeschichte*

(Mitte 19. bis Mitte 20. Jahrhundert) (Wiesbaden: Reichert Verlag, 2003). This book does not provide an extensive coverage of the similarities and intertextual relationships between the Arabic and Turkish traditions, as these critics do. Rather, it fleshes out the Ottoman canon's multilingual character to reassess some key categories used in literary studies and Middle Eastern Studies, such as 'classical Arabic literature' and 'Ottoman literature'.

59. Stephen Sheehi, 'Towards a Critical Theory of *al-Nahḍah*: Epistemology, Ideology and Capital', *Journal of Arabic Literature* 43, no. 2–3 (2012): 293.
60. Adıvar, *Memoirs of Halidé Edib*, 290.
61. Ibid., 396.
62. Cenab Şahabeddin, *Hac Yolunda* (Istanbul: Matbaa-i Ahmet İhsan, 1909), 158.
63. Mary Louise Pratt, *Imperial Eyes: Travel Writing and Transculturation* (New York: Routledge, 2003), 7.
64. For Persian works that were published in Istanbul in the nineteenth century, see Christophe Balaÿ, 'Diasporadaki Fars Edebiyatı: İstanbul 1865–1895', trans. Çiğdem Kurt, in *Tanzimat ve Edebiyat: Osmanlı İstanbulu'nda Modern Edebi Kültür*, ed. Fatih Altuğ and Mehmet Fatih Uslu (Istanbul: Türkiye İş Bankası Kültür Yayınları, 2014), 267–78. For an analysis of Persian literary modernity in a comparative frame, see Kamran Rastegar, *Literary Modernity Between the Middle East and Europe: Textual Transactions in Nineteenth-Century Arabic, English and Persian Literatures* (New York: Routledge, 2007).
65. See Şükran Fazlıoğlu, *Arap Romanında Türkler* (Istanbul: Küre Yayınları, 2006), and Ulrich W. Haarmann, 'Ideology and History, Identity and Alterity: The Arab Image of the Turk from the ʿAbbasids to Modern Egypt', *International Journal of Middle Eastern Studies* 20, no. 2 (1988): 175–96. By foregrounding the unequal power hiearchies within the Ottoman cultural context, *The Ottoman Canon* also undermines the prevalent view in Turkish secondary sources that Western imperialism caused the deterioration of the relations between the Arabs and the Turks who had lived in perfect harmony with each other, since both communities believed in the same religion, Islam.
66. Selim Deringil, '"They Live in a State of Nomadism and Savagery": The Late Ottoman Empire and the Post-Colonial Debate', *Comparative Studies in Society and History* 45, no. 2 (2003): 311–42, and Ussama Makdisi, 'Ottoman Orientalism', *The American Historical Review* 107, no. 3 (2002): 768–96.

1

A Multilingual Ottoman Ocean: Taverns, Exclusions and Ziya Pasha's *Harabat*

When Sultan Selim I (r. 1512–20) conquered Damascus in 1516, one of his first acts there was to restore the mausoleum of Ibn al-ᶜArabī (1165–1240). Marianne Boqvist has remarked that this restoration turned Ibn al-ᶜArabī into the Ottoman patron saint of the city.[1] Ziya Pasha (1829–80) again restored Ibn al-ᶜArabī's mausoleum during his tenure as a governor in Syria in 1877. Süleyman Nazif (1869–1927) noted that Ziya Pasha inscribed the following verses on the door of Ibn al-ᶜArabī's mausoleum:

That grand, holy mausoleum was restored
  It was actually the power of the Sheikh that restored it.
He accepted the special servant Ziya for this task
  As the benevolence of the Sheikh made him the governor of Syria.
Your beneficent gaze surely turns the earth into elixir
  Endow me with munificent favours, O Venerable Sheikh.[2]

Ziya Pasha here suggested that he did not restore this mauseloum; it was rather Ibn al-ᶜArabī himself who did it. Furthermore, Ziya Pasha's verses speak to Ibn al-ᶜArabī, who finds a 'new life' in Ziya Pasha's lines. Ibn al-ᶜArabī turns into an 'Ottoman sheikh' who supports the Ottoman rule in Syria.

While the lines on the mausoleum may suggest that Ziya Pasha would not have much difficulty in governing Syria, Ziya Pasha's tenure was extremely short. Based on archival research, M. Kaya Bilgegil has calculated that Ziya Pasha served as governor of Syria for only 122 days.[3] This short stay suggests that Ziya Pasha may have had difficulty adjusting to Syria. Indeed, Thomas S. Jago, the British Vice Consul, wrote:

> Zia Pasha has expressed to me his astonishment at the state of decay and stagnation which Damascus at present presents; no less his regret and wonder at the intense ignorence [*sic*] and superstition of its inhabitants as exemplified

> in the night of the 27th ultimo when on the occassion of the eclipse of the moon the entire population assembled on the house tops and during two hours, endeavored by a constant fusillade and by beating of tomtoms and tinpots to avert the supposed impending destruction of the orb by the attacks of a beast.[4]

In another letter, Jago noted that 'the fanatical Moslem population of Damascus' expressed a strong distaste against Ziya Pasha's liberal opinions. As a result, he claimed: 'I must not be held to exaggerate when I say that [Ziya Pasha] has not a friend in the country'.[5] It was not only Jago who believed that Ziya Pasha could not get along with the Syrians. Namık Kemal (1840–88) wrote in one of his letters to Menemenlizade Rıfat Bey (1856–1935) that, while Midhat Pasha (1822–84) may have reformed Baghdad, he would not achieve reforming Syria since the Syrians did not have *edep* (good manners). According to Namık Kemal, Syrians would do to Midhat Pasha what they had done to Ziya Pasha and hence force him to escape from Syria.[6]

This chapter will present a close reading of Ziya Pasha's poetry anthology, *Harabat* (Tavern, AH 1291–92 [1874/75–75/76]), to shed light on the Ottoman literary reservoir's multilingual character that makes Ibn al-ᶜArabī an 'Ottoman sheikh'. At the same time, as Jago's and Namık Kemal's observations may suggest, it will also point out the shifting historical and socieconomic contexts in which late Ottoman authors reassessed this reservoir. It will argue that, while *Harabat* affirms the Ottoman reservoir's stability and permanence, both the text itself and its sociopolitical context point to cultural transformations that undermine the Ottoman reservoir's stability. By examining Ziya Pasha's vision for the Ottoman reservoir and indicating the contradictions within the text, I undermine the influence paradigm that has led critics to study Ottoman literature as a precursor of modern Turkish literature only. Unlike the earlier scholarship, this chapter will also claim that *Harabat* does not necessarily capture Ziya Pasha's desire to revive the 'old literature'. *Harabat* reflects the epistemological shifts that would become more overt in later literary histories. For example, in the anthology's introduction, Ziya Pasha claimed that he belonged to a community that was like the Arabs' grandchildren and described Arabic literature as something that had emerged before Turkish literature. *Harabat* also emphasises that Ottoman poets should engage with European culture.

According to Jeffrey Di Leo, 'anthologies are discussed by progressive thinkers in terms of the canonical formations that they propose and the possible political and cultural directions in which they implicate their subject matter'.[7] Following Di Leo, I propose that *Harabat* compiles texts from diverse geographical and temporal origins and, rather than defining them as members of distinct national traditions, projects this compilation as the Ottoman 'reservoir' or canon that constitutes the basis for the artistic direction that Ziya Pasha advocated. My argument draws on Ziya Pasha's characterisation of the Ottoman language as an 'ocean' that encompasses Arabic, Persian and Turkish 'streams' in *Harabat*'s introduction, which was so influential that Ebüzziya Tevfik (1849–1913) published this introduction as a separate book, *Mukaddime-i Harabat* (AH 1311 [1893/94]). *Harabat* itself drew either strong criticism or praise. Yenişehirli Avni Bey (1826–83) wrote a *kaside* poem that praised *Harabat*, just as Lala Mustafaoğlu Hasan Nefi (1854–1917) wrote a praise work titled *Tamir-i Harabat* (Renovation of the Tavern).[8] In contrast, Namık Kemal wrote two books that list the misspellings and factual mistakes in *Harabat*, *Tahrib-i Harabat* (The Destruction of the Tavern, AH 1291 [1874/75]) and *Takib* (Follow-up, AH 1292 [1875/76]).[9]

Texts that belong to a canon affiliated with a particular linguistic tradition can join literary reservoirs, becoming part of another canon that encompasses works of diverse linguistic traditions. The Ottoman literary reservoir has a strictly circumscribed shoreline or boundary that allows intertextualisation only among a select number of texts for generating a canon that can incorporate works from diverse languages and cultures. Texts written in languages other than Arabic, Persian and Turkish also circulated in the Ottoman Empire; however, these linguistic traditions, such as Armenian or Kurdish, did not necessarily shape the cultural reservoir with which most members of the Ottoman literati identified. As I will also demonstrate later in the chapter, not even all Arabic, Persian and Turkish texts could become a part of Ziya Pasha's Ottoman reservoir.

Analysing *Harabat*'s introduction reveals the need for a new conceptual framework for multilingual canons. According to Rey Chow, '[the critique of Eurocentrism] must question the very assumption that nation-states with national languages are the only possible cultural formations that produce "literature" that is worth examining. Otherwise, we will simply see, as we have been seeing, the old Eurocentric models of language and literature study being reproduced ad infinitum in non-European language and literature pedagogy'.[10] Chow has warned against the practice of a literary criticism that often projects literary works as spokespeople of national communities, ignoring that texts can have multiple, even contradicting, cultural identities other than the national. Such a practice perpetuates institutional biases in literary studies today that, for example, would not consider classical Arabic poetry Ottoman because it assumes that texts have a single cultural identity circumscribed by the time and place of their production.

It ignores other ways in which texts from disparate geographical and temporal origins amalgamate and contribute to creating cultural communities, such as the Ottoman literati with which Ziya Pasha affiliated.

This chapter will first describe *Harabat*'s vision of the Ottoman reservoir and then perform a close reading of the sections in which Ziya Pasha wrote about the history of Arabic literature and Arabic poems that *Harabat* cites for revealing this reservoir's exclusionist character. After examining the ocean imagery in Ziya Pasha's anthology, I will discuss the context in which this work was written. While *Harabat* has often been studied as one of the last examples of the classical Ottoman tradition, the chapter will argue that Ziya Pasha's anthology augurs key transformations that would shape modern Arabic and Turkish literatures, since Ziya Pasha provided new perspectives about the relationships among the Ottoman reservoir's diverse linguistic traditions.

Ziya Pasha's Ottoman Ocean and the Formation of Canons

Born in Istanbul, Ziya Pasha, like many members of the Ottoman literati, was well versed in Persian, Arabic and Turkish. He taught himself Arabic and learned Persian through reading its masterpieces, such as the *Shāhnāma* (c. 977–1010) by Firdavsī (c. 940–c. 1020–26).[11] He also showed the same voracious interest in learning French, which increasingly became an essential component of an Ottoman intellectual's formation during Ziya Pasha's time. According to Ebüzziya Tevfik, he could understand whatever he read in French and even translate *Histoire des Arabes et des Mores d'Espagne* (History of the Arabs and Moors of Spain, 1851) by Louis Viardot (1800–83) into Turkish after studying the language for only six months.[12]

Ziya Pasha was a member of the 'Young Ottomans', an influential community of thinkers who believed that the empire was experiencing a political and cultural decline in the face of territorial losses, economic adversities and demographic changes. Thus, these thinkers advocated constitutional government and sought a synthesis between Islamic values and the ideals of the European enlightenment for halting this decline. Many Young Ottomans advocated the political vision of 'Ottomanism'. Annie Greene has defined Ottomanism as a 'civic ideology'[13] that upholds a 'shared patriotic allegiance and political equality for all imperial citizens, based on commitment to and reciprocity between the imperial citizen and the state'.[14] For example, the Ottoman Baghdadi Jewish community could simultanously identify as imperial citizens who sought protection from the Ottoman administration and as Jews who relied on their diasporic networks during times of hardship.[15] At the same time, as Greene has demonstrated, while Ottomanism promised a sense of nominal equality for imperial subjects of different ethnic and religious backgrounds, 'the system favored Sunni Muslim urban elites'.[16] In fact, the exclusion of various literatures such as Ladino (Judeo-Spanish) from *Harabat* suggests that, even though some Young Ottomans advocated Ottomanism as a political ideology, many of them did not necessarily view various works produced in the empire as a stream flowing into the Ottoman literary reservoir. Furthermore, numerous Ottoman thinkers still thought that political visions such as Ottomanism put the Sunni Muslim community at a disadvantage. For example, Ziya Pasha believed that the state had started to give privileges to non-Muslim communities at the expense of Muslims.[17] Likewise, Ziya Pasha once told Hüseyin Vasfi Pasha (d. AH 1296? [1878/79]) that one could not trust the words of an Armenian in Egypt since all Armenians were liars.[18]

Mustafa Fazıl/Muṣṭafā Fāḍil Pasha (1830–75), the brother of the Egyptian khedive Ismāᶜīl (r. 1863–79), decided to contact prominent members of the Young Ottomans in Istanbul because he wanted to use this group to reinforce his interests which often clashed with the Ottoman administration's agenda. Therefore, he invited its two most famous intellectuals, Ziya Pasha and Namık Kemal, to Paris.[19] According to Ebüzziya Tevfik, Mustafa Fazıl/Muṣṭafā Fāḍil Pasha gave the highest stipend to Ziya Pasha, who received 3,000 liras per month and the second-largest to Namık Kemal, who received 2,000 liras per month, suggesting that Ziya Pasha was the group's most eminent member.[20] Furthermore, Mustafa Fazıl/Muṣṭafā Fāḍil Pasha decided to pay 25,000 francs to Ziya Pasha in order to support his publishing activities.[21]

Ziya Pasha initially received financial support from the Egyptian pasha and played the leading role for newspapers that voiced open criticism against the Ottoman government, including the famous *Hürriyet* (Freedom). Mustafa Fazıl/Muṣṭafā Fāḍil Pasha eventually decided to defund the Young Ottomans once the Egyptian pasha had restored amicable relations with the Istanbul administration. This defunding created immense difficulties for the Young Ottomans, which eventually dissolved.

Although the Young Ottomans often had deep disagreements with each other, they shared a disdain for state bureaucrats and advocated a constitutional government, which they thought would curb the power of these bureaucrats. They drew on Western thinkers such as Rousseau (1712–1778), Volney (1757–1820) and Montesquieu (1689–1755) as they formed their political and cultural vision for the empire. At the same time, they also criticised what they considered unbridled Westernisation, which the state bureaucrats spearheaded. The Young Ottomans believed that these bureaucrats adopted 'superficial aspects' of the European culture, such as Western fashion, but dismissed its fundamental values, such as freedom. The Young Ottomans also engaged with Orientalist scholarship. Ebüzziya Tevfik indicated that the Young Ottomans extensively read the British Museum Library's Arabic collection during their exile in London and formed strong friendships with the Orientalists who came to the library.[22] The Young Ottomans engaged in extensive debates with Orientalists such as Ernest Renan (1823–92) and Léon Cahun (1841–1900), sometimes strongly negating their views and sometimes building on their ideas.[23]

One can observe the impact of Ziya Pasha's engagement with Orientalist discourse in his famous newspaper article titled 'Şiir ve İnşa' (Poetry and Prose, 1868). Like many Orientalists of his time, Ziya Pasha in this article argued that the Ottomans could never create original poetry because they imitated the Iranians, who hitherto had imitated the Arabs. Imitation stifled the creativity of the Ottoman poets and prevented the emergence of an authentic Ottoman self.[24] Ziya Pasha also complained about the gap between the intellectuals and the 'common people' (*avam*). This gap had detrimental consequences. No one except for a few people who had received comprehensive scribal training could understand the imperial decrees that were supposed to address all subjects of the empire.[25] When the Tunisians demanded an Arabic translation of the new constitution, the original constitution in Ottoman Turkish was so incomprehensible that no one could translate it into Arabic.[26] Ziya Pasha here complained about the Ottoman language's untranslatability to Arabic.

'Şiir ve İnşa' also claims that the Ottoman subjects remained clueless about cultural and political reforms because the language of intellectuals who demanded these changes sounded too foreign to the public. Therefore, Ziya Pasha called for the formation of a new intellectual who would not remain steeped in useless courtly formalities but craft a new language that would reach society at large. Having asked the reader what Ottoman poetry was, Ziya Pasha himself gave the answer. He insisted that no poet that *Harabat* would praise, including Baki (1526–1600) and Nedim (1681–1730), had composed authentic Ottoman poetry. Ziya Pasha instead praised Turkish folk poetry as authentic Ottoman poetry; therefore, Ziya Pasha called for a return to this poetry's simple language, which would break down the barrier between the elite and the commoners.[27]

Although 'Şiir ve İnşa' depicts Arabic and Persian as sources of influence, *Harabat* suggests that the Arabic and Persian languages are an integral component of the Ottoman language. Arab and Persian poets become members of the Ottoman literary reservoir through a process that John Guillory has called 'the deracination of the text tradition':

> It is just by suppressing culture in the ethnographic sense – or reserving that sense of culture for non-'Western' artifacts – that the traditional curriculum can appropriate the 'great works' of Western civilization for the purpose of constituting an imaginary cultural unity. [. . .] The deracination of the text tradition thus forces us to define the intertextual relation, say, between Aquinas and Aristotle as evidence of the continuity of Western culture, but it allows us to set aside the fact that Aristotle and Aquinas have almost nothing in common *culturally*.[28]

This deracination, slightly or even fully disassociating texts from their immediate contexts, facilitates the formation of the Ottoman literary reservoir. Ziya Pasha frequently mentioned that texts such as the Persian *Gulistān* (1258) by Sa^{c}dī (c. 1213–91/92) or the pre-Islamic *al-Mu^{c}allaqāt* poems transferred him to a mystical world, although he never described this world to the reader and left it mysterious to the uninitiated. For Ziya Pasha, these texts do not necessarily reveal ethnographic information about Persian or Arab communities, as they often lead to a mystical world that those well versed in the Ottoman literary reservoir should have already visited.

Although its three volumes (excluding the introduction) amount to 1,217 pages, *Harabat* does not provide encyclopaedic coverage of the Arabic, Persian and Turkish poetic traditions. It instead selects works from each to affirm a multilingual Ottoman heritage, viewing the Persian and Arabic traditions as integral components of a grand imperial cultural identity. By not simply amalgamating but also making categorical claims on the Persian, Arabic and Turkish poetic heritages in its introduction, *Harabat* marks an Ottoman intellectual's authoritative stance in defining, categorising and analysing these literary corpora.

The work's introduction, written in the *mesnevi* form (poetry composed in rhyming couplets), reveals Ziya Pasha's opinions on the Ottoman reservoir's diverse streams of linguistic traditions. At the beginning of *Harabat*'s introduction, Ziya Pasha praised God[29] and the Prophet Muḥammad (11–17). Then he provided his reasons behind composing this anthology. This section includes mostly biographical information about Ziya Pasha, who, through composing the *Harabat*, wrote down the works of Arab, Turkish and 'Iranian'[30] poets who had shaped his cultural and intellectual formation (18–31). He discussed the Chagatai and Ottoman Turkish poets who had composed their works before the empire acquired vast territories and adopted an imperial, cosmopolitan identity (32–41).[31]

Afterwards, he described the requirements of being a poet, as he argued that poets needed to have both natural talent and comprehensive training in the linguistic sciences (41–55). Ziya Pasha then provided the biographies of *Rum* (an epithet used for Anatolia and Ottoman Turkish) poets who had achieved prominence after the empire had expanded its territories in the fifteenth century (55–80). At the end of this lengthy introduction, he expressed his opinion on 'Iranian poets' (80–97) and then 'Arab poets' (98–102). In the final section, Ziya Pasha lamented his declining health, apologising for any mistakes he might have made while compiling the anthology (103–6).

The lines below, which capture Ziya Pasha's vision for the Ottoman culture, do not project Arabic and Persian literatures as separate 'springs' that nurtured Ottoman civilisation, but instead as seas the confluence of which formed its ocean:

At first, the Turkish language was on its own
  Then Persian elevated and doubled it.
These two jewels [*gevher*] also befitted each other so well
  As if milk and sugar mixed with each other.
Or two seas of knowledge and wisdom
  Came together and became an ocean.
No, three seas came together
  And from their union emerged this majestic ocean.
Since the Persian first
  Attained perfection by uniting with the Arabic language.
This language is the Ottoman language
  So be aware that this is a peerless ocean.
Someone who knows the Ottoman language
  Is an architect with devices.
Who has mastered several tools
  Able to create various transformations. (37–38)

Unlike 'Şiir ve İnşa', which argues that Turkish culture lived under the influence of Persian civilisation, Ziya Pasha in *Harabat* claimed that the Persian language elevated the Turkish language to generate the Ottoman ocean. In the anthology's introduction, Ziya Pasha provided a lengthy description of the Ottoman language, because he defined poetry as the mirror (*ayine*) of language (51). Ziya Pasha called the languages that mixed in the Ottoman ocean *gevher*, which means not only 'jewel' but also 'essence'; therefore, the Ottoman 'ocean' – or what I call reservoir – received the streams of languages and their literary traditions in such a way that several cultural essences intermingled with each other, to the point of becoming indistinguishable, mixing much like fresh water and salt water between river mouth and sea – or, in Ziya Pasha's exact words, like sugar and milk.

Understanding the imagery of the 'ocean', and especially its resonances with Islamic mysticism, leads to crucial insights into the vision for which Ziya Pasha's 'tavern' stood. Mystics have seen themselves as drops that yearn for union with the divine Ocean, God. When Ziya Pasha wrote at the beginning of *Harabat*'s introduction that all created beings continuously repeated the word 'God' (5), he suggested that linguistic discrepancies prevented us from seeing, on both the metaphysical and cultural level, an overarching unity. Ziya Pasha's mystical view of creation resonates with the *Harabat*'s vision of culture and identity. Diverse manifestations of creation seek unity with God as a metaphysical Ocean; diverse poetic heritages unite in the Ottoman reservoir as a cultural ocean that provides vigour, stability and permanence. *Harabat* affirms a non-volatile vision of Ottoman culture, a vision that does not suffer from a cultural crisis or anxiety, as Ziya Pasha in the introduction's final section described *Harabat* as an assembly (*bezm*) in which Arab, Persian and Turkish poets found repose (103).

Most literary histories after *Harabat* claim that Ottoman culture always lived under the influence of another culture and had to find a new source of influence that would revive an ailing empire in crisis in the nineteenth century. For example, Şehabeddin Süleyman (1885–1919) in his *Tarih-i Edebiyat-ı Osmaniyye* (History of Ottoman Literature, 1912/13) claimed that the Eastern 'spring' (*menba*) had nurtured Ottoman literature until the nineteenth century when the Western 'spring' became its primary source.[32] İbrahim Necmi [Dilmen] (1889–1945) in his *Tarih-i Edebiyat Dersleri* (Lessons on Literary History, 1922) similarly argued that, while Ottoman literature had hitherto lived under the influence of Persian and Arabic, it had to seek the Western spring to rejuvenate and create a new literature: Şinasi (1826–71) discovered the spring of the West to revive the Ottoman culture.[33] The imagery of springs also appeared in Turkish literary histories written after the Ottoman Empire's demise. İsmail Hikmet [Ertaylan] (1889–1967) in his *Türk Edebiyatı Tarihi* (History of Turkish Literature, 1925–26) wrote that three springs – that is, Arab, Persian and Byzantine influences – had shaped Ottoman literature.[34] Halid Ziya [Uşaklıgil] (1865–1945) noted that one should seek the 'old spring' of Ottoman literature not among the Ottoman themselves, but instead in something outside the Ottoman milieu.[35] Ahmet Hamdi Tanpınar (1901–62) in his *On Dokuzuncu Asır Türk Edebiyatı Tarihi* (History of Nineteenth-Century Turkish Literature, 1949) noted about the condition of Ottoman poetry that 'it was as if all springs dried up and humankind was left naked',[36] and later, on the art of the same period, that 'the creative spring of life dried up'.[37] What unites all these histories is the assumption that a modern, more rejuvenated Ottoman literature emerged only after it had distanced itself from a culture assumed to be drying up.

Two terms – ocean and spring – stand for different kinds of canon formation circumscribing the texts that a community, such as the Ottoman literati, chooses to preserve and remember. *Harabat* challenges the commonly held notion that a literary canon is a list of texts that belong to only a single linguistic tradition, as it asserts that Arabic, Persian and Turkish traditions mix so perfectly in the Ottoman 'ocean' that they form the canon that an Ottoman poet should master. However, in many histories written after *Harabat*, Ottoman literature could never surpass and merely imitated the Arabic and Persian literatures that had set the standards for eloquence and poetics.

The Ottoman ocean is significantly shaped by its milieu's sociopolitical dimensions. On the one hand, the literary ocean in *Harabat* seems to defy boundaries and even promise a metaphysical transcendence; on the other hand, this ocean has geopolitical boundaries – that is, what Ziya Pasha called 'the Ottoman language'. I thus choose to use the term 'reservoir' to describe this ocean to emphasise that it is, after all, human-made and shaped by the aesthetic biases of the writers who forged, preserved and made claims on it.

Harabat is exclusionist because Ziya Pasha made no mention of texts from diverse linguistic traditions, such as Greek, Armenian, Kurdish, or Albanian, which also circulated widely in the empire. Nor does his anthology strive to include all the works of Arabic, Persian and Turkish poetry. These exclusions serve to reinforce the Ottoman reservoir's boundaries. For example, *Harabat*'s first volume features a section on Arabic *qaṣīda* poems, which includes 42 works in total, revealing insights into the Arabic works that form Ziya Pasha's Ottoman ocean.[38] At the beginning of this section, Ziya Pasha listed the seven *Muᶜallaqāt* in order (1: 214–33). After the *Muᶜallaqāt*, he quoted works from numerous poets in no particular chronological order. For example, after al-Shaykh Muḥammad al-Būṣīrī's (c. 1212–c. 96) famous *Qaṣīdat al-Burda* (The Mantle Ode) (1: 238–43), Ziya Pasha quoted poems from al-Mutanabbī (d. 965) (1: 243). The most frequently quoted poet in this section is al-Mutanabbī, a prominent figure of the Ottoman reservoir, as al-Nahrawālī also observed when Ahmed Çelebi recited his *takhmīs* during his stay in Istanbul in 1558. The section includes four excerpts by al-Mutanabbī (1: 243–44, 1: 244–46, 1: 246–48, 1: 248).[39] Ziya Pasha twice quoted Ibn al-Fāriḍ (1181–1235) (1: 250–51, 1: 251–52), whose mystical poetry most likely held great appeal for the Ottoman poets who affiliated themselves with taverns, and Jamīl ibn ᶜAbd

Allāh ibn Maᶜmar al-ᶜUdhrī (d. 701) (1: 276, 1: 276–77), another poet whose works also feature themes of intense love. This section quotes prominent poets such as al-Shanfarā (d. c. 525) (1: 233–35), al-Maᶜarrī (973–1057) (1: 248–49) and al-Farazdaq (c. 641–728/30) (1: 284–85)[40] only once. All poets included in this section are male, with one exception: al-Khansāᵓ (c. 575–c. 645) (1: 273). *Harabat* also includes works from numerous Andalusian poets such as Ibn ᶜAbdūn al-Andalusī (1050–1134/35) (1: 260–62), Lisān al-Dīn Ibn al-Khaṭīb al-Andalusī (1313–74/75) (1: 262–65) and Ibn Khafāja al-Andalusī (1058/59–1138/39) (1: 265–67); almost all their works are listed one after another. The most 'recent' poet that this section includes is Ibn al-Azraq al-Andalusī (1427/28–91) (1: 270–71). In contrast to the Turkish *kaside* section, which presented works from the seventeenth century and even works by Ziya Pasha himself, this section features no Arabic works written in the Ottoman Empire.

The Arabic poems that *Harabat*'s second volume includes consists of verses and sometimes even just a few lines from various love poems (*tashbībāt*) and short literary selections (*muqaṭṭaᶜāt*). On some pages, Ziya Pasha quoted a few verses, although he did not know who composed the poem (*lā adrī*). For example, he offered excerpts from nine different Arabic poems on page 396 of the second volume and next to them added 'not' (*lā*) to indicate that he did not know who had composed them. The poets that Ziya Pasha did not remember include Imām ᶜAlī (c. 600–661) and Manjak Pasha (1598–1669) (2: 396).[41] Unlike the section on Arabic *qaṣīda* poems in the first volume, *Harabat*'s second volume comprised few Arabic works produced within the Ottoman Empire; yet, the works included are by authors who held imperial administrative positions, such as Sadi Çelebi (d. 1539) (2: 409), Köprülüzade Abdullah Pasha (1684–1735) (2: 384, 2: 387) and Davud Pasha (1774–1851) (2: 394). As E. Khayyat has put it, '[w]ith its peculiar canon of Arabic poetry, [*Harabat*] takes us beyond any idea of Arabic language and literature as the language and literature of Arabs. *Harabat*'s reactionary vision of Arabic could also be interpreted as a progressive model for the study of Arabic today'.[42]

Tahera Qutbuddin has made key observations about the Arabic works in the Topkapı Palace Library's 1502/3–1503/4 inventory written and transcribed by the royal librarian Atufi (d. 1541). In many ways, Ziya Pasha and Atufi made similar choices. For instance, just as al-Mutanabbī's poems are the most frequently quoted Arabic works in *Harabat*, '[t]he *Diwan* (Poetry Collection) of the poetic prodigy al-Mutanabbī is the star of the show (34 copies)'[43] in Atufi's collection. This is followed by 'the lengthy, mystical, love and wine poems of Ibn al-Fāriḍ (30 copies)',[44] just as Ibn al-Fāriḍ is the second-most frequently quoted poet in *Harabat*'s volume on *qaṣīda* poems. Therefore, the 'Ottoman canon of Arabic philology and literature at the turn of the [sixteenth] century'[45] that Qutbuddin has observed in Atufi's inventory did not change significantly. Furthermore, Qutbuddin has noted that the Umayyad poet Jarīr (d. 728?) is missing in Atufi's inventory; Jarīr is not quoted in the first volume of Ziya Pasha's *Harabat* either. At the same time, while 'Andalusian and North African works seem to be almost completely absent in all literary and philological disciplines'[46] in Atufi's sixteenth-century inventory, Ziya Pasha's *Harabat* extensively quotes from Andalusian poets, perhaps reflecting the pasha's engagement with the Orientalist discourse on Andalusia.

Like the section on Arabic poems, the sections on Persian poems in *Harabat* include non-Ottoman and/or pre-Ottoman works. For example, Ziya Pasha quoted twelve different excerpts by Anvarī (c. 1126–1187/88 or 1189/90) (1: 119–38) and five different excerpts from ᶜUrfī (1555/56–1590/91) (1: 167–81) in the section on Persian *qaṣīda* poems in *Harabat*'s first volume. At the same time, this very section also comprises works by members of the Ottoman literati, including Sultan Selim I (1: 158). *Harabat* also does not make a distinction among Persianate works produced in Iran and those produced on the Indian subcontinent. For example, it presents Persian poems by the Indo-Persian poet Masᶜūd Ṣaᶜd Salmān (1046–1121/22) (1: 206–7).[47] The second volume includes short excerpts from Persian poetry. Some of these works feature excerpts from well-known Ottoman figures, such as Fuzuli (d. 1556) (2: 276) and Nefi (d. 1635) (2: 277). The third volume offers the reader excerpts from different Persian *mathnavī* works, such as Rūmī's (d. 1273) *Mathnavī* (3: 227–31), Amīr Khusrav's (1253–1325) *Khusrav u Shīrīn* (3: 238–43), Saᶜdī's *Būstān* (3: 251–66), ᶜAṭṭār's (1145–1221) *Manṭiq al-ṭayr* (3: 289–98), Firdavsī's *Shāhnāma* (3: 298–303), Maktabī's (d. 1510/11) *Laylā u Majnūn* (3: 370–73), Nāẓim Hiravī's (d. 1657) *Yūsuf u Zulaykhā* (3: 379–85) and Vaḥshī's (1532?– 83) *Farhād u Shīrīn* (3: 420–26).

Like the sections on Arabic poetry, *Harabat*'s section on Persian poetry also includes verses next to which Ziya Pasha wrote at the beginning '*lā*' (not), again to indicate that he did not know who composed these verses. Furthermore, Ziya Pasha put a parenthesis around some hemistiches if he did not know who had composed them and wrote '*lā*' before or after these hemistiches, as in this example:

> Not (Each city is as sick as its doctor.)
> (Everywhere the cooped-up bird goes is a garden.) Not (2: 303)

These two hemistiches come from different sources. The first hemistisch is from a poem by Ṣāᵓib Tabrīzī (1592–1676), while the other is from another poem by the same author.[48] In Ziya Pasha's ocean, a particular hemistich from Ṣā'ib Tabrīzī's poem becomes 'deracinated' from the context of its source culture and flows into the Ottoman literary reservoir, as it transforms into the first hemistich of a verse that ends with a hemistich from another poem by Ṣā'ib Tabrīzī. Furthermore, Ziya Pasha did not even indicate that the hemistiches were by Ṣā'ib Tabrīzī. This particular example shows the extent to which the Ottoman reservoir intertextualises different elements of the Persian literary heritage.

According to Ferenc Csirkés, 'premodern anthologies of poetry are spaces for memory as well as models for future works. They are both personal, reflecting the anthologizer's particular taste and potentially communal, serving a whole "textual community", to use Brian Stock's phrase, i. e., a network of people with varying degrees of literacy who might either access a certain text directly by reading it, or indirectly, by listening to its recitation'.[49] Building on Csirkés, I claim that *Harabat* reflects both the anthologiser's taste and the textual community with which Ziya Pasha affiliated himself. Ziya Pasha perpetuated the aesthetic biases of a century-long tradition that one observes in Atufi's inventory, as he also provided new directions to it when he made numerous references to Andalusian works. Ziya Pasha claimed that he 'took whatever he could see' when he composed *Harabat*; he did not merely choose the masterpieces of each tradition.[50] Although Ziya Pasha may have declared to include diverse kinds of works,[51] not just 'masterpieces', 'all what he could see' was shaped by the centuries-old tradition of the Ottoman literati who had filled and shored up the Ottoman literary reservoir. Shifting historical conditions, such as Ziya Pasha's engagement with the Orientalist scholarship that likely contributed to his interest in Andalusia, also circumscribed what he could see.

The section on Arab poets in *Harabat*'s introduction further reveals that Ziya Pasha did not merely list Arabic poems; he also made categorical claims on them (98–102). He praised the *Muᶜallaqāt* poems because they display rhetorical skills (*belagat*). If the Qur'an had not been revealed, these poems would continue to be the most eloquent works. He compared the Qur'an's revelation with the emergence of the sun, whose rise renders other stars – that is, *al-Muᶜallaqāt* – invisible (98). Ziya Pasha wrote that all Arabs, by nature, were poets due to the Arabic language's pliable nature. He then praised various poets such as al-Shanfarā and Kaᶜb ibn Zuhayr (d. c. 646/47) (99). Ziya Pasha criticised the Umayyad period, during which time poetry did not achieve the level of eloquence that the *Muᶜallaqāt* did. The establishment of an Arab caliphate in Damascus led to the deterioration of the Arabs' moral values, as Arab poets started to care only about praising political rulers for material gains (100). Ziya Pasha also claimed that Arabic poetry deteriorated in quality once Arabs intermingled with foreigners. He then praised certain literary figures, such as al-Akhṭal (c. 640–c. 710), al-Jāḥiẓ (776–868/69), al-Mutanabbī, Ibn al-Rūmī (836–96), Abū al-ᶜAtāhiya (b. 748), Abū Tammām (d. 845/46) and Abū Nuwās (d. c. 813–15) (101). He praised Ibn al-Fāriḍ as peerless and beyond comparison in terms of influence. Finally, he emphasised that many great poets had come from Andalusia and listed some of them, such as Abū Rakwa (975–1007), Ibn ᶜAṭiyya (d. 1146/47) and Ibn Khafāja. The last line of this section emphasises that thousands of eloquent Arabs have come to this world, but it is impossible to list them all. Here, Ziya Pasha suggested that he had to make a selection – that is, generate a canon – as he wrote on Arab poets (102). The Ottoman literary reservoir signifies that the empire saw itself at the latest frontier of the Islamic Middle East's complex heritage, both preserving it and taking it to new heights.

Poets of the Ottoman reservoir 'live on' in the 'Ottoman tavern'. Ziya Pasha described the reason behind why he named his anthology *Harabat*:

> Because wandering dervishes meet each other at taverns
> I gave it [the anthology] the title *Tavern*.
> No one would believe in me if I gave it the title *Mosque*,
> Poets do not stay in mosques for long.
> Wine provides companionship to poets.
> The tavern [*harabat*] is the abode of wandering dervishes. (31)

Ottoman poets used the imagery of the tavern, *harabat*, to refer to a space of intense passion and spiritual intoxication. In many Ottoman poems, believers attain mystical divine love in taverns as they contemplate religion's inner essence instead of blindly following rituals in mosques.[52] While the ascetics (*zühhad*) who frequent mosques and meticulously fulfill their religious obligations feel a sense of haughtiness over others, the carefree dervishes (*rindan*) who frequent taverns might be lax in following their religious rituals. However, unlike ascetics, they achieve a proper understanding of God through their genuine devotion.

Harabat quotes the following Persian verses by Niẓāmī (1141–1209), which further reinforce this division between the mosque and the tavern:

> This is not a mosque where its doors are open any moment
> Where you can come late and move quickly to the first row.
> This is the Tavern of Magians, and *rind*s [carefree dervishes] dwell here
> There are beauties, candles, wine, sugar, reed flute and songs.
> Whatever wonders that exists are present here
> (in this tavern there are) Muslims, Armenians,
> Zoroastrian, Nestorians and Jews.[53]

Although the tavern undermines strict social boundaries, it is not like a mosque that is open to everyone. It accepts only a select few. Many poems on taverns in *Harabat* explicitly state that they address a specific group of people – 'people of virtue' (*ehl-i kemal*) (2: 20), or 'people of the tavern' (*erbab-ı harabat*) (2: 6) – which further reinforces the exclusionist character of the Ottoman tavern. Just as Ziya Pasha described himself as one of 'the deserted people of the tavern' (2: 20), Sultan Süleyman I (r. 1520–66) wrote in one of his Turkish poems that he substituted the mosque's lamp with the tavern's (2: 124). The sultan thus also emphasised his affiliation with the poets who belonged to the tavern's circle. In addition to metaphysical unity and transcendence, the tavern stands for a world where poetry and politics live in harmony.

Harabat includes various Arabic, Persian and Turkish poems from Ottoman-era literati, officials and members of the Ottoman dynasty, including Fuzuli (1: 44–46, 2: 124), Köprülüzade Abdullah Pasha (2: 384, 2: 387, 2: 408), Sultan Selim II (r. 1566–74) (2: 80), Sultan Selim III (r. 1789–1807) (2: 80), Sultan Murad III (r. 1574–95) (2: 86), Sultan Bayezid II (r. 1481–1512) (2: 127), Sultan Selim I (1: 158, 2: 187–8, 2: 274, 2: 335, 2: 338, 2: 360, 2: 377) and Şehzade Cem (1459–95) (2: 363).[54] Sultan Murad III (r. 1574–95) expressed the sentiments of a vagabond in his Turkish verses:

> The heart is afflicted with the misery of love; is there any remedy, O God?
> Is there any vagrant like me in this world, O God? (2: 64)

In one of his Persian poems, Sultan Süleyman I lamented his eternal suffering:

> The eye of fire is the heart drowned in my tears
> The effect of this spring is the source of my ruin. (2: 277)

Similarly, the vizier Köprülüzade Abdullah Pasha voiced despair in his Arabic verses:

> Wherever I turned, rain clouds supplied
> Seeds or life, but they did not provide vitality or nourishment.
> My love for her is entrenched in my heart
> Her everlasting beauty is both visible on me and concealed in my soul.
> I reminisced about her departure and my tears
> Suddenly appeared like scattered pearls. (2: 408)

Although Ottoman sultans and viziers may have enjoyed political authority, their poems often expressed powerlessness *vis-à-vis* the beloved and God.[55]

For some late Ottoman thinkers, these expressions of vulnerability may not have fit into an era of political and cultural reforms that wanted to strengthen the empire within the global order shaped by a growing Western European hegemony. According to Süleyman Nazif, Namık Kemal himself depicted *Harabat* as 'a tavern [*meyhane*] that destroys the Young Ottoman ambition to construct a *darülfünun* of literature' in one of the letters he sent to an unspecified addressee.[56] The rivalry between the tavern and the mosque – which refers to disparate ways of living Islam, the former emphasising its mystical and the latter its legalistic dimensions – is recast as a rivalry between the tavern and the *darülfünun*, a European-style university in Istanbul that was established in the nineteenth century. The *darülfünun*, an institution that many scholars have considered the quintessential symbol of Ottoman modernity, which advocated rationality and scientific progress, here takes the role of mosques.[57] This rivalry crystallised burgeoning debates on who had the authority to read, analyse and give future direction to the Ottoman poetic tradition. The new vision of cultural and literary modernity aligned itself with sober responsibility rather than intoxicating transcendence.[58]

Refashioning the Past: Modernity and Harabat

Harabat displays a manifest consciousness about a decline after a golden age, which, in Ziya Pasha's view, corresponded to the reigns of Selim I and Süleyman I. These two sultans receive the loftiest praises in *Harabat*, because they cared as much about the order of language (*tanzim-i lisan*) as about the state.[59] Over time, so Ziya Pasha thought, this harmony between stately order and literary-linguistic order began to vanish. *Harabat* thus suggests that, if language and its mirror, poetry, are neglected, the social order will fall apart and the sultans too will be forgotten. After all, Ziya Pasha insisted that poets crafted words until their last breath, while political leaders perished and were quickly forgotten. In *Harabat*'s introduction, Ziya Pasha wrote regarding the 'thousands of kings who have come to this world':

> That eye which today looks at the daylight
> Decays tomorrow into nests for ants and snakes. (25)

Poetry, unlike sultans, is immortal. The immortality of their works, so he argued, was the ultimate 'revenge of the virtuous literati' (*fuzelanın intikamı*) (55).

Although he may have found some consolation in his poetry that continued to live on after his death, Ziya Pasha encountered many hardships during his lifetime, contributing to his works' cynical tone. Both his famous *Terci-i*

Bend and *Terkib-i Bend* express the existential crisis of a perplexed and even rebellious poet who complains about fate's fickleness, ruthless political affairs and the incomprehensible mysteries of the creation.[60] Due to his harsh criticism of grand viziers such as Ali Pasha (1815–71), Ziya Pasha was punished by exile. He also suffered from serious health issues and witnessed his writings' censorship. He lived in dire poverty in his final years, as governor of Adana. In a letter that he sent to the Ottoman grand vizier Mahmud Nedim Pasha (1818–83), Ziya Pasha described the difficulties he faced while composing *Harabat*. He was bedridden due to ill health and heartbroken due to the disappointments and afflictions of life.[61] In the last lines of *Harabat*'s introduction, Ziya Pasha indicated that his declining health should be apparent to anyone who read his anthology (106). He had only one piece of gold and three *mecidiye*s in his pocket when he passed away in 1880.[62]

As the following lines reveal, Ziya Pasha often complains about these hardships in his work:

The world and the sky have transformed beyond recognition
They call the sky earth and the earth sky now.
Lack of merit counts as talent; stupidity and ignorance count as expertise now.
Deceiving the weak counts as wisdom; telling lies counts as refinement now.
Once upon a time, there used to be things like compassion and diligence
Powerful people seek to quickly get rich now.[63]

Likewise, whereas ignorant people achieve high positions, people with knowledge and wisdom, like Ziya Pasha, suffer like a lamenting nightingale (2: 162). While Ziya Pasha's praise poems suggest that the sultan promises a sense of stability and permanence, his other poems emphasise that people like him cannot obtain the positions that they deserve.

Even the many Arabic poems that *Harabat* includes express a similar sense of displacement and disorientation. The anthology quotes many Arabic *qaṣīda* poems from the Andalusian period, known for its poetry expressing a strong sense of nostalgia, displacement and loss. As Alexander E. Elinson has argued, the 'literary geography of al-Andalus [is] paradoxically rooted in loss', since many Andalusian poets recalled 'that which was either lost or was on the verge of being lost and immortalizing them in poetry'.[64] While some Andalusian poems celebrated the stability and permanence that their political patrons provided for their community, others expressed a strong sense of displacement. The following lines by Abū al-Baqāʾ al-Rundī (1204–85?) are a case in point:

Everything that attains perfection falls into ruins
Then no one should be deceived with good life.

This is the matter of affairs as you have observed
  Whomever time made fortuitous, times made them fall into ruins.
This world does spare anything
  And its affairs do not last forever.
Fate completely tears apart every armour
  As swords and spears recoil. (1: 259)

Ziya Pasha's oeuvre follows the pattern that one can also observe in the collection of Andalusian poems that *Harabat* quotes. In one instance, Ziya Pasha praised the Ottoman sultan, hence imagining his empire as indefatigable and permanent; in another instance, he confronted the fact that everything in his society had turned upside down, leaving no sense of permanence and stability.

Often, critics have tended to study Ziya Pasha's *Harabat* as a complete return to the classical Ottoman tradition that he had rejected in his earlier writings, such as 'Şiir ve İnşa'.[65] However, one can also trace the impact of the Orientalist and Young Ottoman cultural vision in *Harabat*, allowing critics to read it as a 'modern' work. While taverns represent nebulous spaces that reveal spiritual truths to a few initiates, the publication of *Harabat* marks a fundamental transformation. The texts that constituted the Ottoman reservoir became more disassociated from spaces such as taverns or literary gatherings (*meclis*). These texts also circulated to distant parts of the empire – ironically through the publication of works such as *Harabat* as 'the tavern' representing the Ottoman literary reservoir. This reservoir ceased to be an exclusionist, closed and mysterious space, since part of it could be collected in a tangible literary anthology one could pick up and read.

The growing circulation of texts and people contributed to the resignification of the tavern and the Ottoman literary reservoir. Although newspapers acted as an ideal medium for his article 'Şiir ve İnşa', which he had written a few years before the publication of *Harabat* and which advocates a more accessible language and literature, it is ironic that Ziya Pasha called for a more exclusionist vision of Ottoman literature in a *printed* anthology and during the efflorescence of the printing press in the region. According to Johann Strauss, '[t]he idea of printing poetical works even seems to have been completely alien to the Ottomans. [. . .] The Egyptians were thus the first to print, on a large scale, the collected poetical works, known as *divan*. Many *divans* of major Ottoman poetics appeared for the first time in Egypt in print'.[66] Indeed, the Bulaq Press in Cairo published many works of Ottoman *divan* poetry, including *Divan-ı Nefi* (AH 1252 [1836/37]), *Divan-ı Fuzuli* (AH 1254 [1838/39]), *Divan-ı Nedim* (AH 1252–54 [1836/37–38/39]) and *Divan-ı Nabi* (AH 1257 [1841/42]).[67]

These texts became less grounded in a demarcated and exclusionist community as they circulated to distant parts of the empire. Hence, they remained open to alternative ways of being re-signified and re-interpreted for forging alternative visions of culture and literature.

For late Ottoman intellectuals such as Ziya Pasha, Andalusian poems that express a strong sense of loss and displacement could have captured the disorienting aspects of modernity. The Ottoman Empire underwent vast cultural, economic and demographic transformations in the nineteenth century. The declaration of the Gülhane Decree in 1839 and the Islahat Decree in 1856 culminated in statewide reforms on issues ranging from tax collection to military drafting. Russia's territorial expansion created an unprecedented influx of Muslim refugees who migrated from Central Asia to Anatolia, significantly changing the empire's demographic landscape. Furthermore, '[t]he Balkan territorial losses raised Muslims' share of the empire's population from 60 percent before 1878 to 72 percent in the 1880s census and 74 percent in 1906–1907'.[68] The empire also experienced a significant debasement of its currency in this period.[69]

According to Ziya Pasha, one needed to engage with the West in order to halt these shifts. *Harabat* wanted its reader to reach out to Europe. For *Harabat*, reading European masterpieces is more a matter of urgency than of pleasure, since knowing these works would halt 'zealotry and irrationality', traits that contributed to the empire's political and cultural decline according to many Ottoman intellectuals:

> If you want to understand the world
> It is necessary to learn the European language [*Avrupa lisanı*].
> Arts and sciences have advanced there
> Do not refrain from acquiring education.
> It is crucial to learn its arts and sciences
> Leave aside zealotry and irrationality.[70]

When describing the advanced status of arts and sciences in Europe, Ziya Pasha used the Turkish suffix '*miş*', which refers to events that one learns or hears from someone else – a detail that demonstrates that Europe was still a nebulous space in *Harabat*. The word 'there' (*orada*) substantiates the narrator's distance from Europe. Ziya Pasha indicated that one could not become a 'complete poet' without learning what he simply called 'the European language' (*Avrupa lisanı*); nevertheless, his writings never give a clear idea about the exact identity of this 'European language'. While *Harabat* lays out the conditions for becoming a poet and passes authoritative judgments on the Persian, Arabic and Turkish poetic traditions, it does not provide clear guidance on engaging with the European tradition while acknowledging its necessity.

One can compare Ziya Pasha, who showed interest in writers such as Molière (1622–73), with Johann Wolfgang von Goethe (1749–1832), who similarly showed interest in different cultures. Goethe used the imagery of the ocean when writing about world literature. Azadeh Yamini-Hamedani has demonstrated that the Persian poet Ḥāfiẓ (c. 1315–c. 90) played a fundamental role in Goethe's conceptualisation of world literature.[71] Ḥāfiẓ's work, which celebrates the intoxicating divine love that undermines the rigid boundaries between the lover and the beloved as well as the self and the other, would become crucial for Goethe, who shared similar visions of transcendence in *West-östlischer Divan* (*West-Eastern Diwan*, 1819). This work projects the division between East and West, like the division between the lover and the beloved in Ḥāfiẓ's poetry, as something that should be overcome. Reading Ḥāfiẓ's work, Goethe wrote that he entered the Orient and noted: '[I]f one enters it [the Orient] seriously, it is as though one goes into the ocean'.[72] According to Yamini-Hamedani, if national literature were a land, then world literature for Goethe would be the ocean in which one becomes immersed, only to emerge from it as more rejuvenated, enlightened and open-minded.

Despite these similarities between Goethe and Ziya Pasha, Goethe would go so far as to consider Ḥāfiẓ his 'twin' (*Zwilling*);[73] however, Ziya Pasha did not describe Western poets in such affectionate terms and implied a strong sense of unfamiliarity with and even distance from them. Ziya Pasha noted that the Persian poet Sanāʾī (d. 1131?), the Ottoman poet Nefi and the Arab poet al-Farazdaq were irreconcilably different from French writers such as Molière, Lamartine (1790–1869), or Racine (1639–99):

Can Racine and Lamartine
  Craft a *kaside* poem like Nefi!
Is it possible for Sanāʾī and Farazdaq
  To write a theatre play like Molière![74]

While emphasising this cultural discrepancy, *Harabat* also wants its audience to reach out to Europe and learn its arts and sciences.[75] It affirms to the reader that learning another language does not make one an infidel (*kafir*) (48).

Harabat divides the world into different communities that are irreconcilably different from each other, also a key feature of its period's Orientalist scholarship. For example, Ziya Pasha argued that someone in Europe could never be like someone in Africa, since each community had a distinct character (49). He also argued that East and West were irreconcilably different from each other (50). While the anthology itself quotes poets in no strictly chronological order, its introduction, like much of Orientalist scholarship, divides the histories of Arabic, Persian and Turkish poetry into distinct periods listed in a linear, chronological order. On the one hand, *Harabat*'s introduction claims that Arabic, Persian and Turkish mix with each other like sugar and milk; on the other hand, it sometimes reinforces 'the influence paradigm' that has also shaped Orientalist scholarship. For example, Ziya Pasha wrote that, once Ottoman poets started to imitate Iranian poets, the Turkish language lost its purity and eloquence. Because Turkish poetry heavily relies on the *aruz* meter, it becomes impossible to spontaneously (*irticalen*) compose a Turkish poem (22).

On the one hand, Ziya Pasha claimed that Arabic, Persian and Turkish intertwined with each other like sugar and milk; on the other hand, in the same text he also posited that the Arabic stream had emerged *before* Persian and Turkish. Ziya Pasha would go so far as to claim that he belonged to a community who were like the Arabs' grandchildren:

> We are newcomers relative to them
> We are like Arabs' grandchildren [*hafid*].
> Arabic works are the source [*ümm*] of knowledge
> Persian and Turkish are two rivers and Arabic the ocean.
> As I came across that peerless sea
> I, at that moment, grasped the world. (23)

While *Harabat* uses the term 'ocean' to describe the Ottoman language, it also uses the same term to refer to Arabic works only. This testifies to the epistemological shifts that would mark later literary histories depicting Arabic literature as a source of influence that existed prior to Turkish literature. Furthermore, Ziya Pasha used the term 'we' here only in its introduction for marking himself as part of a large community that had descended from the Arabs. His use of the term '*hafid*', a term that literally means 'grandchild', establishes the familial relationship between Arabs and Turks that one can observe in several other texts that *The Ottoman Canon* will examine. Likewise, the term '*ümm*' in the Ottoman source text can be translated as both source and mother, substantiating the familial relations that Ziya Pasha wished to convey in these lines. Furthermore, as the book will also demonstrate, writers such as Ahmet Hamdi Tanpınar used the term 'we' much more frequently and ultimately discussed literature in order to discuss the national community to which this 'we' refers.

Harabat thus reflects the epistemological shifts that would become more visible and prevalent in later literary histories. *Harabat* admits, albeit only in a few lines, that the Ottoman poetic heritage is not as permanent as it initially claimed this heritage to be. In the anthology's introduction, Ziya Pasha argued that he was like Jesus Christ, because poetry had died and now he was reviving it by composing *Harabat* (104). These lines suggest that a 'new literature' had already emerged. At one point claiming the Ottoman poetic heritage to be stable, grand and immutable while at another point declaring it dead, *Harabat* crystallises the transitional aspects of the late Ottoman period.

Notes

1. Marianne Boqvist, 'Visualising the Ottoman Presence in Damascus: Interpreting 16th Century Building Complexes', in *Istanbul as Seen from a Distance: Centre and Provinces in the Ottoman Empire*, ed. Elisabeth Özdalga, M. Sait Özervarlı and Feryal Tansuğ (Istanbul: Swedish Research Institute in Istanbul, 2011), 121.
2. Süleyman Nazif, *İki Dost* (Istanbul: Kanaat Kütüphanesi, 1925), 78. Upon reading this inscription, Süleyman Nazif writes: 'To see the inscription of Turkish verses on the mauseloum of Muḥy al-Dīn Ibn al-ᶜArabī, who is buried in an Arab province, gave me a strong sense of pride and contentment' (79).
3. M. Kaya Bilgegil, *Ziyâ Paşa Üzerinde Bir Araştırma* (Erzurum: Atatürk Üniversitesi Basımevi, 1970), 473. Ziya Pasha arrived in Beirut on 8 February 1877 and in Damascus on 25 February 1877. His appointment as a governor of Syria was announced in the *Ceride-i Havadis* newspaper on 4 January 1877 (473).
4. Quoted in Bilgegil, *Ziyâ Paşa Üzerinde Bir Araştırma*, 411–12.
5. Quoted in ibid., 423.
6. Quoted in ibid., 316.
7. Jeffrey R. Di Leo, 'Analyzing Anthologies', in *On Anthologies: Politics and Pedagogy*, ed. Jeffrey R. Di Leo (Lincoln: University of Nebraska Press, 2004), 2.
8. Mithat Cemal Kuntay, *Namık Kemal: Devrinin İnsanları ve Olayları Arasında* (Istanbul: Milli Eğitim Basımevi, 1949), 409. Ziya Pasha already received significant respect from his peers. For example, Hasan Rıza (d. 1890) and Abdülhak Hamid Tarhan (1852–1937) wrote elegies for him when he passed away. İsmail Hikmet [Ertaylan], *Ziya Paşa: Hayatı ve Eserleri* (Istanbul: Kanaat Kütüphanesi, 1932), 66–67.
9. Zeynelabidin Reşid (1846–1921) criticised *Harabat* because, while Ziya Pasha's anthology included works from egregious authors such as Eşref Pasha (1820–94), Kazım Pasha (1821–90) and Deli Nevres (probably Osman Nevres; d. AH 1293 [1876/77]), it forgets to include works from important poets such as Fehim (probably Süleyman Fehim; d. 1847). M. Kaya Bilgegil, *Harâbât Karşısında Nâmık Kemâl* (Erzurum: Salkımsöğüt Yayınevi, 2014),

112. According to Ebüzziyya Tevfik, Ziya Pasha was one of the founding figures of the 'new literature'. At the same time, he sometimes suffered from 'bad influences' (*tesirat-ı seyyie*). Ebüzziyya Tevfik claimed that it was the Western influence that had helped Ziya Pasha produce good works. See his *Numune-i Edebiyat-ı Osmaniyye* (Istanbul: Matbaa-i Ebüzziya, AH 1308 [1890/91]), 244.

10. Rey Chow, 'In the Name of Comparative Literature', in *Comparative Literature in the Age of Multiculturalism*, ed. Charles Bernheimer (Baltimore: Johns Hopkins University Press, 1995), 109.
11. Ziya Pasha took Persian courses from İsa Efendi at the *Mekteb-i Edebiyye* (Bilgegil, *Ziyâ Paşa Üzerinde Bir Araştırma*, 9).
12. İbnülemin Mahmud Kemal [İnal] (1871–1957) noted that Edhem Pasha translated Viardot's work, but since Edhem Pasha's Turkish was not good, Ziya Pasha improved and edited Edhem Pasha's work. At the same time, the cover page of *Endülüs Tarihi* (the first two volumes published in AH 1276–80 [1859/60–63/64] and all the four volumes published in AH 1304–5 [1886/87–87/88]), the Turkish translation of *Histoire des Arabes et des Mores d'Espagne*, does not mention Edhem Pasha as one of its authors or translators (Bilgegil, *Ziyâ Paşa Üzerinde*, 27).
13. Annie Greene, 'Burying a Rabbi in Baghdad: The Limits of Ottomanism for Ottoman-Iraqi Jews in the Late Nineteenth Century', *Journal of Jewish Identities* 12, no. 2 (2019): 98.
14. Greene, 'Burying a Rabbi in Baghdad', 101.
15. Ibid., 98.
16. Ibid., 117.
17. Hamit Bozarslan, 'The Ottomanism of the Non-Turkish Groups: The Arabs and the Kurds after 1908', *Die Welt des Islams* 56, no. 3–4 (2016): 318.
18. Quoted in Bilgegil, *Ziyâ Paşa Üzerinde Bir Araştırma*, 175–76.
19. Ibid., 100.
20. Ebüzziyya Tevfik, *Yeni Osmanlılar Tarihi* (Istanbul: Kervan Yayınları, 1973–74), 1: 159.
21. Bilgegil, *Ziyâ Paşa Üzerinde Bir Araştırma*, 488.
22. Ebüzziya Tevfik, *Yeni Osmanlılar Tarihi*, 1: 146.
23. Léon Cahun also engaged with the Young Ottomans, although he also thought that they were too naive and had been tricked by European revolutionists (Bilgegil, *Ziyâ Paşa Üzerinde Bir Araştırma*, 111). According to Ebüzziya Tevfik, Hasun Efendi introduced Orientalists to the Young Ottomans when they were in London (Ebüzziya Tevfik, *Yeni Osmanlılar Tarihi*, 1: 147). Ebüzziya Tevfik also notes that Şinasi had personal acquaintance with Orientalists such as Renan and Silvestre de Sacy (1758–1838) (*Numune-i Edebiyat-ı Osmaniyye*, 216).
24. Ziya Paşa, 'Şiir ve İnşa', *Hürriyet* 11 (7 September 1868), 4–5.
25. Ziya Paşa, 'Şiir ve İnşa', 5.
26. Ibid., 5–6.

27. Ibid., 7.
28. Guillory, *Cultural Capital*, 42, emphases Guillory's.
29. Ziya Paşa, *Mukaddime-i Harabat* (Istanbul: Matbaa-i Ebüzziya, AH 1311 [1893/94]), 5–10. Since the anthology's introduction is not page-numbered, I refer to the *Mukaddime-i Harabat*, which has page numbers, when discussing this introduction.
30. While the epithet 'Iranian', as scholars such as Mana Kia have demonstrated, is of modern coinage, Ziya Pasha himself uses the term 'Iran' to refer to authors of Persian poems when he categorises these poets as *şuara-yı İran*. See *Persianate Selves: Memories of Place and Origin Before Nationalism* (Palo Alto: Stanford University Press, 2020), 201.
31. Although *Harabat*'s introduction points out that the anthology would include Chagatai poetry, Ziya Pasha does not create a separate section for Chagatai poetry in his anthology. He includes a few Chagatai excerpts in the sections on Turkish poetry.
32. Şehabeddin Süleyman, *Tarih-i Edebiyat-ı Osmaniyye* (Istanbul: Sancakcıyan Matbaası, 1912/13), 278.
33. İbrahim Necmi [Dilmen], *Tarih-i Edebiyat Dersleri* (Istanbul: Matbaa-i Amire, 1922), 2: 114.
34. İsmail Hikmet [Ertaylan], *Türk Edebiyatı Tarihi I–IV* (Ankara: Türk Tarih Kurumu Basımevi, 2011), xxiv.
35. Ruşen Eşref, *Diyorlar ki*, 53.
36. Tanpınar, *On Dokuzuncu Asır Türk Edebiyatı Tarihi*, 89.
37. Ibid., 142.
38. Ziya Paşa, *Harabat* (Istanbul: Matbaa-i Amire, AH 1291–92), 1: 214–85. *Qaṣīda* poems refer to elaborately structured odes of around 60–100 lines that maintain a single end rhyme throughout the piece.
39. The first three excerpts are poems that are quoted in their entirety. For these poems, see al-Mutanabbī, *al-Dīwān*, 85–88, 398–404, 311–15. After these three poems, Ziya Pasha quotes sections from one single poem by al-Mutanabbī. Although these sections are from different parts of the same poem, Ziya Pasha brings together all these sections in a single, unified excerpt. Therefore, readers have the impression that they read a block quote from the original poem rather than sections that are taken from different parts of this poem. For this poem, see al-Mutanabbī, *al-Dīwān*, 566–69.
40. Al-Farazdaq is the last poet that this section quotes.
41. For the excerpt from Imām ᶜAlī's work, see al-Imām ᶜAlī, *Dīwān Amīr al-Muʾminīn al-Imām ᶜAlī bin Abī Ṭālib raḍiya Allāh ᶜanhu wa karrama Allāh wajhahu*, ed. ᶜAbd al-ᶜAzīz al-Karam (1988), 17. For Manjak Pasha's excerpt, see Manjak bin Muḥammad Bāshā, *Hādhā dīwān al-Amīr Manjak Ibn al-Marḥūm Muḥammad Bāshā* (Damascus: al-Maṭbaᶜa al-Ḥifniyya, AH 1301 [1883/84]), 131.
42. E. Khayyat, 'Bastards and Arabs', in *A Handbook and Reader of Ottoman Arabic*, ed. Esther-Miriam Wagner (Cambridge: Open Book Publishers,

2021), 107. Khayyat has also observed that '*Harabat*'s Arabic contains many errors and typos, some of which could be considered ruinous mistakes in a dissertation on Arabic poetry today' (134). For example, as Khayyat also points out, Ziya Pasha refers to Abū Firās al-Ḥamdānī (932–968) as Abū Firās al-Ḥamdūnī (*Harabat*, 1: 282).

43. Tahera Qutbuddin, 'Books on Arabic Philology and Literature', 1: 609.
44. Ibid., 1: 609.
45. Ibid.
46. Ibid., 1: 614.
47. For Ziya Pasha's understanding of Persian poetry, see also Mehnâz Semenderî and Esedullâh Vâhid, 'Ḥayāt-i adabī-yi Żiyā Pāshā va zabān-i fārsī', *Nüsha: Şarkiyat Araştırmaları Dergisi* 16, no. 42 (2016): 55–68.
48. For the first hemistich, see Ṣāʾib Tabrīzī, *Dīvān-i Ṣāʾib Tabrīzī* (Tehran: Shirkat-i Intishārāt-i ʿIlmī va Farhangī, 1992), 2: 1048. For the second hemistich, see 2: 739.
49. Ferenc Csirkés, 'Turkish/Turkic Books of Poetry, Turkish and Persian Lexicography: The Politics of Language under Bayezid II', in *Treasures of Knowledge: An Inventory of the Ottoman Palace Library (1502/3–1503/4)*, ed. Gülru Necipoğlu, Cemal Kafadar and Cornell H. Fleischer (Leiden: Brill, 2019), 1: 684.
50. Quoted in Mahmud Kemal İnal (ed.), *Son Asır Türk Şairleri* (Istanbul: Milli Eğitim Basımevi, 1970), 11: 2010.
51. Ziya Paşa, *Mukaddime-i Harabat*, 31.
52. For a detailed description of the tavern trope, see İskender Pala, *Ansiklopedik Divân Şiiri Sözlüğü* (Istanbul: L&M Yayınları, 2002), 203–4.
53. Ziya Paşa, *Harabat*, 2: 326. English translation quoted in Siavash Lornejad and Ali Doostzadeh, *On the Modern Politicization of the Persian Poet Nezami Ganjavi* (Yerevan: Caucasian Centre for Iranian Studies, 2012), 191.
54. While Fuzuli and Köprülüzade Abdullah Pasha wrote Arabic works, the sultans composed works in Persian. Fuzuli lived in Baghdad, making him acquainted with Arabic culture, while Köprülüzade Abdullah Pasha had a medrese education that allowed him to compose poetry in Arabic.
55. *Harabat* offers a male-centric cultural vision, as almost all the poets it quotes are men. A few exceptions include Mihri Hatun (c. 1460–c. 1506) (2: 223, 2: 253), and ʿIṣmat Khātūn (d. 1186) (2: 321).
56. Süleyman Nazif, *İki Dost*, 39. Süleyman Nazif surmised that Namık Kemal likely wrote this letter to Recaizade Mahmud Ekrem (1847–1914), since he discovered the letter among Recaizade Mahmud Ekrem's documents.
57. On the importance of the *darülfünun* for Ottoman modernity, see Ekmeleddin İhsanoğlu, *Darülfünun: Osmanlı'da Kültürel Modernleşmenin Odağı* (Istanbul: IRCICA, 2010).
58. Ziya Pasha became acquainted with literary circles in taverns such as Gümüş Halkalı, Servili and Altın-oluk (Bilgegil, *Ziyâ Paşa Üzerinde*, 20).
59. Ziya Paşa, *Mukaddime-i Harabat*, 34.

60. Both *terkib-i bend* and *terci-i bend* refer to poetic forms. They are composed of different sections (*bend*) with a varying number of verses that have the same rhyming scheme. These sections are connected to each other with a 'connecting couplet' (*vasıta beyti*). *Terci-i bend* works use the same couplet as the connecting couplet throughout the work, while *terkib-i bend* works use different verses as connecting verses. Ziya Pasha wrote two poems, one in the *terci-i bend* and another in the *terkib-i bend* form, which became so famous that sometimes the terms '*terci-i bend*' and '*terkib-i bend*' are used to refer to these specific works. Aḥmad Bashīr al-Ḥalabī translated Ziya Pasha's *Terci-i Bend* into Arabic in 1898 (Bilgegil, *Ziyâ Paşa Üzerinde Bir Araştırma*, 271).
61. Bilgegil, *Harâbât Karşısında Nâmık Kemâl*, 101–2.
62. Bilgegil, *Ziyâ Paşa Üzerinde*, 322.
63. Ziya Paşa, *Harabat*, 2: 162.
64. Alexander E. Elinson, *Looking Back at al-Andalus: The Poetics of Loss and Nostalgia in Medieval Arabic and Hebrew Literature* (Boston: Brill, 2009), 15. Ziya Pasha also argues that Europe would not have modernised had Islam not spread to Andalusia (*Mukaddime-i Harabat*, 13). As I will claim below in this chapter, Ziya Pasha's strong interest in Andalusia likely stemmed also from his engagement with the Orientalist discourse.
65. Önder Göçgün, *Ziya Paşa* (Izmir: Kültür ve Turizm Bakanlığı, 1987), 26–27; Bilgegil, *Harâbât Karşısında Nâmık Kemâl*, 104.
66. Johann Strauss, *The Egyptian Connection in Nineteenth-Century Ottoman Literary and Intellectual History* (Beirut: Orient-Institut der Deutschen Morgenländischen Gesellschaft, 2000), 13.
67. Ekmeleddin İhsanoğlu, *The Turks in Egypt and Their Cultural Legacy: An Analytical Study of the Turkish Printed Patrimony in Egypt from the Time of Muhammad 'Ali with Annotated Bibliographies*, trans. Humphrey Davies (Cairo: The American University in Cairo Press, 2012), 'Bibliography I: Books in Turkish Printed in Egypt (1798–1997)', CD-ROM.
68. Carter Vaughn Findley, *Turkey, Islam, Nationalism and Modernity: A History, 1789–2007* (New Haven: Yale University Press, 2010), 175.
69. Şevket Pamuk, *Uneven Centuries: Economic Development of Turkey Since 1820* (Princeton: Princeton University Press, 2018), 104.
70. Ziya Paşa, *Mukaddime-i Harabat*, 47.
71. Azadeh Yamini-Hamedani, 'Foundational Metaphors: Goethe's World Literature; Posnett's Comparative Literature', in *Foundational Texts of World Literature*, ed. Dominique Jullien (New York: Peter Lang, 2011), 155–60.
72. Johann Wolfgang von Goethe, *Briefe: mit Einleitungen und Erläuterungen*, ed. Philipp Stein (Berlin: Otto Eisner, 1905), 7: 4. Translation in Yamini-Hamedani, 'Foundational Metaphors', 156.
73. Johann Wolfgang von Goethe, *West-östlicher Divan* (Leipzig: Insel, 1912), 22. Also quoted in Yamini-Hamedani, 'Foundational Metaphors', 157.
74. Ziya Paşa, *Mukaddime-i Harabat*, 49.

75. Lydia H. Liu has observed a similar dynamic among the May Fourth Chinese writers, who often have been studied as the pioneers of modern Chinese literature. While Goethe 'saw himself presiding over a *world market* wherein all nations offer their *merchandise* to him while he plays the translator magnanimously as he *enriches* himself', the May Fourth writers shared a deep anxiety to make their work accepted and valued within the global literary market in which the West had the upper hand. *Translingual Practice: Literature, National Culture and Translated Modernity – China, 1900–1937* (Palo Alto: Stanford University Press, 1995), 188, emphases Liu's.

2

Jurjī Zaydān, Literary Comparisons and the Formation of Arabic and Turkish Literatures

The following remark by İsmail Hakkı [Eldem] (1871–1944) captures the epistemological shifts of the nineteenth century that one can observe in a few instances in *Harabat*'s introduction: 'Just as the classics start with the Greeks and Romans in Western literature, the classics start with Arab and Persian poets in our literature'.[1] The use of the term 'just as' (*gibi*) emphasises a sense of equivalence between Western literature and Ottoman literature; just as Western civilisation has its classics, so does Ottoman civilisation. According to this statement, Ottoman classics *start with* Arab and Persian poets; therefore, poets such as Abū Tammām (d. 845/46) and al-Mutanabbī (d. 965) constitute an integral component of what İsmail Hakkı called 'our literature'. At the same time, these poets represent 'ancestors' who lived in bygone times, as did the ancient Greeks and Romans. İsmail Hakkı categorised these poets as 'classics', a categorisation that Ziya Pasha did not use in *Harabat*. İsmail Hakkı also used the phrase 'our literature' (*bizim edebiyatımız*) to refer to Ottoman literature, suggesting that literature had become an identity-marker for a large imagined community. Finally, he emphasised that Ottoman literature had started with Arab and Persian *poets* (*Arap ve Acem şuarasından*) rather than with Arabic and Persian *literatures*, suggesting that İsmail Hakkı, unlike many writers after him, did not categorise literature based on ethnolinguistic grounds. This chapter will analyse literary histories of the late Ottoman Empire to further examine the epistemological shifts that İsmail Hakkı's statement captures. Although I will examine works from various historians, including İsmail Hakkı, I will focus in particular on works by Jurjī Zaydān (1861–1914), who has been studied as a pioneering figure of modern Arabic literature.

This chapter builds on Shaden M. Tageldin, who has already revealed the 'epistemological transformations' of the nineteenth century that 'spurred the reinvention of Arabic literature [. . .] as a fundamentally *comparative* literature'.[2] Here, Tageldin has argued that the translations from French to Arabic by Rifāᶜa Rāfiᶜ al-Ṭahṭāwī (1801–73) testified to a moment when numerous *nahḍa* tinkers started to view Arabic and French literatures as comparable with and translatable to each other. The social and political transformations at the beginning of the nineteenth century 'compelled both French and Arabic literatures to rethink themselves in each other's eyes, in translation: in short, to rethink themselves as *comparative* literatures'.[3] While Tageldin has analysed the impact of Western imperialism on Arabic literature, this chapter will take an alternative angle to shed further light on the reinvention of Arabic and Turkish literature as comparative literature. It will claim that Turkish and Arabic literatures also started to rethink 'themselves in each other's eyes, in translation' during the late Ottoman period.[4]

According to Tageldin, comparisons perpetuated a false sense of equivalence between Arabic and Western European literatures (French and English in particular) and thus overlooked the unequal power dynamics in which the West had the upper hand. Late Ottoman literary histories also often generated a sense of equivalence between Arabic and Turkish literatures. This sense of equivalence has perpetuated the assumption in Arabic writings that Turkish literature, like Arabic literature, underwent a similar historical trajectory and experienced *al-nahḍa* in the nineteenth century, after a period of slumber. Late Ottoman Arabic and Turkish literary histories have often overlooked the fact that various intellectual members who drew on the Ottoman literary reservoir engaged with Arabic and Persian texts. In particular, I argue that these works depicted histories of Arabic and Turkish literatures as two trajectories that did not intersect with each other, contributing to the current conceptualisation of classical Arabic heritage as the root from which modern Arabic literature grew. It has become easier to envision Arabic texts only as works of national literature, especially when Arabic literature is compared with Turkish or Ottoman literature.[5] As Alexander Beecroft has put it, 'national literatures are from the beginning constructed as elements of an *inter-national* system of literatures; English literature, in other words, can only exist *as such* if it can be set against French literature, German literature and so on'.[6]

Historians such as Axel Havelmann, Thomas Philipp and Anne-Laure Dupont have already situated Zaydān within the transcultural Ottoman context by demonstrating that, while Zaydān advocated a vision of Arab cultural nationalism, he did not call for the Arabs to secede from the Ottoman Empire. He often advocated the unity of the empire because for Zaydān and other thinkers of his time, such as Muḥammad Kurd ᶜAlī (1876–1953) and Shakīb Arslān (1869–1946), 'Arabism was and should be compatible with Ottomanism, i. e., political loyalty to the empire'.[7] While historians have focused on these thinkers' attitudes towards the Ottoman Empire as a political entity, I pay attention to their attitude towards the Ottoman literary reservoir in which Arabic has had important cultural capital. As Muhsin J. al-Musawi has put it, 'Arabic was used and practiced since the mid-tenth century in the shadow of "world conquerors" and non-Arab empires and dynasties',[8] since leaders such as Timur could claim to become the rulers of the world when they had 'knowledge of other tongues especially Arabic'.[9] This chapter will show that, for Namık Kemal (1840–88), Arabic held great prestige and Arabic works played a crucial role in his vision of a new Ottoman literature.

The first section of this chapter will focus on Jurjī Zaydān's perspectives on Turkish literature. My focus on Zaydān is deliberate, since, as Michael Allan has put it, '[t]o this day, Zaydān's historical understanding of Arabic literature remains a central influence on the formation of the discipline – as much for the methods he undertakes as for the meticulous cataloguing of sources his work provides'.[10] I will demonstrate that Zaydān's works generated a sense of equivalence between Arabic and Turkish literatures, as they highlighted the similarities between the two. I will offer a close reading of an article in the famous journal that Zaydān edited, *al-Hilāl*, on Namık Kemal, who is often regarded as a pioneer of modern Turkish literature. The article describes Namık Kemal as pioneer of a modern 'Turkish *nahḍa*'. By doing so, this article managed to render the Ottoman cultural landscape familiar for Arabic readers and to overlook Namık Kemal's vision of a new Ottoman literature in which Arabic texts played a key role. I will then focus on another article in which Zaydān wrote about the 'history of Turkish language arts' (*tārīkh ādāb al-lugha al-turkiyya*) and point to similarities between this article and one of the most foundational works in the field of Arabic literature, *Tārīkh ādāb al-lugha al-ᶜarabiyya* (The History of Arabic Language Arts,[11] first serialised in *al-Hilāl* in 1894 and 1895 and eventually published as a multivolume work in 1911–14). These similarities reinforce the depiction of Arabic and Turkish literatures as akin to mirror-images, which look alike but never intersect in the Ottoman reservoir.

The second section will demonstrate that late Ottoman literary histories establish a linear historical trajectory for both Arabic and Turkish literatures and emphasise relations of anteriority and posteriority between these literatures. In particular, in the works on Turkish literature, Arabic literature was described only as a source of influence that had existed prior to Turkish literature. To further substantiate these points, I will analyse how these histories employ the term 'classics'. While classics is a 'non-emic' term that did not originate in the literary traditions about which these authors wrote, they mobilised this term to stabilise Arabic and Ottoman literatures within a linear historical trajectory. This chapter will demonstrate that debates on cultural and literary heritage in Arabic writings should be analysed in conjunction with similar debates in Ottoman Turkish writings.

Jurjī Zaydān and the Turkish Nahḍa

As Benjamin C. Fortna and Nergis Ertürk have demonstrated, the Arabic and Turkish works that flowed together into the Ottoman reservoir circulated among a much larger audience in the late Ottoman Empire. This resulted from many socioeconomic changes, such as the establishment of large printing presses in Cairo and Istanbul, which led to the diffusion of not only Western novels but also compilations of Arabic and Ottoman Turkish poetry, as well as the rise of new social communities such as technocrats and intellectuals who constituted an audience for these works.[12] As Ertürk has put it, the '[c]ommunications revolution of the mid-nineteenth century, which freed "Ottoman" from the cultural authority of Arabic and Persian, paved the way for its demise at the same time. [. . .] The late nineteenth- and early twentieth-century rise of Turkish nationalism saw the recoding, through the Orientalist discipline of Turcology, of a "vulgar" Turkic linguistic element (in counterposition with "cultivated" Arabic and Persian) as the foundation of Turkish-speaking Muslim identity'.[13] The rise of Ottomanism opened up new possibilities for people from diverse linguistic, religious and cultural backgrounds in the empire to lay a claim to Ottoman identity. For example, in one of his letters to his son, Zaydān praised his son Amīl because he had started to learn Turkish, 'the language of [their] government',[14] and noted in another letter to Amīl that his son Shukrī's 'patriotic duties demand[ed]' loyalty to the Ottoman Empire.[15] Anne-Laure Dupont has also remarked that Zaydān started to learn Turkish to keep up with the empire's latest political developments.[16]

Zaydān's life testifies to all these economic, technological and political changes. Born into a Greek Orthodox family in Beirut, Jurjī Zaydān came from a modest socioeconomic background, although he later made a vast fortune through his publications. He was self-educated and eventually enrolled in the Syrian Protestant College (today known as the American University of Beirut) in 1881. However, he was dismissed from the college due to his support for a lecturer who advocated Darwin's natural selection theory. He spent his life in different cities and countries, such as Cairo, Istanbul, Beirut and England, all places that shaped his intellectual formation. Zaydān was an extremely prolific writer, as he wrote numerous historical novels as well as works on language and history and edited the highly influential magazine *al-Hilāl*, which, for many critics, played a constitutive role for Arab cultural nationalism.

Zaydān's works often depict histories of Arabic literature and Turkish literature as akin to mirror-images of each other, mirror-images which had parallel historical trajectories and never interacted with each other within the Ottoman reservoir. I observe this kind of depiction especially in two articles in *al-Hilāl*. One of these articles provides a biography of Namık Kemal.[17] The other is part of a series in which Zaydān shares his observations on Istanbul during a visit in 1909.[18]

Much of Zaydān's works reinforces strict distinctions between Arabs and Turks.[19] In her analysis of the representation of Turks in modern Arabic novels, Şükran Fazlıoğlu has noted that Zaydān's novels depicted Turks as the foreign other and even as the enemy.[20] Indeed, Arab, Iranian and Turk often seem clear-cut categories also in *Tārīkh ādāb al-lugha al-ʿarabiyya* (henceforth referred as the *Tārīkh*). Zaydān defined Seljuks and Ottomans simply as Turks and characterised the Abbasid period between AH 232–334 (846/87–945/46) as the 'Turkish age' due to the strong influence of Turks on state affairs.[21] Like many Western thinkers such as Volney (1757–1820), Zaydān argued that the Turkish rule of the Ottoman period harmed Arabic cultural production, since according to him poetry and art underwent a significant decline during the Ottoman rule of much of the Arab world.[22] In another article in *al-Hilāl*, Zaydān wrote that, had the Ottoman Empire completely Turkified its population, one would not have encountered the resurgence of interest in Arabic language and literature in the nineteenth century, suggesting that he may have considered the Ottoman Empire a potential future threat to the cultural revival of the Arab world.[23] At the same time, one needs to keep in mind that Zaydān did not openly call for overthrowing the political system and in many of his writings emphasised that the Ottoman Empire had to remain strong to defend itself against foreign intrusion.[24]

In fact, Zaydān was highly engaged with literary changes in the late Ottoman Empire. For example, *al-Hilāl* dedicated an article to Namık Kemal and depicted him as a pioneer of the 'modern Turkish awakening'.[25] This article was part of a series that appeared in almost every issue of *al-Hilāl*, titled 'The Most Famous Events and the Most Renowned People'. M. Kayahan Özgül has recently called for overcoming the tendency to consider Namık Kemal as pioneer of modern Turkish literature. He has demonstrated that, although earlier scholarship has described Namık Kemal as 'homeland poet' (*vatan şairi*) for popularising among

Turkish readers particular sentiments such as love of the homeland, many poets had already written about the homeland and called for significant thematic and stylistic changes in Turkish literature.[26] This chapter will demonstrate that it was not just Namık Kemal's peers or today's literary critics who considered him the pioneer of modern Turkish literature. Many 'pioneers of modern Arabic literature' such as Jurjī Zaydān and Rūḥī al-Khālidī also viewed Namık Kemal as the pioneer of a modern Turkish *nahḍa*.

Namık Kemal indeed called for a new literature, but this literature also features characteristics that do not neatly fit into what we think of modern Turkish literature today. Although many Arabophone writers may have considered themselves the heirs of a 'highly developed literary, political and religious culture that did not always conform to the culture present at the Ottoman court',[27] works from the classical Arabic poetic heritage constitute a significant inflow into the Ottoman reservoir that shaped the intellectual formation of thinkers such as Namık Kemal. He was drawn to the cultural capital of Arabic for his future aspirations to a new literature. While Namık Kemal criticised Persian literature for its detrimental influence on Ottoman poetry in many of his writings, such as his famous article 'Lisan-ı Osmani'nin Edebiyatı Hakkında Bazı Mülahazatı Şamildir' (Concerning Some Observations about the Literature of the Ottoman Language, 1866),[28] he also emphasised that Arabic literature would provide a good role model for the future of Ottoman poetry. In fact, Namık Kemal considered works from Abū al-ᶜAlāᵓ al-Maᶜarrī (973–1057) and al-Mutanabbī the best examples of poems displaying subtlety (*incelik*)[29] and works from Imruᵓ al-Qays (d. c. 550) the best examples of poems excelling in depiction (*tasvir*).[30]

Although Namık Kemal praised Imruᵓ al-Qays, al-Maᶜarrī and al-Mutanabbī, he often remained silent about Arabic works produced during his lifetime. The magazine *Şark* (East) published the introduction that Namık Kemal wrote for his novel *İntibah* (Awakening, 1876), in which he commented on *nahḍa* Arabic works. He emphasised that Arabic literature consisted only of works produced between the *jāhiliyya* and Abbasid periods in the East and those produced until Andalusia's demise in the West. Namık Kemal then claimed that '*kaside* poems and such things' (*kasideler fülanlar*) recited during his lifetime 'in Egypt, in Tunisia and here there' (*Mısır'da, Tunus'ta, ötede beride*) did not constitute Arabic literature.[31] As an example of what constitutes Arabic literature, Namık Kemal quoted a verse by al-Mutanabbī and another verse by al-Maᶜarrī. Like Ziya Pasha, Namık Kemal made authoritative claims on Arabic poetry. His Ottoman reservoir included works from al-Mutanabbī, but not necessarily Arabic works produced in the Ottoman Empire, in Egypt and Tunisia, in particular. One can interpret this particular attitude of Namık Kemal as that of an author from the hegemonic 'centre', looking down on works from what some historians have described as the empire's 'periphery'.[32]

In contrast, Jurjī Zaydān claimed that Namık Kemal had a special place in the history of Turkish language arts and praised him as pioneer of a Turkish *nahḍa*.[33] At the beginning of his article on Namık Kemal, Jurjī Zaydān indicated that *al-Hilāl* had published an article on Mustafa Reşid Pasha (1800–58) and would publish more works on other famous Ottoman writers.[34] Zaydān then wrote that he had asked a friend living in Istanbul to write a biography (*tarjama*) on the Turkish pioneer, although the reader could not know who composed this article.[35] This anonymous author indicated that he summarised a treatise (*risāla*) by Ebüzziya Tevfik (1849–1913), although the author also admitted that he lacked Ebüzziya Tevfik's eloquence.[36] Here, the author likely referred to Ebüzziya Tevfik's *Merhum Namık Kemal Bey*, because the Arabic article includes translations of excerpts from it. Ebüzziya Tevfik probably wrote this work shortly after Namık Kemal's death, although, as Abdulhakim Tuğluk has pointed out, when the work was actually written has remained subject to debate.[37]

The Arabic article describes Namık Kemal not as 'Turkish' but 'Ottoman' author since it employs the term 'one of the famous Ottomans' to refer to him. At the same time, the article does not mention Namık Kemal's engagement with the classical Arabic heritage, which now seemed to be under the purview of people like Zaydān, who were considered pioneers of a modern Arab identity. Later, the article's author indicated that 'readers of the Arabic and Turkish languages' (*qurrāʾ al-lughatayn al-ʿarabiyya wa-l-turkiyya*)[38] were tied to each other due to their shared 'Ottoman subjecthood' (*al-tābiʿiyya al-ʿuthmāniyya*).[39] Thus, the author promised to provide the Arabic-reading audience with more information on other 'prominent Ottomans', such as Şinasi Efendi, Ahmet Midhat and Ebüzziya Tevfik, in the upcoming issues.

Akin to works that establish a sense of stark rupture between the classical and modern Arabic literatures, the article on Namık Kemal posits the same for classical and modern Turkish literatures. Ebüzziya Tevfik described the newspaper *Tasvir-i Efkar*, edited by Namık Kemal, as 'the initiator of our literature of the new age' (*devr-i cedid edebiyatımızın fatihası*).[40] When the anonymous author translated this sentence, he wrote that *Tasvir-i Efkar* had initiated 'the modern Turkish *nahḍa*' (*al-nahḍa al-turkiyya al-ḥadītha*)[41] and that Namık Kemal was the pioneer of a new Turkish prose (*al-inshāʾ*).[42] While the Arabic article mentions that

Namık Kemal could recite poetry in Arabic, Persian, Turkish and French, it overlooks the fact that Namık Kemal called for a new Ottoman literature that in part would build on works by poets such as al-Mutanabbī.[43] In fact, while Ebüzziya Tevfik claimed that Namık Kemal could recite any poem from the pre-Islamic *al-Mu^callaqāt* 'in such an eloquent manner that one may presume he himself may have composed it',[44] the Arabic article omits this statement. The Arabic article also indicates that Turkish language arts entered a new age with Namık Kemal, as prose branched out into new directions, while Turkish writers before him had shown no innovation in either their prose or their ideas over the past six centuries.[45] Many years later, Zaydān himself would praise Namık Kemal as someone who had 'a special significance in the history of Turkish language arts', in particular for his role in initiating a Turkish *nahḍa*.[46]

Once certain cultural transformations in the late Ottoman Empire are described as 'the modern Turkish *nahḍa*', the history of modern Turkish literature no longer presents a foreign, unfamiliar literary landscape to Arabic readers. It can instead function like a mirror-image that further reinforces among Arabic readers the idea that Arabic literary history had a similar narrative and experienced a complete rupture and its own *nahḍa*. Unlike Namık Kemal, who quoted from classical Arabic poetry and ignored modern Arabic works, intellectuals such as Rūḥī al-Khālidī, Ma^crūf al-Ruṣāfī and Jurjī Zaydān did engage with Namık Kemal's works.[47] I propose that Arabic literature became reinvented as comparative literature also because writers like Zaydān and al-Khālidī translated the 'Turkish *Tanzimat*' into an 'Arabic *nahḍa*', since they described certain changes in the Ottoman literary landscape as a modern Turkish *nahḍa*.

Zaynab Fawwāz's (1860?–1914) *al-Durr al-manthūr fī ṭabaqāt rabbāt al-khudūr* (Pearls Scattered in Times and Places, 1891–94), a book featuring the biographies of 453 women throughout history, also dedicates a section to a key *Tanzimat* writer, Fatma Aliye (1862–1936).[48] Therefore, like Zaydān and al-Khālidī, Fawwāz 'translated' the 'Turkish *Tanzimat*' for *nahḍa* readers. At the same time, a comparison between Fawwāz's and Zaydān's works may provide insights into gender dynamics within *Tanzimat* and *nahḍa* circles. Fawwāz's entry on Fatma Aliye, unlike Jurjī Zaydān's work on Namık Kemal, comprehensively discusses Fatma Aliye's engagement with Arabic and Persian. Not only does it mention that Fatma Aliye took numerous Arabic and Persian lessons, but it also emphasises that Fatma Aliye 'progressed in the Arabic language and all its branches including metre, grammar, style and the rest' when she lived in Syria.[49] At the same time, although Jurjī Zaydān described Namık Kemal as the author 'who opened up new venues for Turkish prose',

Fawwāz defined Fatma Aliye in no such terms. While women writers such as Fawwāz and Fatma Aliye were key actors in *Tanzimat* and *nahḍa* literary circles, it was almost always the male authors, such as Zaydān and al-Khālidī, who sought to identify 'pioneers' of literature. The need to identify 'pioneers' of Arabic or Turkish literature contributed to the view that an 'old literature' had already existed and that a pioneer had transformed this old literature into a 'new literature'. Critics thus have become habituated to thinking that authors such as Namık Kemal and Jurjī Zaydān merely modernised a national literature that has always existed since time immemorial, rather than that they laid down the concepts, frameworks and paradigms that prepared the ground for the construction of Turkish and Arabic literature as national literatures.

Zaydān wrote about what he called 'the history of Turkish language arts', which contributed to this construction. 'Tārīkh ādāb al-lugha al-turkiyya' has notable similarities with his more famous *Tārīkh ādāb al-lugha al-ᶜarabiyya*, which provides a comprehensive history of Arabic works in a wide range of forms, such as poetry, history, encyclopedia, newspaper and geography, from the pre-Islamic period to the twentieth century. Likewise, 'Tārīkh ādāb al-lugha al-turkiyya' presents a history of Turkish works in a wide range of forms produced in the Ottoman Empire. The history of Turkish language arts constitutes part of a series of articles in which he shared his observations on the Young Turk Revolution. Zaydān travelled to Istanbul in 1909 to share his observations about this revolution and wrote extensively about his trip in *al-Hilāl*.[50] He informed his readers about various aspects of Istanbul, including its geographical location, monuments, palaces, museums and political situation. At the beginning of the section titled 'Its Scientific and Literary Condition', Zaydān indicated that one needed to study the Turkish language arts to understand Istanbul's cultural landscape, since Istanbul was a Turkish place. Furthermore, Ottoman became the marker of a particular Turkish identity when Zaydān claimed that one needed to distinguish Ottoman Turks from other Turks, such as the Azeris.[51]

While Zaydān did not write extensively about what he called 'the history of Turkish language arts' in contrast to the voluminous *Tārīkh ādāb al-lugha al-ᶜarabiyya*, both works share many characteristics. They both describe not just works of 'literature' in the modern sense, but also works of historiography, geography and philosophy. The Arabs experienced *nahḍa*s during certain moments in the Abbasid period, while the Turks experienced a *nahḍa* during the reign of Sultan Süleyman the Magnificent (r. 1520–66).[52] *Al-nahḍa* functions as a point of rupture for the Turkish language arts, which is evident in the section titles, such as 'The Last Scientific *Nahḍa*'.[53] If 'Tārīkh ādāb al-lugha al-turkiyya' emphasised numerous times that the Turkish language arts had recently entered a *nahḍa* after a long slumber, *Tārīkh ādāb al-lugha al-ᶜarabiyya* claimed that the Arabic language arts had entered its last *nahḍa* after a period of decline.[54]

Furthermore, 'the last *nahḍa*' of both Arabs and Turks corresponded to the late nineteenth and early twentieth centuries and displayed similar qualities, such as a deeper engagement with the Western language arts and aspects of modern civilisation.[55] Both 'Tārīkh ādāb al-lugha al-turkiyya' and *Tārīkh ādāb al-lugha al-ᶜarabiyya* list libraries, journals and printing presses in their histories of 'the last *nahḍa*' of the Turkish and Arabic language arts.[56] Zaydān's writings envision both Turkish and Arabic language arts as two parallel trajectories that do not, despite their deep similarity, ever meet in the cultural confluence that filled the Ottoman literary reservoir. As they lay the foundation of Zaydān's vision for Arabic literature, both 'Tārīkh ādāb al-lugha al-turkiyya' and *Tārīkh ādāb al-lugha al-ᶜarabiyya* overlook the new 'Ottoman afterlife' that Arabic texts attained in the Ottoman 'tavern' or 'ocean' that Ziya Pasha's *Harabat* upholds.

In the *Tārīkh*, Zaydān indicated that all the communities belonging to Islamic civilisation, including Turks and Iranians, became 'Arabised' and produced Arabic works in diverse fields such as language arts, grammar, history, medicine, science and philosophy.[57] Unlike Zaydān's writings on Namık Kemal that de-emphasise the cultural intersections between Arabic and Turkish literatures, the *Tārīkh* here acknowledges the influence of Arabic texts on Ottoman writers. However, the *Tārīkh* depicts Arabic works mainly as a source of influence that Arabised Ottoman writers and not as the works in a reservoir that are read to grow and water an Ottoman identity. Therefore, much like the article on Namık Kemal, the *Tārīkh* encourages readers to imagine Arabic texts as works that cultivate only Arab or Arabised communities.

Arabic Literature and the Debate on the Classics

Even if many of their writings may have de-emphasised the Ottoman reservoir's multilingual characteristic, authors like Zaydān were part of the translingual and transcultural space of the Ottoman Empire. Some authors who today are considered pioneers of modern Arabic literature did read works of the *turāth* during their time in Istanbul. Maḥmūd Sāmī al-Bārūdī (1839–1904), who has been 'recognized and recreated as the founder of Arab nationalism coinciding with the revitalization of the utopian vision of this movement',[58] worked as a civil administrator in Istanbul. *Miṣbāḥ al-sharq*, the Arabic newspaper founded by Muḥammad al-Muwayliḥī (1858–1930) in 1898, included 'extracts from Arabic literature, including essays by al-Jāḥiẓ and poems from the *Dīwān* of Ibn al-Rūmī, which Muḥammad had transcribed in Istanbul's Fatih Library during his stay there'.[59] One of the most prominent figures of the *nahḍa*, Aḥmad Fāris al-Shidyāq (1805/6–87) also made extensive use of literary works while in Istanbul. As Geoffrey Roper has indicated, '[h]is assiduous work in the libraries of Europe and Turkey enabled him to study, appreciate, copy and later edit great works of the Arabic literary heritage, many of which had not yet been published and had lapsed into obscurity in their homeland'.[60] Many Orientalists encountered what they considered classical masterpieces of Arabic literature in Istanbul's libraries. For example, Rūḥī al-Khālidī stated that the prominent Orientalist Richard Boucher discovered the works of al-Farazdaq (c. 641–728/30) in the Ayasofya Library in Istanbul, before providing a commentary on them and translating them into French.[61] Therefore, all these writers engaged with Arabic texts that some members of the Ottoman literati likely deemed worth preserving.

Zaydān also drew on the Arabic texts that had formed the Ottoman reservoir. Furthermore, Zaydān himself observed that most works in Istanbul's libraries were written in Arabic during his visit to Istanbul.[62] He wrote at the beginning of Book 3 of the *Tārīkh* that Aḥmad Taymūr (1871–1930) had provided him with a list of books from Istanbul.[63] The Arabic sources that Zaydān consulted for the *Tārīkh* include *al-Fihrist* by Ibn al-Nadīm (d. 995/98), as well as works by the Ottoman literati, such as *Kashf al-ẓunūn* by Katib Çelebi (1609–57) and *Miftāḥ al-saᶜāda* by Taşköprüzade Ahmed Efendi (1495–1561).[64]

At the same time, literary histories from the late Ottoman period, such as the *Tārīkh*, used the term 'classics' to situate Arabic texts within the evolution of a national literature. Thought to be first used by the late antique Greek writer Aulus Gellius (c. 130–80), the term 'classics' eventually came to signify a work of first quality among Roman thinkers and retained this signification to this day. In this sense, the term has had a broad appeal since writers such as T. S. Eliot (1888–1965) have defined classics as works representing the apex of a nation's linguistic expression. Furthermore, since many Western European intellectuals have sought their cultural roots in ancient Greek and Roman works, they have also eulogised these works and categorised them as classics.[65]

Ultimately tied to the project of canonisation, debates on the classics in Arabic and Turkish writings, as İsmail Hakkı's remark on Ottoman literature demonstrates, attempted to project their respective literatures as akin to Western literatures that also had their own classics. Many intellectuals who are today viewed as pioneers of Arabic and Turkish literature, such as Zaydān and Ahmet Hamdi Tanpınar (1901–62), forged their vision of 'the classics' as they engaged with Western literatures. Works by these authors often use the term 'classics' to demarcate the canon of texts that their readers should read. For example, as this chapter will show, many Ottoman Turkish writings treat Arabic writings as their classics, while Arabic works such as the *Tārīkh* also classify these works as the classical pedestals of a modern Arabic literature.

How Zaydān used the term 'classics' reveals the manifold comparisons that he made in order to situate Arabic literature within a global literary field. The term 'classics' comes up twice in Zaydān's *Tārīkh*, both times in Volume 2. In the first instance, he used the term to describe how a style that became prevalent in the late Abbasid period was imitated by later generations: 'This time-period stands out with the full maturation of arts and sciences, including the composition of large lexicons and the establishment of a prose style that became the norm for the following centuries, a style that Europeans call "classics"'.[66] Zaydān put a quotation mark around the word 'classics', suggesting that this concept, a European expression, was foreign to his audience. Zaydān suggested that, although his audience may have been unfamiliar with the term 'classics', this concept helped to describe a particular style of Arabic writings.

Zaydān also employed the term 'classics' to emphasise the high quality of particular Arabic works and compared them with the Greek and Roman classics to emphasise the critical role that they played for the cultural formation of their respective communities: '[E]pistolary prose writing of this age became the style that later generations took as a model to be pursued. It is the scholastic style that is called in the words of Europeans (classics). In other words, the school of Arabic epistolography reached its fullest expression in this age, just as the Roman prose style reached its fullest expression in the age of Cicero and then began to decline after that'.[67] Here, Zaydān claimed that prose writing had achieved its golden age in the final years of the Abbasid Empire. This classical tradition to which Zaydān was referring had various features such as rhymed prose (*sajᶜ*), paronomasia (*jinās*) and rhetorical embellishment (*badīᶜ*).[68] Because the word 'classics' is in parenthesis, this statement once again suggests that the word 'classics' was a concept with which Zaydān's readers were not familiar. At the same time, Zaydān also emphasised that, even though the Europeans and Arabs may have come up with different expressions to describe a particular style, they shared similar historical trajectories. Zaydān, like numerous literary historians of the late Ottoman Empire, not only used the term 'classics' simply to mark his relationship *vis-à-vis* the past but also to signify an affinity with Western civilisation, which also had its own classical heritage.

Furthermore, Zaydān did not employ parentheses or quotation marks when using the terms '*naḥw*' (the science of grammar) and '*al-jāhiliyya*' to describe certain aspects of Greek or French writings throughout the *Tārīkh*. Indeed, Zaydān constantly emphasised the similarities between Greeks and Arabs to show that the Arabs, like the Greeks, belonged to an influential civilisation. He wrote that both debated extensively about their poets' talent; both shared a period of *jāhiliyya*; both developed *naḥw*.[69] Like Zaydān, many influential authors such as Tawfīq al-Ḥakīm (1898–1987), Ṭāhā Ḥusayn (1889–1973) and Sulaymān al-Bustānī (1856–1925) would frequently compare their communities to the Greeks and Romans.[70]

The list of the sources that Zaydān consulted for the *Tārīkh* reinforces my portrayal of him as a comparatist. One of these sources consists of a foundational text of the discipline of Comparative Literature, *Histoire des littératures comparées des origines au XXe siècle* (A History of Comparative Literatures from the Earliest Times to the Twentieth Century, 1903) by Frédéric Loliée (1856–1915).[71] Zaydān's work resonates with the Comparative Literature discipline of the nineteenth century, especially as it was developed by German and French scholars, which compared literatures from different cultures of the world to pass judgment on how 'civilised' these cultures were.[72] In a similar vein, Zaydān argued in the beginning of the *Tārīkh* that literary histories provided information on the social and intellectual progress of a particular community *vis-à-vis* other civilisations.[73]

The list of sources that Zaydān consulted also includes histories of Italian, Indian, Persian, French and Greek literatures, such as *Histoire de la littérature italienne* (The History of Italian Literature, 1867) by François-Tommy Perrens (1822–1901), *A Literary History of Persia* (1902) by Edward Granville Browne (1862–1926) and *A Literary History of India* (1898) by Robert Watson Frazer (1854–1921). Similarly, he included the names of libraries from different parts of the world, where the manuscripts that he had used for his history were located, including the British Museum Library in London and the Ayasofya and Beyazıt Libraries in Istanbul.[74]

Another work that generated comparisons between Arabic and Western literatures, Rūḥī al-Khālidī's *Tārīkh ᶜilm al-adab ᶜinda al-Ifranj wa-l-ᶜArab wa-Fīktūr Hūkū* (History of the Science of Literature among the Europeans and the Arabs and Victor Hugo, 1904), also depicts Arabic literature as a past source of influence for Ottoman literature rather than as a stream flowing into the Ottoman reservoir. The publication of this work marked, according to H. Al-Khateeb, 'the beginning of the study of comparative literature in the Arab world'.[75] Al-Khālidī has written about the controversy around the anthology *Harabat* by Ziya Pasha:

> In criticising the ancients, Minister Ziya Pasha followed in the footsteps of Boileau. He composed an anthology he titled *al-Kharābāt*, which criticised many poems by Arabs, Persians and Turks who had preceded him. He passed away in Bursa in AH 1295 [1878]. He was succeeded by Kemal Bey, the pioneer of literature in the Ottoman language, who wrote a critique of the anthology which he titled *Takhrīb al-Kharābāt* published by Ebüzziya Press. The pioneers of Ottoman literature such as the two above-mentioned authors [Ziya Pasha and Namık Kemal], Abdülhak Hamid Bey, who was a counselor at the London embassy, Ekrem Bey, Said Bey, who was a member of the Shura Council, Muallim Naci Efendi, who had passed away a few years ago, and the rest of modern prose writers all aimed to purify their language from foreign Persian exaggerations. To that end, they followed in the footsteps of Boileau, Racine, Corneille, Molière and the other litterateurs who lived during Louis XIV's reign.[76]

Like Zaydān, this paragraph 'translates' the Ottoman literary landscape in several ways and thus renders it familiar to its Arabic readers. First, it calls Ziya Pasha's anthology *al-Kharābāt*, thereby using the Arabic definite article. It then used the Arabic *iḍāfa* construction in reproducing the title of Namık Kemal's work as *Takhrīb al-Kharābāt* rather than the Turkish *Tahrib-i Harabat*, further endowing these works with a sense of familiarity for Arabic readers. Second, al-Khālidī has 'misread' *Harabat* by claiming that the anthology criticises old poets, although, as Chapter 1 has demonstrated, Ziya Pasha did not call for a complete disavowal of the literary tradition. Finally, al-Khālidī has classified diverse figures such as Reşad Ekrem, Muallim Naci and Abdülhak Hamid Bey as 'new writers' and overlooked the discrepancies among them.

Furhermore, like Zaydān, al-Khālidī has described Namık Kemal as 'the pioneer of literature in the Ottoman language' but has nothing to say about his engagement with Arabic literature. In her analysis of nineteenth-century Arabic translations of European novels, Rebecca C. Johnson has argued that critics should not study the 'mistranslations', 'bad translations' and 'misreadings' that characterise these Arabic works as failures, but instead as facilitators of Arabic literary modernity. In a similar vein, 'misreadings' of the Turkish and Ottoman literary landscape in Zaydān's and al-Khālidī's works served a similar function of facilitating Arabic literary modernity.[77]

Al-Khālidī has pointed out similarities between Ottoman and French writers. For example, he has indicated that Ziya Pasha and Namık Kemal 'followed in the footsteps' of Boileau who also called for a strict separation between ancient and modern literatures and established what al-Khālidī has referred to as a style that is 'scholastic (classics)'. Al-Khālidī has compared the period of Louis XIV with the period of Augustus and the time of Pericles of Greeks.[78] By comparing Ottoman writers with poets from Louis XIV's reign, al-Khālidī has generated a sense of equivalence between authors like Ziya Pasha and Namık Kemal and their French counterparts, such as Boileau, Racine and Molière. He has also indicated throughout his book that the French authors 'followed in the footsteps' of earlier Arab writers from Andalusia and then stated that Ziya Pasha followed in the footsteps of Boileau.[79] The Arabs first contributed to the emergence of the classics as they influenced French authors like Boileau, who ultimately shaped the intellectual formation of authors such as Namık Kemal and Ziya Pasha. Al-Khālidī has thus generated a particular genealogy that starts with the Arabs and ends with Ziya Pasha through his use of the term 'classics', with the French acting as a temporal bridge between the two.

Therefore, as al-Khālidī, in Yaseen Noorani's words, 'align[s] the Arabic literary heritage of the previous fourteen centuries with a European-instituted world order of literature made up of universal literary genres and national literatures',[80] his work also depicts Arabic as a source of influence that predated the emergence of Ottoman literature but never existed as a part of its reservoir. The classics, which established comparisons between Arabic and European literatures, also stabilised the classical Arabic heritage within a linear historical trajectory in works by both Zaydān and al-Khālidī. 'The similarities between Zaydān's position and al-Khālidī's are striking but not surprising', Haifa Saud Alfaisal has written, 'considering that the two men moved in the same circles'.[81]

Namık Kemal's *Tahrib-i Harabat* (The Destruction of the Tavern, AH 1291 [1874/75]), a book-length diatribe against Ziya Pasha's *Harabat*, also testifies to the epistemological shifts that one observes in Arabic *nahḍa* texts by Zaydān and al-Khālidī. Namık Kemal first praised Ziya Pasha for his works, such as *Terkib-i Bend*, and then indicated that he could not understand why Ziya Pasha had decided to compose such a lousy anthology.[82] Namık Kemal claimed that *Harabat* was as detrimental for his community as a tavern (159) and emphasised that people like Kaᶜb ibn Zuhayr (d. c. 646/47), Sultan Süleyman I (r. 1520–66), or Ebussuud Efendi (d. 1574) had not spent their life drinking wine, as *Harabat* suggests (44). *Tahrib-i Harabat* claims that composing a work like *Harabat* is a matter of great responsibility, because the anthology quotes great works created over the past 1,200 years (158). Therefore, Namık Kemal did not accept Ziya Pasha's excuse that he may have made mistakes when composing the anthology due to his declining health. He also criticised Ziya Pasha, since the latter also included some of his own work among such great poems (119).

Namık Kemal analysed certain lines from *Harabat*'s introduction and pointed out the factual mistakes in them. For example, although Ziya Pasha wrote that Nefi was from Van, Namık Kemal pointed out that he actually was from Erzurum (31). He also criticised Ziya Pasha for his use of hackneyed expressions and the wrong *aruz* metre while also singling out many contradictions in his work. On the one hand, Ziya Pasha claimed that the Persian language elevated the Turkish language; on the other hand, he argued that it corrupted the Turkish language (32, 34). Namık Kemal also criticised Ziya Pasha for omitting specific key figures from his anthology. He reported that *Harabat*'s introduction did not mention the eleven Persian poets that were included in the index (135). According to *Tahrib-i Harabat*, Ziya Pasha dedicated only seventy pages to Arabic poetry, while he should have devoted more pages to Arabic poetry (153).[83] Namık Kemal accused Ziya Pasha of forgetting to include some essential poems, such as Labīd's (c. 560–c. 661) work featuring the hemistich 'Verily, everything except God is untrue' (*alā kullu shayʾin mā khalā Allāha bāṭilu*) (9) and Abū Tammām's 'The sword is more telling than books' (*al-sayfu aṣdaqu anbāʾan min al-kutubi*) (153). By pointing out these omissions and mistakes, Namık Kemal implied that Ziya Pasha did not live up to the canon that *Harabat*'s introduction praised and the standards that this canon upheld.

At the same time, his other remarks in *Tahrib-i Harabat* testify to the 'reinvention of Arabic and Turkish literature as comparative literatures'. Criticising Ziya Pasha's remarks on both Rūdakī (d. 940/41) and the critics who had studied Rūdakī as the first Persian poet, Namık Kemal made the following remark: 'On the contrary, the greatest poets have come to the world with the emergence of literature [*edebiyatın ibtidasıyla*] in the communities to which they belonged [*mensup oldukları milletlerde*] – poets of the *Muᶜallaqāt* for the Arabs, Homer for the Greeks, Virgil for the Romans, Cervantes for the Spanish, Shakespeare for the British, Corneille and Molière for the French, and Schiller and Goethe for the Germans' (136). Namık Kemal also emphasised that Ziya Pasha should have followed a universal value system, as the greatest poets in all communities emerged once they started to have literature. Namık Kemal, like other late Ottoman intellectuals, often re-evaluated the linguistic traditions of the Ottoman reservoir as they engaged with Western traditions.

Namık Kemal disagreed with Ziya Pasha who insisted that East and West were incomparable and incompatible, as the latter had suggested in *Harabat* that Sanāʾī and al-Farazdaq could not compose a theatre play as Molière had done. One should not exaggerate cultural differences. As Victor Hugo's (1802–85) *Les Orientales* (Eastern Poems, 1829) had already demonstrated, Western writers imitated those aspects of Eastern literature that they deemed valuable and acceptable. However, according to Namık Kemal, one should not expect eighteenth- and nineteenth-century writers who enjoyed the fruits of civilisation to adopt the features of old, classical works by poets such as Nefi and Sanāʾī. If Lamartine and Racine had truly wanted to do so, they could have composed works with many exaggerations and literary wordplays, as did Nefi; after all, telling lies was not just a feature of Persians and Turks (50). Likewise, if talented poets such as Sanāʾī and al-Farazdaq had wanted to do so, they could have written theatre plays; they just had not been born into a community that wrote works in the form of theatre plays (51). Although China was 'part of the Far East according to them [Ottomans]', it had produced theatre plays already before Europe (52). The world had not turned upside down since the Turks had started to write theatre plays over the past few years (52).

Just as 'the *nahḍa*', according to Tageldin, 'unfolded in translation' by transporting 'French and English into Arabic [and thus] appear[ing] to "preserve" Arabic – all the while *translating* it',[84] 'Ottoman poetry', as Veli N. Yashin has put it, 'becomes (new Turkish) literature, inasmuch as it can be recognized in European terms – fitted into its form and translated into its history'.[85] The use of the term 'classics' in late Ottoman writings, then, fits into the context of the epistemological shifts that are manifest in the comparisons and 'translations' that Zaydān, al-Khālidī and Namık Kemal made between the Arabic, Turkish and European literatures. I propose that the term 'classics' also shaped these authors' attitudes towards the Arabic literary heritage since it helped these authors envision Arabic texts as the predecessors of Ottoman Turkish writings rather than as streams feeding the Ottoman reservoir.

The term 'classics' foregrounds the relations of anteriority and posteriority that this reservoir did not emphasise in such stark terms. Indeed, Fatih Altuğ has argued that Arabic, Persian and Turkish literatures were intertwined in the Ottoman cosmopolitan tradition in a heterogeneous and centreless manner (*heterojen ve merkezsiz*), making it hard to separate these traditions.[86] Altuğ's observation of these traditions' intertwinement would resonate well with the description of the Ottoman ocean in Ziya Pasha's *Harabat*. Unlike *Harabat*, many late Ottoman texts 'stabilise' Arabic and Ottoman Turkish literatures such that Arabic literature always predates Ottoman Turkish literature as a source of influence. Like many European writers in the nineteenth century who studied the Mediterranean as the basin of a Greco-Roman heritage that gave birth to modern Western civilisation, writers such as İsmail Hakkı also sought the roots of their 'civilisation' in Arabic and Persian works as their classics.[87] Thus, Ottoman literature could be resignified as Turkish literature and classical Arabic poetry as a source of influence that had once shaped this literature and eventually could be set aside for the constitution of a new, modern culture.

Regarding the role of classical Roman and Greek traditions in the current imagination of Western culture and its use by the British imperial discourse, Mark Bradley has written: 'For the self-conscious discourses of modernity, the classical world was both the "other", pushed back into the distant past *and* the evidence of unbroken tradition evoked to bestow legitimacy on the present'.[88] Although Bradley has focused on representations of the classical Greek and Roman traditions in the nineteenth-century British Empire, his observations capture the dynamic between classical and modern works in the literary histories that I have been examining. These histories relegate the texts that they deem classical to a distant past while still maintaining a sense of continuity between past and present.

Even if numerous Turkish literary histories do not use the term 'classics' *per se*, they share with İsmail Hakkı the same attitude towards Arabic literature. Mehmed Fuad Köprülü (1890–1966) and Şehabeddin Süleyman (1885–1919) claimed that, just as French literature came into existence by imitating Greek and Latin literatures, Ottoman literature came into existence by imitating Persian literature in particular.[89] Likewise, Ahmet Hamdi Tanpınar compared the influence of Arabic on Cevdet Pasha (1822–95) to the influence of Latin on French writers.[90] These histories project Persian and Arabic texts as the 'classics' that once influenced Ottoman Turkish literature and claim that Ottoman literature began by imitating classical Arabic and Persian works, just as Western literature had begun by imitating classical Greek and Roman works. In these works, Ottoman literature constitutes the final destination in a teleological Islamic history, which becomes the mirror-image of European history with a similarly teleological trajectory whose origins lie in ancient Greece and Rome.

This particular use of the term 'classics' demonstrates that numerous members of the Ottoman intelligentsia viewed the empire less as a cosmopolitan state that upheld a multilingual cultural reservoir and more as a Muslim-Turkish state that no longer viewed Arabic and Persian literary traditions as waters feeding the Ottoman reservoir. These heritages were not necessarily discarded but instead resignified as 'classics'. Perhaps ironically, as Chapter 4 will further discuss, these shifts correspond to an unprecedented circulation of these 'classics', including Ibn Khaldūn's (1332–1406) *Muqaddima* (1377) or Mutanabbī's poems throughout the empire,[91] as well as an extensive number of translations from Arabic and Persian works into Turkish.[92]

This revived interest in the 'classics' was deeply intertwined with the emergence of the discipline of Orientalism in the nineteenth century. For example, in her history of Ottoman poetry, Dora d'Istria (1828–88) compared the influence of Arabic and Persian poetry on Ottomans with the influence of Greek and Latin works on the French.[93] As their use of terms such as 'classics' or 'Far East' also reveals, writers such as Zaydān and Namık Kemal engaged with this Orientalist discourse, sometimes building on it and sometimes critiquing it.[94] Aamir R. Mufti has argued that Orientalism perpetuated a nationalist-philologist understanding of culture and thus projected the world as an amalgamation of disparate civilisations, each possessing an authentic, classical tradition.[95] For Mufti, this changing understanding of the world led to the use of the concept 'literature' as an umbrella category that encompasses many non-Western works not necessarily considered literary by their own communities. These texts, which circulated more extensively around the globe during this period, began to be categorised as classics and as cultural pedestals in which non-Western civilisations were rooted. Only then, so Mufti has argued, could the discipline of world literature be imagined as an object of study.

Karim Mattar has built on Mufti's insights but also pointed out a key distinction between Middle Eastern and South Asian contexts: while 'Orientalist scholars and colonial administrators' imposed this modern conception of literature in South Asia, intellectual elites in the Middle East, according to Mattar, often appropriated this European conception of literature for their cultural and political visions.[96] This chapter proposes that such an appropriation took place in conjunction with a reassessment of the Ottoman reservoir. The shared engagement of late Ottoman Arabic and Turkish writings with this reservoir also contributed to the formation of Arabic and Turkish literatures as modern objects of study.

While this chapter has examined epistemological shifts, these shifts are also deeply tied to the socioeconomic transformations that shaped the late Ottoman period. Stephen Sheehi has criticised the tendency in *Nahḍa* Studies to see 'authors as producers' whose writings initiated modernity.[97] The same tendency is also prevalent in the *Tanzimat* Studies that view Namık Kemal as pioneer of modernity. Rather, one can interpret Zaydān's and Namık Kemal's works as effects of and responses to the particular socioeconomic transformations of their time. Stephen Sheehi has reminded us that we need to pay more attention to these transformations, rather than considering 'pioneers' such as Zaydān as jump-starting modernity. The next chapter will explore late Ottoman socioeconomic transformations, such as the laissez-faire economic policies and land reforms that generated, in Sheehi's words, a both literal and epistemological 'deterritorialisation' that contributed to the reinvention of Arabic and Turkish literatures.[98]

Notes

1. İsmail Hakkı, *Muallim Naci Efendi* (Istanbul: Nişan Berberyan Matbaası, AH 1311 [1893/94]), 88. İsmail Hakkı built on critics such as Johann Wolfgang von Goethe (1749–1832) and Charles Augustin Sainte-Beuve (1804–69) while defining the term 'classics'. He defined it once as 'old poetry' (90) and another time as works from the past that have a high literary value (83). İsmail Hakkı shared his thoughts on classics at the end of his biography of Muallim Naci (1849–93), praising him as one of the last poets who used the classical style. According to İsmail Hakkı, Muallim Naci would not receive the praise that he deserved, because more authors looked down on the classical style.
2. Tageldin, *Disarming Words*, 115.
3. Shaden M. Tageldin, 'One Comparative Literature?: "Birth" of a Discipline in French-Egyptian Translation, 1810–1834', *Comparative Literature Studies* 47, no. 4 (2010): 443.
4. Hannah Scott Deuchar and Bridget Gill have made a similar point while analysing how Arabic and Turkish translations of William Shakespeare's (1564–1616) *Othello* (c. 1603–4) characterise Othello as an Arab hero and represent relations between Venice and the Ottoman Empire: '[I]n both languages [Arabic and Turkish], the translated text becomes a space in which "Arabs" and "Ottomans" – two uncertain and overlapping categories – may look at one another'. '"Pour Our Treasures into Foreign Laps": The Translation of *Othello* into Arabic and Ottoman Turkish', in *Ottoman Translations: Circulating Texts from Bombay to Paris*, ed. Marilyn Booth and Claire Savina (Edinburgh: Edinburgh University Press, 2023), 82.
5. Zaydān did not use the term 'national literature' *per se*. Nor did he use terms such as 'Lebanese literature' or 'Egyptian literature' in his literary histories; therefore, he did not categorise literatures based on territorial identities. Still, his works reinforce a national-literature paradigm that draws a one-to-one correspondence between a textual tradition and an ethnolinguistic community, hence his use of the term 'Arabic language arts'. As a result, his works suggested that Arabic literature refers to works that only Arab or Arabised communities produced.
6. Alexander Beecroft, *An Ecology of World Literature: From Antiquity to the Present Day* (London: Verso, 2015), 199, emphases Beecroft's.
7. Axel Havemann, 'Between Ottoman Loyalty and Arab "Independence": Muḥammad Kurd ʿAlī, Ǧırǧī Zaydān and Šakīb Arslān', *Quaderni di Studi Arabi* 5/6 (1987–88): 351. Axel Havemann has also demonstrated that Zaydān's belief in this compatibility was 'rather typical for the intellectual

and political mood of his time' (353). See also Thomas Philipp, 'Jurji Zaidan and the Ottoman Revolution: Between Arab Nationalism and Ottomanism, 1908–1914', in *Jurji Zaidan: Contributions to Modern Arab Thought and Literature*, ed. George C. Zaidan and Thomas Philipp (Bethesda: Zaidan Foundation, 2013), 145–63, and Anne-Laure Dupont, *Ǧurǧī Zaydān (1861–1914), Écrivain réformiste et témoin de la Renaissance arabe* (Damascus: Institut Français du Proche-Orient, 2006), 543–626.

8. Muhsin J. al-Musawi, *The Medieval Islamic Republic of Letters: Arabic Knowledge Construction* (Notre Dame: University of Notre Dame Press, 2015), 40.
9. al-Musawi, *The Medieval Islamic Republic of Letters*, 76.
10. Allan, *In the Shadow of World Literature*, 83–84. At the same time, I do not claim that all other *nahḍa* thinkers shared Zaydān's opinions about Turkish literature. I focus on Jurjī Zaydān and Namık Kemal since much of the scholarship has studied these two intellectuals as pioneering figures who have shaped how we envision Arabic and Turkish literatures today. However, the late Ottoman period witnessed multiple and even contradictory understandings of the concepts that I discuss throughout this chapter, such as *al-nahḍa* and Ottoman culture. Further research can examine other authors from the late Ottoman period for providing alternative perspectives on these concepts.
11. Critics have provided different translations of the title due to the multilayered character of the term '*ādāb*'. I here use Michael Allan's translation, 'language arts', because it captures the capacious nature of the term (Allan, *In the Shadow of World Literature*, 85).
12. For the impact of these printing presses, especially for disseminating classical Arabic and Turkish works in the Ottoman Empire, see Ami Ayalon, *The Arabic Print Revolution: Cultural Production and Mass Readership* (Cambridge: Cambridge University Press, 2016); Benjamin C. Fortna, *Learning to Read in the Late Ottoman Empire and the Early Turkish Republic* (London: Palgrave Macmillan, 2011); and Nergis Ertürk, *Grammatology and Literary Modernity in Turkey* (Oxford: Oxford University Press, 2013).
13. Ertürk, *Grammatology and Literary Modernity*, 14.
14. Jurjī Zaydān, *The Autobiography of Jurji Zaidan: Including Four Letters to His Son*, trans. and ed. Thomas Philipp (Washington, DC: Three Continents Press, 1990), 78.
15. Zaydān, *The Autobiography of Jurji Zaidan*, 84.
16. Dupont, *Ǧurǧī Zaydān*, 579.
17. 'Muḥammad Nāmiq Kamāl Bek', *al-Hilāl* 5, no. 5 (1896): 161–67.
18. Muḥammad Ḥarb, *Riḥlat Jurjī Zaydān ilā al-Āstāna ᶜām 1909* (Cairo: Dār al-Hilāl, 2004). Ḥarb's book is a compilation of Zaydān's articles in *al-Hilāl* about his journey to Istanbul. Ḥarb also provides an introduction to Zaydān's life and works. For articles on Istanbul in *al-Hilāl*, see Jurjī Zaydān, 'al-Astāna al-ᶜaliyya', *al-Hilāl* 18, no. 1 (1909): 3–38; Jurjī Zaydān,

'al-Astāna al-ᶜaliyya', *al-Hilāl* 18, no. 2 (1909): 67–107; and Jurjī Zaydān, 'al-Astāna al-ᶜaliyya', *al-Hilāl* 18, no. 3 (1909): 131–65. For his perspectives on Turkish literature, see Jurjī Zaydān, 'al-Astāna al-ᶜaliyya', *al-Hilāl* 18, no. 2 (1909): 93–107.

19. Zaydān's writings constantly employ the categories of 'Arab' and 'Turk'. As Kamran Rastegar puts it, '[w]hile my own compulsion is to pluralize the term Arab society, to do so may do a kind of violence to Zaydān's own thinking – he clearly worked within a conceptual framework that idealized a singular Arab culture and society'. 'Literary Modernity between Arabic and Persian Prose: Jurji Zaydan's *Riwayat* in Persian Translation', *Comparative Critical Studies* 4, no. 3 (2007): 374.
20. Fazlıoğlu, *Arap Romanında Türkler*, 253.
21. Jurjī Zaydān, *Tārīkh ādāb al-lugha al-ᶜarabiyya* (Beirut: Dār al-Fikr, 2011), 2: 168, 3: 127.
22. Zaydān, *Tārīkh ādāb al-lugha al-ᶜarabiyya*, 3: 307.
23. Jurjī Zaydān, 'Ājāl al-duwal aw iᶜmārahā qadīman wa ḥadīthan', *al-Hilāl* 21, no. 8 (1913): 459.
24. Thomas Philipp, *Jurji Zaidan and the Foundations of Arab Nationalism: A Study* (Syracuse: Syracuse University Press, 2014), 115. Muḥammad Ḥarb also indicates that Zaydān supported the Ottoman rule, considering this rule an important defense mechanism against European intrusion (*Riḥlat Jurjī Zaydān*, 20).
25. 'Muḥammad Nāmiq', 164. Namık Kemal is mainly known for popularising the concepts of freedom, nation and homeland among Turkish readers. After attending numerous educational institutions such as the Beyazıt Rüşdiyesi and Valide Mektebi, Namık Kemal worked at the Translation Bureau in Istanbul, which played a fundamental role in the intellectual formation of many other late Ottoman *Tanzimat* intellectuals. He would eventually join the Young Ottomans. Namık Kemal suffered under exile and censorship due to his political viewpoints deemed controversial during his lifetime. His exile in Europe would make him a stronger advocate for the values of civilisation and progress. Some of his most famous works include *Vatan yahut Silistre* (Homeland or Silistre, 1873), *İntibah* (Awakening, 1876) and *Cezmi* (1880).
26. M. Kayahan Özgül, *Kemâl'le İhtimal yahut Nâmık Kemâl'in Şiirine Tersten Bakmak* (Istanbul: Dergâh Yayınları, 2014).
27. Bruce Masters, *The Arabs of the Ottoman Empire, 1516–1918: A Social and Cultural History* (Cambridge: Cambridge University Press, 2013), 6.
28. Namık Kemal, *Külliyat-ı Kemal. Birinci Tertib. 3. Makalat-ı Siyasiyye ve Edebiyye* (Istanbul: Selanik Matbaası, n. d.), 116–17. For his praise of Arabic, see 106–8.
29. Namık Kemal, *Namık Kemal'in Talim-i Edebiyat Üzerine Bir Risalesi*, ed. Necmettin Halil Onan (Ankara: Milli Eğitim Basımevi, 1950), 46.
30. Namık Kemal, *Namık Kemal'in Talim-i Edebiyat Üzerine Bir Risalesi*, 54.

31. Namık Kemal, 'Kemal Bey'in Bir Makalesi', *Şark*, ed. Mustafa Reşid, 1, no. 5 (AH 1298 [1880/81]): 99. Although Namık Kemal wrote this introduction for *İntibah*, this piece was not included in the novel when it was published. Therefore, the editor of *Şark*, Mustafa Reşid, wrote in the beginning of this article that he had decided to publish it because he thought that it contained valuable insights (97).
32. I use the terms 'centre' and 'periphery' cautiously here and put them in quotation marks since they often obscure rather than shed light on the complex cultural dynamics of the Ottoman Empire. The central Istanbul administration infringed on domestic affairs in many regions of the empire more than ever in its final years; nevertheless, the paradigm of a clash between a hegemonic imperial Turkish 'centre' and an Arab 'periphery', which has significantly influenced the field of Ottoman Studies, cannot capture the complex literary relations in the late Ottoman Empire, especially because Arabic had high cultural capital for the Ottoman reservoir.
33. Writers considered pioneers of modern Persian literature had a deep engagement with the Persian translations of Zaydān's works. See Rastegar, 'Literary Modernity between Arabic and Persian Prose'. For a comprehensive description of how some Ottoman Turkish writings appropriated Orientalist themes and tropes to describe cultures and places that their authors consider 'less civilised', see Christoph Herzog and Raoul Motika, 'Orientalism *Alla Turca*: Late 19th/ Early 20th Century Ottoman Voyages into the Muslim "Outback"', *Die Welt des Islams* 40, no. 2 (2000): 139–95.
34. 'Muḥammad Nāmiq', 162. Zaydān shares many characteristics with another author from Ottoman Turkish literature, Ahmet Midhat (1844–1912): both were prolific writers, came from modest socioeconomic backgrounds and wrote many historical novels to educate their audience. Dupont has also remarked that Zaydān may have become familiar with and even seen himself in Ahmet Midhat (*Ğurğī Zaydān*, 28). In fact, Zaydān wrote a brief biography of Ahmet Midhat in *al-Hilāl* after he passed away. This biography introduces Ahmet Midhat as one of the most important Turkish authors. See Jurjī Zaydān, 'Aḥmad Midḥat: al-kātib al-turkī al-shahīr', *al-Hilāl* 21, no. 6 (1913): 355–57. Esra Taşdelen has also provided a comprehensive comparison between Jurjī Zaydān and Ahmet Hikmet Müftüoğlu. See her 'Literature as a Mirror of History: A Comparative Study of the Historical Fictions of Ahmet Hikmet Müftüoğlu (1870–1927) and Jurjī Zaydān (1861–1914)' (Unpubl. PhD dissertation, University of Chicago, 2014).
35. The same piece with minor changes would appear later in *Tarājim mashāhīr al-sharq fī al-qarn al-tāsiʿ ʿashar* (Biographies of Prominent People of the Orient in the Nineteenth Century, 1902–3) by Zaydān. See Jurjī Zaydān, *Tarājim mashāhīr al-sharq fī al-qarn al-tāsiʿ ʿashar* (Beirut: Manshūrāt Dār Maktabat al-Ḥayāh, n. d.), 2: 115–21. In the *Tarājim,* Namık Kemal figures in the same section as other important *nahḍa* figures, such as Aḥmad Fāris al-Shidyāq, Ibrāhīm al-Muwayliḥī and Ibrāhīm al-Yāzijī.

36. 'Muḥammad Nāmiq', 162.
37. Abdulhakim Tuğluk, 'Ebüzziya Tevfik'in "Merhûm Nâmık Kemâl Bey" Adlı Eseri (İnceleme-Metin)', *Türkiyat Mecmuası* 28, no. 1 (2018): 179–99. Tuğluk has pointed out that different versions of Ebüzziya Tevfik's work appeared under various titles, such as *Kemal, Kemal Bey'in Terceme-i Hali* and *Merhum Namık Kemal Bey* (182).
38. 'Muḥammad Nāmiq', 162.
39. Ibid.
40. Ebüzziya Tevfik, *Merhum Namık Kemal Bey* (Istanbul: 1911/12), 6.
41. 'Muḥammad Nāmiq', 164.
42. Ibid., 165.
43. Ibid., 166.
44. Ebüzziya Tevfik, *Merhum Namık Kemal Bey*, 19.
45. 'Muḥammad Nāmiq', 165.
46. Ḥarb, *Riḥlat Jurjī Zaydān*, 134.
47. As Chapter 4 will demonstrate, Maᶜrūf al-Ruṣāfī translated Namık Kemal's *Rüya* (Dream, 1908) into Arabic as *al-Ruᵓyā fī baḥth al-ḥurriya* (Dream about the Search for Freedom, 1909). See Maᶜrūf al-Rūṣafī, *Āthāruhu fī al-naqd wa-l-adab*, ed. Dāwūd Sallūm, ᶜĀdil Kuttāb Naṣīf al-ᶜAzzāwī and ᶜAbd al-Ḥamīd al-Rashūdī (Beirut: Manshūrāt al-Jamal, 2014), 3: 613–42.
48. For the section on Fatma Aliye, see Zaynab bint ᶜAlī bin Ḥusayn bin ᶜUbayd Allāh bin Ḥasan bin Ibrāhīm bin Muḥammad bin Yūsuf Fawwāz al-ᶜĀmilī, *al-Durr al-manthūr fī ṭabaqāt rabbāt al-khudūr* (Bulaq: al-Matbaᶜa al-Kubrā al-Amiriyya, AH 1312 [1894/95]), 368–426. For a comprehensive study of *al-Durr*, see Marilyn Booth, *Classes of Ladies of Cloistered Spaces: Writing Feminist History through Biography in fin-de-siècle Egypt* (Edinburgh: Edinburgh University Press, 2015). This entry also includes an Arabic translation of Fatma Aliye's *Nisvan-ı İslam* (Women of Islam, AH 1309 [1891/92]) in its entirety. For a detailed comparison between *Nisvan-ı İslam* and its Arabic and French translations, see Marilyn Booth and A. Holly Shissler, 'Fatma Aliye's *Nisvan-ı İslam*: Istanbul, Beirut, Cairo, Paris, 1891–6', in *Ottoman Translations: Circulating Texts from Bombay to Paris*, ed. Marilyn Booth and Claire Savina (Edinburgh: Edinburgh University Press, 2023), 327–88.
49. Fawwāz, *al-Durr*, 369.
50. Ḥarb, *Riḥlat Jurjī Zaydān*, 125.
51. Ibid.
52. Ibid., 130.
53. Ibid., 133.
54. Zaydān, *Tārīkh*, 4: 9.
55. Ḥarb, *Riḥlat Jurjī Zaydān*, 133, and Zaydān, *Tārīkh*, 4: 13.
56. Zaydān also wrote about what he called 'foreign newspapers' (*al-ṣuḥuf al-ajnabiyya*), which included 'newspapers in Turkish language with Armenian alphabet' (*jarāᵓid ḥarfuhā armanī wa lughatuhā turkiyya*), 'Greek newspapers

with Greek alphabet and Turkish words' (*jarāʾid rūmiyya ḥarfuhā yunānī wa lafẓuhā turkī*) and 'Spanish newspapers with Hebrew alphabet' (*jarāʾid asbāniyya ḥarfuhā ʿibrānī*) (Ḥarb, *Riḥlat Jurjī Zaydān*, 143). His designation of these newspapers as 'foreign' suggests that he did not view these works as a part of what he called the 'Turkish language arts'.

57. Zaydān, *Tārīkh*, 1: 22.
58. Terri DeYoung, *Mahmud Sami al-Barudi: Reconfiguring Society and the Self* (Syracuse: Syracuse University Press, 2015), 2.
59. Roger Allen, 'Introduction', in Muḥammad al-Muwayliḥī, *What ʿĪsā ibn Hishām Told Us, or, A Period of Time*, ed. and trans. Roger Allen (New York: New York University Press, 2015), 1: xiii.
60. Geoffrey Roper, 'Aḥmad Fāris al-Shidyāq and the Libraries of Europe and the Ottoman Empire', *Libraries & Culture* 33, no. 3 (1998): 234.
61. Rūḥī al-Khālidī, *Tārīkh ʿilm al-adab ʿinda al-Ifranj wa-l-ʿArab wa-Fīktūr Hūkū* (Damascus: Ittiḥād al-Kuttāb wa-l-Ṣuḥufiyyīn al-Filasṭīniyyīn, 1984), 80.
62. Ḥarb, *Riḥlat Jurjī Zaydān*, 151.
63. Zaydān, *Tārīkh*, 3: 3.
64. Ibid., 1: 5.
65. Gregory Jusdanis, *Belated Modernity and Aesthetic Culture: Inventing National Literature* (Minneapolis: University of Minneapolis Press, 1991), 173–74.
66. Zaydān, *Tārīkh*, 2: 255.
67. Ibid., 2: 294.
68. Ibid.
69. Zaydān, *Tārīkh*, 1: 181, 1: 236, 2: 11.
70. See Peter E. Pormann, 'The Arab "Cultural Awakening (*Nahḍa*)", 1870–1950 and the Classical Tradition', *International Journal of the Classical Tradition* 13, no. 1 (2006): 3–20.
71. Zaydān, *Tārīkh*, 1: 10.
72. For a more comprehensive description of the first works in the discipline of Comparative Literature, see Natalie Melas, *All the Difference in the World: Postcoloniality and the Ends of Comparison* (Palo Alto: Stanford University Press, 2007), 1–43.
73. Zaydān, *Tārīkh*, 1: 6.
74. Ibid., 1: 10–11. Especially Book 4 of the *Tārīkh* provides extensive information on the libraries in Cairo, Alexandria, Istanbul and many European cities such as London and Paris (Zaydān, *Tārīkh*, 4: 97–140). Zaydān also wrote about famous Orientalists (*Tārīkh*, 4: 150–70) and praised the meticulous attention that European Orientalists displayed to works written in Arabic (*Tārīkh*, 4: 167).
75. H. Al-Khateeb, 'Rūḥī al-Khālidī: A Pioneer of Comparative Literature in Arabic', *Journal of Arabic Literature* 18 (1987): 82. See also al-Khaṭīb (Al-Khateeb), *Rūḥī al-Khālidī: rāʾid al-adab al-ʿarabī al-muqāran*

(Amman: Dār al-Karmal, 1985). Like Zaydān, al-Khālidī also was a part of the transcultural context of the Ottoman Empire. He read Arabic, Persian, Turkish and French and received his education in numerous cities, such as Beirut, Istanbul and Paris. He was elected deputy to the Ottoman parliament multiple times (Al-Khateeb, 'Rūḥī al-Khālidī', 86).

76. al-Khālidī, *Tārīkh ᶜilm al-adab*, 140–41.
77. Johnson, *Stranger Fictions*, 2.
78. al-Khālidī, *Tārīkh ᶜilm al-adab*, 138.
79. Ibid., 126.
80. Noorani, 'Translating World Literature into Arabic and Arabic into World Literature', 236. In a similar vein, Haifa Saud Alfaisal has argued that it is impossible to think of modernity as apart from coloniality; therefore, the literary comparisons that *nahḍa* authors such as Rūḥī al-Khālidī made cannot be thought apart from the colonial and inter-imperial political context in which these comparisons were made. For example, al-Khālidī naturalised the French ideal of *liberté* and internalised the notion that the Arabs experienced a decline during the late Ottoman period. See Haifa Saud Alfaisal, 'The Politics of Literary Value in Early Modernist Arabic Comparative Literary Criticism', *Journal of Arabic Literature* 50, no. 3–4 (2019): 251–77.
81. Haifa Saud Alfaisal, 'Liberty and the Literary: Coloniality and Nahdawist Comparative Criticism of Rūḥī al-Khālidī's *History of the Science of Literature with the Franks, the Arabs and Victor Hugo* (1904)', *Modern Language Quarterly* 77, no. 4 (2016): 543. Alfaisal has also noted that al-Khālidī frequently made contributions to *al-Hilāl* (Alfaisal, 'Liberty and the Literary', 543).
82. Namık Kemal, *Tahrib-i Harabat* (Istanbul: Matbaa-i Ebüzziya, AH 1303 [1885/86]), 4.
83. Although Namık Kemal here referred to the number of pages in the anthology's first volume only, *Harabat* itself dedicates 193 pages to Arabic poetry.
84. Tageldin, *Disarming Words*, 5, emphases Tageldin's.
85. Yashin, 'The True Face of the Work', 166.
86. Fatih Altuğ, 'Namık Kemal'in Edebiyat Eleştirisinde Modernlik ve Öznellik' (Unpubl. PhD dissertation, Boğaziçi University, 2007), 185.
87. For this understanding of the Mediterranean in European writings, see Iain Chambers, *Mediterranean Crossings: The Politics of an Interrupted Modernity* (Durham, NC: Duke University Press, 2008).
88. Mark Bradley, 'Introduction', in *Classics and Imperialism in the British Empire*, ed. Mark Bradley (New York: Oxford University Press, 2010), 11, emphases Bradley's.
89. Mehmed Fuat Köprülü and Şehabeddin Süleyman, *Malumat-ı Edebiyye* (Istanbul: Kanaat Matbaası, 1914/15), 18.
90. Tanpınar, *On Dokuzuncu Asır Türk Edebiyatı Tarihi*, 182.

91. Şerif Mardin, *The Genesis of Young Ottoman Thought: A Study in the Modernization of Turkish Political Ideas* (Syracuse: Syracuse University Press, 2000), 203.
92. Saliha Paker, 'Turkish Tradition', in *Routledge Encyclopedia of Translation Studies*, ed. Mona Baker (New York: Routledge, 2001), 577.
93. Dora d'Istria, *La poésie des Ottomans* (Paris: Maisonneuve, 1877), 42–43.
94. For an anthology of works that both draw on and critique the Orientalist discourse, see Zeynep Çelik, ed., *Avrupa Şark'ı Bilmez: Eleştirel Bir Söylem (1872–1932)* (Istanbul: Koç Üniversitesi Yayınları, 2020).
95. Aamir R. Mufti, *Forget English!: Orientalisms and World Literatures* (Cambridge: Harvard University Press, 2016).
96. Karim Mattar, *Specters of World Literature: Orientalism, Modernity and the Novel in the Middle East* (Edinburgh: Edinburgh University Press, 2020), 21.
97. Sheehi, 'Towards a Critical Theory of *al-Nahḍah*', 269–98.
98. Ibid., 293.

3

The Ottoman Tarboosh: Disguise and the Novel Genre in Ahmet Midhat's *Hasan Mellah* and Muḥammad al-Muwayliḥī's *What ᶜĪsā ibn Hishām Told Us*

Namık Kemal criticised people who wanted to create a dictionary for Turkish by drawing on parts of the Arabic dictionary by al-Fīrūzābādī (1329–1414/15), *al-Qāmūs al-Muḥīṭ* (Comprehensive Dictionary, c. 1410), and parts of the Persian dictionary by Muḥammad Ḥusayn ibn Khalaf Tabrīzī (d. c. AH 1062 [1651/52]), *Burhān-i qāṭiᶜ* (Conclusive Proof, AH 1062 [1651/52]): '[I]t is in no way possible to use *Kamus* [*al-Qāmūs al-Muḥīṭ*] and *Burhan* [*Burhān-i qāṭiᶜ*] for the Turkish language by making some rearrangements in them, which is like hoping that an Arab and an Iranian would join the Turkish community when they are forced to wear a fez [tarboosh]. If a dictionary is written for Ottomans, it should address their needs'.[1] Namık Kemal's use of the term 'Ottoman' in this statement testifies to the shifting conceptions of Ottoman identity and culture in the nineteenth century, as the term 'Ottoman' here refers to a Turkish-reading audience who would derive no benefits from *al-Qāmūs al-Muḥīṭ* or *Burhān-i qāṭiᶜ*.

Mütercim Asım Efendi's (1755?–1819) Turkish translation of the *Qāmūs*, *Kamus Tercümesi*, was published under the supervision of Sultan Mahmud II in AH 1230–33 (1814/15–17/18).[2] However, Namık Kemal claimed that, even if one rearranged the order of words in the *Qāmūs* based on their first letter rather than the last consonant of an Arabic word's root, 'a man who [did] not master Arabic grammar'[3] would not be able to find what he was looking for in this dictionary. Furthermore, Namık Kemal suggested that the fez (tarboosh), 'a brimless hat of red felted wool with a flat circular top and a tassel',[4] had served as a means of disguise for Arabs and Iranians who wanted to join Turkish society. He suggested that the circulation of the *Qāmūs* was no different from those Arabs who disguised themselves under a tarboosh. In other words, Namık Kemal implied that an Arabic text could never have an 'Ottoman afterlife'; it could only disguise itself as Ottoman.

This chapter will examine the imagery of disguise within the changing socioeconomic context of the late Ottoman period. Şevket Pamuk has demonstrated that, while nation-states such as Turkey could adopt protectionist and interventionist economic policies in the early twentieth century, the Ottoman Empire in its final years had to 'pursue laissez-faire policies and keep the economy open to foreign trade and foreign investment'.[5] The empire, unlike much of the non-Western world in the nineteenth century, was not colonised by a Western European power that had established full hegemony over its economy and trade networks. At the same time, in order to maintain its territorial integrity and receive support for its reforms, the empire often sought the aid of European powers, which then put pressure on the Ottoman administration to pursue laissez-faire economic policies that provided more benefits to these powers than to local communities. Pamuk has noted that this open economy model would come to an end only in World War I. For example, '[d]uring the financial crisis and the political turmoil in Lebanon in 1860–61, the Ottoman state agreed to lower the customs duties collected on exports to 1 percent, where it remained until World War I'.[6] During its final years, the empire also suffered from the highest rates of inflation and monetary debasement in its history.[7]

Therefore, Stephen Sheehi has called for studying the *Tanzimat* 'not only as an ordering regime but also a deterritorializing force'.[8] Both late Ottoman Arabic and Turkish writings, testifying to the socioeconomic shifts of their time, engage with this deterritorialising force. As the Ottoman Empire became more integrated into global capitalist networks during the nineteenth century, late Ottoman works featured a world of increasing mobilities. Their authors shared a strong sense of displacement that resulted from socioeconomic changes and sometimes reacted towards this displacement by describing what scholars have studied as markers of modernisation, such as the tarboosh headgear and the literary form of the novel, as means of disguise.

Sheehi has proposed that late Ottoman works often 'camouflaged' the deterritorialising impact of the *Tanzimat*: 'The concept of backwardness camouflaged or housed the alienation inevitable in capitalism's radical nature of economy, money and selfhood, the alienation resulting from individuating and ripping subjects away from "traditional" communal polities into *nahḍawī* ethos of national and citizen'.[9] As *nahḍa* authors emphasised the need to march towards civilisation, their writings, according to Sheehi, 'camouflaged' the deterritorialisations that global capitalism caused. This chapter will discuss the imagery of disguise first in *Hasan Mellah yahud Sır İçinde Esrar* (Sailor Hasan, or, Secrets within Secrets,

AH 1291 [1874/75]; henceforth referred to as *Hasan Mellah*) by Ahmet Midhat (1844–1912) and *Ḥadīth ᶜĪsā ibn Hishām aw Fatra min al-zaman* (*What ᶜĪsā ibn Hishām Told Us, or, A Period of Time*, first serialised between 1898–1902 and then published as a book in 1907; henceforth referred to as *What ᶜĪsā ibn Hishām Told Us*) by Muḥammad al-Muwayliḥī (1858–1930). I will then pay attention to late Ottoman articles on the novel genre. In particular, I claim that late Ottoman works sometimes served to 'camouflage' the process by which Arabic and Turkish literatures were constructed and ultimately conceptualised as national literatures in a global order of world literature.

Nergis Ertürk has already analysed how disguise became a key aspect of İsmail Gasprinskii's (1851–1914) literary works, such as *Frengistan Mektupları* (European Letters, 1887), *Kadınlar Ülkesi* (Country of Women, 1890–91) and *Molla Abbas Fransevi'ye Tesadüf* (Chance Encounter with Mulla Abbas Fransevi, 1908), as they also engage with the deterritorialising impacts of modernity. These works feature characters who travel in disguise, as they claim to have full control over the languages they speak and translate. However, they ultimately confront the unstable, uncanny (*unheimlich*) and arbitrary character of all languages and identities. Gasprinskii, often studied as the founder of Turcology, adopted the European Orientalist notion of a unified, authentic Turkic identity in order to 'domesticate the *Unheimlichkeit* of a wandering self and language',[10] an *Unheimlichkeit* that modernity renders visible and to which his literary writings testify.

In a similar vein, Ahmet Midhat's works testify to the deterritorialising impacts of a global capitalist modernity, characterised by the telecommunications revolution – that is, the 'intensification of printing and translational activity'.[11] As Ertürk points out, this deterritorialisation renders visible a sense of alienation that, contrary to typical scholarly assumption, does not result from an encounter between an authentic 'self' and the Western 'other'. Rather, this alienation stems from the arbitrariness and uncanniness that characterises all languages and identities. Instead of letting readers confront this situation, however, Ahmet Midhat's novels attempt to domesticate this alienation by calling for a 'politics of identitarian essentialism'.[12] As a result, Ahmet Midhat 'instrumentalize[d] literature as a device for suppressing the arbitrariness of modern identity'.[13]

This chapter will point out the juxtaposition between the late Ottoman Empire's material conditions that generated displacement and those authors who claimed to have agency in controlling these changes as they used the imagery of disguise. To study the implications of this disguise imagery, this chapter will first present a close reading of *Hasan Mellah* and *What ᶜĪsā ibn*

Hishām Told Us. I will then flesh out a homology between the characters in *Hasan Mellah* and *What ᶜĪsā ibn Hishām Told Us* moving around under the guise of new clothes and works such as *Hasan Mellah* and *What ᶜĪsā ibn Hishām Told Us* circulating under the guise of different forms such as novel, *nazire* and *maqāma*. Late Ottoman authors classified works from different periods, such as *The One Thousand and One Nights*, as novels, even though literary scholars today would not categorise them as such. Their writings reinforce the impression that the proliferation of the novel genre did not stem (even in part) from the social and cultural displacements that the shifting economic conditions generated. Instead, they suggest that the novel was merely a guise that old tales such as *The Thousand and One Nights* could adopt. Disguise reinforces the notion that these markers merely signify shifts in appearance, rather than the results of displacement and deterritorialisation. The imagery of disguise thus serves as a discursive strategy for authors who wanted to give the impression that they had a sense of agency and control over the transformations of their time.

As late Ottoman authors suggested that people from different ethnic, religious and linguistic communities should affiliate themselves with a larger Ottoman community, they disguised the increasing solidification of communal boundaries. Likewise, as they used the term 'novel' for a wide range of texts, they depicted the novel as a transhistorical form rather than an effect of deterritorialising socioeconomic forces that also contributed to the solidification of communal boundaries. The chapter's final section will point out that the widely accepted notion in the current scholarship – that is, the novel signifies a stark rupture from classical to modern literatures – 'disguises' the relatively recent invention of 'Arabic literature' and 'Turkish literature' as modern categories of analysis.

People in Disguise

Heroes and rulers in many Arabic and Turkish tales, such as Bamsı Beyrek in the epic tales of Dede Korkut and the Abbasid ruler Hārūn al-Rashīd (r. 786–809) in *The One Thousand and One Nights*, change clothes to move around in disguise. Political rulers themselves changed clothes to wander around in disguise. For example, Sultan Osman III (r. 1754–57) roamed the streets of Istanbul as commoner so that he could ensure that his subjects strictly followed dress regulations. He condemned women who wore clothes that were too tight or men who used gold thread on their horses.[14] Similarly, Sultan Selim III (r. 1789–1807) moved in disguise among Istanbul's bread makers so as to control the quality of the bread in the city.[15] Although Islamic rulers could change their clothes, their subjects often faced regulations that strictly controlled what one could wear. Due to these regulations, dress became a key marker of identity. For example, according to Julia A. Clancy-Smith, 'the primary marker of identity in the streets of Tunis was first and foremost dress, which provided immediate information on the religion, social class, profession and ethnic belonging of individuals sharing different kinds of spaces'.[16]

Numerous *nahḍa* and *Tanzimat* texts featured characters who wandered around in disguise. For example, in *Vatan yahut Silistre* (Homeland or Silistre, 1873), Namık Kemal's famous play, one of the main characters, Zekiye, puts on a military uniform, disguises herself as a man and joins the Ottoman army while adopting a new name, Adem. One of the main characters in Şemseddin Sami's (1850–1904) *Taaşşuk-ı Talat ve Fitnat* (Talat and Fitnat Falling in Love, 1872–73), Talat, visits his beloved, Fitnat, by disguising himself as a woman. In Jurjī Zaydān's (1861–1914) *al-ᶜAbbāsa ukht al-Rashīd* (*The Caliph's Sister: Harun al-Rashid and the Fall of the Persians*, 1906), al-Faḍl confronts the soldiers of the state who wander around in disguise. In these texts, rulers do not roam in disguise. Rather, they feature 'everyday characters' who 'don' different identities. In late Ottoman writings such as *Hasan Mellah*, disguise does not necessarily serve as a surveillance strategy employed by rulers to control their subjects. Instead, the characters change their clothes so that they can explore and move among the different milieux of the Ottoman Empire without experiencing any radical shift in their 'essence' or 'original identity'. As characters move among the empire's different territories, they, similar to what Namık Kemal described as 'Arabs and Iranians who put on a fez', can adopt different guises. However, these late Ottoman works substantiate the assumption that what lies beneath these guises is a stable national, ethnic and linguistic self – that is, 'an Arab' or 'an Iranian'.

Gender and Religious Difference in Ahmet Midhat's Hasan Mellah

Ahmet Midhat was a famous Ottoman journalist, writer and translator. Unlike many other late Ottoman intellectuals, he came from a modest socioeconomic background. He worked as a civilian officer in Baghdad between 1869 and 1871 and wrote his first works there. Ahmet Midhat then continued publishing his works in Istanbul. He established a printing press and published many famous novels there. Ahmet Midhat continued to produce works in multiple genres, including novels, short stories, newspaper articles and manifestos. His novels featured diverse settings such as villages in the Congo, or Iowa in the United States. Ahmet Midhat was so prolific that he has been known as 'a writing machine', even among today's critics.

Hasan Mellah narrates the adventures of the pirate Hasan Mellah. Hasan is the son of a Moroccan prince who was killed by his enemies. He then receives a naval education in Cádiz and goes to Morocco to avenge his father's death. Having been kidnapped by pirates, Hasan Mellah is forced to burglarise the wealthy merchant Senior Alfons's house and steal his possessions. Alfons wants his daughter, Cuzella, to marry the merchant Pavlos, whose actual name is Dominico Badia and who, as it eventually turns out, also killed Hasan Mellah's father.[17] When Hasan Mellah intrudes into Alfons's house, Cuzella and Hasan Mellah encounter each other and immediately fall in love. Nevertheless, Hasan Mellah has to leave the house when Alfons's guards are about to capture him. Pavlos eventually kidnaps Cuzella. Afterward, the novel narrates Hasan Mellah's various adventures during his quest for Cuzella. In the end, Hasan Mellah manages to find Cuzella and marries her. Ahmet Midhat also informs the readers that Pavlos is eventually murdered, although this murder takes place after 'the event that he narrates as a story' (461) comes to an end.

In the preface, Ahmet Midhat wrote that *Hasan Mellah* was his contribution to his community's growing intellectual circle during its age of progress (*asr-ı terakki*) (2). He also repeated that his community needed to 'progress' and 'move forward'. For example, he wrote: 'Rather than remaining stuck in one place, it is of course more preferable to move forward, even if we lose ourselves in the process' (3). While lovers may not attain a final union in many classical stories of the Islamic tradition, Ahmet Midhat created a love story in which the lovers actually live happily ever after. Hasan Mellah fulfills his dreams at the end of his journey, just as Ahmet Midhat wanted his readers to believe that the Ottomans will transform into civilised society, a destination that they need to reach. As he emphasised that Ottomans always needed to move forward, disguise could serve to ease the anxieties that accompany the 'movement' that he discussed. Disguise reinforces a sense of control and agency over the disorientating aspects of modernity, suggesting that one can sometimes adopt different identities and then go back to the 'original self' by simply changing clothes.

The characters in *Hasan Mellah* adopt different identities with ease. Hasan introduces himself to other pirates: 'My current name is Hasan. Before that, my name was Safatino. The name before that, that is, my actual name, is Turgo' (60). He is described as Christian, Muslim and Jew, as well as Spanish, French and Arab. Hasan Mellah tells Madame İlya that, 'just as Pavlos was an Arab while being Spanish, [he] can go to Paris as a Spaniard while being an Arab' (194). Hasan Mellah also describes Pavlos with the following words: 'The man we are looking for is a Christian, a Muslim and a Jew. He can be a Spaniard, a Frenchman and an Arab' (193–94). People describe Alfons as 'Easterner' (7), because he made a vast fortune during his travels in Egypt and Algeria. Many characters speak multiple languages with ease. For example, Pavlos's Arabic is so good that he can introduce himself as a Muslim to any Arab (390). Hasan Mellah speaks Spanish in a way that is more eloquent than the Spanish that the cardinal of Madrid speaks (59). Even Hasan Mellah's ship is described as a French ship in Alexandria and as a Moroccan ship in Istanbul (271).

Furthermore, *Hasan Mellah* suggests that one can change identities as one puts on new clothes, and that it is easy to claim one's 'original identity' again. Hasan Mellah changes both his name (*tebdil-i nam*) and appearance (*tebdil-i sima*) (38) to travel in diverse milieux such as Paris and the villages of Morocco (123, 217). Hasan Mellah also wanders in disguise as a priest (119, 123). Pavlos himself observes that he may have seen in Marseilles five Arabs who wander around in Spanish clothes (*İspanyol kıyafetine girmiş belki beş Arap*) (141). Later, Hasan 'disguises himself once again in Muslim clothes' (*yine Müslüman kıyafetine bi't-tebdil*) when he goes to Tangier one more time (152). Cuzella describes Pavlos first as someone 'who goes out with Muslim clothes' (418) and later as a 'person who puts on Muslim clothes to deceive Muslims' (419). When Hasan Mellah visits the coffeehouse to ask about Pavlos, the Damascenes understand that Hasan Mellah is a foreigner based on his clothes, demonstrating that dress is one of the most salient markers of identity (402). Alonzo tells Hasan Mellah that, even though Hasan Mellah may be a thief in appearance (*surette haydut*), in essence (*sirette*) he is someone who can prevent thieves from committing horrendous acts (70). No one in Damascus believes that Dominico actually is a Christian when he preaches religious sermons to Muslims and disguises himself as Seyyid Ali (394).

In fact, *Hasan Mellah* sometimes suggests that there is no difference between Islam and Christianity. When Mari reminds Cuzella that her beloved, Hasan, is a Muslim, Cuzella defends herself with the following words:

> In my opinion, all religions want people to worship one God who created the heavens and the earth, the entire universe. No religion views us mortals as more sacred than the Highness. No religion prays more for us mortals than for the Creator. Do not all religions support good and prohibit evil? (116)

Cuzella indicates that 'all religions' share the same characteristics and speaks about Ottoman sultans who have married Christian women (117). Likewise, as a 'good Muslim', Hasan claims that he knows Christian and Jewish customs. For example, he tells his friend that he has read the Torah (171). *Hasan Mellah* emphasises that there is practically no difference among Christianity, Judaism and Islam, suggesting that no hierarchies existed among their followers in the Ottoman Empire.[18]

At the same time, the Ottoman Empire's integration into global capital networks developed in conjunction with the rise of identity cleavages within the empire. Relative to their Muslim counterparts, non-Muslim merchants benefited more from the empire's socioeconomic shifts, as European powers preferred to establish trade relations with these non-Muslim merchants. As Şevket Pamuk has argued, Sultan Abdülhamid (r. 1876–1909) wanted to mobilise the resentment among the conservative Muslim elites who felt discontent partly due to the legal privileges and growing economic power of non-Muslim communities.[19] The empire generated a more favourable environment for the Muslim-Turkish bourgeisie only during World War I, when the empire started to adopt more protectionist economic policies and when this bourgeisie 'also acquired the lands and other assets of the departing Greeks and Armenians'[20] who were either massacred or forced to leave Anatolia.

Jeffrey Sacks has argued that that the late Ottoman period witnessed '[t]he expansion of capital and capitalist relations, which loosens and devastates language, as language is recaptured in relation to "the juridical equality of all subjects", an equality for which the violence of the law calls'.[21] This emphasis on the 'equality of subjects' that one especially sees in the empire's 1856 Decree can also reinforce communal boundaries when it provides a clear-cut definition for the empire's communal subjects. Like this emphasis on the juridicial equality of all subjects, the use of disguise helps readers to overlook the material and 'epistemic' violence that critics such as Sacks have pointed out. It posits categories such as the novel, not as the consequence of vast socioeconomic deterritorialisations, but as a new vestment that 'old texts' can simply put on and then take off whenever they wish.

Therefore, the disguise imagery may cause readers to overlook the identity cleavages that arose from the *Tanzimat*'s deterritorialising impact. At the same time, *Hasan Mellah* also includes a few instances that suggest that, after people have wandered around in disguise, they cannot necessarily go back to their original, 'stable' self. *Hasan Mellah* reveals that gender roles may have shifted to the point of no return when Esma, a character whom Hasan Mellah first meets in Alexandria during his travels, disguises herself in Istanbul as a young boy (*nev-civan*) whose facial hair has not yet grown in and whose beauty will make anyone who sees him go mad (351). Fatma Hanım falls in love with this beautiful boy who does not speak Turkish and who is 'either Egyptian or Algerian' (369). When she sneaks into this boy's house, they have the following conversation:

> Kid – Yes! I am also like you.
> Woman – O, my sir, I am now getting mad. Are you a woman?
> Kid – Don't you see?
> Woman – Truly, I can't believe this! Yes! These breasts are a woman's breasts! (373)

The boy does not give a clear answer to the question 'Are you a woman?' After revealing his breasts, the novel continues to describe the child as a 'young boy'. This particular scene in *Hasan Mellah* reveals the difficulty of maintaining strict gender distinction.

Esma always walks around 'in men's clothes' (374) in Istanbul, and Ahmet Midhat described her as follows:

> Esma no longer carried the Esma-ness that she had in Caucasia, a freshness came to her skin and her behaviours carried a sense of freedom. [Arslan] could not recognize her either with his perception [*feraset*] and high intelligence [*fetanet*] as she mixed Turkish with Arabic and changed her clothes. (380)

Later, Ahmet Midhat also noted that Esma 'immediately returned to womanhood by changing clothes' (*derhal karılığa tebdil-i kıyafetle avdet eyledi*) (382). Rather than suggesting that she appears as a woman as she puts on women's clothes, this phrase emphasises that Esma enters womanhood. Therefore, changing clothes does not generate a shift in appearance only. The transformations that occur in society are beyond the control of any individual. Arslan asks Cuzella: 'What was your name when you walked around in men's clothes?' (430). These examples suggest that characters like Esma significantly change as they wander around in disguise.

The novel also suggests that people have turned into animals, to such an extent that they cannot return to their 'original selves'. Ahmet Midhat wrote regarding Madame İlya that one 'started to observe changes in the lady's behaviours' (202) after she spoke with Trillo, who convinced her that protecting sexual honour is not important for women. Afterwards, the novel describes Madame İlya as a beast, as she was fighting against her desire 'with her claws' (204). Hasan Mellah acquires similar animal-like characteristics when he shows his physical strength (265). People do not necessarily wander around in disguise; they sometimes metamorphose and even change beyond recognition.

While Hasan Mellah starts his journey as a Moroccan, he ends his journey as a soldier in the Ottoman domains. Hasan Mellah settles in Algeria and starts to 'live under the Ottoman flag': 'Seyyid Hasan is creating a troupe as he takes control of the administration and hoisting the Ottoman flag. They can live in comfort and peace of mind since Algeria is a bountiful land, as it also has many places with a cool climate' (446). *Hasan Mellah* thus ends with a 'happy ending', as Cuzella and Hasan Mellah live happily ever after under the Ottoman flag. However, even if they live under the Ottoman flag or roam the Ottoman domains by disguising themselves as Ottoman subjects, the novel's ending provides no information on whether these characters have started to view themselves as Ottomans or even become Ottoman.[22]

In her analysis of Hovsep Vartan Pasha's (1813–79) *Akabi Hikâyesi* (Akabi's Story, 1851), a Turkish-language work written in Armenian script and sometimes studied as the first Turkish novel, Neveser Köker has argued that, '[a]s the Ottoman state became increasingly preoccupied with creating an overarching category of "Ottomanness" for its subjects',[23] perhaps ironically, the empire witnessed among its subjects a stronger emphasis on 'communal selves' such as Arab, Armenian and Greek as well as the growing need of these communal selves to differentiate themselves from 'communal others'.[24] My close reading reveals a dynamic that Köker has also observed in *Akabi Hikâyesi*. People from different backgrounds may share similar spaces and identify themselves as Ottoman; however, they are also assigned to stable ethnic, national and linguistic communities that are starkly differentiated from 'communal others'.

Taming the Ghost in Muḥammad al-Muwayliḥī's What ᶜĪsā ibn Hishām Told Us

Muḥammad al-Muwayliḥī (1858–1930) came from a family of silk merchants. The family received significant support from Egypt's ruler, Khedive Ismāᶜīl (r. 1863–79), who ordered his entourage to wear al-Muwayliḥī silks only. After spending a significant period in Naples, Paris and Istanbul, the city in which he would acquire a deep familiarity with pre-modern Arabic masterpieces such as al-Jāḥiẓ's and al-Maᶜarrī's works, he settled in the city of his childhood, Cairo, and started to work with his father, Ibrāhīm al-Muwayliḥī. Together, they published the famous newspaper *Miṣbāḥ al-sharq* (Torch of the East). The reputation of the newspaper reached its zenith during the publication of a series of episodes, titled *Fatra min al-zaman*, between 1898 and 1902. The series was published eventually in book form for the first time in 1907, under the name *Ḥadīth ᶜĪsā ibn Hishām* (*What ᶜĪsā ibn Hishām Told Us*).

What ᶜĪsā ibn Hishām Told Us narrates the adventures of two main characters, ᶜĪsā ibn Hishām and Aḥmad Pāshā al-Manīkalī (later referred to as 'the Pasha' throughout the work). As ᶜĪsā ibn Hishām strolls around a graveyard, he meets the Pasha, who has just resurrected from the dead. Several events unfold after the Pasha's resurrection. After getting into a feud with a farmer, the Pasha makes observations about the new Egyptian legal system. Later, the Pasha hears about the plague that afflicts Egypt and seeks ways to avoid it. The book then describes a series of assemblies during which the Pasha encounters people from diverse professions and backgrounds. In the final section, which constitutes the shortest part of the book, the Pasha and ᶜĪsā ibn Hishām visit a cultural fair in Paris.

As ᶜĪsā ibn Hishām walks around the graveyard, he witnesses the resurrection of Aḥmad Pāshā al-Manīkalī:

> Deep in thought about the extraordinary things which fate brings about, I was trying to probe the secrets of the resurrection. Suddenly, there was a violent tremor behind me, which almost brought my life to an end. In terror, I looked behind me. I discovered that one of the graves had opened and a man had appeared. He was tall and imposing, carried himself with dignity and a majestic aura and displayed all the signs of nobility and high birth. I felt as stunned and terrified as Moses on the day when the mountain was destroyed.[25]

ᶜĪsā ibn Hishām experiences a strong sense of displacement and deterritorialisation, as he feels as 'terrified as Moses on the day when the mountain was destroyed'.

This sense of disorientation comes to an end when the Pasha starts to disguise himself. The Pasha tells ᶜĪsā ibn Hishām that, 'in the time of [their] regime, it was considered appropriate for governors and senior officials to change their appearance, disguise themselves and substitute unfamiliar attire for their usual uniform', so that they could 'maintain contact with the common people' (2: 5). Furthermore, the plot unfolds in *What ᶜĪsā ibn Hishām Told Us* because the Pasha explores Cairo and Paris in disguise. The Pasha puts on ᶜĪsā ibn Hishām's overcoat and tarboosh and then declares: 'I have disguised myself [*ᶜalā ṭarīqat al-takhaffī wa-l-tabdīl*] in even shabbier clothes than this' (1: 41). Having already moved around in disguise in his previous life, the Pasha now uses a tarboosh to disguise himself. Almost no one notices the Pasha as a stranger intruding into people's private spaces; even his grandchildren cannot recognize the Pasha (1: 165).

Muḥammad al-Muwayliḥī employed two Arabic terms, '*tabdīl*' and '*takhaffī*', to refer to disguise. While '*takhaffī*' is commonly used to refer to disguise in Arabic today, this particular use of the term '*tabdīl*' captures the impact of the increasing Arabic–Turkish cultural interactions in the nineteenth century. As Chapter 4 will also discuss, Maᶜrūf al-Ruṣāfī wrote *Daf^c al-hujna fī irtiḍākh al-lukna* (Overcoming the Flaws of Speech Defects, AH 1331 [1912/13]) to provide a list of solecisms that became popular among Arabic speakers due to 'bad' translations from Turkish to Arabic. Al-Ruṣāfī complained that some Arabs had started to use words that were 'Arabic in terms of structure and Turkish in terms of meaning'.[26] *Tabdīl* was one of them. While Ottoman Turkish texts used the term '*tebdil gezmek*' to refer to the act of 'wandering around in disguise' ('*tebdil geziyordu*' *aw kharaja mutanakkiran*), this usage did not exist in the Arabic language.[27] Al-Ruṣāfī lamented that Arabs who did not care about their language had started to pick up this usage of *tabdīl/tebdil*. Muḥammad al-Muwayliḥī's use of the term '*tabdīl*' to refer to disguise reveals the impact of the linguistic exchanges that characterised the late Ottoman period.

Furthermore, the Pasha puts on a tarboosh in order to disguise himself. The fez or tarboosh has a long history, as people in modern-day Tunisia and Algeria have worn it for centuries. Sultan Mahmud II (r. 1808–39) required his army to wear the fez once he had abolished the Janissary system, through legal stipulations such as the *kıyafetname*. The Egyptian khedive Mehmed Ali/Muḥammad ^cAlī also 'started to wear the tarbush [tarboosh], the new sartorial sign of being an Ottoman subject'.[28] Thus, '[f]ifty thousand fezzes were duly ordered from the governor-general of Tunis, Mustafa Efendi, who was thereupon appointed minister in charge of production and supply'.[29] Ultimately, to meet the growing demand for this headgear, the Imperial Fez Factory was established in Istanbul, and it was initially staffed by workers from Tunis.[30]

As Namık Kemal's statement regarding the use of Arabic dictionaries also demonstrates, the fez was sometimes seen as a means of disguise. It reinforced the notion that an Arab could move in the Ottoman community by putting on a fez and hence appear as Ottoman while remaining an Arab 'in essence'. As more people felt improverished during the nineteenth century, Sultan Mahmud II criticised state bureaucrats who wore ostentatious clothes that incited the desire of the general populace to spend money and led to bankruptcy. The 1829 clothing laws partly served to undermine the display of wealth on the streets.[31] The sultan decided to adopt the headgear that some of his soldiers from the Maghreb wore – the fez, its name allegedly deriving from the place where it was originally worn, Fes in Morocco.[32] Although this law designated seventeen different groups of officials and described the clothing that each group should wear, it prescribed for all these groups to wear the same head covering, the fez. 'Thus, *all* fez-wearing officials, be they *kaymakams* or clerks would appear the same'.[33] Similarly, non-Muslims 'disguised their religious affiliation',[34] when they wore a fez. While non-Muslims and Muslims with high economic status accepted this law unquestioningly, many Ottoman workers reacted against the law. Donald Quataert has noted that, ultimately, 'the plain fez worn by the Muslim and non-Muslim bureauracts and by the non-Muslim merchants represented support for the laissez-faire economic policies of the sultan'.[35] Likewise, Bülent Somay has argued that the fez/tarboosh 'as a universal equaliser' marked the transition from pre-capitalist societies in which clothing and sartorial identity served as a marker of class.[36]

Quataert has demonstrated that, unlike many clothing regulations that aimed to make social and economic distinctions more visible, the 1829 law requiring Ottoman men to wear a fez was intended to generate social and cultural homogeneity.[37] After all, 'non-Muslims dressed like Muslims and subordinate Muslims dressed like their social superiors. As the state intended, upper- and middle-strata Muslims and non-Muslims superficially, sartorially, came to resemble one another in an unprecedented manner'.[38] The fez as a sign of Ottomanism signified a more egalitarian vision of Ottoman culture and identity than what the Ottoman literati often envisioned. After all, writers from different backgrounds, such the Arab Christian Jurjī Zaydān and the Armenian Zabel Yessayan (1878–1943),[39] identified themselves as members of an Ottoman community in their writings, although the Ottoman literati would not often envision non-Muslims as part of Ottoman culture.

Although the fez/tarboosh became a symbol of modern Ottoman subjecthood in the nineteenth century,[40] Wilson Chacko Jacob has shown that many Egyptian intellectuals, such as Maḥmūd ᶜAzmī (1889–1954), recoded it 'as a specifically Egyptian nationalist symbol'[41] during the World War I, because the act of wearing a tarboosh eventually became a symbol of resistance against the Western occupying forces, such as the British. Later, Mustafa Kemal Atatürk (1881–1938), the founder of the Republic of Turkey, banned the tarboosh in 1925, as it turned into a symbol of Islamic conservatism and a decadent Ottoman past. When an Egyptian delegate wearing a tarboosh visited Atatürk in 1932, Atatürk asked the delegate to remove it. Some Egyptians viewed this request, also known as the 'tarboosh incident', as a sign of disrespect and humiliation, demonstrating how the tarboosh had turned also into a key constituent of modern Egyptian identity.

The Pasha's transformation after he puts on the tarboosh in *What ᶜĪsā ibn Hishām Told Us* captures the shifting understandings of Ottoman culture and identity. The tarboosh helps him integrate into modern Egyptian society; it also helps the Pasha to look like a modern Ottoman subject. At the same time, as he puts on the symbol of Ottoman modernisation, he no longer speaks a language that consists of Arabic and Turkish words. The Pasha may 'look' Ottoman; at the same time, he does not work in a high administrative position or recite the Turkish or Persian poetry that signifies his acquaintance with the Ottoman literary reservoir.[42]

Although initially described simply as 'the ghost' (*al-shabaḥ*),[43] Aḥmad al-Manīkalī is simply later called 'the Pasha'. Therefore, in Karim Mattar's words, *What ᶜĪsā ibn Hishām Told Us* narrates the attempt to tame the Pasha's 'ghost'. Mattar has examined how global capitalist modernity led to the emergence of the Middle Eastern novel and argued that, although the modern novel displaced earlier local traditions, traces of these traditions continue to appear in Middle Eastern novels; in other words, these traditions 'haunt' the modern novel.[44] In a similar vein, one may argue that the Ottoman pasha 'haunts' modern Arabic writing, as *What ᶜĪsā ibn Hishām Told Us* reveals the struggles and even failures that come with the attempts to domesticate the Ottoman Pasha and a deterritorialising modernity.

The Pasha realises that what makes someone an Egyptian has changed, as he asks ᶜĪsā ibn Hishām: 'Tell me, for heaven's sake, which country are you from? You can't be an Egyptian. There's no one in the whole country who doesn't know where my house is. I'm Aḥmad Pāshā al-Manīkalī, the Egyptian Minister of War!' (1: 39) For al-Manīkalī, a true Egyptian is someone who knows Egypt's ruling class. ᶜĪsā ibn Hishām, instead, insists that what makes someone Egyptian is a solid grasp of the Arabic language when the Pasha 'misuses' words such as 'lentils' and 'greens': 'It's clear to me that you're the one who's not Egyptian. The only use we have for such words is for food. We've never heard of their being used to convey permission to travel at night' (1: 43). Later, ᶜĪsā ibn Hishām also tells the Pasha: 'Believe me, Pāshā, I'm from pure Egyptian stock' (1: 41). ᶜĪsā ibn Hishām emphasises that he understands the Arabic language better than the Pasha, who tends to get confused as he cannot understand some Arabic expressions. For example, the Pasha asks ᶜĪsā ibn Hishām what the term 'police' means, and ᶜĪsā ibn Hishām replies: 'It's what you used to call "Kavvas"' (1: 49). Although the term '*qawwās*' initially meant archer in Arabic, it acquired a new meaning in Turkish (*kavvas*) to refer to the guardians of officials and ministers. Likewise, the Pasha misunderstands the Arabic word *shahāda* and thinks that it means 'martyrs', although the term means 'certificate' (1: 65).

The Pasha claims that he belongs to a particular community that has ruled Egypt but does not have a particularly good command of Arabic. For example, Muḥammad ᶜAlī/Mehmed Ali Pasha 'managed to rule the

Egyptian people for a long time and to conquer Arab lands without ever speaking Arabic' (1: 179). When someone thanks Muḥammad ᶜAlī/Mehmed Ali Pasha with an Arabic phrase, he misunderstands it as the Turkish phrase '*ne eşek*' (what an ass) (1: 179). Likewise, someone uses the Turkish term '*başıbozuk*' (*al-bāshibūzuq*, irregular soldier) (1: 165) to refer to the Pasha and '*cennetmekan*' (*jannatmakān*, a term that literally means 'dwelling in paradise' and is used for venerable people who have passed away) (1: 301) to refer to Muḥammad ᶜAlī/Mehmed Ali.[45]

What ᶜĪsā ibn Hishām Told Us suggests that the Pasha is a representative figure of the Ottoman era: 'He was completely unfamiliar with the present state of affairs and had no idea that, with the passage of time since his own era and the decline of the dynasty of his time into the folds of decay, things had changed' (1: 59). The Pasha himself later admits that 'dynasties have succeeded one another, conditions have changed' (1: 61). All these statements suggest that modern Egypt has managed to leave behind the traces of the Ottoman past. The Pasha does not merely need to disguise himself as a modern subject; he may become one as he 'improves' his Arabic.

The Pasha and ᶜĪsā ibn Hishām do not engage with each other on equal terms, as the Pasha, unlike ᶜĪsā ibn Hishām, undergoes significant character transformations. The Pasha, 'as [is] his wont' (2: 197), tends to ask questions about certain aspects of modern society. ᶜĪsā ibn Hishām strives to 'tame' the Pasha and educate him, so that the Pasha can adjust to modern Egyptian society. The Pasha serves ᶜĪsā ibn Hishām's aim to expose the shortcomings of modern Egyptian society and ultimately becomes a role model for Egyptian readers about how one should modernise. ᶜĪsā ibn Hishām experiences 'delight in [. . .] realizing with joy how far [the Pasha had] progressed in his thinking, appreciation and psychological state' (2: 13).

What ᶜĪsā ibn Hishām Told Us also reveals the rivalry between the 'people of the tarboosh' (*arbāb al-ṭarbūsh*) and the 'people of the turban' (*arbāb al-ᶜimāma*). For example, a religious scholar complains about the 'people of the tarboosh': 'You can say whatever you like about these times when tarboosh-wearers have the absolute effrontery to discuss, argue, disagree and compete with turbaned shakyhs about their area of scholarship' (1: 389). Although the turban may be seen as symbol of tradition and the tarboosh as symbol of modernity, ᶜĪsā ibn Hishām declares that not everyone who wears a tarboosh is necessarily modern 'in essence': 'Beneath the tarboosh you'll often find some people more ferociously destructive than wild beasts' (1: 203). A person may appear modern and civilised as he puts on a tarboosh; however, this may be just an illusion.

These words suggest that the tarboosh serves as a mere instrument of disguise that allows the circulation of the 'old', such as the Pasha, under new guises. This example also suggests that people may look modern in appearance; however, they have changed only at a superficial level.

Although disguise gives the impression that socioeconomic shifts may have a short-term impact, *What ᶜĪsā ibn Hishām Told Us* also reveals that society has transformed to such an extent that one cannot retain tradition. The Pasha describes these vast transformations in the following words: 'In my lifespan I've witnessed remarkable transformations and alterations which neither pens can describe, nor notebooks contain within their covers. From now on, the sun may well start rising in the West and the earth release the dead from their graves!' (1: 157). Indeed, the plot unfolds in *What ᶜĪsā ibn Hishām Told Us* as a dead person – the Pasha himself – rises from his grave.

What ᶜĪsā ibn Hishām Told Us exposes the dissolution of old economic, cultural and political hierarchies. ᶜĪsā ibn Hishām declares to the Pasha: 'Just observe how circumstances have made us equals' (1: 103). The Pasha feels shocked that 'the old elite' no longer has a monopoly on knowledge: 'How can they possibly claim that knowledge is the sole province of the young to the exclusion of older people? I've only encountered genuine learning in people whose backs have been bent by old age and whose hairline has been whitened by experience' (1: 115). The Pasha complains about the destruction of old political and cultural hierarchies: 'Is the mighty man on par with the lowly, the powerful dignitary the equal of the small, the great man the equal of the despised, the servant the equal of the master? Has the Qurayshī no longer any superiority over the Abyssinian and is a Turkish amir not of higher status than a mere Egyptian?' (1: 61). When the Pasha sees a 'prince', someone from the Egyptian khedive's family, at a tavern that 'common people' also visit, he complains: 'How can such a royal person enter a tavern? We've never heard before of such personages lowering themselves to mingle with common people in places like this' (2: 67). This dissolution of old hiearchies is not peculiar to Egypt; for example, the Pasha laments that most members of France's Chamber of Deputies 'belong to the merchant class and the general populace' (2: 361).

All social and political distinctions become undermined in a society driven by profits and economic gains. *What ᶜĪsā ibn Hishām Told Us* criticises different professions, such as law and medicine, whose practitioners only 'want to broaden their revenue sources and earn more money' (1: 267). Socioeconomic shifts have deprived the Pasha of his wealth. The Shop Owner, who used to oversee the Pasha's lands, tells the Pasha that 'not a single trace of [his] wealth remains. Lands, money, wealth and posessions – they're all gone' (1: 159). Muḥammad al-Muwayliḥī pointed out that the stock exchange had become the key signifier of modernisation: 'To sum it all up, the difference in speedy profits between people who work on the one hand in commerce, agriculture and industry and on the other in the Stock Market is like the difference between traveling by camel and flying on the wings of steam' (2: 27). *What ᶜĪsā ibn Hishām Told Us* also suggests that these economic shifts are tied to global shifts, as the Frenchman lays out the strong link between France's civilising mission and global capitalism: '[H]ow are we supposed to make our goods available and find a market for our industry, the things for which our own country is too small and upon which our livelihood depends, if people like these weak, puny, yellow-faced Chinese dare to confront us?' (2: 215).

Ibrāhīm al-Muwayliḥī, Muḥammad al-Muwayliḥī's father, also laid bare the deterritorialising facet of the late Ottoman period in his *Mā hunālika* (*Spies, Scandals and Sultans*; literally 'Out Yonder', first serialised in *al-Muqaṭṭam* in 1895 and 1896 and eventually published as book in 1896), which describes his observations on Istanbul during his stay there.[46] Ibrāhīm al-Muwayliḥī wrote that his main intention in composing this work was to prevent the imminent collapse of the Islamic caliphate by exposing the corrupt practices taking place in the capital.[47] Although he advocated an Ottoman political unity, Ibrāhīm al-Muwayliḥī observed the solidifications of identity cleavages during his stay in Istanbul. *Spies, Scandals and Sultans* reveals that Arabs in Istanbul could suffer from discrimination. For example, Ibrāhīm al-Muwayliḥī claimed that Abū al-Hudā did not get the job he deserved – the position of *şeyhülislam* – simply because he was an Arab.[48] One of the sultan's doctors, Arif Pasha, uses the term 'Arab' as an insult: '"If I don't do such and such to you", [he] said in a fury, "then I'm an Arab". No one should be allowed to do such things in the seat of the Caliph of the Arab Prophet'.[49]

Ibrāhīm al-Muwayliḥī noted that, in Istanbul, al-Mutanabbī's verse was chanted,[50] Abū al-Hudā acted like his 'colleague' (*raṣīf*) Imruᶜ al-Qays in his search for glory,[51] and the imams in the mosques repeated the Prophet's sayings.[52] However, he pointed out a disturbing fact: the Ottoman government had banned many Arabic books, including ᶜAbd al-Ghanī al-Nābulusī's (d. 1731) *al-Ṭarīqa al-Muḥammadiyya*, Abū Ḥafṣ ᶜUmar al-Nasafī's (d. 1142) *al-ᶜAqāʾid al-Nasafiyya* and al-Māwardī's (d. 1058) *al-Aḥkām al-sulṭāniyya*.[53] Even if some of these works had been written centuries ago, before the establishment of the empire, they, according to Ottoman bureaucrats, evoked in readers the desire to rebel against the state. These Arabic texts no longer constituted a crucial component of the Ottoman canon, as these bureaucrats thought that people now resignified and reinterpreted these texts in subversive ways that undermined Ottoman authority.

Texts in Disguise

Elizabeth M. Holt has analysed the deep imbrication between the rise of global capitalism and the Arabic novel in the nineteenth century. She has argued that Arabic serialised novels which became prevalent in the nineteenth century fit into an era of global capitalism. Holt has steered attention to economic transformations, such as the Ottoman Empire's bankruptcy in 1875 and Egypt's stock market crash in 1907. By analysing the impact of global capitalism on Arabic literature, Holt has undermined the association of modernity with enlightenment and pointed out the discrepancy between the discourse of intellectuals such as Jurjī Zaydān, who promised progress and enlightenment, and their society's shifting material conditions that generated a sense of displacement and disorientation among their communities.[54]

Holt has also pointed to a form of 'disguise' that characterised *nahḍa* works. She has demonstrated that the late-nineteenth-century Arabic printing press capitalised on the garden imagery, as both gardens and fruits were important tropes for literary production in the Islamic tradition. Many writers thus projected their works as both 'Eden' (*janna*) and 'gardens of knowledge' (*majlis*) when writers such as Buṭrus al-Bustānī (1819–83) named their journals and newspapers after gardens and natural landscapes. Nevertheless, Holt has also shown that the Ezbekiyya garden in *nahḍa* texts represented a 'counter-allegory' that undermines the association between gardens and refinement or knowledge acquisition.[55] In Zaydān's novels, the Ezbekiyya is an 'un-Edenic' space, a site of burglary, drinking and illicit encounters.[56] The Ezbekiyya is also a place of debauchery and extravagance in *What ᶜĪsā ibn Hishām Told Us*. During their stroll in the garden, ᶜĪsā ibn Hishām and the Pasha observe the corrupt behaviours of the Playboy, the Merchant and ᶜUmdah (2: 13–17). Although *nahḍa* works belong to a milieu of capitalism and industrialisation, they 'disguise' themselves as serene gardens where one can find refinement and escape from industrialisation.

Late Ottoman Turkish writings also employ the metaphor of disguise when they discuss language and literature. For example, Ahmet Vefik Pasha (1823–91) wrote that some Arabic and Persian words 'changed clothes' (*kılığı tebdil olunarak*) and obtained new meanings once people used these words in the Ottoman language.[57] Namık Kemal compared one author's attempt to 'convey a colourful meaning with strange expressions' that characterised what he called the 'old literature' with an attempt to 'hide a black woman with a bedizenned bridal veil'.[58] Şemseddin Sami claimed that late Ottoman texts 'cover[ed] enlightened Western ideas with an Eastern garment' (*Garp efkar-ı münevveresini Şark kisvesine bürümek*).[59] Here, Şemseddin Sami did not describe his time-period as a strong rupture between tradition and modernity; rather, he suggested that 'tradition' could disguise itself under markers of 'modernity', just as 'modernity' could disguise itself under markers of 'tradition'.

In fact, as many late Ottoman writings discuss the novel form, they, unlike many critics today, do not always describe the novel as signifier of a stark rupture between classical and modern traditions. Mizancı Murat (1854–1917) castigated other late Ottoman writers who used the term 'novel' to categorise any kind of text, regardless of its content. He complained that writers described classical love tales as examples of 'the national novel'.[60] What writers called a 'novel' was no different from classical tales such as *Leyla and Mecnun*, since, when writers claimed to produce a new novel, they simply changed the character names of classical tales while adopting those same tales' plots.[61]

In a similar vein, Ahmet Midhat argued that the novel's 'true form' (*suret-i asliyye*) consisted of wondrous tales and described *The One Thousand and One Nights* as 'one of the best works in the novel valley [*roman vadisinde*] of its age'.[62] In *Ahbar-ı Asara Tamim-i Enzar* (A General Overview of the History of the Novel, AH 1307 [1889/1900]), he emphasised that one should not think of Émile Zola's (1840–1902) works as the sole examples of the novel genre. Instead, he argued that the novel had a transhistorical character when he wrote that 'the works that one calls a novel merely convey the ideas that an author wants to convey to his readers in forms [*zarflarda*] by setting up a time [*zarf-ı zaman*] and a setting [*zarf-ı mekan*] that suits every age and the inclinations of people in that age'.[63] Also according to Ahmet Midhat, English writers described shocking events in France in 'the form of novels' (*romanlar suretinde*).[64] He wrote about 'the form that is called historical novel [*roman-historique*]' in *Süleyman Musli*'s (AH 1294 [1877/88]) introduction, as he referred to 'stories that are based on history', such as *Süleyman Musli* and *Hasan Mellah*.[65] Ahmet Midhat emphasised that, when authors write stories, they should create a 'form of a reality that is one step more real than reality itself' (*gerçekten bir kat daha gerçek sureti*).[66] He wrote that one could generate the 'image' of a novel by investigating the details of an actual event, such as the marriage of a man to his second wife.[67] Ahmet Midhat again described the novel as an image when he claimed that a novelist could use 'all kinds of colours' in a work.[68]

Late Ottoman Arabic writings used the term '*riwāya*', today a term for novel, for a wide range of literary forms. For example, *What ᶜĪsā ibn Hishām Told Us* describes theatre plays as '*riwāyāt al-tashkhīṣ*': 'These theatrical plots [*riwāyāt al-tashkhīṣ*] are loaded down with depictions of father-killers and men marrying their mothers or sisters' (2: 177). Stephan Guth has already examined the shifting understandings of the term '*riwāya*' in Arabic works from the nineteenth century to the present day. Guth has demonstrated that today's critics would use a wide range of genre classifications, such as biography, drama, opera, autobiography, novel and history, to categorise the texts classified as *riwāya* by writers such as ᶜUthmān Jalāl (1829–89), Saᶜīd al-Bustānī (1859–1901) and Zaynab Fawwāz (1860?–1914).[69] In fact, Muḥammad ᶜAbduh (1849–1905) used the term '*rūmāniyya*', most likely coined from the French term '*roman*', to refer not only to Fénelon's (1651–1715) *Télémaque* (1699), but also to Ibn al-Muqaffaᶜ's (d. c. 759) *Kalīla wa Dimna* and Ibn ᶜArabshāh's (1392–1450) *Fākihat al-khulafāʾ* and *Marzubānnāma*. Guth has observed a 'clear overlapping of ᶜAbduh's classifciation of "*rūmāniyyāt*" with the characteristics of texts that otherwise [. . .] are termed "*riwāyāt*"'.[70] Furthermore, 'while the classical term "*riwāya*" is beginning to incorporate modern-type novels, a modern generic term loaned from French is made to include texts from the classical *adab* tradition'.[71]

Guth has attributed this 'semantic expansion of the term *riwāya*'[72] partly to shifting class dynamics in late Ottoman society:

> The genre's usefulness in the context of nation-building, its down-to-earthness and anchoring in real life were of course values especially appreciated by the new educated elite, the *afandiyya*, or 'engineers'. It was only natural for the new social group who had to find their place in society somewhere between the old elite and the masses, to propagate a genre that, with its focus on real life and the world, could serve as a counter-concept of all those genres of traditional literature, associated with the religious and literary establishment.[73]

In a similar vein, Samah Selim has argued that the novel became the site that testified to 'the hegemony of the European liberal-juridical concept of the subject, with its related institutions of authorship and copyright in the literary domain',[74] as well as 'the disciplinary project of a middle class in the process of constituting itself as a national bourgeoisie'.[75]

Drawing on Guth's and Selim's insights, this chapter claims that the circulation of texts under different guises such as *riwāya* and *maqāma*, akin to people moving around with the tarboosh, served this new educated elite's interests. Samah Selim has pointed out how the shifting socioeconomic dynamics led many *nahḍa* authors to assert the sense of a bounded, autonomous self who has full control over the disorienting conditions of their times: 'In its effort to forge its own destiny, the autonomous self is made to contain and resolve the existential contradiction produced by the new social order'.[76] As I have pointed out earlier, many late Ottoman authors also claimed to inaugurate a 'new literature' that differentiated itself from an 'old literature'; therefore, the disguise imagery may seem to undermine their claim to be pioneers of a new literature and of modernity. However, as these authors claimed to leave aside the old tradition, they simultaneously described the changes of their period as something that was not disconcerting or deterritorialising. Rather, the 'progress' or 'new civilisation' that they celebrated in their works was described as a point of destination that readers should desire. Likewise, disguise reinforced the view that the social shifts that these authors advocated would not entail the violence and deterritorialisation that critics such as Sacks and Sheehi have pointed out. Therefore, their works could depict the changes they called for as harmless, if not desirable.

Arabic works also use the imagery of disguise to refer to the literary shifts of their period. The article on Namık Kemal in *al-Hilāl*, which the previous chapter has discussed, claims that the Turkish language 'put on the clothes of a new age'.[77] As he believed that historical novels should educate the audience and improve society, Jurjī Zaydān hoped to write history in the form of a novel (*ṣūrat al-riwāya*) according to the introduction of his *al-Ḥajjāj bin Yūsuf* (1902). He argued that it would be more beneficial to publish history works in the form of a novel. Many European writers shared historical facts as their novels put on 'the garb of reality' (*thawb al-ḥaqīqa*).[78] One can find such descriptions of the novel even shortly after the demise of the Ottoman Empire when, for example, Khalīl Baydas (1874/75–1949) wrote in 1924: '[Novelists] disseminate their representations of emotions and truths among the people in the garb [*fī athwāb*] of diversion and entertainment'.[79]

If characters put on different clothes to disguise their identities in works such as *Hasan Mellah* and *What ᶜĪsā ibn Hishām Told Us*, then numerous late Ottoman authors such as Ahmet Midhat and Jurjī Zaydān suggested that their texts too 'wore' different literary forms such as novel or *maqāma*. In other words, texts, like people, can wander around in disguise and undertake '*tebdil/tabdīl*'. These authors described forms such as novels as clothes – or 'verbal vestures', as Stephen Dedalus has called them in James Joyce's (1882–1941) *A Portrait of the Artist as a Young Man* (1916)[80] – that can endow texts with the ability to circulate within a particular audience. For example, both Ahmet Midhat and Jurjī Zaydān emphasised the importance of 'dressing' their texts 'with the form or clothes of a novel' so that their audience could have a better understanding of their histories. Just as the clothes of a poor merchant helped Sultan Selim III move among Istanbul's bread-makers, the novel as a 'garment' helped works such as *Hasan Mellah* circulate among Ahmet Midhat's readers who, according to the author, sought civilisational progress. Furthermore, just like a tarboosh that gave people from different class, religious and cultural backgrounds a similar appearance, the novel as a 'garment' generated a sense of similarity among texts that were produced in different cultures and time periods.

Unlike late Ottoman writers, many critics today have agreed that it is hard or even impossible to designate a particular genre identity to *nahḍa* and *Tanzimat* texts such as *What ᶜĪsā ibn Hishām Told Us* or *Hasan Mellah.* While both works carry characteristics of traditional genres, the former *maqāma* and the latter *meddah* (oral story), they also share characteristics that critics have often associated with the modern novel, such as character development and a well-structured plot.[81] As Muhammad Siddiq has put it, 'Muḥammad al-Muwailiḥī's epochal work *Ḥadīth ᶜĪsā ibn Hishām* (The Discourse of ᶜĪsā ibn Hishām) is transitional in every respect. Written at the close of the nineteenth century and initially published serially in a newspaper before it appeared in book form in 1907, *Ḥadīth,* perhaps more than any other work of modern Arabic literature, owes much of its lasting appeal to its interstitial state'.[82]

Although more scholarly works today have emphasised that it is anachronistic to use the term 'novel' to designate texts such as *The Thousand and One Nights* or *What ᶜĪsā ibn Hishām Told Us*, this chapter reflects on why some late Ottoman authors designated such 'interstitial texts' as novels. I here build on Hans Robert Jauss, who has argued that 'literary genres cannot be deduced or defined, but only historically determined, delimited and described',[83] and Tzvetan Todorov, who has argued that genres are 'classes of texts that have been historically perceived as such'.[84] While I do not call for designating these works as novels, I propose that some late Ottoman writers tended to describe the novel as a means of disguise that any text can adopt. Thus, they reinforced the notion that the novel does not necessarily signify the displacement and deterritorialisation that global capitalism causes. Although texts such as *Hasan Mellah* may carry new characteristics, their authors implied that these works were not radically different from texts produced centuries ago – that is, old 'novels' such as *The Thousand and One Nights*.

Hasan Mellah also points to the numerous changes that industrialism and capitalism caused in Ottoman society. Ahmet Midhat lamented that people had given up old forms of entertainment (356) since newspapers, theatre plays (354) and printing presses had not existed back then (355). At the same time, Ahmet Midhat did not express uncritical nostalgia for old times. Instead, he emphasised that his community should always 'move forward'. He praised the publishing industry, which had achieved immense progress (2). Ahmet Midhat wrote about the positive aspects of modern reforms, including the abolition of the Janissaries (354–55). He considered himself as one of the few brave pioneers who dared to write prose works, however elementary, that would transform the empire into an advanced civilisation (2). Unlike Western writers who came from 'a civilisation that has been producing novels and philosophical treatises for the past 300 years' (2), he was from a 'community that started writing its first serious prose works only three years ago' (2–3). Ahmet Midhat thus thought that he needed to work hard so that readers would be informed about the empire's history and geography through his writings.

Ahmet Midhat emphasised that *Hasan Mellah* was not a figment of the imagination and then made the following statement: 'Some of the people I have mentioned in [*Hasan Mellah*] are so important that, if one were to write directly their adventures, it would mean to write a long novel' (4). He undermined the distinction between fiction and reality when he compared the world to a theatre play (459). In another article, 'Romancı ve Hayat' (The Novelist and Life), Ahmet Midhat noted that one could encounter anyone in the street who 'runs towards the novel'[85] and also stated: 'Everyone is more or less a character in a novel's plot'.[86] As he emphasised that life provided the actual material for a novel, Ahmet Midhat posited the novel as a universal and transhistorical form. Like *Hasan Mellah*, *What ʿĪsā ibn Hishām Told Us* undermined the distinction between fiction and reality, when an inspector noted that he had gathered the information he needed from the *Miṣbāḥ al-sharq* in which Muḥammad al-Muwayliḥī was publishing his work: 'I've already studied the angles of the case in *Miṣbāḥ al-sharq*' (1: 109).

Ahmet Midhat reminded his readers that *Hasan Mellah* was not similar to other texts. For example, he did not want to provide all the details about Alonso's feast; otherwise, *Hasan Mellah* would become the 'journal of a pantryman' (32). Ahmet Midhat emphasised that *Hasan Mellah* differed from earlier works because it did not have a 'a poetic style': 'If our work [*Hasan Mellah*] had the shortcomings of a poetic imagination, then we would have made Hasan faint whenever we make Cuzella see Hasan' (406–7). At the same time, Ahmet Midhat also suggested that *Hasan Mellah* was not radically new. He did not describe *Hasan Mellah* as an imitation or translation, but instead as a *nazire* of

Le Comte de Monte-Cristo (*The Count of Monte Cristo*; 1844–46) by Alexandre Dumas (1802–70) (2).[87]

A *nazire* poem adopts the rhyme, rhythm and often the vocabulary of the source poem. Walter G. Andrews has argued that, while translation (*terceme*) implies difference, *nazire* suggests similarity.[88] In other words, while translations often reinforce borders among cultures, *nazire* poems efface them, as poets write *nazire* poems of works that come from a culture similar to their own.[89] Andrews has also emphasised that, as classical Ottoman poets wrote *nazire* poems of Persian works, they considered Persian and Ottoman Turkish poems as part of the same literary 'episteme' or universe. Therefore, when Ahmet Midhat wrote that *Hasan Mellah* was not a translation (*terceme*) but instead a *nazire* of *The Count of Monte Cristo*, he implied that he and Alexander Dumas belonged to the same literary episteme, rather than to two distinct traditions of East and West. Furthermore, Ahmet Midhat suggested that *Hasan Mellah* did not signify a complete rupture with the past. Instead, like *What ᶜĪsā ibn Hishām Told Us*, which can 'appear' as a *maqāma*, *Hasan Mellah* can 'appear' as a form that Ottoman poets have used for centuries – that is, a *nazire*.

In a similar vein, like many late Ottoman authors, Monsieur Mitchell, a French character in *Hasan Mellah*, uses the term 'novel' (*roman*) to describe the translations of old Persian tales such as *Kerem and Aslı*:

> I have a friend who has stayed in Istanbul for a while. Even though he has been in Istanbul for decades, guess what he started to become interested in: he hired a teacher who specialised in Turkish translations of novels [*romanlar*] that were composed by classical Persian writers. He learned some Turkish. With his teacher's help, he translated a few of these novels into French. I came across one of these works. In it, there was a lover called Kerem. Because his father took his beloved, Aslı, away from him, Kerem started to look after her. (211)

Ahmet Midhat suggested that *Hasan Mellah* was unlike earlier 'novels' in specific ways, but it was not too different, since old works, like *Kerem and Aslı*, may also be 'novels' after all.

Ahmet Midhat's designation of *Hasan Mellah* as a *nazire* in the work's introduction and as a work that 'has the form of a novel' in *Süleyman Musli*'s introduction may look like a paradox. In the introduction to his short story 'Ölüm Allah'ın Emri' (Death is God's Commandment, 1873), Ahmet Midhat indicated that he was known as Istanbul's first novelist,[90] and he later wrote that he felt particularly proud of *Hasan Mellah*, since 'no other adventure novel has surpassed it'.[91] At the same time, Ahmet Midhat may have wanted to emphasise that his work could appear under different 'guises', as *Hasan Mellah* could circulate both as a novel and as a *nazire*. As his writings describe works such as *The Thousand and One Nights* and *Kerem and Aslı* as a novel, Ahmet Midhat reinforces the assumption that the novel is a transhistorical concept rather than an *effect* of various socio-economic changes. At the same time, the novel was not one of the 'clothes' that Ahmet Midhat freely chose and made his texts wear; he often had to write his novels in serialised form since this was an ideal medium to address the new reading publics that emerged with the dissolution of old gender, class and political hierarchies. The form of the novel helped him meet the exigencies of the market.

What ᶜĪsā ibn Hishām Told Us also captures the desire to depict modernity's shifts in 'recognisable guises'. Muḥammad al-Muwayliḥī serialised *What ᶜĪsā ibn Hishām Told Us* in the newspaper *Miṣbāḥ al-sharq* between 1898 and 1902. It was published as book in 1907 and then as textbook by Egypt's Ministry of Education in 1927.[92] Muḥammad al-Muwayliḥī's work carries many characteristics of the *maqāma* genre – that is, narratives of episodic adventures of a rogue trickster endowed with elaborate language. Muḥammad al-Muwayliḥī's work is a direct reference to Badīᶜ al-Zamān al-Hamadhānī's (959–1008) *Maqāmāt Badīᶜ al-Zamān al-Hamadhānī*, whose narrator is also called ᶜĪsā ibn Hishām and which is often studied as the first example of the *maqāma*.[93] Although Muḥammad al-Muwayliḥī's work, in many ways, is a product of the publishing industry and the world of global capitalism, it can also circulate among its readers under the 'guise' of a tenth-century *maqāma*.

As Wen-chin Ouyang has noted, the late nineteenth and early twentieth centuries witnessed a revival of the *maqāma* genre in Arabic letters. A key aspect of this genre is the freedom of mobility since both the narrator and the protagonist in the *maqāmāt* often travel freely between different places. Furthermore, '[m]obility in [*What ᶜĪsā ibn Hishām Told Us*], like the *Maqāmāt* of al-Hamadhānī and al-Ḥarīrī, is paradoxical; it is both powerlessness and power'.[94] For example, the Pasha remains marginalised due to the shifting socioeconomic and political transformations in the late Ottoman Empire, while people like ᶜUmdah attain powerful positions in this new social order. At the same time, the Pasha's mobility gives him the ability to enter diverse spaces and to expose the shortcomings of the institutions that cause his marginalisation. Furthermore, his mobility, much like the mobility of Hasan Mellah in Ahmet Midhat's work, gives a sense of control over the large territorial domains in which this mobility is rarely, if ever, interrupted. Therefore, the rise of the *maqāma* testifies to a tension that this chapter has laid out: as characters experience a sense of deterritorialisation due to the shifting conditions of the late Ottoman period, they also seek to maintain a sense of control over vast territories as they move across them, sometimes in disguise. Mobility and disguise can ease the identitarian anxieties that may characterise the late Ottoman Empire, since '[c]ontrol of space comes hand in hand with self-mastery, it seems; where one possessses no control over space, one loses the sense of self-mastery as well'.[95]

Although the characters in *What ᶜĪsā ibn Hishām Told Us* strive to control space and ultimately achieve a sense of self-mastery, newspapers also capture the extent to which society has undergone a deterritoralising modernisation and transformed to an irrevocable extent. During his observations on Cairo, ᶜĪsā ibn Hishām makes the following remark: 'Just then, we heard a newspaper vendor shouting in a voice so hideous that it was even worse than a donkey braying: "*Al-Muᵓayyad* and *Al-Muqaṭṭam*, *Al-Ahrām* and *Miṣr*, all four for a piastre"' (1: 99). The Pasha expresses his utter shock: 'What incredible things I keep hearing! Have mosques, mountains, monuments and countries become things one can purchase by auction in the market?' To this ᶜĪsā ibn Hishām responds: 'Those names aren't monuments or countries! They're used as titles for daily newspapers' (1: 99). The Pasha points out the strong link between the increasing popularity of newspapers and global capitalism. The works that 'disguise' themselves as 'mosques, mountains, monuments and countries' are mere commodities of the market.

As Kamran Rastegar has demonstrated, Middle Eastern Studies have associated the birth of modern national identities in the region with the birth of the modern novel in the nineteenth century. While critics may have classified texts such as *What ᶜĪsā ibn Hishām Told Us* as novels to substantiate nationalistic frameworks, some late Ottoman writers also upheld what Kamran Rastegar has called a 'novelistic framework', as they characterised many works such as *The Thousand and One Nights* as novels.[96] However, unlike most current critics, they did not necessarily make this categorisation to lay the basis of a nationalistic cultural vision. Nergis Ertürk's following statement, which uses the metaphor of disguise, from her analysis of Ahmet Midhat's works can provide an explanation for why late Ottoman authors used a novelistic framework:

> The structural condition of possibility of such domestication had certainly already been established by Midhat and other mid-nineteenth-century writers, who we could say habituated their readers to translative modernity by enabling them, so to speak, to 'wear' the foreign in the form of a 'moral' novel, the system of 'good' capitalism, or the mask of Islamicized Armenian Christian difference *while* guaranteeing identical self-sameness.[97]

As this chapter has shown, *Tanzimat* and *nahḍa* writers themselves used the imagery of clothing and disguise to describe the shifts of their period. The disguise imagery 'habituates' readers to view the changes of their time as mere shifts in appearance and not in 'essence'.

Late Ottoman authors could have reinforced the belief among their readers that markers of modernity, such as the tarboosh headgear and the novel genre, were mere 'clothes' that one could easily put on and then take off again, rather than the signifiers of displacement and deterritorialisation that new socioeconomic conditions generated. As characters and texts disguise themselves in late Ottoman works, these works can ultimately imply that one can have full control of modernity, which becomes a matter of changing 'clothes'. They also solidify the notion that one can reclaim a well-defined authentic self or classical tradition with ease: all one needs to do is to replace the tarboosh with the turban (*ᶜimāma*) and the novel with the *maqāma* or the *nazire*. Once these works shape our understanding of what the 'clothes' of tradition and modernity look like, they camouflage the irrevocable sense of alienation and deterritorialisation that spares neither those who claim to be on the side of modernity nor those who claim to be on the side of tradition.

According to Stephen Sheehi, the new social groups (such as the technocrats, intellectuals and merchants) of the late Ottoman period 'naturalized material and ideological conditions of nation-state and bourgeois selfhood'.[98] Both Muḥammad al-Muwayliḥī and Ahmet Midhat fit into this new community that Sheehi has analysed. Muḥammad al-Muwayliḥī came from a family of silk merchants and published the newspaper *Miṣbāḥ al-sharq*. In a similar vein, Ahmet Midhat, known as 'the writing machine', made a vast fortune through his writing and publishing business. He even wrote a book that praises the value of hard work, *Sevda-yı Say ü Amel* (Love of Effort and Work, 1879). Erol Köroğlu has noted that, unlike many late Ottoman thinkers such as Namık Kemal or Recaizade Mahmud Ekrem (1847–1914) who came from prominent families, Ahmet Midhat came from a much more modest socioeconomic background and ultimately made a significant fortune through his writing and publishing activities. Köroğlu has thus shown that other writers adopted a 'classicist and elitist' approach towards Ahmet Midhat, as they claimed that Ahmet Midhat did not produce 'serious literature', but only aimed to entertain the masses with his low-quality output.[99] For these authors, Ahmet Midhat could have embodied the displacements that the late Ottoman socioeconomic changes had caused.

Late Ottoman writers could also designate certain parts of the Ottoman literary reservoir, such as classical Persian tales, as 'novels'. For writers like Ahmet Midhat, the Ottoman reservoir turned into a source of guises (including the *nazire*) under which their texts could circulate. In a changing socioeconomic milieu, the Ottoman reservoir's power to cement a community of literati diminished. The repertoire of the Ottoman reservoir, which included forms such as the *maqāma* and the *nazire*, ultimately became a repertoire under which texts could disguise themselves – 'cover[ing] enlightened Western ideas with the Eastern garment', as Şemseddin Sami put it – so that Ottoman readers ultimately would consume the products of the publishing industry.

Much of the earlier scholarship in Arabic and Ottoman Studies has sought to pinpoint 'the first novel'. For example, it has been debated whether Muḥammad Ḥusayn Haykal's (1888–1956) *Zaynab* (1913/14), Aḥmad Fāris al-Shidyāq's (1805/6–87) *Al-Sāq ʿalā al-Sāq* (*Leg over Leg*, 1855), or Muḥammad al-Muwayliḥī's *Ḥadīth ʿĪsā ibn Hishām* should be counted as the first Arabic novel. Attempts to identify the first novel could have reinforced the assumption that a classical literature already existed before 'pioneers of literary modernity', such as Ahmet Midhat and Muḥammad al-Muwayliḥī, introduced a new genre to their respective national traditions. I argue that the attempts to identify the first Arabic novel or first Turkish novel have habituated critics to view Arabic and Turkish literatures as transhistorical categories. However, the 'rise of the novel' in the late Ottoman Arabic and Turkish contexts also tallies with the conceptualisation of Arabic literature and Turkish literature as national literatures. Attempts to identify 'the first novel' in the Arabic and Turkish traditions, in Sacks's words, 'domesticate[s] loss through a practice of historiographical reading'[100] – that is, the loss that the *Tanzimat*'s deterritorialising impact generated for both *nahḍa* and *Tanzimat* authors.

The imagery of disguise domesticates loss and habituates readers to view vast socioeconomic transformations as non-threatening and even pleasent. The argument that the novel form has always existed 'camouflages' modernity's deterritorialising forces that would ultimately help these authors envision themselves as members of an autonomous national subject that produces a national literature. Once both late Ottoman authors and today's critics pinpoint 'the first novel', they can claim to identify and speak about what exactly they left behind – 'tradition', 'old literature', 'classical genres', or 'classical literature' – rather than confront modernity's losses and deterritorialisations that one cannot represent through language.

The emergence of the novel form has been studied as one of the key markers of the transition from classical to modern literatures in both Ottoman and Arabic Studies. Critics do not have to take at face-value what late Ottoman writings propose, including their claim that the novel signifies a rupture between classical and modern literatures, but can instead focus on what they 'camouflage'. The prevalent notion that the emergence of the novel form marked the transition from classical to modern literature in the fields of both Arabic and Turkish literatures 'disguises' a key transformation: late Ottoman writings often habituated their readers to view 'Arabic literature' and 'Turkish literature' as transhistorical concepts rather than as constructions that took shape within the context of late Ottoman socioeconomic shifts.

Notes

1. Namık Kemal, *Külliyat-ı Kemal*, 113–14.
2. This Turkish translation would later be published again in Egypt in AH 1250 (1834/35) and then in Istanbul in AH 1268–72 (1851/52–55/56) and in AH 1304–5 (1886/87–87/88). Mütercim Asım Efendi also translated *Burhān-i qāṭi*ᶜ into Turkish, *Burhan-ı Katı Tercümesi*, which was first published in Istanbul in AH 1214 [1799/1800] and then in Bulaq, Cairo, in AH 1251 [1835/36] and AH 1268 [1851/52].
3. Namık Kemal, *Külliyat-ı Kemal*, 113.
4. Wilson Chacko Jacob, *Working Out Egypt: Effendi Masculinity and Subject Formation in Colonial Modernity, 1870–1940* (Durham, NC: Duke University Press, 2011), 331–32. Following much of the scholarship, I use the terms 'fez' and 'tarboosh' interchangeably in this chapter, although some sources point out that a tarboosh is slightly taller than a fez ('Fez or Tarbush', *Textile Research Centre Leiden*, https://trc-leiden.nl/trc-digital-exhibition/index.php/from-kaftan-to-kippa/item/54-fez-and-tarbush). At the same time, while the Ottoman administration wanted all officials to wear the same kind of fez, this fez ultimately started to exhibit variations among different communities and economic classes. For example, Donald Quataert notes that '[b]y wearing fezes wrapped in a wide variety of fabrics, workers aimed to differentiate themselves from the Ottoman official classes, international merchants and other laissez-faire advocates who had so quickly adopted the plain fez'. See his 'Clothing Laws, State and Society in the Ottoman Empire, 1720–1829', *International Journal of Middle East Studies* 29, no. 3 (1997): 417. Therefore, the variations one may observe in the fez/tarboosh cannot be attributed solely to ethnic and/or national differences. Rather, the Arabic word 'tarboosh' is a derivation of the Persian word that one also uses in Ottoman Turkish, *serpuş*, which literally means 'headcovering'. F. ᶜAbd al-Raḥīm, *Muᶜjam al-dakhīl fī al-lugha al-ᶜarabiyya al-ḥadītha wa lahjātuhā* (Damascus: Dār al-Qalam, 2011), 142.
5. Pamuk, *Uneven Centuries*, 16.

6. Ibid., 98.
7. Ibid., 104.
8. Stephen Sheehi, *The Arab Imago: A Social History of Portrait Photography, 1860–1910* (Princeton: Princeton University Press, 2016), 160.
9. Sheehi, *The Arab Imago*, 183.
10. Nergis Ertürk, 'An Uncanny Turkic: İsmail Gasprinskii's Language Lesson', *Middle Eastern Literatures* 19, no. 1 (2016): 43.
11. Ertürk, *Grammatology and Literary Modernity in Turkey*, 34.
12. Ibid., 44.
13. Ibid., 62.
14. Quataert, 'Clothing Laws', 410.
15. Fahrettin Tızlak, 'Hatt-ı Hümayunlar Işığında III. Selim Dönemi'nde İstanbul'da Fırınların ve Ekmeklerin Tebdil-i Kıyafetle Denetimi', *Cedrus* 3 (2015): 337–50.
16. Julia A. Clancy-Smith, *Mediterraneans: North Africa and Europe in an Age of Migration, c. 1800–1900* (Berkeley: University of California Press, 2011), 276.
17. Different characters, including Hasan Mellah himself, have the nickname 'Pavlos' because they work for Pavlos's company. The owner of this company, whose actual name is Pavlos, is an old man who supports Hasan Mellah. Dominico is the 'fifth Pavlos'. Ahmet Midhat, *Hasan Mellah yahud Sır içinde Esrar* (Istanbul: Şark Matbaası, AH 1291 [1874/75]), 93–94.
18. Nüket Esen has demonstrated that, while his novels often express a positive attitude toward non-Muslims, Ahmet Midhat made discriminatory statements against Greeks and Armenians in his letters. Nüket Esen, *Hikâye Anlatan Adam: Ahmet Mithat* (Istanbul: İletişim Yayınları, 2014), 88.
19. Pamuk, *Uneven Centuries*, 95.
20. Ibid., 167.
21. Jeffrey Sacks, *Iterations of Loss: Mutilation and Aesthetic Form, Al-Shidyaq to Darwish* (New York: Fordham University Press, 2015), 79.
22. Ahmet Midhat wrote another work, *Zeyl-i Hasan Mellah yahud Sır İçinde Esrar* (Addendum to Hasan Mellah, or, Secrets within Secrets, AH 1292 [1875/76]), which further narrates the adventures of Dominico Badia. The main arguments of this chapter also hold true for *Zeyl-i Hasan Mellah*, which features characters who wander in disguise in Tunisia, Algeria, Egypt, Morocco and Syria. Like numerous other critics such as Berna Moran, I focus on *Hasan Mellah* in this chapter, also because it has been sometimes studied as the first Turkish novel. For Moran's analysis of *Hasan Mellah*, see his *Türk Romanına Eleştirel Bir Bakış 1: Ahmet Mithat'tan Ahmet Hamdi Tanpınar'a* (Istanbul: İletişim Yayınları, 2004), 1: 25–46.
23. Neveser Köker, 'Inconvertible Romance: Piety, Community and the Politically Disruptive Force of Love in *Akabi Hikayesi*', in *Ottoman Culture and the Project of Modernity: Reform and Translation in the Tanzimat*

Novel, ed. Monica M. Ringer and Etienne E. Charrière (London: I. B. Tauris, 2020), 140.

24. Köker, 'Inconvertible Romance', 142.
25. al-Muwayliḥī, *What ^{c}Īsā ibn Hishām Told Us*, 1: 39. Allen's edition also includes the Arabic source text; thus, I also use Allen's work when referring to the Arabic source text. All original Arabic quotes appear one page before the English translations.
26. Ma^{c}rūf al-Ruṣāfī, 'Daf^{c} al-hujna fī irtiḍākh al-lukna', in *Āthāruhu fī al-naqd wa-l-adab*, ed. Dāwūd Sallūm, ^{c}Ādil Kuttāb Naṣīf al-^{c}Azzāwī and ^{c}Abd al-Ḥamīd al-Rashūdī (Beirut: Manshūrāt al-Jamal, 2014), 2: 151.
27. al-Ruṣāfī, 'Daf^{c} al-hujna fī irtiḍākh al-lukna', 2: 168.
28. Adam Mestyan, *Arab Patriotism: The Ideology and Culture of Power in Late Ottoman Egypt* (Princeton: Princeton University Press, 2017), 36. While this chapter focuses on the use of the tarboosh/fez in the nineteenth century, Youssef Ben Ismail has demonstrated that the tarboosh had a wide appeal in many urban centres of the empire in the seventeenth and eighteenth centuries. It was only in the nineteenth century that 'fez-wearing [. . .] had acquired a new connotation: it came to symbolize support for the new socio-political order instituted by the sultan'. Youssef Ben Ismail, 'A History of the Ottoman Fez Before Mahmud II (ca. 1600–1800)' *Muqarnas* 38, no. 1 (2021): 176.
29. Patricia L. Baker, 'The Fez in Turkey: A Symbol of Modernization?', *Costume* 20, no. 1 (1986): 75.
30. Baker, 'The Fez in Turkey', 76.
31. Quataert, 'Clothing Laws', 411.
32. Ibid., 412.
33. Ibid., 413, emphases Quataert's.
34. Ibid., 414.
35. Ibid.
36. Bülent Somay, *The Psychopolitics of the Oriental Father: Between Omnipotence and Emasculation* (New York: Palgrave Macmillan, 2014), 117.
37. Quataert, 'Clothing Laws', 420.
38. Ibid., 420. For another comprehensive study of the fez, see also Namık Sinan Turan, '16. Yüzyıldan 19. Yüzyıl Sonuna Dek Osmanlı Devletine Gayri Müslimlerin Kılık Kıyafetlerine Dair Düzenlemeler', *Ankara Üniversitesi SBF Dergisi* 60, no. 4 (2005): 239–67. Turan has argued that, since all Ottoman men of office were required to wear a fez in the nineteenth century, the fez became a symbol of Ottomanism.
39. For example, Zabel Yessayan wrote: 'The day that Yıldız fell, even the long-awaited Day of the 101 Cannons, proved to be our unhappiest day. Yet our weeping eyes learned to smile again; and, when the whole Ottoman world was filled with the greatest happiness, our hearts beat harder than all the rest'. Zabel Yessayan, *In the Ruins: The 1909 Massacres of Armenians in Adana, Turkey*, trans. G. M. Goshgarian (Boston: AIWA Press, 2016), 3.

40. At the same time, some Egyptian intellectuals viewed the tarboosh as a symbol of Ottoman tyranny (Jacob, *Working Out Egypt*, 218).
41. Jacob, *Working Out Egpyt*, 191.
42. Later in the text, the Merchant tells the Playboy and the ᶜUmdah: 'As the saying goes, eat whatever you like, but wear clothes that please other people!' (al-Muwayliḥī, *What ᶜĪsā ibn Hishām Told Us*, 2: 41). Here, the Merchant suggests that people disguise themselves for acquiescing to social expectations.
43. al-Muwayliḥī, *What ᶜĪsā ibn Hishām Told Us*, 1: 39.
44. Mattar, *Specters of World Literature*.
45. For more examples of Turkish words in *What ᶜĪsā ibn Hishām Told Us*, see ᶜAbd Allāh ᶜAbd al-Muṭṭalib Aḥmad, *al-Muwayliḥī al-Ṣaghīr: ḥayātuh wa adabuh* ([Cairo]: al-Hayᵓa al-Miṣriyya al-ᶜĀmma li-l-Kitāb, 1985), 323.
46. The Egyptian political journalist and writer Ibrāhīm al-Muwayliḥī (1844–1906) was born into a wealthy Egyptian family of silk merchants that traced its ancestry back to the town of Muwayliḥī on the coast of the Red Sea. He criticised the Ottoman government in the newspaper *al-Ittiḥād* (Union); the commentaries against the empire irritated Sultan Abdülhamid (r. 1876–1909). While in France, Ibrāhīm al-Muwayliḥī continued to publish in the same newspaper articles that criticised the government, and so the sultan asked the French authorities to eventually exile him and his son to London. Afterwards, Ibrāhīm al-Muwayliḥī started to write articles that supported the Ottoman regime, and the sultan invited Ibrāhīm to Istanbul. Ibrāhīm al-Muwayliḥī first sent his son, Muḥammad al-Muwayliḥī, to make sure that it would be safe for him to travel to Istanbul, and he eventually joined his son in the Ottoman capital.
47. Ibrāhīm al-Muwayliḥī, *Spies, Scandals and Sultans: Istanbul in the Twilight of the Ottoman Empire*, trans. Roger Allen (Lanham: Rowman & Littlefield Publishers, 2008), 155; Ibrāhīm al-Muwayliḥī, *Mā hunālika* (Cairo: Maṭbaᶜat al-Muqaṭṭam, 1896), 222.
48. al-Muwayliḥī, *Spies, Scandals and Sultans*, 151; al-Muwayliḥī, *Mā hunālika*, 219. Sultan Abdülhamid could not speak Arabic and understood only a few expressions in the Hijazi dialect, which he had picked up from the Sudanese eunuchs (al-Muwayliḥī, *Spies, Scandals and Sultans*, 165; al-Muwayliḥī, *Mā hunālika*, 240).
49. al-Muwayliḥī, *Spies, Scandals and Sultans*, 93; al-Muwayliḥī, *Mā hunālika*, 115.
50. al-Muwayliḥī, *Spies, Scandals and Sultans*, 30; al-Muwayliḥī, *Mā hunālika*, 25.
51. al-Muwayliḥī, *Spies, Scandals and Sultans*, 40; al-Muwayliḥī, *Mā hunālika*, 40.
52. al-Muwayliḥī, *Spies, Scandals and Sultans*, 106; al-Muwayliḥī, *Mā hunālika*, 133.
53. al-Muwayliḥī, *Spies, Scandals and Sultans*, 25–26; al-Muwayliḥī, *Mā hunālika*, 19–20.

54. Holt, *Fictitious Capital*.
55. Elizabeth M. Holt, 'From Gardens of Knowledge to Ezbekiyya after Midnight: The Novel and the Arabic Press from Beirut to Cairo, 1870–1892', *Middle Eastern Literatures* 16, no. 3 (2013): 234–37.
56. Holt, 'From Gardens of Knowledge', 242.
57. Ahmed Vefik Paşa, 'Lehce-i Osmanî Mukaddimesi', in *Yeni Türk Edebiyatı Antolojisi III*, ed. Mehmet Kaplan, İnci Enginün, Birol Emil and Zeynep Kerman (Istanbul: Marmara Üniversitesi Yayınevi, 1994), 3: 3.
58. Namık Kemal, *Mukaddime-i Celal* (Istanbul: Matbaa-i Ebüzziya, AH 1309 [1891/92]), 13–14.
59. Şemseddin Sami, 'Şiir ve Edebiyattaki Teceddüd-i Ahîrimiz', in *Yeni Türk Edebiyatı Antolojisi III*, ed. Mehmet Kaplan, İnci Enginün, Birol Emil and Zeynep Kerman (Istanbul: Marmara Üniversitesi Yayınevi, 1994), 3: 322.
60. Mizancı Murat, *Turfanda mı yoksa Turfa mı* (Istanbul: Mahmud Bey Matbaası, AH 1308 [1890/91]), 2.
61. Mizancı Murat, *Turfanda mı yoksa Turfa mı*, 2.
62. Ahmet Midhat, *Ahbar-ı Asara Tamim-i Enzar* (Istanbul: AH 1307 [1889/1900]), 25–26. The increasing circulation of old tales such as *The Thousand and One Nights* contributed to the novel genre's popularisation. As Reuven Snir puts it, '[w]hat is clear is that the new genres developed quickly thanks to the popularity of non-canonical narrative literature, with *Alf Layla wa-Layla, Siyar al-Anbiyāʾ* and the various epics of ʿAntara, Baybars and Banū Hilāl all paving the way for modern narrative prose'. Reuven Snir, *Modern Arabic Literature: A Theoretical Framework* (Edinburgh: Edinburgh University Press, 2017), 207.
63. Ahmet Midhat, *Ahbar-ı Asara*, 114.
64. Ibid., 116.
65. Ahmet Midhat, *Çengi, Kafkas, Süleyman Muslî* (Ankara: Türk Dil Kurumu, 2000), 396.
66. Ahmet Midhat, 'Hikâye Tasvir ve Tahriri', in *Yeni Türk Edebiyatı Antolojisi III*, ed. Mehmet Kaplan, İnci Enginün, Birol Emil and Zeynep Kerman (Istanbul: Marmara Üniversitesi Yayınevi, 1994), 3: 57.
67. Ahmet Midhat, 'Romancı ve Hayat', in *Yeni Türk Edebiyatı Antolojisi III*, ed. Mehmet Kaplan, İnci Enginün, Birol Emil and Zeynep Kerman (Istanbul: Marmara Üniversitesi Yayınevi, 1994), 3: 66.
68. Ahmet Midhat, *Ahbar-ı Asara*, 135.
69. Stephan Guth, 'From Water-Carrying Camels to Modern Story-Tellers, or How "*riwāya*" Came to Mean [Novel]: A History of an Encounter of Concepts', in *Borders and Beyond: Crossings and Transitions in Modern Arabic Literature*, ed. Kerstin Eksell and Stephan Guth (Wiesbaden: Harrassowitz Verlag, 2011), 153–55.
70. Guth, 'From Water-Carrying Camels to Modern Story-Tellers', 159. In this chapter, I translate the term '*roman*' in late Ottoman Turkish writings as 'novel', although late Ottoman Turkish novels do not always have all the

characteristics that many critics would associate with the modern novel. Likewise, I choose to translate the term '*riwāya*' in late Ottoman Arabic writings as 'novel', although the term '*riwāya*' was used to categorise a wide range of texts. I make this choice partly due to the strong overlap that Guth has also observed between *rūmāniyyāt* and *riwāyāt*. Furthermore, while authors of late Ottoman Arabic works used a term from pre-modern times, '*riwāya*', to define their texts, they also often emphasised that these texts featured modern characteristics that pre-modern texts did not.

71. Ibid., 159. Guth has shown that the consolidation of the term '*riwāya*'s' meaning as novel in the modern sense occurred due to the growing secular elite's impact on their society and an increasing globalisation that led modern writers to engage with the global literary field (172).
72. Ibid., 157.
73. Ibid., 166. Guth has also used the term 'engineers' to refer to the *afandiyya* 'because of their pragmatic approach to life and their view of society as a mechanical entity' (152).
74. Samah Selim, 'Translation, Popular Fiction and the Nahdah in Egypt', in *Other Renaissances: A New Approach to World Literature*, ed. Brenda Deen Schildgen, Gang Zhou and Sander L. Gilman (New York: Palgrave Macmillan: 2006), 45.
75. Selim, 'Translation, Popular Fiction and the Nahdah in Egypt', 38.
76. Samah Selim, 'The Narrative Craft: Realism and Fiction in the Arabic Canon', *Edebiyat: Journal of Middle Eastern Literatures* 14, no. 1–2 (2003): 113.
77. 'Muḥammad Nāmiq Kamāl Bek', 165.
78. Jurjī Zaydān, *al-Ḥajjāj bin Yūsuf* (Cairo: Maṭbaᶜat al-Hilāl, 1902), [i]. Wen-chin Ouyang has pointed out a similar dynamic: '[Matti] Moosa, by calling his book *The Origins of Modern Arabic Fiction*, is able to imply that the Arabic novel, despite its "Western" garb, in fact represents the continuity of an indigenous tradition of fiction that has existed since before the advent of the Western influence'. *Poetics of Love in the Arabic Novel: Nation-State, Modernity and Tradition* (Edinburgh: Edinburgh University Press, 2012), 7. As this chapter will also later discuss, Ouyang has noted that the search for the origin of the modern Arabic novel cannot be thought apart from the search for an authentic self in Arabic critical writings: 'This kind of *taᶜṣīl* process [the proces of authentication] can give new literary genres, such as the Arabic novel, authenticity in the form of a history derived primarily from the "self", and authority to shape contemporary Arab culture. The legitimacy of this authorial voice is in turn avowed on the basis of how authentic this voice is, in other words, of how central literature is to the formulation of cultural modernity' (Ouyang, *Poetics of Love in the Modern Arabic Novel*, 14).
79. Khalil Baydas, 'Stages for the Mind', intro. and trans. Spencer Scoville, in *The Arab Renaissance: A Bilingual Anthology of the* Nahda, ed. Tarek El-Ariss (New York: The Modern Language Association, 2018), 208. For the Arabic original of the quote, see 214.

80. James Joyce, *A Portrait of the Artist as a Young Man* (New York: Oxford University Press, 2008), 180.
81. Roger Allen, for instance, has noted that *What ᶜĪsā ibn Hishām Told Us* is the quintessential work marking the transition from classical to modern in Arabic literature. See his '*Hadith ᶜIsa ibn Hisham* by Muhammad al-Muwailihī: A Reconsideration', *Journal of Arabic Literature* 1, no. 1 (1970): 103–5.
82. Muhammad Siddiq, *Arab Culture and the Novel: Genre, Identity and Agency in Egyptian Fiction* (New York: Routledge, 2007), 38.
83. Hans Robert Jauss, 'Theory of Genres and Medieval Literature', in *Modern Genre Theory*, ed. David Duff (New York: Routledge, 2000), 131.
84. Tzvetan Todorov, 'The Origin of Genres', in *Modern Genre Theory*, ed. David Duff (New York: Routledge, 2000), 198.
85. Ahmet Midhat, 'Romancı ve Hayat', 3: 66.
86. Ibid., 3: 67.
87. For a comprehensive comparison between *Hasan Mellah* and *Le Comte de Monte-Cristo*, see Ali Yağlı, 'Une étude comparative entre *Le Comte de Monte-Cristo* d'Alexandre Dumas Père et *Denizci Hasan* (Hasan le Marin) d'Ahmet Mithat Efendi', *RumeliDE Dil ve Edebiyat Araştırmaları Dergisi* 18 (2020): 457–69.
88. Walter G. Andrews, 'Starting Over Again: Some Suggestions for Rethinking Ottoman Divan Poetry in the Context of Translation/ Transmission', in *Translations: (Re)shaping of Literature and Culture*, ed. Saliha Paker (Istanbul: Boğaziçi University Press, 2002), 33.
89. Andrews, 'Starting Over Again', 33.
90. Ahmet Midhat, 'Ölüm Allah'ın Emri', in *Letaif-i Rivayat* (Istanbul: Kırk Anbar Matbaası, AH 1290 [1873/74]), 8: 4.
91. Quoted in Esen, *Hikâye Anlatan Adam*, 121.
92. The textbook version omits many parts of the serialised version, such as the harsh criticisms against Egypt's rulers and the prominent centre of Islamic learning, al-Azhar University.
93. Jaakko Hämeen-Anttila, *Maqama: A History of a Genre* (Wiesbaden: Harrassowitz Verlag, 2002), 53–54.
94. Ouyang, *Poetics of Love in the Arabic Novel*, 96.
95. Ibid., 105.
96. Rastegar, *Literary Modernity between the Middle East and Europe*.
97. Ertürk, *Grammatology and Literary Modernity in Turkey*, 76, emphases Ertürk's.
98. Sheehi, 'Towards a Critical Theory of *al-Nahḍah*', 272.
99. Erol Köroğlu, 'Tanpınar'a Göre Ahmet Midhat: Esere Hayattan Girmek yahut Eseri Hayatla Yargılamak', in *Merhaba Ey Muharrir!: Ahmet Mithat Üzerine Eleştirel Yazılar*, ed. Nüket Esen and Erol Köroğlu (Istanbul: Boğaziçi Üniversitesi Yayınevi, 2006), 332.
100. Sacks, *Iterations of Loss*, 172.

4

Ka^c^b ibn Zuhayr Weeps for Sultan Murad IV: Baghdad, Translation and the Turkish Language in Ma^c^rūf al-Ruṣāfī's Works

Amīn al-Rayḥānī (1876–1940) wrote that the Iraqi poet Ma^c^rūf al-Ruṣāfī (1875–1945) experienced significant transformations during his stay in Istanbul. According to al-Rayḥānī, al-Ruṣāfī took 'a leap from the mosque to the tavern' (*min al-masjid ilā al-ḥāna*) there.[1] In Istanbul, al-Ruṣāfī also eventually discarded his turban (*'imāma*) and replaced it with the tarboosh.[2] As this chapter will show, he became acquainted with many prominent Ottoman intellectuals during his stay there. At first, these details may suggest that al-Ruṣāfī, coming from the empire's 'periphery', acquiesced to the cultural and political superiority of the imperial 'centre'. However, this chapter will reveal that, as al-Ruṣāfī translated and engaged with Turkish works, he also challenged some of their perspectives on culture and language. It will analyse al-Ruṣāfī's, Namık Kemal's (1840–88) and Süleyman Nazif's (1869–1927) works in order to further nuance the typical understanding of cultural power dynamics within the empire. I will demonstrate that, while the Istanbul administration may have infringed on the Iraqi provinces more than ever during the empire's final years, al-Ruṣāfī transmitted the ideas he deemed useful in Turkish writings to his Arabic readers, as he also maintained a boundary between the Arabic and Turkish languages. Furthermore, al-Ruṣāfī did not advocate a vision of the Ottoman literary reservoir in which poets such as Ka^c^b ibn Zuhayr (d. c. 646/47) and al-Mutanabbī (d. 965) played a key role.

The beginning of this chapter will provide the contextual background for al-Ruṣāfī's life and for the Iraqi provinces. It will also demonstrate that political power dynamics do not neatly map onto cultural power dynamics within the empire. As a case-study, I will examine al-Ruṣāfī's intertextual engagements with Turkish works and the Turkish language. First, I will perform a close reading of his *Daf^c^ al-hujna fī irtiḍākh al-lukna* (Overcoming the Flaws of Speech Defects, AH 1331 [1912/13]), which provides a list of Arabic words borrowed from Turkish. Al-Ruṣāfī claimed that these words had become more popular among Arabic speakers because 'unskilled translators' had popularised them through their translations from Turkish to Arabic.

The chapter will then examine *al-Ruʾyā fī baḥth al-ḥurriya* (A Dream on the Search for Freedom, 1909), which is al-Ruṣāfī's Arabic translation of *Rüya* (Dream, published posthumously in 1908) by Namık Kemal (1840–88). In particular, I compare the source text *Rüya* with its Arabic translation *al-Ruʾyā* to understand the choices that al-Ruṣāfī made as a translator. While al-Ruṣāfī's translation remains 'faithful' to the source text in terms of content, it replaces the expressions that he would later list in *Dafᶜ al-hujna* as corrupt borrowings from Turkish with what al-Ruṣāfī considered their 'true' Arabic equivalents. Through translation, al-Ruṣāfī transmitted Namık Kemal's vision of modernity, but he also generated strict boundaries between the Arabic and Turkish languages. Finally, I will examine Süleyman Nazif's work on the Ottoman defeat in Iraq, *Firak-ı Irak* (The Separation from Iraq, 1918) and al-Ruṣāfī's poem 'Nuwāḥ Dijla' (The Lamentation of the Tigris). Both authors provided similar interpretations of the same historical event, as they expressed deep sorrow over the Ottoman defeat in Iraq. At the same time, Süleyman Nazif suggested that Kaᶜb ibn Zuhayr, Ḥassān ibn Thābit (d. 674) and Fuzuli (d. 1556) had become orphans after this defeat, implying that this political event was also a cultural watershed moment. However, al-Ruṣāfī lamented the Ottoman Empire's political and military losses while not describing Baghdad as a place whose loss various poets of the Ottoman reservoir lamented. In other words, while al-Ruṣāfī showed support for the Ottoman Empire, he did not necessarily advocate the cultural vision of the Ottoman literary reservoir that depicted Kaᶜb ibn Zuhayr and al-Mutanabbī as 'Ottoman poets' who showed great concern for the cultural and political developments in the empire and lived in the same world as the famous poet Nefi (d. 1635). The chapter will conclude that al-Ruṣāfī's engagement with Turkish works contributed to the emergence of a shared repertoire of images, ideas and themes in both Arabic and Turkish writings. However, this engagement also set up boundaries between the Arabic and Turkish languages, as well as between Süleyman Nazif's vision of the Ottoman canon and al-Ruṣāfī's vision of Arabic heritage. After all, in *Firak-ı Irak*, Kaᶜb ibn Zuhayr speaks Turkish.

Iraq and the Arabic Literary Modernity

The Istanbul administration had a growing presence in the Iraqi provinces during the late Ottoman period.[3] These provinces differed from much of the empire in terms of their demographical composition, which included many Kurds and Shiites. Al-Ruṣāfī's father, ᶜAbd al-Ghanī Maḥmūd, was affiliated with the Kurdish tribe of Jabbāra.[4] Some Ottoman Turkish writings depict Iraq as 'backward' when compared to the rest of the 'civilised' Ottoman world. In his travelogue *Afak-ı Irak* (The Horizons of Iraq, 1914–16), Cenab Şahabeddin (1870–1934) wrote that Iraq had been deprived of its Abbasid glory for the past eight centuries.[5] Selim Deringil has also examined in Ottoman works the attitude of a 'civilising mission' towards Iraq.[6] Gökhan Çetinsaya has argued that the comprehensive reforms concerning the Iraqi provinces were not significantly different from France's 'civilising mission' towards its colonies, such as Algeria and Tunisia. Tahsin Pasha (1845–1918) described the relationship between the Ottoman 'centre' and its Iraqi 'periphery' in his memoir with the following words:

> Sultan Hamid employed a special policy towards distant regions like Iraq and Yemen, which might be called a colonial policy. Sultan Hamid, having appreciated that the people of these regions could not be administered like those settled in other parts of the country or with a uniform law and methods, accepted a system of administration in accordance with the capacities of the population of these regions.[7]

Iraq thus underwent the socioeconomic transformations and 'deterritorialisations' that the previous chapter has discussed in greater depth. Midhat Pasha (1822–83), who previously had served as governor of the Danube (Tuna) district, became the governor of Baghdad between 1869 and 1872. He undertook extensive reforms, as he played a crucial role in establishing the region's first tramway, public park, modern hospital, technical school and government newspaper.[8] Ottoman officials such as Süleyman Hüsnü also suggested that the government needed to construct schools in Baghdad so that its residents who belonged to, in the pasha's view, 'unorthodox' Muslim sects would accept the Sunni Islam to which the members of the Ottoman ruling class belonged.[9]

The major shifts in the cultural and political frontiers also led the Istanbul administration to invest more in the Iraqi provinces since, as Emine Ö. Evered has put it, Ottoman statespeople 'saw Iraq and Syria as potential areas to be developed to make up for the empire's economic losses from lost territories in the Balkans. Later reforms thus were aimed at developing the Iraqi provinces in ways that would increase productivity'.[10] The centralisation policies deprived various communities of their primary source of income, the waqf (endowment) revenues, which had also sustained madrasas and the ulama. As the

Ottoman Empire became integrated more into the capitalist networks of a global market economy through railroads and telegraphs, the merchant class became more influential.[11] One of the consequences of this socio-economic shift was the rise of a 'middle-class' intelligentsia of writers, lawyers, engineers and doctors to which Marᶜūf al-Ruṣāfī belonged.[12] As Annie Greene, Orit Bashkin, Lital Levy, Reuven Snir and Avi-ram Tzoreff have shown in their analysis of Jewish-Iraqi cultural production, many Iraqi intellectuals of different ethnic, religious and linguistic affiliations engaged with the cultural and political developments within the empire.[13]

With the Ottoman administration's growing presence in the Iraqi provinces, al-Ruṣāfī was able to attend imperial schools, learn Turkish and rise trough the empire's administrative ranks. Al-Ruṣāfī did not read European languages and never travelled to Europe. He instead had access to European works through their Arabic or Turkish translations.[14] At the same time, like other intellectuals such as Rifāᶜa Rāfiᶜ al-Ṭahṭāwī (1801–73) and Namık Kemal who read Western languages, al-Ruṣāfī also espoused values associated with modernity, such as freedom and women's rights. Marᶜūf al-Ruṣāfī was among the most influential poets in Iraq during the late nineteenth and early twentieth centuries. He attended the Rüşdiye School that the Ottoman administration had established and experienced a difficult time there, because he had to adjust to the strict military discipline and did not have a high Turkish proficiency. He indicated that even his Arabic language classes were conducted in Turkish.[15] He then took lessons from Maḥmūd Shukrī al-Ālūsī (1857–1924), a famous Iraqi theologian and writer, who offered comprehensive training in Arabic language and literature.[16] After completing his education, al-Ruṣāfī worked as a primary school teacher and later as a teacher of Arabic language and literature in a civilian senior high school in Baghdad.[17]

Ahmet Cevdet (1862–1935), the editor of the journal *İkdam* (Working with Zeal), invited Marᶜūf al-Ruṣāfī to Istanbul in 1909 so that al-Ruṣāfī could publish an Arabic edition of that paper.[18] Al-Ruṣāfī accepted this invitation. During his first brief stay in Istanbul, al-Ruṣāfī shared a home with al-Zahāwī (1863–1936).[19] When he later returned to Istanbul, al-Ruṣāfī worked for another daily, *Sabīl al-rashād* (The Path of Integrity).[20] During his stay in Istanbul, he also became acquainted with Zeki Megamiz (1871–1932), who translated some of Jurjī Zaydān's works into Turkish.[21] Al-Ruṣāfī became a member of Ottoman parliament, the *Meclis-i Mebusan*, in 1912.[22] He would become familiar with one of the most important members of the Committee of the Union and Progress, Talat Pasha (1874–1921), who asked al-Ruṣāfī to teach him Arabic.[23]

He was also married to Belkıs, a Turkish woman, whom he described as 'his gazelle' in one of his poems, although he could never see his wife after the empire's demise.[24] In Istanbul, he held two teaching positions as instructor of Arabic, one in the imperial civil service school and another in the preachers' school.[25] During one of his last visits to Istanbul, he met Süleyman Nazif, who had been a governor in Baghdad. Al-Ruṣāfī sought Süleyman Nazif's help to acquire Turkish citizenship in 1922, although he failed in this endeavour.[26]

Like Jurjī Zaydān, al-Ruṣāfī did not call for political secession from the Ottoman Empire and was deeply engaged with the Turkish cultural milieu. At the same time, al-Ruṣāfī also wanted to protect the Arabic language from 'foreign' influences, including Turkish. He was well-versed in Arabic belles-lettres. He wrote numerous works on the history of Arabic literature[27] and on poets such as al-Mutanabbī[28] and al-Maᶜarrī (973–1057).[29] Al-Ruṣāfī believed that literature could transform the world, as he wrote in one of his poems that he lived in an age in which 'the sword submits to the pen'.[30] Al-Ruṣāfī, like many other intellectuals of his time, thought that the empire was experiencing political and cultural decline and that language reform could halt this decline. Al-Ruṣāfī compared himself to a medical doctor, noting that, while the doctor examined the human body, the litterateur, *adīb*, examined the universe through his writing.[31]

After the Ottoman Empire's demise, al-Ruṣāfī became a member of the National Assembly of Iraq in 1930. Although he served as deputy in the Iraqi parliament for five sessions,[32] he complained about his salary[33] and believed that 'he had not been offered the position and prestige which he had enjoyed during the Ottoman era'.[34] He disapproved of the British mandate and did not have amicable relations with King Faisal I (r. 1921–33). Al-Ruṣāfī spent most of his final years in isolation, and Nuᶜmān Māhir al-Kanᶜānī (1919–2010) noted that there was a sense of emptiness, coldness and silence around his deathbed when al-Ruṣāfī passed away in 1945.[35]

Translation, Social Reform and Anxieties about a New Language

Yasir Suleiman has argued that the Arabic language transformed 'from a decentred medium of communication to a centred view of it as an object of modernisation' for authors in the late Ottoman period, such as Ibrāhīm al-Yāzijī (1847–1906).[36] For these authors, Arabic was a subject of scientific inquiry and analysis. The Arabic language was also an object of modernisation in al-Ruṣāfī's works since he emphasised in many of his writings that one needed to reform language in order to reform society. While al-Ruṣāfī displayed both deep familiarity and engagement with Turkish culture, he stressed the need to maintain a firm boundary between Arabic and Turkish in works such as *Daf^c^ al-hujna*.

Al-Ruṣāfī wrote at the beginning of *Daf^c^ al-hujna* that *laḥn*, the Arabic word for solecism or deviations from the norms of a language, lately had become widespread among Arabic speakers. *Laḥn* has various connotations, such as idiom, speech style and tone. It also designates the peculiar manner of speaking of a particular individual or ethnic community. As Amidu Sanni has shown, it has further meanings, such as 'perceptiveness', 'veiled or obscure allusion', 'solecism, [which] also entails barbarism and malapropism' and 'musical melody, song, or tune'.[37] Al-Ruṣāfī built on this multivalence of the term '*laḥn*' for his project of modernising the language.

For much of Islamic history, solecism had served to set up communal boundaries. As Islam spread into new territories, more people started to use incorrect idioms in everyday speech and made frequent mistakes in their recitation of the Qur'an, giving rise to a *laḥn al-^c^āmma* (literally 'solecisms of common people') literature. Later, '[t]he Umayyad period (661–775) brought about a change in the attitude towards solecism. Whereas the association between language and religion was paramount in the early Islamic period, greater weight started to be given to the association of language and people in the Umayyad period'.[38] While solecism had hitherto been considered a linguistic mistake that everyone could make when reciting the Qur'an, it eventually became a marker of non-Arab identity.

Al-Ruṣāfī drew on this understanding of solecism that eventually became a signifier of cultural and ethnic identity. He also wrote on the history of the Arabic language and solecisms. Al-Ruṣāfī argued that solecisms became widespread with the rise in foreigners 'who adopted Arab customs' (*al-musta^c^ribūn*).[39] After the Abbasid Empire had lost its strength, non-Arab empires took control of the region, leading to a decline in the Arabic language that continued to that day. Al-Ruṣāfī claimed that the art of oration had become inert (*bārid*) and imitative, while poetry had become more barren.[40] He wrote that only those who specialised in Arabic in Western universities such as Oxford and the Sorbonne had a solid knowledge of the Arabic language.[41]

For al-Ruṣāfī, this deterioration of the Arabic language signified the decline of Arab civilisation. While al-Ruṣāfī, like his predecessors, viewed language as a marker of identity differentiation, he, unlike many of his predecessors, believed that literature captured a community's sentiment (*ᶜāṭifa*) and intellect (*ᶜaql*).[42] When he was asked whether Egypt was the cultural leader in the Arab world, he lamented that Egypt, like the rest of the 'Eastern Arab nations', only imitated the sciences and literatures of the West.[43]

In discussing the Arabic language, al-Ruṣāfī also wrote about the Ottoman language. In his introduction to *Dafᶜ al-hujna*, al-Ruṣāfī indicated that one should not conflate the Ottoman language with the Turkish language. He defined the Ottoman language as a mixture of four languages (Turkish, Arabic, French and Persian) and considered this heterogeneity an obstacle to civilisational advancement. He compared the Ottoman language with a mixture of wine and water, hence suggesting that it could never attain a perfect sense of organic unity.[44] In this sense, al-Ruṣāfī's vision of Ottoman culture differs from *Harabat*'s 'Ottoman ocean', since Ziya Pasha, as Chapter 1 has shown, wrote that the Arabic, Persian and Turkish streams perfectly mixed in the Ottoman reservoir. Al-Ruṣāfī also criticised what he called expressions that were 'Arabic in terms of structure and Turkish in terms of meaning', which started to proliferate in Arabic (2: 151). While many Arabic expressions can have a Turkish meaning and an Arabic meaning, al-Ruṣāfī wanted each Arabic term to express the Arabic meaning only and considered it a mistake to use an Arabic expression with a Turkish meaning.

To prevent such incorrect usage, *Dafᶜ al-hujna* lists Arabic terms in the Ottoman language that the Ottomans themselves coined based on Arabic grammar rules (2: 151–59), those that changed only in meaning (*maᶜnā*) (2: 159–89), those that changed only in form (*lafẓ*) (2: 189–96) and those that changed in both form and meaning (2: 197–98). Sometimes, al-Ruṣāfī dismissed a misused expression when he wrote 'this is not correct' (2: 169), or 'its [the word's] meaning is not like that in Arabic language' (*laysa maᶜnāhu kadhālika fī al-ᶜarabiyya*) (2: 164). In other instances, he suggested that certain words have not transformed in meaning but in their letter composition – that is, their form (*hiya muḥarrafa lafẓan*) (2: 189).

Dafᶜ al-hujna addresses 'the Arab people' (*abnāᵓ al-ᶜArab*) (2: 147). The phrase, which one can literally translate as 'the sons of Arabs', already suggests that Arabic speakers, unlike 'people of the Ottoman language' (*ahl al-lisān al-ᶜuthmānī*) (2: 147), have a familial and even affective bond with each other. While many Arabs criticised Ottoman intellectuals who wanted to purge Arabic expressions from Ottoman Turkish, al-Ruṣāfī was convinced that the Arabs would benefit from this simplification of the Ottoman language (2: 150). He observed that many Arabs picked up solecisms from the Ottoman language, thus corrupting the Arabic language. At the end of the introduction, he wrote that one found a 'Turkish style' (*uslūb turkī*) in the works of unskilled translators who translated works from Turkish to Arabic (2: 199). Al-Ruṣāfī also described extensive debates in Ottoman Turkish writings about the role of language. Al-Ruṣāfī argued that Arabic terms played such a crucial role for Ottomans that they could not explain even the most fundamental concepts in the sciences if they excised Arabic expressions from their language (2: 149).

The 'commoners' (*al-^{c}awāmm*) seem much less concerned about the purity of their language, as al-Ruṣāfī wrote numerous times in *Daf^{c} al-hujna* that the 'commoners' borrowed 'foreign' Turkish expressions and put little effort in protecting the Arabic language from foreign influences. Al-Ruṣāfī complained about 'commoners' who kept borrowing misused Arabic words (*akhadhuhu al-^{c}awāmm*), such as *^{c}amal*, from Ottoman books or newspapers (2: 177, 2: 179, 2: 180, 2: 193, 2: 196). Due to their lack of education in government schools, the 'commoners' likely may not have had as good a command of Turkish as al-Ruṣāfī did. Still, his remarks testify to the various linguistic exchanges that resulted from the extensive circulation of Turkish texts and their Arabic translations among Arabic readers. *Daf^{c} al-hujna* also testifies to different authorities over the Arabic language. In the entry on the word '*mola*' (rest), al-Ruṣāfī quoted Şemseddin Sami (1850–1904), the composer of an Arabic–Turkish dictionary, that the Ottoman word '*mola*' was borrowed from Italian. Al-Ruṣāfī insisted that this word was, in fact, a deviation of the Arabic word '*muhla*' (2: 196). He criticised alternative authorities on the Arabic language, including Ottoman Turkish texts discussing Arabic.

Both Şemseddin Sami and al-Ruṣāfī aimed to 'master' each other's language so that they could purify their language and made it conform to its 'essence'. The late Ottoman period witnessed the publication of numerous Turkish writings on the Arabic language and Arabic writings on the Turkish language.[45] It also witnessed the publication of dictionaries, language textbooks and treatises on grammar and rhetoric, including *Kavaid-i Osmaniyye* (Grammar of the Ottoman Language, 1851) by Ahmet Cevdet Pasha, *Lisan* (Language, AH 1303 [1885/86]) by Şemseddin Sami and *Muḥīṭ al-muḥīṭ: ay qāmūs muṭawwal li-l-lugha al-^{c}arabiyya* (Ocean of the Ocean, or, Comprehensive Dictionary of the Arabic Language, 1867–70) by Buṭrus al-Bustānī. Many of these works also called for the purification of their language from 'foreign loanwords'. Şemseddin Sami, the composer of the Arabic–Turkish dictionary, claimed that even though the Ottoman language consisted of a mixture of Turkish, Arabic and Persian, the Ottoman language was, in essence, Turkish, while Arabic and Persian expressions were merely foreign loanwords in this language. Hence, Şemseddin Sami argued that the Ottoman language could have preserved its 'Turkish grammar and syntax', even though it heavily borrowed expressions from Arabic and Persian.[46]

This increasing interest in each other's language also corresponded to an increase in the number of translations between Arabic and Turkish during the late Ottoman period, which has not received much attention in earlier scholarship. The rise in the number of translations from Western Europe, France in particular, has been viewed as the key marker of Arabic and Turkish literary modernity in the late Ottoman Empire. Just as Muhammad Badawi has defined the Egyptian *nahḍa* as the 'the Age of Translations and Adaptations',[47] Nurullah Ataç has defined the *Tanzimat* as the 'age of translation'.[48] In 1820, the Egyptian khedive Mehmed Ali/Muḥammad ᶜAlī set up the Bulaq Press, which translated works from multiple languages into Arabic and Turkish, just as the Ottoman government in 1832 set up the Translation Chamber, which translated many French, Persian and Arabic works into Turkish.[49] The earlier focus on translations from Western languages has overlooked numerous translations between Arabic and Turkish in the nineteenth century. However, Shayyāl has noted that the Turkish language had never been as prevalent as it was during the age of Khedive Mehmed Ali/Muḥammad ᶜAlī in Egypt.[50] Saliha Paker has also shown that the number of translations between Arabic and Turkish reached a peak during this period.[51]

As this chapter will demonstrate through its examination of al-Ruṣāfī's Arabic translation of Namık Kemal's *Rüya*, translations between Arabic and Turkish contributed to a shared repertoire of ideas and themes in Arabic and Turkish works. At the same time, they also may have contributed to modernisation movements that emphasised that languages should remain free from foreign influences, ultimately leading to the Ottoman reservoir's dissolution. A comparison between al-Ṭahṭāwī's famous *Takhlīṣ al-ibrīz fī talkhīṣ Bārīz aw al-dīwān al-nafīs bi-Īwān Bārīs* (*An Imam in Paris*, 1834; literally 'Extracting Gold in the Abridgment of Paris or the Valuable Compendium in Palatial Paris') and its Turkish translation, *Tercüme-i Rıhlet-i Rifaa* (Translation of Rifaa's Travel, AH 1255 [1839/40]) reveals these dynamics. Rüstem Besim, the text's translator, kept the Arabic poems untranslated. One does not observe large discrepancies between the translation and the source text in terms of content. However, the choices that Rüstem Besim made as translator may have eventually contributed to movements that aimed to purify languages from 'foreign' influences. For example, al-Ṭaḥṭāwī used the term '*ifranj*'[52] to refer to Europeans, while Rüstem Besim translated this term as '*Frenkistan*',[53] even though the term '*efrenc*' also exists in Ottoman Turkish. In fact, Rüstem Besim wrote a few pages later '*taife-i efrenc indinde yani Frenkistan'da*' (among the community of Europeans, that is, the land of Franks).[54] Therefore, Rüstem Besim may have wanted to avoid using expressions that existed in both Arabic and Turkish. Furthermore, he translated the phrase '*fī kasb mā lā ta^crifuhu*' (in attaining what they [the Islamic lands] did not know)[55] as '*tahsil*'.[56] Later, al-Ruṣāfī would write in *Daf^c al-hujna* that the Turks used the term '*taḥṣīl*' to refer to getting educated, although, as al-Ruṣāfī also observed, the Arabs had started to borrow this usage.[57]

Likewise, Zeki Megamiz, who translated some of Jurjī Zaydān's works into Turkish,[58] often remained 'faithful' to the source text in terms of content. For example, there is no significant discrepancy between Zaydān's *Tārīkh al-tamaddun al-islāmī* (History of the Islamic Civilisation, 1902–6) and the Turkish translation, *Medeniyet-i İslamiyye Tarihi* (History of the Islamic Civilisation, 1910–12) in terms of content. At the same time, Megamiz translated some Arabic terms in Zaydān's texts into terms the forms of which comply with Turkish grammar rules. For example, the Turkish text translates the terms '*khiyām*'[59] (tents) and '*qabā^ɔil*'[60] (tribes) in the Arabic source text as '*haymeler*'[61] and '*kabileler*',[62] even though Ottoman Turkish can also use the Arabic plural forms of these expressions (*hıyam* and *kabail*). Furthermore, Zeki Megamiz translated the term '*tuwuffiyya*'[63] (passed away) in the Arabic source text as '*irtihal eyledi*'.[64] *Daf^c al-hujna* indicates that the Turks use this term to refer to death, although more Arabs, under the influence of the Turks, also started to use the term '*irtiḥāl*' for exclusively referring to death (2: 160). Translating '*tuwuffiyya*' as '*irtihal eyledi*' may have perhaps contributed to the notion that the term '*irtihal/irtiḥāl*' was used to refer to death only in Turkish and not in Arabic.

However, Megamiz did not necessarily intend to undertake a practice of translation that always served to 'purify' the Arabic and Turkish languages from foreign loanwords. In their analysis of Zeki Megamiz's and Asmai's/Yusuf Samih's (d. 1942) Turkish translations of Qāsim Amīn's (1863–1908) *Taḥrīr al-mar^ɔa* (*The Liberation of Women*, 1899), Ilham Khuri-Makdisi and Yorgos Dedes have observed that both translations 'deployed recherché Arabic terms and expressions that were not in common use', 'inject[ed] or reinject[ed] specific Arabic words into Ottoman Turkish' and 'experiment[ed] with and expand[ed] the Ottoman Turkish lexicon'.[65] Therefore, like the 'unskilled' translators about whom al-Ruṣāfī complained, Megamiz and Asmai undertook a translation practice that did not set up a strict boundary between Arabic and Turkish. In contrast, a comparison between Namık Kemal's *Rüya* and al-Ruṣāfī's Arabic translation, *al-Ru^ɔyā*, suggests that some translations between Arabic and Turkish may have reinforced the boundary between the two languages. After all, shortly before the demise of the Ottoman Empire, al-Ruṣāfī himself would call for Arabic translations that no longer introduced into the Arabic language 'solecisms' or terms that were 'Turkish in meaning and Arabic in form'.

In *Daf^c al-hujna*, al-Ruṣāfī wanted his audience to consult the classical Arabic heritage, *al-turāth*, rather than Turkish works, in order to coin expressions that capture the scientific and technological advancements of his age. For example, he noted that, as archeology has started to establish itself as a scientific field, Turks have started to use the term '*mustaḥātha*' to describe an old piece from antiquity. This specific use of the term '*mustaḥātha*' also became popular among Arabs, although they had actually used this term to refer to anything extracted from earth (*mustakhraj*). (2: 183–84). He also indicated that people should use the terms '*taṣ^{c}īd*' and '*ṣa^{c}ida*' instead of '*tabkhīr*' to describe the process of steam formation because, while '*tabkhīr*' was a loanword from Ottoman Turkish, '*ṣa^{c}ida*' was extensively used in classical Arabic sources (2: 167–68). İhsan Fazlıoğlu has argued that, once more engineering schools (*mühendishane*) were established in the Ottoman Empire, Turkish started to become a language of science throughout the Muslim world.[66] Therefore, many Arabic speakers in the nineteenth century used 'Turkish loanwords' to describe modernisation's technological and scientific developments.[67] Al-Ruṣāfī did not want the 'commoners' to resort to what he described as Ottoman language for scientific explanations and envisioned a 'pure' Arabic that drew on the *turāth*, classical Arabic heritage, that could address the need to coin new scientific terms.

Turkish texts circulated more widely among Arabic speakers, and the 'commoners' picked up expressions from these texts. Furthermore, an intellectual like al-Ruṣāfī could learn Turkish and rise through the administrative ranks. Even though *Daf^c al-hujna* advocated the need to retain the Arabic language free of foreign influences, al-Ruṣāfī did not argue against translating Turkish works into Arabic. The next section will examine an actual translation by al-Ruṣāfī of a Turkish source text, Namık Kemal's *Rüya*. I suggest that al-Ruṣāfī set a role model for a translation that would not introduce solecisms into the Arabic language. In a similar vein, his Arabic poem 'Nuwāḥ Dijla' refuses to 'translate' Süleyman Nazif's vision of Ottoman culture for his Arabic readers, as the poem describes the Ottoman defeat in Iraq as a watershed moment in terms of politics but not culture.

Language, Heritage and the Ottoman Defeat in Iraq

Although al-Ruṣāfī criticised bad translations from the Turkish language that introduced solecisms into Arabic language, Erol Ayyıldız has also revealed that Iraqi Arabic texts of the nineteenth and early twentieth centuries made numerous references to Ottoman Turkish texts. For example, al-Ruṣāfī's poetry makes references to Turkish works by Recaizade Mahmud Ekrem (1847–1914) and Tevfik Fikret (1867–1915). Furthermore, al-Ruṣāfī's poetry engages with numerous themes that one observes in late Ottoman Turkish poetry, such as gender equality, tyranny (*istibdād*) and Istanbul.[68] In a similar vein, al-Ruṣāfī's work transmits Namık Kemal's ideas by offering translations of the latter's texts. At the same time, al-Ruṣāfī's translation sets a strict boundary between Namık Kemal's Turkish and his own Arabic. Al-Ruṣāfī did not alter the source text's content in his translation; however, he made an effort not to include in his translation the solecisms that emerged due to the cultural exchanges between Arabic and Turkish during the late Ottoman Empire. This section will examine al-Ruṣāfī's works on language and political developments in the Ottoman Empire to demonstrate how his works undermine the empire's power hierarchies.

Shared Dreams, Separate Languages: al-Ruṣāfī's Translation of Namik Kemal's Rüya

Namık Kemal's *Rüya* describes a social utopia. In the beginning, the narrator sits in a mansion as he looks at the Bosphorus. He then observes sudden transformations in his surroundings, such as the darkening sky. Afterwards, he falls asleep in immense pain. He wakes up when a young and beautiful woman, who introduces herself as 'Freedom' (*Hürriyet*), appears in a fire cloud. She laments the horrendous decline of the narrator's society and emphasises the need to reform it to put an end to its deep slumber. Freedom possesses supernatural qualities; in fact, the narrator compares her with the Greek goddess of beauty. She complains about the decline and stagnation of the narrator's society and then tells the narrator what his society should do. His society should develop in terms of science, express interest in other cultures and civilisations, and promote social equality and freedom of speech. Later, the setting suddenly changes, and Freedom shows the narrator the panorama of an ideal society in which everything works perfectly. Finally, the narrator wakes up and expresses a strong desire to see this dream again.

Rüya exhibits various features that make the work easy to translate. The Turkish source text includes excerpts of Arabic poetry that al-Ruṣāfī also kept in his translation. Furthermore, due to the lack of specific geographical and temporal markers throughout much of the story, it is easy to imagine that *Rüya* could take place anywhere. In other words, the narrator describes the social decline as a natural disaster more than a product of particular social and economic conditions. When Freedom advocates virtues such as equality and scientific progress, these virtues no longer seem imports from Western society but rather become like irrefutable commandments against which the narrator can never argue.

Al-Ruṣāfī's translation is 'accurate', as the content of the translation shows no significant discrepancies from the content of the source text. At the same time, for the translation, al-Ruṣāfī does not choose the expressions that he would later list in *Dafᶜ al-hujna*. This decision is fundamental because al-Ruṣāfī at the end of *Dafᶜ al-hujna* wrote that numerous translations from Turkish to Arabic had introduced solecisms into the Arabic language. Al-Ruṣāfī may have translated Namık Kemal's work not only to transmit the content of his writings, but also to set himself apart from other translators who introduced solecisms into the Arabic language. For example, while Namık Kemal used the word '*eserler*',[69] al-Ruṣāfī translated it as '*maᵓāthir*'.[70] While al-Ruṣāfī noted that Ottoman Turkish writings used the word '*eser*' to refer to books and works, he also claimed that this particular use of *eser/athar* was not Arabic.[71] He may thus have wanted to use the term '*maᵓāthir*' (glorious deeds) instead. Likewise, he criticised that people misused the word '*waram*' in Arabic. This word refers to tuberculosis in Turkish; however, al-Ruṣāfī emphasised that the word '*waram*' simply meant any form of swelling.[72] Therefore, to differentiate this more common meaning from the disease of tuberculosis, he used the expression '*dāᵓ al-waram*'[73] (sickness of swelling) for translating '*verem*' in the source text.[74] While Turks use the expression '*vücud*' for referring to the body, al-Ruṣāfī wrote that this expression solely meant 'existence' in Arabic.[75] He thus translated the word '*vücud*' in the source text[76] as '*abdān*' (bodies).[77] Likewise, al-Ruṣāfī translated the term '*aza*' in the Turkish source text[78] as '*farāᵓiṣ*' (flanks or muscles below the shoulder blade).[79] In *Dafᶜ al-hujna*, al-Ruṣāfī noted that, although the term '*aᶜḍāᵓ*' could refer to a single limb in Turkish, the term actually meant limbs (in plural) in Arabic.[80]

While al-Ruṣāfī's translation avoids introducing to his readers the 'solecisms' that became widespread with the growing circulation of Turkish works, it contributes to generating a shared repertoire of imagery, themes and genres in the Arabic and Turkish literatures of the late Ottoman period. Both al-Ruṣāfī's and Namık Kemal's works feature a woman character who carries characteristics of the ideal beloved in many classical Arabic and Turkish love poems in terms of physical appearance: pearl-like teeth and beautiful neck.[81] While Freedom shares physical features with the idealised beloved, she is not an object of observation and rupture. Freedom speaks back as she practices agency and provides instructions on how one should modernise. Furthermore, this work builds on the dream genre of the Islamic literary tradition. Aslı Niyazioğlu has demonstrated that the dream genre often expressed the career aspirations of high-ranking Ottoman officials.[82] In the late Ottoman period, dreams started to express future visions of a social utopia. According to Erol Ayyıldız, after Maᶜrūf al-Ruṣāfī translated Namık Kemal's *Rüya* into Arabic, many other Iraqi authors produced similar works in what has been called the 'dream genre', which describes dreams that convey the narrator's future aspirations for society. This genre proliferated in Iraq and became a staple genre of the nationalist movement.[83] Many writings in different languages throughout the empire thus express a shared dream of modernisation.

Despite this shared dream, al-Ruṣāfī's translation displays a key difference from the source text, Namık Kemal's *Rüya*. Namık Kemal glorified the Ottoman flag in the following words:

> The flag of the Ottoman felicity lies at the hand of Freedom
> Praise be to God, the glorious Ottoman future has arrived.[84]

Al-Ruṣāfī translated these lines as follows:

> O, the flag at the hand of Freedom rises
> With glory and victory, elevating every Ottoman.[85]

Al-Ruṣāfī used the term 'every Ottoman' (*kull ᶜuthmānī*), an expression that does not exist in the Turkish source text. Al-Ruṣāfī wanted to bring the subjects of the Ottoman Empire – including the Iraqi population whom the Istanbul administration often neglected – to a more central stage. This difference captures the unequal power dynamics that shaped the Ottoman cultural landscape. While Namık Kemal's lines suggest that Freedom will carry the Ottoman flag into a glorious future, al-Ruṣāfī's lines emphasise that the Ottoman people, like al-Ruṣāfī himself, will benefit from Freedom's guidance. The next section will also show that, while al-Ruṣāfī indeed supported the Ottoman Empire's political unity, what he valued differed from what the Ottoman literati tended to favour.

Shared Grief, Separate Cultural Visions: Al-Ruṣāfī's 'Nuwāḥ Dijla' and *Süleyman Nazif's* Firak-ı Irak

Various editions of al-Ruṣāfī's poetry collection point out that al-Ruṣāfī wrote the poem 'Nuwāḥ Dijla' in response to a *qaṣīda* poem by Süleyman Nazif upon the Ottoman defeat in Baghdad during World War I.[86] If this claim is true, this poem may be 'Dicle ve Ben' (Tigris and I), one of the works compiled in *Firak-ı Irak*. Indeed, Erol Ayyıldız and Muḥammad Ḥāmid Sālim have analysed the similarities between 'Nuwāḥ Dijla' and 'Dicle ve Ben'.[87] Regardless of whether al-Ruṣāfī wrote 'Nuwāḥ Dijla' as a response to Süleyman Nazif's work, al-Ruṣāfī's 'Nuwāḥ Dijla' and Süleyman Nazif's *Firak-ı Irak* share important characteristics since they both lament the British victory and Ottoman defeat in Iraq during World War I. At the same time, while the Ottoman Empire's defeat in Iraq becomes the shared source of suffering for al-Ruṣāfī and Süleyman Nazif, they provide different interpretations of the same historical event.

In *Firak-ı Irak*, Süleyman Nazif expressed a strong sense of grief over the loss of the Iraqi provinces. The book includes a compilation of works, such as a poem titled 'Kübalılar' (Cubans), which praises the Cubans and castigates the Spanish, who, as Süleyman Nazif writes, had driven the Muslims out of Andalusia hundreds of years ago,[88] and a short story, 'Şehidin Babası' (The Martyr's Father), which describes a father who has lost his son in World War I and yet still cannot accept the reality of his son's death.[89] Al-Ruṣāfī expressed the same sentiments as Süleyman Nazif in his poem; however, unlike Süleyman Nazif, al-Ruṣāfī did not depict Iraq as a core element of a cosmopolitan Ottoman identity. Süleyman Nazif associated Baghdad with poets such as Fuzuli and al-Mutanabbī and suggested that all these poems lamented Baghdad's defeat. Al-Ruṣāfī, in contrast, described the Ottoman defeat in Baghdad as a watershed moment in terms of politics but not culture.

Born in Diyarbakır, Süleyman Nazif received his primary education in Harput. He served as governor in various urban centres of the empire, such as Trabzon, Mosul and Baghdad. After serving as governor of Baghdad for six months, he returned to Istanbul. Later, he continued to write for various newspapers, such as *Peyam-ı Sabah* (The Morning Message). His writings advocated political and social reform; they also expressed sorrow and hopelessness as he witnessed the Ottoman Empire's declining strength.

In *Firak-ı Irak*, Süleyman Nazif argued that the Ottomans had neglected Baghdad for the past 400 years and failed to appreciate Baghdad's true worth. He described the Ottoman defeat in Iraq as a tragedy for the entire Muslim world. He addressed his mother's grave in the beginning, describing that he was no longer an orphan simply because he had lost his parents. After the Ottoman defeat in Iraq, he also became an orphan of his homeland (*yetim-i vatan*) and of history (*yetim-i tarih*). Throughout his work, Süleyman Nazif emphasised numerous times that he considered Iraq a part of his homeland and claimed that both Iraq and Baghdad remained orphaned after the Ottoman defeat.

In his poem 'Dicle ve Ben' (Tigris and I), Süleyman Nazif compared the Tigris River with a woman and claimed that the Tigris had given up her sexual honour. The Tigris remained indifferent towards his grief. Later, however, he fell into a moment of self-reflection. The Ottomans should experience a deep sense of regret because they had ignored Iraq for centuries:

> Hush, I know our crime, too!. . .
> Perhaps we are more sinful than you are,
> As we have neglected it [Baghdad] for the past 400 years,
> We are now seeking a scapegoat.[90]

He later wrote that, even though the Iraqi provinces might eventually forgive the Ottomans, neither history nor God would forgive the empire.

Firak-ı Irak suggests that the Ottoman administration's negligence of Iraq comes at the expense of the Ottoman literary reservoir's dissolution. The Ottomans experienced not only a political and military defeat, but also a cultural one. *Firak-ı Irak* includes an index listing the poets and political leaders whom Süleyman Nazif's work mentions. Süleyman Nazif did not list these figures in chronological order or enumerate them in separate lists with titles such as 'Arab poets', 'Persian poets' and 'Turkish poets'. For example, he listed Kaᶜb ibn Zuhayr right after Fuzuli and before the Prophet Muḥammad.[91] The narrator speaks with key figures from the Ottoman past, Sultan Süleyman and Fuzuli, in *Firak-ı Irak*. He describes Iraq as Fuzuli's lands and uses the epithet 'from Baghdad' (*Bağdadi*) when referring to Fuzuli. As narrator, Süleyman Nazif speaks with Fuzuli (d. 1556) and his grave, claiming that he already achieved great familiarity with Baghdad by reading Fuzuli's poetry.[92]

In 'Fuzuli-i Bağdadi'den Nefi-i Erzurumi'ye' (From Fuzuli of Baghdad to Nefi of Erzurum), another work included in *Firak-ı Irak*, Fuzuli explains to the sixteenth-century poet Nefi how he joined the 'world of eternal ones' (*ebedîler âlemi*) that includes composers of Arabic, Persian and Turkish poetry. 'All poets who recite the Qur'an' gather around Ḥassān ibn Thābit and compose *qaṣīda*/*kaside* poems to Saladin (r. 1174–93), Mahmud of Ghazni (r. 998–1030) and Sultan Selim I (r. 1512–20) in their language. Then Fuzuli describes the dialogue between Kaᶜb ibn Zuhayr and Ḥassān ibn Thābit, which took place when Nefi was executed:

> Kaᶜb ibn Zuhayr suddenly trembled. The excitement that he felt when he recited his *kaside*,
>
> Suᶜād has departed and today my heart is sick,

in the presence of the Prophet was revived again. He said:
– Since my arrival here, the star that I have dwelled on in the afterlife has been revolving around its own sun more than one thousand times. Also, whenever something extraordinary happened to one of the poets who recite the Qur'an, I was here trembling, shaking, suffering in pain and feeling torment. I still could not find the eternal peace my Prophet had promised to me when he bestowed upon me his honourable mantle.

Ḥassān ibn Thābit replied to Kaᶜb ibn Zuhayr:
– I am also like you, my dear brother, he said. Until the last person from our spiritual family remains in the world and that person recites his last line, we will not receive our promised share of eternal peace.

Kaᶜb ibn Zuhayr continued to speak to Ḥassān ibn Thābit with compassion:
– However, I have never felt what I am feeling now, he said. I did not feel shattered to this extent even when thieves tore to pieces the repenting poet Abū Ṭayyib al-Mutanabbī. At this moment, which incidents target us, being shot like arrows from invisible heavens? . . .[93]

Both Ḥassān ibn Thābit and Kaᶜb ibn Zuhayr here refer to the poet Nefi's execution by Sultan Murad IV (r. 1623–40), who felt offended by Nefi's infamous and biting satire poems (*hiciv*). Nefi, who comes to these poets with his two hands 'soaked in blood', tells the other poets that the sultan treated him unjustly, as Nefi had also composed wonderful panegyric poems for the sultan. Nefi's death causes Kaᶜb ibn Zuhayr to experience a pain he had not felt even at al-Mutanabbī's death. Other poets deeply care about Nefi, too; for example, the Persian poets Anvarī (c. 1126–1187/88 or 1189/90) and ᶜUrfī (1555/56–90/91) describe Nefi as 'the poet [they] gave as a gift to the Ottoman community'.[94]

Later, Fuzuli observes Nefi praying to God, as Nefi regrets that he wrote poems that castigated Sultan Murad IV and asks the sultan for forgiveness. Nefi then shows to the other poets the moment when Sultan Murad IV re-conquered Baghdad in 1638, as the Safavids had previously overtaken the city while it was under Ottoman rule in 1624. He claims that the Tigris and the Euphrates under Safavid rule were crying and became orphans of history and homeland. Once Sultan Murad IV takes over Baghdad again, Nefi feels great joy and asks God to forgive Sultan Murad IV in case the sultan committed a sin by executing Nefi. He wishes that he had a thousand lives so that the sultan could execute him a thousand times.[95] After Nefi's speech, all poets cry profusely and pray to God so that Sultan Murad IV may be forgiven.[96] Fuzuli and Nefi then lament that all of them, including poets such as Kaᶜb ibn Zuhayr, who belong to the 'spiritual family' and call each other 'brother', have become orphans of history and homeland due to the Ottoman defeat in Iraq in 1917.

According to Süleyman Nazif, Ḥassān ibn Thābit and Ka^cb ibn Zuhayr are not distant ancestors who passed away in bygone times; instead, they have an 'Ottoman afterlife', as they live in the same world as Nefi and reflect on historical events that shape the Ottoman Empire, such as World War I. If Ka^cb ibn Zuhayr is seen as a progenitor of Islamic poets, he also becomes, in Süleyman Nazif's words, the progenitor of a spiritual family that includes poets such as Fuzuli and Nefi. Therefore, the Ottoman defeat in Baghdad is a tragedy not only for Ottoman society or the poets who lived during the Ottoman period, such as Nefi or Fuzuli. Süleyman Nazif suggested that this event also had cataclysmic consequences for the poets of the Ottoman canon, such as Ḥassān ibn Thābit, who now all spoke Turkish.

Süleyman Nazif described poets such as Ḥāfiẓ (c. 1315–c. 90), al-Mutanabbī and Fuzuli as poets who believed in the Qur'an, rather than as poets who gathered in a tavern, as did Ziya Pasha. This overt association between the Qur'an and these poets reveals the growing impact of pan-Islamism on how intellectuals such as Süleyman Nazif envisioned Ottoman identity and the Ottoman cultural reservoir, as many authors confronted an increasing Western imperialism. While Ziya Pasha also had made numerous Islamic references in *Harabat*, Süleyman Nazif put even stronger emphasis on the Islamic character of these poets.

Al-Ruṣāfī's poem expresses the deep sense of grief that characterises *Firak-ı Irak*; however, one can also observe significant discrepancies between Süleyman Nazif's and al-Ruṣāfī's interpretation of the event. Süleyman Nazif suggested in *Firak-ı Irak* that the Tigris was a traitor who had lost her sexual honour; however, 'Nuwāḥ Dijla' emphasises that the river laments the defeat and hates the enemy. In other words, it is a loyal Ottoman subject. Except for the occasional use of the word 'today' (*al-yawm*), 'Nuwāḥ Dijla', like Namık Kemal's *Rüya*, includes almost no historical details and depicts the defeat almost as a supernatural event akin to doomsday:

It is my eye and its tears are overflowing
  Every affliction drawing its waters.
How can I not shed tears, as my pride
  Is annihilated, perishing under the flood of humiliation?
The hand of time cast me away into a great misery
  Into endless nights.
As the darkness eclipsed the sky off my sight
  Darkness in which ghosts hide.

The gleaming honour of my people
Slowly faded from my sight.
I woke up to a day with no protectors, spears, or blades
To defend me against injustice.
Today I am like a ship sailing
Without a sail or a helmsman.[97]

Later, the river complains about its intense suffering and indicates that no one will protect it in the future.

In his analysis of another poem by al-Ruṣāfī, 'Baᶜda al-Nuzūḥ' (After Exile, 1922), Hussein N. Kadhim has noted that 'the river occupies a prominent position in twentieth-century Arabic poetry as part of a distinct poetics that sought to construct an anti-colonial national (as opposed to pan-Arab) identity. It is also at this period that poets begin to be identified with certain rivers – the best-known case of such identification is that of the Egyptian poet Ḥāfiẓ Ibrāhīm (1871–1932) known as *shāᶜir al-Nīl* (the bard of the Nile)'.[98] In fact, while al-Ruṣāfī described himself as 'son of the river' in 'Baᶜda al-Nuzūḥ', the narrator becomes the river itself in 'Nuwāḥ Dijla'. Furthermore, the river describes itself not as an orphan child, as Süleyman Nazif suggested, but instead as a lover who longs for the beloved. The river speaks, something that one does not observe in *Firak-ı Irak*. At the same time, 'Nuwāḥ Dijla' does not lament a sense of exile, as does 'Baᶜda al-Nuzūḥ'. Nor does it make references to diverse 'homelands' (*mawāṭin*), such as Beirut, Baghdad and Jerusalem, to which al-Ruṣāfī wanted to get accustomed, as he wrote in 'Baᶜda al-Nuzūḥ':

They are the homelands that I draw near while they drive me away
Like adversities that I test while they afflict me.[99]

If 'Nuwāḥ Dijla' features a narrator who seeks union with a single beloved for a sense of stability and serenity, al-Ruṣāfī sought many homelands in 'Baᶜda al-Nuzūḥ'. This time, however, al-Ruṣāfī did not mention Istanbul as one of them.

'Nuwāḥ Dijla' also uses the imagery of desiccation to emphasise the situation's gravity. However, what desiccates here is not the Ottoman reservoir, as Süleyman Nazif implied, but the Tigris itself.[100] Furthermore, al-Ruṣāfī foregrounded the emotional bonds (*widād*) between him and the Ottoman political leaders rather than among the poets who recited the Qur'an:

The valley of the Tigris wears the crown of Osman's glory,
Bears the crescent flag, the military sash.

I remain loyal even when
My heart was wounded by those I loved.[101]

At first, one may read these lines only as an expression of particular deference towards Ottoman authority. At the same time, al-Ruṣāfī put emphasis on Ottoman political and military power rather than on the richness of its culture, the canon of which maintained a sense of camaraderie among poets such as al-Mutanabbī and Fuzuli.

Kadhim has argued that al-Ruṣāfī uses a 'language' that feels familiar to him, classical Arabic, to make sense of the chaotic colonial situation which generates a strong sense of alienation.[102] I propose that al-Ruṣāfī's use of classical Arabic may serve another function. While Süleyman Nazif emphasised the familial bonds between Kaᶜb ibn Zuhayr and Fuzuli to reinforce his vision of the Ottoman canon, al-Ruṣāfī drew on classical Arabic poetry, to respond to the alienating reality as well as to situate poets such as Kaᶜb ibn Zuhayr within a lineage of the Arabic *turāth* rather than of the Ottoman literary reservoir.

'Nuwāḥ Dijla' can be divided into two parts. The first part of the poem emphasises the magnitude of the river's suffering. The poet used the term 'teardrops' (*dam*ᶜ or *dumū*ᶜ) in numerous verses throughout the section. However, the narrator asks a question for the first time in verse 17 and starts a dialogue with the Turkish soldiers and leaders:

Where are the protectors, did they leave me as loot
At the hands of enemies and then leave?[103]

Al-Ruṣāfī never used the term 'tear' or 'tears' in the second section, which employs a less figurative and ornamental language than the first section. The river suggests that the addressee does not know the extent of its suffering since, if the Ottomans saw it as a captive of the enemy, they would also cry and wail. Here, the 'beloved' – the Ottoman political leaders – would become exactly like the wailing lover if they witnessed the river's humiliation. However, this time, the lover will not achieve union with the beloved nor attain a sense of stability and serenity. Like Suᶜād who departed (*bānat*) and left behind Kaᶜb ibn Zuhayr, the Turkish armies also left behind (*bānū*) the Tigris. However, while Kaᶜb ibn Zuhayr undertakes a journey and achieves the sense of stability and security that the poets attain in the praise (*madḥ*) section of their panegyric odes, the river itself cannot undertake such a journey:

My evenings are not evenings anymore
And my mornings are not mornings since they left me.
I wish I could fly to them
With wings but where are they?[104]

The Tigris complains that it does not have wings and that only winds can carry its complaints. The river will never achieve union with the beloved.

At the same time, the dialogue between the river and the Ottoman political figures has not ended, as the winds will continue to carry its grievances:

My complaints today are about them and to them
Oh winds, deliver my grievances to them.[105]

Firak-ı Irak and 'Nuwāḥ Dijla' were both composed during World War I, which led to the Ottoman Empire's demise and the emergence of various nation-states throughout the Middle East. This demise also substantiated the epistemological shifts that Chapter 2 has discussed. Many authors of the new nation-states reinforced nationalistic frameworks, hence equating Ottoman literature with Ottoman Turkish works. They also categorised Arabic and Persian poems not as waters crucial for filling the Ottoman reservoir, but rather as sources of influence for Ottoman literature. The next chapter will demonstrate that even late Ottoman authors who claimed that the Ottoman language or literature was no different from the Arabic language or literature would reinforce these epistemological shifts.

Notes

1. Quoted in ᶜAbd al-Laṭīf Sharārah, *al-Ruṣāfī: dirāsa taḥliliyya* (Beirut: Dār Ṣādir, 1960), 7.
2. Yūsuf ᶜIzz al-Dīn, *al-Ruṣāfī yarwī sīrat ḥayātih: sijill li-l-ḥayā al-ijtimāᶜiyya wa-l-siyāsiyya wa-l-fikriyya bi-kull jarāᵓa wa-ṣarāḥa* (Damascus: Manshūrāt al-Madā, 2004), 99–100. Likewise, the Rüşdiye School in Baghdad that al-Ruṣāfī attended also required students to wear a tarboosh. ᶜAbd al-Ḥamīd al-Rashūdī, *Al-Ruṣāfī: ḥayātuh–āthāruh–shiᶜruh* (Beirut: Manshūrāt al-Jamal, 2012), 21.
3. One should not conflate modern-day Iraq with what historians have called Ottoman Iraq. Ottoman Iraq consisted of three provinces – Mosul, Baghdad and Basra – although some nineteenth-century Ottoman sources also used the term 'Iraq'. Following much of the secondary scholarship, I sometimes use the term 'Iraq' or 'Ottoman Iraq' throughout the chapter, while remaining cognisant of the relatively recent coinage of these terms.
4. While ᶜAbd al-Ghanī Maḥmūd knew Arabic, Kurdish and Turkish (al-Rashūdī, *al-Ruṣāfī*, 18), al-Ruṣāfī himself indicated that he did not know Kurdish (ᶜIzz al-Dīn, *al-Ruṣāfī yarwī*, 148).
5. Cenap Şahabettin, *Âfâk-ı Irak: Kızıldeniz'den Bağdat'a Hatıralar*, ed. Bülent Yorulmaz (Istanbul: Dergâh Yayınları, 2002), 91.
6. For more on this 'civilising mission' towards Iraq, also see Deringil, '"They Live in a State of Nomadism and Savagery"'.

7. Tahsin Paşa, *Abdülhamit: Yıldız Hatıraları* (Istanbul: Muallim Ahmet Halit Kitaphanesi, 1931), 150; translated and quoted in Gökhan Çetinsaya, *Ottoman Administration of Iraq, 1890–1908* (Abingdon: Routledge, 2017), 147.
8. As Nabil al-Tikriti puts it, '[t]his Ottoman assertion of centralized imperial power effectively required a virtual reconquest in the early nineteenth century. Once this was accomplished in Baghdad with the expulsion of Da'ud Pasha in 1831, the imperial center stamped its presence over local governance, reestablishing central power one town at a time in Mosul, Karbala, Najaf, Basra and Suleymaniyah'. Nabil al-Tikriti, 'Ottoman Iraq', *The Journal of the Historical Society* 7, no. 2 (2007): 206.
9. Karen M. Kern, *Imperial Citizen: Marriage and Citizenship in the Ottoman Frontier Provinces of Iraq* (Syracuse: Syracuse University Press, 2011), 9.
10. Emine Ö. Evered, *Empire and Education under the Ottomans: Politics, Reforms and Resistance from the Tanzimat to the Young Turks* (London: I. B. Tauris, 2012), 160.
11. Çetinsaya, *The Ottoman Administration of Iraq*, 140.
12. al-Rashūdī, *al-Ruṣāfī*, 18.
13. Greene, 'Burying a Rabbi in Baghdad', 97–123; Orit Bashkin, '"Religious Hatred Shall Disappear from the Land": Iraqi Jews as Ottoman Subjects, 1864–1913', *International Journal of Contemporary Iraqi Studies*, 4, no. 3 (2010): 305–23; Lital Levy, 'The *Nahḍa* and the *Haskala*: A Comparative Reading of "Revival" and "Reform"', *Middle Eastern Literatures*, 16, no. 3 (2013): 300–16; Reuven Snir, 'Arabic Journalism as a Vehicle for Enlightenment: Iraqi Jews in the Arabic Press During the Nineteenth and Twentieth Centuries', *Journal of Modern Jewish Studies* 6, no. 3 (2007): 219–37; Reuven Snir, '"If I Forget Thee, O Baghdad": The Demise of Arab-Jewish Identity and Culture'. *Asian and African Studies* 30, no. 1 (2021): 173–88; and Avi-ram Tzoreff, 'Acknowledging Loss, Materializing Language: Translation and Hermeneutics of Gaps in Nineteenth Century Baghdad', *Middle Eastern Studies* 59, no. 1 (2023): 1–21. For example, Reuven Snir has noted that late Ottoman Iraqi Jews, such as Sassoon Efendi (1860–1932) who was a representive of Baghdad in the Ottoman parliament, became more engaged with both European and Ottoman political and cultural developments and attained a highly cosmopolitan character as they could read newspapers in multiple languages, such as Arabic, Ottoman Turkish, Hebrew, Judeo-Arabic and French. This transformation resulted partly from the reforms that Ottoman officials such as Tahsin Pasha had initiated (Snir, 'Arabic Journalism', 225). After the demise of the Ottoman Empire, Iraqi Jews would uphold a political and cultural vision that viewed Baghdad as a place where different religions and cultures co-existed. They could not realise this vision, however, mainly because of the establishment of the Israeli state. Snir has viewed this vision as 'the product of a very limited period (mainly the 1920s and the 1930s), a very confined space

(specifically Baghdad), and a very singular history (that of the crumbling Ottoman empire and prior to the increasing power of Zionism)' (Snir, '"If I Forget Thee, O Baghdad!"', 186).

14. Abdul Wahhab Abbas al-Qaysi, 'The Impact of Modernization on Iraqi Society during the Ottoman Era: A Study of Intellectual Development in Iraq, 1869–1917' (Unpubl. PhD dissertation, University of Michigan, 1958), 141.
15. ᶜIzz al-Dīn, *al-Ruṣāfī yarwī*, 148.
16. al-Rashūdī, *al-Ruṣāfī*, 23.
17. Maᶜrūf al-Ruṣāfī, *al-Risāla al-ᶜirāqiyya fī al-siyāsa wa-l-dīn wa-l-ijtimāᶜ, yalīhi Kāmil al-Jādirjī fī ḥiwār maᶜa al-Ruṣāfī* (Beirut: Manshūrāt al-Jamal, 2012), 230.
18. al-Rashūdī, *al-Ruṣāfī*, 30.
19. Ibid.
20. Ibid.
21. 'Izz al-Dīn, *al-Ruṣāfī yarwī*, 71, 96–98. Al-Ruṣāfī complained that, although he did not know enough Turkish, he succeeded in his Turkish classes at the Rüşdiye School, because he would merely memorise for the exam without having an actual understanding of the content (al-Rashūdī, *al-Ruṣāfī*, 21).
22. ᶜIzz al-Dīn, *al-Ruṣāfī yarwī*, 96.
23. Ibid., 95. Al-Ruṣāfī tried to teach Arabic to Talat Pasha upon the pasha's request; however, later he understood that Talat Pasha did not actually want to learn the language but wanted to take lessons from him to learn about al-Ruṣāfī's political views.
24. al-Rashūdī, *al-Ruṣāfī*, 32; Qaysi, 'The Impact of Modernization', 189. For the poem, see al-Maᶜrūf al-Ruṣāfī, *Dīwān al-Ruṣāfī*, ed. Muṣṭafā ᶜAlī (Baghdad: Manshūrāt Wizārat al-Iᶜlām fī al-Jumhūriyya al-ᶜIrāqiyya, 1977), 5: 187–88. Unless otherwise indicated, I refer to the 1972–77 edition of al-Ruṣāfī's poetry collection when I quote his verses.
25. al-Rashūdī, *al-Ruṣāfī*, 30.
26. ᶜIzz al-Dīn, *al-Ruṣāfī yarwī*, 87–88.
27. al-Ruṣāfī, *Āthāruhu fī al-naqd wa-l-adab*, 1: 45–100.
28. Ibid., 1: 175–217.
29. Ibid., 1: 401–457.
30. al-Ruṣāfī, *Dīwān al-Ruṣāfī*, 2: 168.
31. al-Ruṣāfī, *Āthāruhu fī al-naqd wa-l-adab*, 1: 126–27. For some critics, al-Ruṣāfī's ideas on social reform contradicted the main tenets of Islam. While his ideas challenged what he described as Iraq's traditional customs, al-Ruṣāfī constantly emphasised that his ideas did not contradict these tenets. His writings not only criticised society's traditional customs that led to its corruption, but also the intellectuals who viewed Islam as the main cause of this corruption. He wrote a biography of Prophet Muḥammad, *al-Shakhsiyya al-Muḥammadiyya*, in order to convince his audience that Islam advocates modernity's values, including liberty and women's rights.

32. al-Rashūdī, *al-Ruṣāfī*, 42.
33. Ibid., 44.
34. Qaysi, 'The Impact of Modernization', 205.
35. ᶜAbd al-Ḥamīd al-Rashūdī, *Dhikrā al-Ruṣāfī* (Baghdad: Maktabat al-Zawrāᵓ, 1950), 233.
36. Yasir Suleiman, *The Arabic Language and National Identity: A Study in Ideology* (Edinburgh: Edinburgh University Press, 2003), 103. Suleiman has also noted that Ziya Gökalp (1876–1924), a key intellectual who is often considered to have established the ideology of Turkish nationalism, held similar views on language. Ziya Gökalp considered language reform as a stepping-stone for reforming other aspects of society, such as science (76).
37. Amidu Sanni, 'The Discourse on *Laḥn* in Arabic Philological and Literary Traditions', *Middle Eastern Literatures* 13, no. 1 (2010): 2.
38. Suleiman, *The Arabic Language*, 53.
39. al-Ruṣāfī, *Āthāruhu fī al-naqd wa-l-adab*, 1: 61.
40. Ibid., 1: 73.
41. Ibid., 1: 74.
42. Ibid., 2: 437.
43. Ibid.
44. al-Ruṣāfī, 'Dafᶜ al-hujna fī irtiḍākh al-lukna', 2: 148.
45. Some of the Turkish works include the Arabic lexicon *Nuhbe-i Vehbi* (Exquisite Selections from Vehbi, 1799) by Sünbülzade Vehbi, *Sanihat ül-Arap* (Proverbs of the Arabs, AH 1304 [1886/87]) by Muallim Naci and *Kamus-ı Arabi* (Arabic Dictionary, AH 1313–14 [1896/97–97/98]) by Şemseddin Sami; the Arabic works include *Kitāb Kanz al-lugha al-ᶜuthmāniyya* (The Book of the Treasure of the Ottoman Language, 1881) by Muṣṭafā Sulaymānzādah al-Sharīf al-Ḥalabī, *Ghāyat al-amānī fī tafṣīl qawāᶜid al-lisān al-ᶜuthmānī* (Aspirations of Elaborating the Rules of the Ottoman Language, AH 1314 [1896/97]) by Muḥammad Kāmil and *al-Tuḥfa al-ḥamidiyya fī al-lugha al-ᶜuthmāniyya* (The Hamidian Gift for the Ottoman Language, AH 1314 [1896/97]) by Miṣbāḥ bin Salīm al-Labābīdī. Many Arabic titles use the term 'Ottoman language'. Hayati Develi has argued that the term 'Ottoman language' became popular only in the nineteenth century and attributed this increasing popularity to the rise in Ottomanism. See Hayati Develi, *Osmanlı'nın Dili* (Istanbul: 3F Yayınevi, 2006), 65.
46. Şemseddin Sami, *Lisan* (Istanbul: Mihran Matbaası, AH 1303 [1885/86]), 103.
47. M. M. Badawi, *A Short History of Modern Arabic Literature* (Oxford: Clarendon Press, 1993), 11.
48. Hikmet Dizdaroğlu, Nurullah Ataç and Sami N. Özerdim, *Ataç: Ataç Üzerine, Söyleşiler, Nurullah Ataç Bibliyografyası* (Ankara: Ankara Üniversitesi Basımevi, 1962), 251.

49. For a comprehensive list of translations from the Bulaq Press, see Jamāl al-Dīn al-Shayyāl, *Tārīkh al-tarjama wa-l-ḥaraka al-thaqāfiyya fī ^{c}aṣr Muḥammad ^{c}Alī* (Cairo: Dār al-Fikr al-^{c}Arabī, 1951), Appendix: [7–36].
50. al-Shayyāl, *Tārīkh al-tarjama wa-l-ḥaraka al-thaqāfiyya fī ^{c}aṣr Muḥammad ^{c}Alī*, 222.
51. Saliha Paker, 'Turkish Tradition', 577. Many works that were translated were official documents, such as the 1839 and 1856 Imperial Decrees.
52. Rifā^{c}a Rāfi^{c} al-Ṭahṭāwī, 'Takhlīṣ al-ibrīz fī talkhīṣ Bārīz aw al-dīwān al-nafīs bi-Īwān Bārīs', *al-A^{c}māl al-kāmila li-Rifā^{c}a Rāfi^{c} al-Ṭahṭāwī*, ed. Muḥammad ^{c}Amāra (Cairo: Dār al-Shurūq, 2010), 2: 25.
53. Rifaa et-Tahtavi, *Tercüme-i Rıhlet-i Rifaa*, trans. Rüstem Besim (Cairo: Matbaa-i Sahib es-Saadet el-Ebediyye, AH 1255 [1839/40]), 12. Although the title of al-Ṭahṭāwī's work is *Takhlīs al-ibrīz fī talkhīṣ Bārīz*, the translator, Rüstem Besim, writes that people in Egypt know the work as '*Seyahatname*' (Rifaa et-Tahtavi, *Tercüme-i Rıhlet-i Rifaa*, 7).
54. et-Tahtavi, *Tercüme-i Rıhlet-i Rifaa*, 15.
55. al-Ṭaḥṭāwī, 'Takhlīṣ al-ibrīz', 2: 23.
56. et-Tahtavi, *Tercüme-i Rıhlet-i Rifaa*, 10.
57. al-Ruṣāfī, 'Daf^{c} al-hujna', 2: 170.
58. Zeki Megamiz's other translations of Jurjī Zaydān's works include *Ebu Müslim-i Horasani* (translation of *Abū Muslim al-Khurāsānī*, 1914/15), *Cihan Hatun, Fergane Güzeli* (translation of *^{c}Arūs Farghāna*, 1927) and *Selahaddin-i Eyyubi ve İsmaililer* (translation of *Ṣalāḥ al-Dīn al-Ayyūbī*, 1927). Two of these translations, *Cihan Hatun Fergane Güzeli* and *Selahaddin-i Eyyubi ve İsmaililer* were produced after the Ottoman Empire's demise.
59. Jurjī Zaydān, *Tārīkh al-tamaddun al-islāmī* (Cairo: Maṭba^{c}at al-Hilāl, 1902), 1: 18.
60. Ibid., 1: 18.
61. Corci Zeydan, *Medeniyet-i İslamiyye Tarihi*, trans. Zeki Megamiz (Istanbul: İkdam Matbaası, 1912/13), 1: 19.
62. Zeydan, *Medeniyet-i İslamiyye Tarihi*, 1: 19.
63. Zaydān, *Tārīkh al-tamaddun*, 1: 24.
64. Zeydan, *Medeniyet-i İslamiyye Tarihi*, 1: 26.
65. Ilham Khuri-Makdisi and Yorgos Dedes, 'Translating Qasim Amin's Arabic *Tahrir al-mar$^{\supset}$a* (1899) into Ottoman Turkish', in *Ottoman Translations: Circulating Texts from Bombay to Paris*, ed. Marilyn Booth and Claire Savina (Edinburgh: Edinburgh University Press, 2023), 252.
66. İhsan Fazlıoğlu, 'Osmanlı Döneminde "Bilim" Alanında Türkçe Telif ve Tercüme Eserlerin Türkçe Oluş Nedenleri ve Bu Eserlerin Dil Bilincinin Oluşmasındaki Yeri ve Önemi', *Kutadgubilig* 3 (2003): 172.
67. While al-Ruṣāfī emphasised the need to protect the Arabic language from foreign influences, Rebecca Gould has demonstrated that translators in the early Islamic tradition who translated from Arabic to Persian did not aim to make their translations accessible to a large audience, since they translated

for an intelligentsia familiar with both source and target languages. In fact, they kept some of the words untranslated. As Rebecca Gould has put it, '[w]hile modern linguistics commonly understands language as a form of communication, neither al-Jurjānī's *naẓm* nor Rādūyānī's *naql* deploy language for the purpose of communication. In Islamic literary culture, translation was available to make foreignness legible'. Rebecca Gould, 'Inimitability versus Translatability: The Structure of Literary Meaning in Arabo-Persian Poetics', *The Translator* 19, no. 1 (2013): 99–100.

68. For an extensive documentation of how al-Ruṣāfī intertextualises modern Turkish literature, see Erol Ayyıldız, *Irak Şiirinde Yeni Türk Edebiyatı Tesiri* (Bursa: Uludağ Üniversitesi İlahiyat Fakültesi, n. d.), 36–54.
69. Namık Kemal, *Rüya ve Magosa Mektubu* (Egypt: Matbaa-i İctihad, 1908), 29. For another explication of *Rüya*, see İsmail Parlatır, 'Rüya'nın Fikir Örgüsü', *Doğumunun Yüzellinci Yılında Namık Kemal* (Ankara: Atatürk Kültür Merkezi Yayınları, 1993), 59–66.
70. Maʿrūf al-Ruṣāfī, 'al-Ruʾyā fī baḥth al-ḥurriya', in *Āthāruhu fī al-naqd wa-l-adab*, ed. Dāwūd Sallūm, ʿĀdil Kuttāb Naṣīf al-ʿAzzāwī and ʿAbd al-Ḥamīd al-Rashūdī (Beirut: Manshūrāt al-Jamal, 2014), 3: 631.
71. al-Ruṣāfī, 'Dafʿ al-hujna', 2: 159.
72. al-Ruṣāfī, 'Dafʿ al-hujna', 2: 187.
73. al-Ruṣāfī, 'al-Ruʾyā fī baḥth al-ḥurriya', 3: 633.
74. Namık Kemal, *Rüya ve Magosa Mektubu*, 33.
75. al-Ruṣāfī, 'Dafʿ al-hujna', 2: 187.
76. Namık Kemal, *Rüya ve Magosa Mektubu*, 23.
77. al-Ruṣāfī, 'al-Ruʾyā fī baḥth al-ḥurriya', 3: 628.
78. Namık Kemal, *Rüya ve Magosa Mektubu*, 25.
79. al-Ruṣāfī, 'al-Ruʾyā fī baḥth al-ḥurriya', 3: 629.
80. al-Ruṣāfī, 'Dafʿ al-hujna', 2: 163.
81. al-Ruṣāfī, 'al-Ruʾyā fī baḥth al-ḥurriya', 3: 626.
82. Aslı Niyazioglu, *Dreams and Lives in Ottoman Istanbul: A Seventeenth Century Biographer's Perspective* (New York: Routledge, 2017), 80.
83. Erol Ayyıldız, *Arapça Bir Rü'ya Fantezisi, Tercemesi ve Namık Kemal'in 'Rü'ya'sı ile Mukayesesi* (Bursa: Uludağ Üniversitesi İlahiyat Fakültesi, n. d.), 1. For example, al-Ruṣāfī's 'al-Nashīd al-waṭanī' (Homeland Anthem) has intertextual references to Tevfik Fikret's 'Vatan Şarkısı' (Homeland Anthem), just as al-Ruṣāfī's 'Fī maṭbakh al-dustūr' (In the Constitution Kitchen) includes intertextual references to Tevfik Fikret's 'Han-ı Yağma' (The Restaurant of Plunder). See Maʿrūf al-Ruṣāfī, 'Al-Nashīd al-waṭanī', *Dīwān al-Ruṣāfī*, 5: 479–81; Maʿrūf al-Ruṣāfī, 'Fī maṭbakh al-dustūr', *Dīwān al-Ruṣāfī*, 5: 393; Tevfik Fikret, 'Vatan Şarkısı', *Rübab-ı Şikeste* (Istanbul: Tanin Matbaası, 1910/11), 305–6; Tevfik Fikret, 'Han-ı Yağmâ', *Rübâb-ı Şikeste ve Tevfik Fikret'in Bütün Diğer Eserleri*, ed. Fahri Uzun (Istanbul: İnkilâp Kitabevi, 1985), 36–37.
84. Namık Kemal, *Rüya ve Magosa Mektubu*, 39.

85. al-Ruṣāfī, ‘al-Ruʾyā fī baḥth al-ḥurriya’, 3: 637.
86. Maᶜrūf al-Ruṣāfī, *Dīwān al-Ruṣāfī* (Beirut: Maṭbaᶜat Dār al-Maᶜraḍ, 1931), 399; al-Ruṣāfī, *Dīwān al-Ruṣāfī* (1975), 3: 320; and Maᶜrūf al-Ruṣāfī, *Dīwān al-Ruṣāfī*, ed. Muṣṭafā al-Saqqā (Cairo: Dār al-Fikr al-ᶜArabī, 1953), 420. As I also indicate in note 24, I use the 1972–77 edition throughout the chapter whenever I quote al-Ruṣāfī’s poetry.
87. See Muḥammad Ḥāmid Sālim, ‘Rithāʾ al-mudun bayna al-shāᶜir al-turkī Sulaymān Naẓīf wa-l-ᶜirāqī Maᶜrūf al-Ruṣāfī: “Baghdād” numūdhajan’, *Majallat al-Dirāsāt al-Sharqiyya* 57 (2016): 441–523, and Ayyıldız, *Irak Şiirinde Yeni Türk Edebiyatı Tesiri*, 53. While this chapter points out similarities between these two particular poems, I also compare ‘Nuwāḥ Dijla’ with *Firak-ı Irak*, of which ‘Dicle ve Ben’ was a part. Since al-Ruṣāfī personally knew Süleyman Nazif, he was likely familiar with Süleyman Nazif’s works.
88. Süleyman Nazif, *Firak-ı Irak* (Istanbul: Mahmud Bey Matbaası, 1918), 62–63.
89. Süleyman Nazif, *Firak-ı Irak*, 34–53.
90. Ibid., 13.
91. Ibid., 65–66.
92. Ibid., 19–20.
93. Ibid., 22–23. The translation of Kaᶜb ibn Zuhayr’s verse is from Suzanne Pinckney Stetkevych, *The Mantle Odes: Arabic Praise Poems to the Prophet Muḥammad* (Bloomington: Indiana University Press, 2010), 38.
94. Süleyman Nazif, *Firak-ı Irak*, 24.
95. Ibid., 26.
96. Ibid., 27.
97. al-Ruṣāfī, ‘Nuwāḥ Dijla’, *Dīwān al-Ruṣāfī* (1975), 3: 320–21. For the Arabic source text and the poem’s English translation, see C. Ceyhun Arslan, ‘Kaᶜb ibn Zuhayr Weeps for Sultan Murad IV: Baghdad, Heritage and the Ottoman Empire in Maᶜrūf al-Ruṣāfī’s Poetry’, in *The Routledge Handbook of Arabic Poetry*, ed. Suzanne Pinckney Stetkevych and Huda J. Fakhreddine (London: Routledge, 2024), 207–209.
98. Hussein N. Kadhim, *The Poetics of Anti-Colonialism in the Arabic* Qaṣīda (Leiden: Brill, 2004), 106.
99. Translated and quoted in Kadhim, *The Poetics of Anti-Colonialism*, 91. For the Arabic poem, see al-Ruṣāfī, ‘Baᶜda al-Nuzūḥ’, 3: 137–42.
100. al-Ruṣāfī, ‘Nuwāḥ Dijla’, 3: 322.
101. Ibid., 3: 324.
102. Kadhim, *The Poetics of Anti-Colonialism*, 130.
103. al-Ruṣāfī, ‘Nuwāḥ Dijla’, 3: 322.
104. Ibid., 3: 323.
105. Ibid., 3: 324.

5

From 'Ottoman Literature is Arabic Literature' to 'Arabs Possess a Literature': Hacı İbrahim, Ahmet Rasim and the Fetters of Influence

In his memoir, Ahmet Rasim (1864–1932) wrote about the moment when he learned that Hacı İbrahim (1826–88) would be his literature instructor. He noted that the term 'literature' was like a newly invented term back then.[1] Likewise, Recaizade Mahmud Ekrem (1847–1914) wrote at the beginning of his *Talim-i Edebiyat* (Textbook on Literature, AH 1296 [1878/79]) that no one had provided a definition of 'literature' or written a history of it, although it had become one of the most frequently used words over the past few years.[2] Both authors described literature as something new and 'modern'.

This chapter will reveal the similarities between what has been studied as two opposing camps among late Ottoman authors – that is, defenders of 'old literature' and of 'new literature'. Even writers who vehemently opposed Westernisation did not hesitate to use the 'modern' category of literature in their works. Some authors who defended the 'old literature' claimed that one should adore the Arabic language and that the Ottomans had added nothing new to Arabic language or literature. In fact, as this chapter will show, an anonymous author in the newspaper *Malumat* (Information) even suggested that Ottoman literature was Arabic literature. Those who defended the 'new literature' emphasised that Turks were not Arabs and hence Ottoman literature was not Arabic literature. Although both sides seemed to advocate arguments that contradicted each other, their works capture the influence paradigm that depicts Arabic literature as a source of influence which one should either adore or shun.

Furthermore, even late Ottoman Turkish works that defend the need for Ottomans to learn and read Arabic or that advance the claim that Ottoman literature is ultimately Arabic literature very rarely, if ever, make references to 'Ottoman Arabic works' – that is, Arabic works written during their lifetime. As this chapter will show, when late Ottoman Turkish works discuss Arabic literature, they tend to draw more on pre-Ottoman works such as Imruʾ al-Qays's (d. c. 550) *Muʿallaqa* ode than on *nahḍa* writings which also feature extensive discussions of Arabic culture and language. Even Ahmet Rasim's work on the 'civilisational development of Arabs' makes no reference to the *nahḍa*, although many *nahḍa* authors claimed that Arab civilisation was progressing during their lifetime.[3]

The first section of this chapter will analyse Hacı İbrahim's works. Although Hacı İbrahim has been studied as a 'conservative thinker' who resisted modernisation, I will reveal similarities between Hacı İbrahim and other 'modern' authors. The second section wil point out a 'contradiction': while the newspaper *Malumat* on its pages features photos from late Ottoman Syria, the same pages do not present articles on the cultural, political and economic transformations in the Ottoman Syrian provinces, but excerpts from pre-Ottoman Arabic poems and their Turkish explications. Although one may interpret pre-modern poems as signifiers of tradition and photos as signifiers of modernity, I claim that both photos and poetry excerpts capture the key shifts of the late Ottoman period: whereas the photos reveal that the Ottoman provinces became an object of the gaze for Ottoman readers, pre-Ottoman Arabic poems testify to a moment when Arabic works are seen as 'translatable' for the same readers. The final section will focus on Ahmet Rasim's translation of the Orientalist Gustave Le Bon's (1841–1931) *La Civilisation des Arabes* (The Arab Civilisation, 1884). Ahmet Rasim's translation omits Le Bon's remarks about the Turks's 'indebtedness' to the Arabs; however, Ahmet Rasim translated and hence transmitted Le Bon's view that literature ultimately is a possession to which communities such as the Arabs lay claim.

The Ottoman Diet: Al-Mutanabbī's Poems as Iron Chickpeas

Hacı İbrahim has been studied as a 'conservative' intellectual who defended 'old literature' and resisted the *Tanzimat*.[4] Even late Ottoman authors tended to categorise Hacı İbrahim as a supporter of the 'old literature'. For example, Ahmet Rasim noted that, when he was a student at the *Darüşşafaka* school, his class witnessed a divide between those who supported Ahmet Midhat ('new literature') and those who supported Hacı İbrahim ('old literature').[5] Supporters of Hacı İbrahim accused Ahmet Midhat of eating pork and advocating Darwin's ideas.[6] According to Hacı İbrahim, writers such as Ahmet Midhat thought that, if a community needed to progress, it had to hate anything related to the Arabs and adore everything related to Europe.[7]

Born in Tophane, Istanbul, Hacı İbrahim was the son of İsmail Efendi, the butler of Şerif Pasha.[8] After the Ottoman administration appointed Şerif Pasha as governor of the Hijaz province, Hacı İbrahim spent the earlier years of his life in Mecca, where he learned Arabic. He then worked in various administrative positions in Istanbul and Erzurum and retired in 1882. After retirement, however, Hacı İbrahim continued to teach classes at various institutions. Sultan Abdülhamid II (r. 1876–1909) appointed him as literature instructor at the *Mekteb-i Mülkiyye* (School of Administration). He also taught courses on composition and rhetoric (*belagat*) at the *Darüşşafaka* (where Ahmet Rasim took classes from him) and courses on oratory skills and Ottoman rhetoric at the *Mekteb-i Hukuk* (Law School). He founded a two-year private secondary school, *Darüttaalim*, which aimed to teach students Arabic in an accelerated fashion. The school became highly popular; even Muslims from Russia attended the *Darüttaalim* to learn Arabic. He engaged in controversial debates on language and literature with many thinkers of his time, such as Recaizade Mahmud Ekrem and Ahmet Midhat.

An article in the 1115th issue of the newpaper *Tercüman-ı Hakikat* (Interpreter of Truth), titled 'Belagat-ı Osmaniyye' (Ottoman Rhetoric), insisted that a Turk could not be expected to appreciate Arabic poetry because a prominent Arab poet compared camel dung to black pepper: 'Is it an abomination if a Turk finds nothing admirable when one of the prominent Arab poets finds beauty in camel dung, compares it to black pepper in terms of its blackness and records it in his poem?'[9] Hacı İbrahim responded to this particular question in his article in the 1121st issue of the *Tercüman-ı Hakikat*. First, Hacı İbrahim inquired which Arab poet had composed such a work that compared camel dung to black pepper. He also emphasised that both Turkish and non-Turkish poets could write about abominable (*müstekreh*) things and that it was merely a matter of taste rather than the quality of the work if someone did not enjoy reading poems dealing with abominable issues.[10]

Hacı İbrahim later discussed the 'Ottoman diet': he emphasised that his readers liked both Çamlıca water and Zemzem/Zamzam water; likewise, both Çavuş grapes – a particular grape variety that grows in the Marmara and Central Anatolian regions today – and Medina dates taste delicious to an Ottoman. Hacı İbrahim claimed that people who ate no meat or cheese had come into this world, but this did not mean that people should be banned from eating meat or cheese.[11] In a similar vein, those who found an Arabic poem abominable could not prevent other people from consuming Arabic poetry. Hacı İbrahim wrote about the Arabic lessons that students at the *Mekteb-i Sultaniyye* took for two days every week. These students learned the conjugation of Arabic verbs. As a result, they could understand the poems of Abū Tammām (d. 845/46) and al-Mutanabbī (d. 965), whose works were seen as 'roasted chickpeas made of iron' (*demirden leblebi*) due to their great difficulty.[12] While the *Tercüman-ı Hakikat* may have suggested that it was not natural for an Ottoman reader to read al-Mutanabbī's work, which 'may break one's teeth',[13] Hacı İbrahim insisted that simple education in Arabic could help students to consume them easily. For Hacı İbrahim, al-Mutanabbī was part of an Ottoman's 'natural diet'.

The following description of the Ottoman language by Hacı İbrahim further reinforces his view of Arabic poems as part of the natural diet of an Ottoman subject, as it also resonates with Ziya Pasha's description of the Ottoman ocean:

> Lemonade, which is something everyone always drinks, is composed of water, lemon and sugar. Each of these three things is a reality of its own. Lemonade cannot turn into sugar; water cannot turn into sugar; and sugar cannot turn into any of these things. But, when these three things mix with each other, they turn into lemonade. Likewise, our language is composed of Arabic, Turkish and Persian, and each of them has a nature of its own. Arabic cannot turn into Turkish, Turkish cannot turn into Arabic. Persian cannot turn into any of them. Yet, mixing and blending these three languages gives rise to the Ottoman language.[14]

Ottoman Turkish articles on Arabic poetry often end up being about what it means to be an Ottoman subject and the texts which constitute a part of this subject's 'diet'.[15]

A later article in the 1130th issue of *Tercüman-ı Hakikat* indicates that the 'prominent Arab poet' that the newspaper referred to in its 1115th issue was Imruᵓ al-Qays. At the same time, the anonymous author of the article also admitted his mistake: Imruᵓ al-Qays had not referred to camel dung; instead, he wrote about antelope dung. He then quoted Imruᵓ al-Qays's verse:

> There, in desolate courtyards and in empty plains
> You see droppings of white antelope scattered
> like seeds of pepper.[16]

In response, Hacı İbrahim pointed out that these lines might not belong to Imruᵓ al-Qays since they were not recorded in al-Zawzanī's (d. 1093) *Sharḥ al-Zawzanī* and Abū al-Fatḥ al-ᶜAbbāsī's (1463–1556) *Maᶜāhid al-tanṣīṣ*. Furthermore, he claimed that the metre of this verse did not conform to the metre of the other verses in the same poem. Hacı İbrahim indicated that, even if Imruᵓ al-Qays had actually composed these lines, one should not find fault in them: a strongly infatuated person could naturally compare something valuable with camel dung. If an Arab quoted the Turkish proverb 'Compared to shit, dung is like a pure ambergris' (*boka nisbetle tezek amber-i sara gibidir*), then the Turks had nothing to say in order to defend themselves. Therefore, one could not claim that Turks and Arabs were different simply because Imruʾ al-Qays wrote about dung.[17]

Recaizade Mahmud Ekrem criticised Hacı İbrahim, who had quoted a verse from the *jāhiliyya* poet Zuhayr ibn Abī Sulmā (c. 520–c. 609) in order to attack Recaizade Mahmud Ekrem's views on *istiare* (figure of speech), since *Talim-i Edebiyat* was about Ottoman and not Arabic literature.[18] Still, Hacı İbrahim continued to criticise Recaizade Mahmud Ekrem; in fact, he claimed that *Talim-i Edebiyat* simply borrowed the definition of the term 'literature' from French sources:

> What is meant by 'scholars' [*erbab-ı tedkik*] in the 'Preface' [*kable'ş-şuru*] section is the scholars of France. The definition of 'literature' in French literature books is like how the author himself defined it. This means that there is no contradiction when the author first notes that 'we have not come across a definition that is worthy of the literati' and then that 'this is how the literati define it' because this definition [of literature] belongs to France. After all, it is a matter of cultural differences. Likewise, do not believe in *Talim-i Edebiyat* when it claims in its preface: 'I did not show any hesitation when transmitting foreign scholarly works that are compatible with us'. Entire sections of the book are taken from them.[19]

Musa Aksoy has observed that Recaizade Mahmud Ekrem did not disagree with Hacı İbrahim.[20] In other words, Hacı İbrahim pointed out that Recaizade Mahmud Ekrem not only borrowed Western forms, but also the term 'literature' itself.

Although he criticised Recaizade Mahmud Ekrem for borrowing ideas from France, Hacı İbrahim himself made references to Orientalist works while discussing Ottoman and Arabic literatures. He also advocated some 'modern' ideas: first, he sometimes described Ottoman language as Arabic language. Second, he stressed the difficulty of learning Arabic. Finally, he put strong emphasis on the need to translate Arabic into Turkish. Hacı İbrahim occasionally claimed that he saw no difference between the Arabic and Ottoman languages, even if this claim contradicted his description of the Ottoman language as a 'lemonade' that mixed Arabic, Turkish and Persian. In fact, according to Hacı İbrahim, anyone who claimed that Ottoman and Arabic were separate languages wanted the empire to be partitioned.[21] In response to an anonymous author in *Tercüman-ı Hakikat* who insisted that the Arabic language was different from the Ottoman language, Hacı İbrahim noted that the actual literary language of Ottomans was Arabic:

> The perfect and complete version of our language is the Arabic language. Hence, from this point of view, it can be said that the Arabic language and the Ottoman language are the same thing and differ only in terms of grammar. Therefore, one should devote oneself to learning Arabic grammar in an enthusiastic manner. Those who do not know Arabic grammar will not receive their share of literature, and their writings will not be devoid of faults and mistakes.[22]

Three supporters of Hacı İbrahim, Faik, Esad and Ali Sedad, wrote another article for *Ceride-i Havadis*, in which they insisted that the Ottomans should protect Arabic, since Arabic was a key tenet of their language.[23] An article in the newspaper *Malumat* claimed that Ottoman literature meant Arabic literature because the Ottoman and Arabic languages shared the same terms, just as Ottoman grammar was based on Arabic grammar: 'Now I want attention to this point, O readers! [. . .] At this point, no one doubts that Ottoman literature means Arabic literature if this matter is examined from a number of angles'.[24] According to this statement, the 'fact' that Ottoman literature is Arabic literature is not a subjective supposition; it is a truth that anyone can discover when examining the issue from multiple angles.

Hacı İbrahim also sometimes emphasised that it was difficult to 'master' Arabic: 'No one – including children and adults – knows Arabic literature, and even Arabs who serve literature [*edebiyata hizmet eden Araplar*], even if their language is Arabic, do not have full mastery of Arabic literature'.[25] These words express that one can never master Arabic literature and experience a sense of superiority *vis-à-vis* Arabic. In a similar vein, in the 1599th issue of the newspaper *Tarık*, Hacı İbrahim described Arabic literature as an ocean that no one has ever crossed from one end to the other and Arabic as '[our] literary language' (*lisan-ı edebîmiz*).[26] These statements do not reinforce the notion that Ottoman language or literature is more elevated than Arabic language or literature. Nor do they suggest that the Arabic language is merely one river feeding the Ottoman ocean. Therefore, Arabic literature turns into a challenge that authors need to overcome, rather than a stream that contributes to the construction of the Ottoman language. The use of the imagery of a journey is also key here: one needs to cross the Arabic ocean from one end to the other; the ocean turns into an insurmountable challenge rather than a signifier of imperial grandeur. The Ottomans needed Arabic because the Ottoman language was lacking significantly, and Arabic helped the Ottomans to overcome this lack.

Hacı İbrahim also noted that many read and perhaps even understood Arabic poems; however, they could not translate them. Hacı İbrahim considered the ability to translate as a criterion for one's mastery of the Arabic language. According to him, only readers who fully understood a text could successfully translate it. He defined the term 'reading' in the following manner: 'What we mean by reading here is not to read something on a surface level and understand it; rather, it is to understand something and have the ability to translate it'.[27] While earlier Ottoman Turkish authors may not even have felt the need to translate Arabic works, Hacı İbrahim posited translation as the ultimate skill that a person knowing Arabic should have.

Several students who graduated from Hacı İbrahim's school *Darüttaalim* published important translations. For example, Hersekli Hacı Mehmed Kamil Bey (d. 1900) published the Turkish translations of the *Muᶜallaqāt* in *Tercüme-i Muallakat-ı Seba* (Translation of the Seven *Muᶜallaqāt*, AH 1305 [1887/88]). Likewise, Midillili Ali Fuad (1878–1957) published the Turkish translation of Ibn al-Jawzī's (c. 1116–1201) *Kitāb al-Adhkiyāʾ* (Book of the Intelligent) when he was only fifteen years old. Hacı İbrahim himself wrote that, if fifteen-year old children could read and translate works of Arabic literature such as *Muḥādarāt* and *Maqāmāt* and works of Ottoman literature such as Veysi's (1561/62–1628) and Baki's (1526–1600) poems with ease, then grown-ups who could not translate *Muḥādarāt* and *Maqāmāt* should feel proud of the youngster rather than jealous.[28] He claimed that only ten or fifteen people in Istanbul – most of them his students – could translate al-Rāghib's (d. 1108/9) *Muḥādarāt*.[29]

İbrahim Avni, one of Hacı İbrahim's students, described the examination process that Hacı İbrahim conducted for his students in the newspaper *Tarık*: İbrahim Avni read excerpts from al-Ḥarīrī's (d. 1122) *Maqāmāt*, while Faziletlü Bekir Efendi, another student, read eight pages from the Alexandrian *Maqāmāt* and translated three pages from it.[30] Likewise, Sadık Bey asked a student of the *Darüttaalim* to translate some lines from al-Ḥarīrī's *Maqāmāt* and then explicate some lines from Nefi's (d. 1635) 'July *kaside*'. Whenever a student could translate al-Ḥarīrī's *Maqāmāt* into Turkish, everyone felt great joy.[31] When another student could accurately translate some Arabic verses into Turkish, Münif Pasha 'cried from happiness'.[32]

Various articles in late Ottoman journals, such as *Servet-i Fünun* (Wealth of Arts and Sciences) and *Malumat*, also showed significant engagement with issues related to Arabic–Turkish translations. For example, the 157th issue of the newspaper *Malumat* included an article on mistakes in '*Bedayi-i Arap*' (Marvels of Arabs), a section in the

Servet-i Fünun that provided Turkish translations of excerpts from Arabic poems.[33] The author of the 'Sual' (Question) section in the 164th issue of *Malumat* indicated that the newspaper had received a letter that pointed out the mistakes in the newspaper's translations from Arabic to Turkish. As a result, the author once again wrote down both the original Arabic source text and its Turkish translation to leave it up to the readers to decide whether *Malumat*'s translations were accurate.[34] In the 169th issue, another author identified translation mistakes in excerpts from Maᶜarrī's poetry. For example, he noted that the Arabic term '*abītu*' had been translated as '*gece gündüz*' (day and night) rather than as '*gecelemek*' (to spend the night).[35]

In addition to putting emphasis on the need to accurately translate Arabic into Turkish, Hacı İbrahim's works display another 'modern' character that one does not necessarily find in early modern Ottoman works: Hacı İbrahim made the kind of comparisons that Chapter 2 has laid out, which posited the relationship between Arabic and Ottoman as akin to the relationship between ancient Greek or Latin and French. He also made references to Orientalist works in order to validate his claims. Hacı İbrahim defended why one should use the term 'Ottoman literature' rather than 'Turkish literature': 'Europeans call literary books written in our language (*littérature ottomane*), which means [in our language] 'Ottoman literature', rather than (*littérature turque*)'.[36] Hacı İbrahim used recently invented terms such as literature and drew examples from Orientalist scholarship.

According to Hacı İbrahim, the Ottomans, like people from the West, should *adore* Arabic literature. Hacı İbrahim claimed that, while Western people 'elevate[d] Arabic to the skies with their praise, [Ottomans brought] it to the ground with their criticism'.[37] Western authors picked eloquent expressions from Arabic literature and described them as good examples of world literature. However, Hacı İbrahim noted that they looked down on Ottoman works: 'What do they understand from your gibberish! If some [European] newspapers have discussed your nonsense works, it is not for a serious matter. They were only having fun with carefree people like you'.[38] The high praise for the Arabs in Orientalist scholarship sometimes caused some intellectuals such as al-Ṭahṭāwī to overlook the unequal power dynamics underlying a global system shaped by Western European hegemony.[39] Hacı İbrahim's adoration for Arabic, too, does not have to be interpreted as a sign of 'conservatism' or 'resistance against modernity', as he gave examples from Orientalist writings when justifying why Ottomans 'ought to praise' Arabic. While Hacı İbrahim expressed his frustration towards other Ottoman authors, he never overtly questioned Western Orientalists who made specific value judgments on Ottoman and Arabic literatures. Hacı İbrahim did not openly criticise the unequal power dynamics of the global system, as he did with the proponents of the 'new literature'.

Furthermore, Hacı İbrahim noted that, just as the French learned Latin to understand the essence of philosophy and mathematics, '[the Ottomans] also need[ed] to learn Arabic in order to understand the essence of science'. According to him, the Ottomans were not as nationalist as the Greeks, since the Greeks studied Homer (c. eighth–twelfth century BC) and other ancient writers; the French learned Latin in order to understand their own language.[40] In a similar vein, he insisted that the Ottomans, like their Western counterparts, needed to learn Arabic in order to understand Ottoman. Like the authors discussed in Chapter 2, Hacı İbrahim noted that, much like the French needed to learn Greek and Latin in order to understand the essence of French, one needed to learn Arabic in order to understand the essence of the Ottoman language.

On the one hand, Hacı İbrahim posited a strong distinction between East and West or Ottoman literature and French literature. On the other hand, his engagement with Orientalist scholarship shaped his perception of the relationship between Arabic and Ottoman. In order to substantiate his argument that Ottomans needed to learn Arabic, Hacı İbrahim emphasised in many of his articles that the French needed to learn Latin and ancient Greek. For instance, Hacı İbrahim quoted an anynonmous writer in *Tercüman-ı Hakikat* who claimed that 'one can find only 40 people among 40 million French people [. . .] who would feel a sense of lack because they do not know ancient Greek and Latin'.[41] Hacı İbrahim responded to this author by discussing an official French decree (*kararname-i resmiyye*) published on 24 July 1874. According to this decree, the exam on literature in French high schools (*mekteb-i sultaniyye*) tested students's knowledge on French, Latin and Greek literatures. He referred to this law to substantiate his view that a significant number of French citizens could read Greek and Latin. He then noted that a member of the French Academy claimed that Latin constituted the essence of French.[42]

Hacı İbrahim's adoration for Arabic was not 'traditional', and his works argue for a new relationship with the Arabic heritage that one does not necessarily see in earlier Ottoman Turkish works. Late Ottoman Turkish works often describe Arabic literature either as an object the superiority of which should be adored or a master whose influence should be shunned. As the Ottomans' relationship with the Arabic heritage was reconfigured along Western and European lines, proponents of 'old literature' sometimes posited Ottoman literature as Arabic literature – and nothing more.

Furthermore, as *jāhiliyya* poets such as Zuhayr ibn Abī Sulmā and Imruʾ al-Qays were 'deracinated' from their original context, they found 'a new life' as their works became a central component in discussions about language, literature and modernisation in Ottoman Turkish writings. At the same time, *nahḍa* works, such as Zaydān's *Tārīkh ādāb al-lugha al-ᶜarabiyya* (1911–14), were rarely mentioned in debates on Arabic language in Ottoman Turkish writings. As an exception to this rule, the 174th issue of the newspaper *Malumat* included a section titled 'Felicitious News for the Lovers of True Progress!' (*Terakkiyat-ı Ciddiye Muhibbanına Müjde!*). This section announced that *Malumat* had translated Jurjī Zaydān's *al-Alfāẓ al-ᶜarabiyya wa-l-falsafa al-lughawiyya* (Arabic Expressions and the Philosophy of Language, 1886) into Turkish. The anonymous author described Jurjī Zaydān with the following words:

> This book is the work of a young Arab [*civan-ı Arabiyye*], whose name is Jurjī Zaydān Efendi. He is an Ottoman writer who is a member of the Congress of Orientalists and whose deep erudition in all sciences on Arabic literature is already well established through his work on that matter. He has been publishing for many years the scientific journal *al-Hilāl* in Egypt. Zaydān has quickly prepared and presented his work to Orientalists. For his work, he received immense praise that is worthy of his reputation.[43]

This is one of the few instances in which an Ottoman Turkish newspaper made a reference to a *nahḍa* author. As the author discussed Zaydān's contributions to diverse sciences in Arabic literature, he emphasised that Zaydān was an authoritative figure because Orientalists had accepted and understood the importance of his work. At the same time, Hacı İbrahim, like many other authors who wrote in Ottoman Turkish, did not give reference to Zaydān's works when discussing works on Arabic language and literature. Debates on Arabic language and literature in late Ottoman Turkish works revolved around *jāhiliyya* poems more so than around *nahḍa* works such as Zaydān's *Tārīkh ādāb al-lugha al-ᶜarabiyya.*

Literature as a Matter of Debts and Transactions

To further flesh out this indifference towards 'Ottoman Arabic' works in Ottoman Turkish writings, this section will examine works by Ahmet Rasim as well as the poems and photos in the newspaper *Malumat*. Like Ahmet Midhat, Ahmet Rasim had been raised in a modest socioeconomic milieu. He became acquainted with important literary and social movements in the Ottoman Empire after he attended the *Darüşşafaka* School in 1876. He graduated as valedictorian in 1883 and worked as civil servant in the Mail and Telegraph Division. The newspaper *Malumat* sent him to Syria during the German Emperor Wilhelm II's (r. 1888–1918) expedition in 1898; later, in 1916, the newspaper *Sabah* sent him to Romania. He was eventually elected as parliament member in 1927. Ahmet Rasim was a prolific writer; he wrote more than a hundred works.

Ahmet Midhat praised Ahmet Rasim since his works 'put to shame wine and tavern poets'.[44] While Ahmet Midhat here marked Ahmet Rasim as an advocate of the 'new literature' who distanced himself from 'tavern poets', Ahmet Rasim himself noted that the 'old literature' had not disappeared; one could still find it in taverns: 'The tavern belongs to the poet' (*meyhane şairindir*).[45] Ahmet Rasim himself noted that, as fewer newspapers published works of old literature, they were recited in establishments serving alcohol (*işretgâh*).[46] According to him, he could 'touch with his hands and body the spiritual manifestations of his ancestors' in taverns, although one could never meet these ancestors in 'western-style beer houses' (*alafranga birahaneler*).[47]

Ahmet Rasim indeed was familiar with the canon of the Ottoman literati. He noted that some of his favourite authors were Victor Hugo (1802–85), Lamartine (1790–1869), Voltaire (1694–1778), Delile (1738–1813), Alfred de Musset (1810–57), al-Maᶜarrī (973–1057), Ḥāfiẓ (c. 1315–c. 90), Shakespeare (1564–1616) and al-Mutanabbī (d. 965).[48] Ahmet Rasim, like many other late Ottoman intellectuals who defended the 'new literature', showed interest in Western European writers such as Lamartine and Shakespeare, but did not ignore authors of the 'Ottoman literary reservoir' such as al-Mutanabbī and Ḥāfiẓ. He listed al-Mutanabbī right after Schiller and before Racine. Therefore, just as he did not make a particular distinction between Eastern and Western authors, Ahmet Rasim did not make a strong distinction between classical and modern authors.

Ahmet Rasim witnessed crucial social and economic transformations during his lifetime. Just as he translated a work on 'the Arab civilisation', he also wrote about 'Arabs' in the different provinces of the empire. Just as he provided news on Taif, Egypt and Alexandria, Ahmet Rasim wrote about al-Shidyāq's (1805/6–87) newspaper *al-Jawāʾib*, which was published in Istanbul.[49] According to Ahmet Rasim, Ottomans were ignorant of international laws and regulations. Therefore, unless an uprising took place, people did not understand what was going on 'in Egypt, Yemen, Syria, Iraq, Kurdistan, Caucasia, Crimea, Bulgaria, Serbia, Wallachia and Montenegro'.[50]

Although the newspaper *Malumat* sent Ahmet Rasim to Syria, its issues provided little knowledge about the Syrian provinces to its readers; rather, it included photos taken during Wilhelm II's expedition there.[51] In fact, the issues and sometimes even the pages that feature photos from Ottoman Syria also feature pre-Ottoman Arabic poems. The 'Muktetafat' (Selected

Excerpts) section, which provides excerpts of these poems, does not list the poems in chronological order and almost never gives information on who wrote them. Rather, an author named Zeki (perhaps Zeki Megamiz, translator of Jurjī Zaydān's works) presented a Turkish explication of the Arabic excerpts. The author cared more about conveying each excerpt's meaning in Turkish than about offering exact information on its author and the date of its production.

The authors of these poetry excerpts became 'deracinated' from their original milieux and incorporated into a new context. For example, the 171st issue[52] includes excerpts by Maḥmūd al-Warrāq (d. c. 844/45),[53] Imām ᶜAlī ibn Abī Ṭālib (c. 600–661),[54] Imām al-Shāfiᶜī (767–820)[55] and al-Mutanabbī,[56] although it does not mention their names. In fact, it is one of the rare issues where the 'Muktetafat' section actually mentions the three authors whom it quotes – Ibn al-Wardī (1292–1349), Abū al-Faḍl al-Riyāshī (d. AH 257 [870/71]) and Ḥātim al-Ṭāʾī (d. c. 605) – in contrast to many other issues, such as the 164th issue, which mentions none of the authors it quotes.[57] None of these poets belonged to the *nahḍa* era. Furthermore, their excerpts are not listed in chronological order.

Other than 'Muktetafat', *Malumat* features another section titled 'Şemmet ül-Edeb' (The Smell of Literature), which includes excerpts from al-Maᶜarrī's *Luzūm mā lā yalzam* (The Obligation of What is Not Obligatory). Each excerpt is followed by its Turkish explication (*hülasa-i mana*).[58] This section was prepared by 'From Aleppo: Refet' (Haleb'den: Refet), showing that *Malumat* had readers and contributors from Aleppo. Refet stated that he had decided to write about al-Maᶜarrī's works to share pieces of wisdom with his readers.

At the same time, one finds only scant information about the Syrian lands in *Malumat*. Rather, the newspaper features numerous photos likely taken during Ahmet Rasim's expedition to the Syrian provinces. These photos put great emphasis on the empire's modernisation efforts, as they feature the German emperor's visits to factories, ports and railroads throughout the empire.[59] Other photos display various sites of worship in Ottoman Palestine and Syria, such as the Protestant church at Jerusalem,[60] Masjid al-Aqsa,[61] the Mosque of Omar[62] and the mosque that Sultan Selim I (r. 1512–20) had built.[63] Unlike *Malumat*, the newspaper *İkdam* gave a detailed account of the expedition. İsmail Zühdü, the journalist whom *İkdam* had sent to report on the German emperor's expedition, provided detailed information about the itinerary and often foregrounded the Ottoman Empire's progress when, for example, he praised the roads that the Ottomans had built.[64]

Most captions for images of Ottoman Palestine and Syria use the French term '*vue*' and the Turkish term '*manzara*', which both mean 'view'.[65] These captions suggest that Ottoman provinces became an object of the gaze, as the late Ottoman Empire underwent what Ahmet A. Ersoy has called 'a pictorial turn' in his analysis of photographs in journals that circulated throughout the empire, such as *Malumat*: 'The journals were, therefore, both a manifest sign and a powerful agent of the global culture of modernity. They testified to a new era that would come to be hegemonised by the image and which ushered in a volatile, visually intense and kaleidoscopic sense of the world informing daily experiences as well as historical imagination'.[66] This pictorial turn, according to Ersoy, signifies a key characteristic of Ottoman modernisation.

While photos in *Malumat* provide information on Ottoman Syria, sections on some pages with these photos present the reader with excerpts from pre-Ottoman Arabic works rather than articles on the Syrian provinces. At the same time, I claim that one does not have to interpret these pages featuring excerpts from pre-Ottoman Arabic poems and photos of Ottoman Syria as example of a paradox or clash between signifiers of tradition (classical poems) and signifiers of modernity (photos of Ottoman Syria and of the empire's factories and railroads). Rather, the 'Muktetafat' section can also be studied as a characteristic of Ottoman modernity, as it posits each Arabic excerpt as something that can be explicated in or translated into Turkish. It resonates with a context in which authors such as Hacı İbrahim also put strong emphasis on the need to translate Arabic works into Turkish, which ultimately contributed to the refashioning of the pre-modern Arabic heritage.[67]

Another article in *Malumat* constitutes a key example of this refashioning, as it claims that Kaᶜb ibn Zuhayr (d. c. 646/47) was such a good poet that he, like some European writers, spent one entire year to produce a single *qaṣīda* poem and sought feedback from other writers. However, Ottoman writers, unlike Zuhayr, cared more about quantity than quality; therefore, they produced too many works of horrible quality. The article thus suggests that, since Ottoman writers recently became more like European writers, they inevitably started to resemble Zuhayr as they were more diligent about their work. The author suggested that, as Ottoman authors 'Westernised', they could become more like Kaᶜb ibn Zuhayr.[68]

In addition to comparisons and translations between Arabic and Turkish, Orientalist discourse also contributed to a refashioning of the Arabic heritage. Orientalist works, such as Le Bon's *La Civilisation des Arabes*, often praised the Arabs at the expense of the Turks: if the Arabs represented the apex of language, literature and culture, then the Turks served as a foil who acted as a military force and produced nothing 'original' or 'authentic'. Instead, they 'borrowed everything from the Arabs'.

Many nineteenth-century Orientalist works on Ottoman poetry suggest that Arabic literature constituted its main source of influence. Dora d'Istria (1828–88) wrote: 'When one knows how rich Arabic literature is, one understands what a fortunate influence it must have had on those who studied Arabic'.[69] Elias John Wilkinson Gibb (1857–1901) used a language of economic transactions in describing literary relations: 'Here the Turks were borrowing what was itself a loan, as almost every detail connected with the structure of Persian verse had been adopted by the Persians from the Arabs'.[70] Carl Brockelmann (1868–1956) made the following remark about Arabic literature in Istanbul: 'Turkish literature in the nineteenth century experienced a great national awakening, which took special care of its national idiom, and thus displaced Arabic'.[71]

Another writer who expressed great admiration for Arabic literature was Gustave Le Bon, who, as Anne-Laure Dupont has remarked, was also highly popular among *nahḍa* figures such as Zaydān.[72] Le Bon noted that he consulted 'authentic' sources in order to substantiate the validity of his claims. *La Civilisation des Arabes* emphasises that its author had visited the places that he studied.[73] Its title page claims to use 'absolutely authentic' photographs and documents. Le Bon praised the accuracy of photographs over drawings: photos drew readers into the authentic setting of the Arabs.[74] Therefore, he wanted his readers to believe in the credibility of his claims about the Arabs.

At the same time, *La Civilisation des Arabes* was read not only by those who wanted to learn more about Arabs. When Fakhr-i Dāᶜī (d. 1964/65) translated Gustave Le Bon's *La Civilisation des Arabes* into Persian, he relied on Sayyid ᶜAlī Bilgrāmī's (1851–1911) Urdu translation of Le Bon's text. Fakhr-i Dāᶜī believed that his translations could contribute to 'the Iranian genius' and help Iranians have a better understanding of themselves.[75] Ahmet Rasim may also have had similar motivations and translated parts of *La Civilisation des Arabes* not only to introduce Arabs to his Ottoman readers, but also to guide his readers about how to progress. After all, Ahmet Rasim may have wanted to understand how the Arabs had 'achieved to create one of the most brilliant civilisations',[76] and he may have wanted his Ottoman readers to understand important aspects of this civilisation as they sought to modernise. It was not only Ahmet Rasim who engaged with Gustave Le Bon's works; late Ottoman writers such as Abdullah Cevdet (1869–1932), Abdurrahman Fehmi (d. 1904) and Mehmed Fuad Köprülü (1890–1966) also translated Gustave Le Bon's works or engaged with his ideas in their writings.[77]

For Le Bon, Ottomans learned Arabic and even sometimes wrote in Arabic, not because they wanted to signify their imperial grandeur, but because they experienced cultural inferiority *vis-à-vis* the Arabs. According to Le Bon, the Turks merely 'propagated the influence of [the Arabs]' (170),[78] since the Turks were 'impotent to create a civilisation' (*impuissants à créer une civilisation*) (640). Although the Turks 'politically replaced the Arabs in Egypt', their 'ethnographic influence was always null' (53). Therefore, Le Bon noted regarding diverse communities that had ruled 'the Orient' that, while their 'political influence has always been grand, their civilisational influence has generally been weak' (610). In contrast to the Turks, the Arabs 'very quickly created a civilisation that was extremely different from those who had preceded them' (116).

Likewise, Le Bon used a discourse of sovereignty as he discussed Turkish–Arab relations: although the Arabs may have lost political sovereignty over the past few centuries, 'their civilisation continued to reign' in Ottoman lands (128). Since the Turks had always beeen warriors, they did not have the qualities that allowed them to become civilised. He claimed that 'the entire Orient did nothing but imitate the Arabs, just as the Occident has imitated and continues to imitate the Greeks and Romans' (542). Le Bon made a similar observation on the Greeks and Romans: 'While they were the masters of the world, Romans never displayed an observable intellectual superiority in the arts or sciences. In regard to everything intellectual, the Greeks were their masters, even if the Romans had enslaved them' (671–72). Therefore, he insinuated that, even though the Ottomans may have politically ruled the Arabs, they merely served the Arabs. Le Bon thus emphasised that the Turks could never escape from the influence of the Arabs, as he wrote: 'Turks, Monghols etc. took their traditions and posited themselves as propagators of their [the Arabs'] influence throughout the entire world' (612).

In accordance with the rise of global capitalism that also characterised the late Ottoman period, Le Bon frequently used 'economic' terms such as 'possess', 'profit' and 'borrow' while describing literary and cultural interactions. One of the words that he frequently used was 'profit'. He noted that many communities that overthrew empires 'had profited from the civilisation of the people they had conquered' (60). Likewise, he indicated that 'each generation first profit[ed] from the treasures that earlier civilisations have accumulated' (539), before they added something new to it – that is, if they were capable to do so. Profit shaped one's relationship to earlier cultures: 'Arabs, Greeks, Romans, Phoenicians, Hebrews and so on, all of them, in one word, have profited from the past' (539–40). Likewise, Le Bon emphasised that the Turks attempted to 'profit from the heritage of those who preceded them' (130). He claimed that all the Turks could do was 'to profit arduously from what their subjects had possessed' (116). He later wrote: '[The Turks's] supreme effort was to try to profit from the subjects that they had under control. Sciences, arts, industry, commerce, they borrowed all of them from the Arabs [*Sciences, arts, industrie, commerce, ils ont tout emprunté aux Arabes*]. The Turks showed progress in none of the knowledge areas in which the Arabs shone' (640). Therefore, Le Bon's work viewed cultural interactions as a matter of profits and transactions.

In the beginning of his *Arapların Terakkiyat-ı Medeniyyesi*, which translates excerpts from *La Civilisation des Arabes*, Ahmet Rasim complained about the lack of Ottoman works on the Arab civilisation. Therefore, his book aimed to enlighten his readers about this civilisation of which they had little knowledge.[79] Ahmet Rasim did not translate Le Bon's claims that the Qur'an was 'quite incoherent' (94) and that Islam may be 'a more simplified version of Christianity' (102), since he, as a Muslim, likely did not agree with these statements. Ahmet Rasim, like the many other Ottoman authors that the edited volumes *Migrating Texts* and *Ottoman Translations* have examined,[80] selectively appropriated an Orientalist's remarks.

Arapların Terakkiyat-ı Medeniyyesi, Ahmet Rasim's translation, starts with the following statement: 'This book that I dared to publish, *The Civilisational Progress of Arabs*, is a work that came into existence as I compiled excerpts from *The Civilisation of Arabs*, which was recently written by one of the renowned French authors, Gustave Le Bon'.[81] Ahmet Rasim here noted that he 'dared' to publish this work because no Ottoman before had written a work on Arab civilisation. He then indicated that he used the means of *iltikat* to write this book. *İltikat* refers to the process of gathering information by consulting different books.[82] For example, Ahmet Rasim stated that the section on the Prophet Muḥammad was taken from Cevdet Pasha's (1823–95) *Kısas-ı Enbiya* (Stories of the Prophets) rather than from Gustave Le Bon's *La Civilisation des Arabes*.[83] He chose excerpts from Le Bon's work in a selective manner, noting that he only 'took excerpts' (*parça almak*) on the development of the Arab civilisation (*terakkiyat-ı medeniyye-i Arabiyye*) and discarded all the rest.[84] For instance, Ahmet Rasim left out those sections in which Le Bon argued that the Turks had borrowed everything from the Arabs. Although Le Bon claimed that the Turks suffered from decadence (640), Ahmet Rasim did not translate this particular statement.

Ahmet Rasim's work, like Le Bon's book, praised the Arabs: 'The Arabs are the most civilised and the most knowledgeable community'.[85] Ahmet Rasim also claimed that, although the Arabs enjoyed a significant civilisational advancement, their civilisation experienced decline and decadence.[86]

The book insinuates that the Ottomans should start to follow the 'civilisational progress' that the Arabs had shown during the Abbasid period. The *Tanzimat* then could be envisioned, not as a complete rupture from tradition, but instead as a re-enactment of the Abbasid period, when the Arabs had already demonstrated how one could achieve civilisational progress as they 'imitated' the Greeks and Iranians without giving up their authentic cultural essence. As intellectuals such as Ahmet Rasim became more invested in progress and civilisational advancement, they could also have seen Arab civilisation as a model to emulate. Therefore, on the one hand, the earlier ages of Arab civilisation became an object of desire for authors such as Ahmet Rasim; on the other hand, many Ottoman governors and writers saw the Arabs who lived in the Ottoman Empire as subjects who should become civilised and reformed, as Chapters 1 and 4 have shown in particular.

Like Le Bon, Ahmet Rasim described literature as an object of transaction and possession. He pointed out the strong relationship between civilisation and language. First, he wrote that Ottomans 'posssesed no knowledge of the Arabs's distant past'. Later, he wrote: 'A community's civilisation is its language's civilisation [*Bir kavmin medeniyeti lisanının medeniyetidir*]. Both of them manifest themselves all of a sudden in history; however, they have a particular essence, and it takes time for them to appear in the world'.[87] This statement implies that, if a community desires to belong to a civilisation, it needs to possess a language and a literature. Le Bon wrote: '*[À] l'époque du prophète, les Arabes possédaient déjà une littérature et une langue très développées*' (At the time of the Prophet, the Arabs already possessed a highly developed literature and language).[88] Ahmet Rasim translated this sentence in the following manner: '*Peygamberimizin zamanında Araplar fevkalade müterakki bir lisan ve edebiyata malik idiler*'.[89] Ahmet Rasim provided a highly accurate translation of the French statement.[90] He even translated '*possédaient*' as '*malik idiler*'. While Ahmet Rasim omitted many statements from the French source text, he did not hesitate to convey in very exact terms the statement that rendered literature a commodity that a national subject possessed.

Other Ottoman authors also depicted literature as an object of possesssion. Nigar Hanım (1862–1918) claimed: 'What we have so far is this: first, the property of Arabic and Persian literature, then of European literature. There is no doubt about that'.[91] Hamdullah Subhi (1855–1966) noted that he always aspired to 'possess' a literature like the Polish and Russian literatures.[92] Ziya Gökalp (1876–1924) believed that the Turks had possessed a literature for centuries before they came under the influence of the Arabs and Iranians.[93] All these authors talked or wrote of an autonomous national subject and viewed literature as a possession to which this subject could lay a claim. As these writers affiliated themselves with a modern, autonomous national subject, they could have become subjugated to the power structures of the global capitalist modernity; however, they also claimed agency as they expressed a will to possess a literature and acted freely within the context of this modernity. As Bülent Somay has put it: 'Subjectivisation [. . .] is always an antithetical act: while subordinating, it also empowers; while dragging hitherto unconnected hetreogeneous entities within the confines of an ordered existence where they will occupy a homogenous subordinate position, it also transforms them into subjects/ agents vying for freedom'.[94]

If the *nahḍa* project aimed to constitute the bounded, autonomous and modern Arab subject,[95] I would argue that literature as a possession served to substantiate the boundaries of this subject. As many *nahḍa* and *Tanzimat* writers 'imagined' and 'constituted' in their works a bounded Arab or Turkish subject, they also emphasised that this subject had full control over the language it spoke and possessed a literature it had produced throughout the ages. Both philology and history as disciplines also substantiated the sense of control that these national subjects had over the languages and literatures that they possessed.

Hacı İbrahim's works remind us, as Ali Behdad has put it, of 'the impossibility of occupying a position outside the orientalist formation'.[96] On the surface, Hacı İbrahim may seem to have defended a tradition that remained unaffected by modernity, capitalism and Orientalism; however, the 'traditional' views he defended cannot be thought apart from the context of global capitalist modernity in which Orientalism played a constitutive role. Two claims – 'Ottoman literature is Arabic literature' and 'Arabs possess a literature' – may seem to represent two differing worldviews, as the former comes from a proponent of 'old literature' and the latter from a proponent of 'new literature'. However, both statements employ the category of 'literature' to begin with. They also contribute to the conceptualisation of Arabic and Turkish literatures as literatures that are translatable to and comparable with each other. Authors who defended the 'old literature' and the 'new literature' formed their opinions as they engaged with Orientalist discourse. Furthermore, like Hacı İbrahim, Ahmet Rasim made no mention of *nahḍa* Arabic works in his writings, even though both authors could read Arabic.

Ahmet Rasim's *İlk Büyük Muharrirlerden Şinasi* (One of the First Great Authors: Şinasi, 1927), his post-Ottoman work on the biography of Şinasi (1826–71), also captures the epistemological shifts that posit a dichotomy between the 'old literature' and the 'new literature'. Even the book's title stresses the 'pioneers' who modernised an entire literary tradition. To substantiate his points, Ahmet Rasim quoted from works by Ebüzziya Tevfik and Abdülhak Hamid Tarhan (1852–1937), who used excerpts from Arabic writings as they expressed their views on the Ottoman language. For example, Ahmet Rasim shared the following words by Abdülhak Hamid Tarhan on Şinasi:

> Şinasi has demonstrated that one would need to take literature from the West [*Şinasi edebiyatın Garb'dan alınmak lazım geleceğini gösterdi*]. Like the excerpt in the introduction of Ḥarīrī's *Maqāmāt*,
> If I cried with desire for Suᶜdā before she did,
> I would have cured my soul instead of falling into regret.
> Yet she cried before me. Her tears agitated mine.
> I said: Superior are those who act early.
> we too should hold Şinasi, the innovator of literature, in high esteem and not dishonour this virtuous man's honourable tomb as grave robbers do.[97]

Abdülhak Hamid Tarhan did not translate the Arabic lines into Turkish but left them in the original. Neither did Ahmet Rasim feel the need to translate them when he conveyed Tarhan's views on modernisation. While much of the current scholarship has depicted Şinasi as the author who generated the transition from old to new literature, Abdülhak Hamid Tarhan rather described Şinasi as someone who 'brought literature from Europe', hence acknowledging that the category 'literature' itself was something new. According to this excerpt, late Ottoman writers should act early, like Suᶜdā, so that they do not fall into regret. The desire to progress was not the result of a new, capitalist order; instead, Abdülhak Hamid Tarhan suggested that this desire had already found expression in al-Ḥarīrī's *Maqāmāt*. Excerpts from pre-Ottoman Arabic texts, the waters that filled a significant volume of the Ottoman literary reservoir, featured in works that emphasised the need to progress and leave behind the past or 'old literature' even during post-Ottoman times.

Ahmet Rasim also suggested that Şinasi had pioneered a new literature as he quoted Ebüzziya Tevfik who described late Ottoman authors as 'Şinasi's children' in his *Numune-i Edebiyat-ı Osmaniyye* (Excerpts from Ottoman Literature, AH 1296 [1878/79]). This depiction of Şinasi as a 'father-figure' stands in stark contrast to how one author described himself in an article in the newspaper *Malumat*. This author told his readers: '[We are] the children of Arabs' (*evlad-ı Arap*).[98] In contrast, Şinasi served as a father-figure as he also became the pioneer of a new literature according to Ebüzziya Tevfik, who was then quoted in Ahmet Rasim's post-Ottoman book:

> It is beyond my means to say anything about a genius savant who brought a new life to literature such as Şinasi, even if what I will say is high praise. As far

> as I can tell, he is the Azrael of literary mistakes and the father of the elevated abilities we see in the new literature, which has the language of truth. Thanks to him, our intelligent people who have the power to put things into words can write down what they think, read what they write and make their readers like what they write; thus, we all are spiritual children [*manevi evlad*] of Şinasi.[99]

Unlike writers who described themselves as the 'children' or 'grandchildren of the Arabs', Ebüzziya Tevfik described himself as a child of Şinasi, seen as the pioneer of a new literature. This quote insinuates that the Turks had finally managed to find their authentic selves as Şinasi had given birth to authentic subjects with full control over what they spoke and wrote. Yet, as Abdülhak Hamid Tarhan's statement also suggests and as the next chapter will show, visions from the past 'haunted' post-Ottoman works that desired to generate a new genealogy, father-figure and family lineage.

Notes

1. Ahmet Rasim, *Matbuat Hatıralarından: Muharrir, Şair, Edib* (Istanbul: Kanaat Kütüphane ve Matbaası, 1924), 59.
2. Recaizade Mahmud Ekrem, *Talim-i Edebiyat* (Istanbul: Mihran Matbaası, AH 1299 [1881/82]), 11.
3. Elisabetta Benigni has observed a similar dynamic in the work of the Italian Arabist Michele Amari (1806–89). As he wrote about the twelfth-century work *Sulwān al-muṭāᶜ fī ᶜudwān al-atbāᶜ* (Consolation for the Ruler during the Hostility of Subjects) by Ibn Ẓafar al-Ṣiqillī (d. AH 566 [1170/71]), Amari emphasised that medieval Arab Sicily could serve as a model for the progress of Italian civilisation. At the same time, Amari, like other Italian thinkers and writers of his time, paid little attention to works of the *nahḍa* when they wrote about topics such as progress and civilisation. Rather, '[t]heir gaze was directed toward an imagined Arab Mediterranean past, which in their eyes epitomized a fruitful space to conceptualize the present "rising" of the Italian nation'. Elisabetta Benigni, '"Metempsychosis" and "Marvelous Affinities": Re-Imagining the Past in the *Ilyāḏah* by Sulaymān al-Bustānī (1904) and in the *Divano di ᶜOmar ben al-Fared* by Pietro Valerga (1874)', *Oriente Moderno* 101 (2021): 276.
4. For example, see Musa Aksoy, *Moderniteye Karşı Geleneğin Savaşçısı: Hacı İbrahim Efendi* (Ankara: Akçağ, 2005), and Abdülkadir Dağlar, 'Klâsik Türk Edebiyatı Şerh Geleneği ve Hacı İbrâhim Efendi'nin Şerh-i Belâgat'ına Dâir', *Turkish Studies* 2, no. 2 (2007): 161–78.
5. Agâh Sırrı Levend, *Ahmet Rasim* (Ankara: Ankara Üniversitesi Basımevi, 1965), 49.
6. Ahmet Rasim, *Matbuat Hatıralarından*, 77.

7. Hacı İbrahim, 'Tercüman-ı Hakikat'in 1305 Numaralı Nüshasındaki İtirazata Cevab', *Vakit* 8, no. 2501 (21 October 1882): 3.
8. Şerif Pasha here likely refers to Şerif Muhammed bin Abdülmuin (d. 1858) who was the governor of Hijaz between 1827 and 1851 and then between 1856 and 1858.
9. 'Mevadd-ı Fenniyye: Belagat-ı Osmaniyye. İbrahim ve Abdülrahman Efendilere Mukabele', *Tercüman-ı Hakikat* 1115 (6 March 1882): 3.
10. Hacı İbrahim, 'Mevadd-ı Fenniyye: Tercüman-ı Hakikat'in 1115 Numaralı Nüshasına Belagat-ı Osmaniyye Mübahasesine Dair Münderic Olan Makale Üzerine Mütalaa', *Tercüman-ı Hakikat* 1121 (13 March 1882): 3.
11. Hacı İbrahim, 'Mevadd-ı Fenniyye', 3.
12. Ibid.
13. 'İbrahim Efendi Hazretlerine Mukabele', *Tercüman-ı Hakikat* 1130 (23 March 1886): 3.
14. Hacı İbrahim, 'Saadetlü El-Hac İbrahim Efendi Hazretlerinin Bu Kere Dahi İrsal Buyurmuş Oldukları Varakadır', *Vakit* 8, no. 2510 (31 October 1882): 3.
15. Usman Ahmedani and Dženita Karić have explored a similar dynamic as they examine the image of the Arab in Abdülhak Hamid Tarhan's *Tarık* (1879), in its modern Turkish rendering (1960), as well as in its Bosnian (1915), Dari Persian (1922), Urdu (1943) and Arabic (1959) translations. For example, the Ottoman Turkish source text praises the virtuous characters of Arabs; the Urdu translation can translate the term 'Arab' in the source text as 'Muslim'; the Bosnian translation displays a strong fascination with Arab culture; and the modern Turkish edition does not dwell too much on Tarık's Arabness. How these works engage with the image of the Arab, therefore, can reveal crucial insights into the visions of communal identity that they uphold. Usman Ahmedani and Dženita Karić, 'Finding the Lost Andalusia: Reading Abdülhak Hamid Tarhan's *Tarık or the Conquest of al-Andalus* in its Multiple Renderings', in *Ottoman Translations: Circulating Texts from Bombay to Paris*, ed. Marilyn Booth and Claire Savina (Edinburgh: Edinburgh University Press, 2023), 203–4.
16. 'İbrahim Efendi Hazretlerine Mukabele'.
17. Hacı İbrahim, 'Mevadd-ı Fenniyye', *Tercüman-ı Hakikat* 1132 (30 March 1882): 3.
18. Recaizade Mahmud Ekrem, 'Mevadd-ı Fenniyye: Arz-ı Mazeret ve Beyan-ı Nedamet', *Tercüman-ı Hakikat* 1304 (17 October 1882): 2–3.
19. Hacı İbrahim, 'Saadetlü El-Hac İbrahim Efendi Hazretleri Tarafından Bu Kere Dahi Tevarüd Eden Varakadır', *Vakit* 8, no. 2514 (4 November 1882): 3. The last two sentences of this excerpt likely meant that Recaizade Mahmud Ekrem did not merely quote a few sections from French books; he plagiarised entire sections and chapters. Hacı İbrahim again criticised the 'Kable'ş-şuru' section in the 1293rd issue of the *Tercüman-ı Hakikat* newspaper. Hacı İbrahim, 'Mülahazat', *Tercüman-ı Hakikat* 1293 (4 October 1882): 3.

20. Aksoy, *Moderniteye Karşı*, 222. As Paker has noted, Recaizade Mahmud Ekrem drew on Émile Lefranc's (1798–1854) *Traité théorique et pratique de littérature* (A Theoretical and Practical Treatise on Literature, 1837) (Paker, 'Poetic Practices', 36).
21. Hacı İbrahim, 'Bahs ve Münazaradan Husule Gelen Netayic', *Tercüman-ı Hakikat* 1113 (3 March 1882): 3.
22. Hacı İbrahim, 'Teşekkür ve Temenni', *Tercüman-ı Hakikat* 1146 (12 April 1882): 2.
23. Faik, Esad and Ali Sedad, 'Aynen Varakadır', *Ceride-i Havadis* 43, no. 4893 (4 March 1882): 3.
24. 'Lisan-ı Osmani', *Malumat* 7, no. 162 (8 December 1898): 839.
25. Hacı İbrahim, 'Saadetlü el-Hac İbrahim Efendi Hazretlerinin Varakalarından Ma Bad', *Tarık* 5, no. 1600 (9 September 1888): 3.
26. Hacı İbrahim, 'Saadetlü el-Hac İbrahim Hazretlerinden Varid Olan Varakadır', *Tarık* 5, no. 1599 (8 September 1888): 3.
27. Hacı İbrahim, 'Saadetlü el-Hac İbrahim Efendi Hazretlerinden Mevrud Varakadır', *Tarık* 5, no. 1575 (25 August 1888): 3.
28. Hacı İbrahim, 'Saadetlü el-Hac İbrahim Efendi Hazretlerinin Varakalarından', *Tarık* 5, no. 1600 (9 September 1888): 3.
29. Hacı İbrahim, 'Saadetlü el-Hac İbrahim Efendi Hazretlerinden Varid Olan Varakadır'.
30. İbrahim Avni, 'Saadetlü el-Hac İbrahim Efendi Hazretlerinin Varakalarında Beyan Olunan Ruzname-i İmtihandan Ma Bad', *Tarık* 5, no. 1651 (30 October 1888): 3.
31. Hacı İbrahim, 'Saadetlü el-Hac İbrahim Efendi Hazretlerinin Varakalarında Beyan Olunan Ruzname-i İmtihandan Ma Bad', *Tarık* 5, no. 1650 (29 October 1888): 3.
32. Hacı İbrahim, 'Saadetlü el-Hac İbrahim Efendi Hazretlerinden Mevrud Varakadır'.
33. 'Galatat', *Malumat* 7, no. 157 (3 November 1898): 740–43.
34. 'Sual', *Malumat* 7, no. 164 (22 December 1898): 887.
35. 'Cevab', *Malumat* 8, no. 169 (26 January 1899): 970–71.
36. Hacı İbrahim, 'Bakiye-i İbret', *Tercüman-ı Hakikat* 1257 (23 August 1882): 3.
37. Hacı İbrahim, 'Mevadd-ı Fenniyye', *Tercüman-ı Hakikat* 1136 (30 March 1882): 2.
38. Hacı İbrahim, 'Rusûhi, Ali Râif Efendi'ye Cevab', *Saadet*, no. 338 (18 April 1886); quoted in Aksoy, *Moderniteye Karşı*, 451.
39. See Tageldin, *Disarming Words*.
40. Hacı İbrahim, 'El-Hac İbrahim Efendi Hazretlerinin Bu Kere Dahi İrsal Eylemiş Oldukları Varakanın Aynıdır', *Vakit* 2506 (27 October 1882): 3.
41. Hacı İbrahim, 'Mevadd-ı Fenniyye', *Tercüman-ı Hakikat* 1136 (30 March 1882): 3.
42. Ibid.

43. 'Terakkiyat-ı Ciddiye Muhibbanına Müjde!', *Malumat* 8, no. 174 (9 March 1899): 1082.
44. Ahmed Rasim, *Matbuat Hatıralarından*, 199.
45. Ibid., 185.
46. Ibid., 174.
47. Ibid., 187.
48. Ibid., 84.
49. Ahmet Rasim, *İki Hatırat, Üç Şahsiyet: Said Paşa* (Istanbul: Matbaa-i Hayriyye ve Şürekası, 1916/17), 93.
50. Ahmet Rasim, *Matbuat Hatıralarından*, 83.
51. The 'Resimlerimiz' (Our Photos) section in the newspaper provided factual information on photos of various districts in Syria, but they often made general remarks on Damascus rather than describing details of the expedition. For an example, see 'Resimlerimiz', *Malumat* 8, no. 175 (16 March 1899): 1110–11.
52. Zeki, 'Muktetafat', *Malumat* 8, no. 171 (16 February 1899): 1018–19.
53. For the excerpt, see Maḥmūd al-Warrāq, *Dīwān Maḥmūd al-Warrāq: shāʿir al-ḥikma wa-l-mawʿiẓa* (Ajman: Muʾassasat al-Funūn, 1991), 102.
54. For the excerpt, see al-Imām ʿAlī ibn Abī Ṭālib, *Dīwān Amīr al-Muʾminīn al-Imām ʿAlī Abī bin Ṭālib raḍiya Allāh ʿanhu wa karrama Allāh wajhah*, ed. ʿAbd al-ʿAzīz al-Karam (1988), 70.
55. For the excerpt, see Muḥammad bin Idrīs Shāfiʿī, *Dīwān al-Shāfiʿī*, ed. Muḥammad ʿAbd al-Munʿim Khafājī (Cairo: Maktabat al-Kulliyāt al-Azhariyya, 1985), 87.
56. For the excerpt, see al-Mutanabbī, *Dīwān al-Mutanabbī*, 491.
57. Zeki, 'Muktetafat', *Malumat* 7, no. 164 (22 December 1898): 883.
58. Haleb'den: Refet, 'Şemmet ül-Edeb', *Malumat* 7, no. 161 (1 December 1898): 823.
59. 'Almanya İmparator ve İmparatoriçesi Hazaratının Hereke Fabrika-i Hümayun Köşkü Kapusunda', *Malumat* 7, no. 159 (17 November 1898): 780; 'Almanya İmparator ve İmparatoriçesi Hazaratının Kudüs Şimendöferine Rükubları', *Malumat* 7, no. 163 (15 December 1898): 869; 'Haşmetlü Almanya İmparatoru Hazretlerinin Suriye'ye Vuku Seyahatleri Hasebiyle "Hohenzollern" Yatıyla Birlikte Beyrut Taraflarına Gitmek Üzere Köprüden Huruc Eden "İclaliyye" Zırhlı-i Hümayunun Resmini de Bu Nüshamızda Dercediyoruz', *Malumat* 7, no. 168 (19 January 1899): 960.
60. 'İmparator ve İmparatoriçe Hazaratının Protestan Kilisesini Ziyaretleri', *Malumat* 7, no. 163 (15 December 1898): 868.
61. 'Almanya İmparator ve İmparatoriçesi Hazaratanın Kadim Mescid-i Aksa'dan Çıkışları', *Malumat* 7, no. 160 (24 November 1898): 800.
62. 'Almanya İmparator ve İmparatoriçesi Hazaratının Hazret-i Ömer (r. d.) Cami Havlisinde Duruşları', *Malumat* 7, no. 160 (24 November 1898): 796.
63. 'Şam'da Sultan Selim Cami-i Şerifi', *Malumat* 8, no. 173 (2 March 1899): 1053.

64. İsmail Zühdü, 'Muhbir-i Mahsusamızın Mektupları 2 (Kudüs Hatıratı)', *İkdam* 5, no. 1553 (5 November 1898): 1. For more on this expedition, see also İbrahim Sarıtaş, 'Alman İmparatorluğu'nun Türk Dünyasına Yönelik Propaganda Faaliyetleri: Arkeolog Max Freiherr von Oppenheim ve Doğu Haber Ajansı', *Bilig* 91 (2019): 113–35; Ö. Kürşad Karacagil, 'II. Wilhelm'in Osmanlı İmparatorluğu'nu Ziyareti ve Mihmandarı Mehmed Şakir Paşa'nın Günlüğü (1898)', *Türkiyat Mecmuası* 24, no. 2 (2014): 73–97. A brief article at the beginning of the 155th issue of the newspaper *Malumat* also indicates that the Germans had highly advanced technology and that they also showed immense rapport with the Ottomans. 'Şevketlü Padişahımız Gazi Büyük Abdülhamid Han-ı Sani Efendimiz Hazretleri ve Almanya İmparatoru Haşmetlü İkinci Wilhelm Hazretleri', *Malumat* 7, no. 155 (20 October 1898): 705.
65. For example, see 'Kudüs-ü Şerif Manazarından Jeriko Şehriyle Bahr-ı Lut', *Malumat* 7, no. 168 (19 January 1899): 957, and 'Haleb Kalesinden Kışla-i Hümayune Doğru Bir Manzara', *Malumat* 8, no. 178 (6 April 1899): 1159.
66. Ahmet A. Ersoy, 'Ottomans and the Kodak Galaxy: Archiving Everyday Life and Historical Space in Ottoman Illustrated Journals', *History of Photography* 40, no. 3 (2016): 332.
67. The 160th issue of *Malumat* features a similar dynamic as it displays the photo of Wilhelm II's expedition to Bethlehem, and below the photo is an excerpt from al-Mutanabbī's poem, although the newspaper does not mention the excerpt's author. The excerpt is followed by a Turkish explication. Zeki, 'Muktetafat', *Malumat* 7, no. 160 (24 November 1898): 801. For the excerpt, see al-Mutanabbī, *Dīwān al-Mutanabbī*, 292.
68. 'Mülahazat', *Malumat* 7, no. 165 (30 December 1898): 901.
69. d'Istria, *La Poésie des Ottomans*, 187.
70. E. J. W. Gibb, *A History of Ottoman Poetry* (England: Luzac & co.,1900), 1: 70.
71. Carl Brockelmann, *Geschichte der arabischen Litteratur* (Leipzig: C. F. Amelangs Verlag, 1909), 254.
72. Dupont, *Ǧurǧī Zaydān (1861–1914)*, 28.
73. Gustave Le Bon, *La Civilisation des Arabes* (Paris: Librairie de Firmin-Didot et Cie, 1884), [2–3]. Le Bon differentiated '*Arabes nomades*' (nomadic Arabs) from '*Arabes sedentaires*' (sedentary Arabs). Ahmet Rasim translated these terms as '*bedevi Arap*' (Bedouin Arab) and '*medeni Arap*' (civilised Arab). Ahmet Rasim, *Arapların Terakkiyat-ı Medeniyyesi* (Istanbul: Şirket-i Mürettibiyye Matbaası, AH 1304 [1886/87]), 9.
74. Le Bon, *La Civilisation des Arabes*, xii.
75. Jabbari, 'From Persianate Cosmopolis to Persianate Modernity', 624.
76. Le Bon, *La Civilisation des Arabes*, 60.
77. See Abdurrahman Fehmi, *Medreset ül-Arap* (Istanbul: Matbaa-i Ebüzziya, AH 1304 [1886/87]); Gustave Le Bon, *Avrupa Harbinden Alınan Psikolociyai* [Psikolojik] *Dersler*, trans. Abdullah Cevdet (Istanbul: Kanaat Matbaası, 1918); Gustave le Bon, *Ruh ül-Cemaat*, trans. Mehmed Fuad Köprülü and

Sadreddin Celal (Istanbul: Uhuvvet Matbaası, AH 1327 [1909/10]); Gustave Le Bon, *Ruh-ı Siyaset ve Müdafaa-i İctimaiyye*, trans. Mehmed Fuad Köprülü (Istanbul: Ahmet İhsan ve Şürekası Matbaacılık Osmanlı Şirketi, 1910).

78. Le Bon also claimed that even the Turkish architecture displayed strong influences of other civilisations. For example, all the mosques built by Turks merely reflect the influence of the Hagia Sophia. Therefore, a Turk can never generate original, authentic constructions (Le Bon, *La Civilisation des Arabes*, 242).
79. Ahmet Rasim, *Arapların Terakkiyat-ı Medeniyyesi*, 3.
80. Booth (ed.), *Migrating Texts*, and Booth and Savina (eds), *Ottoman Translations*.
81. Ahmet Rasim, *Arapların Terakkiyat-ı Medeniyyesi*, 3.
82. Şemseddin Sami, *Kamus-ı Türki* (Istanbul: İkdam Matbaası, AH 1317–18 [1899/1900–1900/1]), 154.
83. Ahmet Rasim, *Arapların Terakkiyat-ı Medeniyyesi*, 39.
84. Ibid., 4.
85. Ibid.
86. Ibid.
87. Ibid., 13.
88. Le Bon, *La Civilisation des Arabes*, 59.
89. Ahmet Rasim, *Arapların Medeniyet-i Terakkiyesi*, 15.
90. The main difference is that, while Le Bon used the term '*prophète*' (prophet), Ahmet Rasim wrote '*peygamberimiz*' (our prophet).
91. Ruşen Eşref, *Diyorlar ki*, 30.
92. Ibid., 203.
93. Ibid., 223.
94. Somay, *The Psychopolitics of the Oriental Father*, 29.
95. Tarek El-Ariss, *Leaks, Hacks and Scandals: Arab Culture in the Digital Age* (Princeton: Princeton University Press, 2019), 167.
96. Ali Behdad, *Belated Travelers: Orientalism in the Age of Colonial Dissolution* (Durham, NC: Duke University Press, 1994), 111.
97. Ahmet Rasim, *İlk Büyük Muharrirlerden Şinasi* (Istanbul: Yeni Matbaa, 1927), 69. Ahmet Rasim noted that this excerpt is taken from one of the letters that Abdülhak Hamid Tarhan sent from the island of Lesbos.
98. 'Lisan-ı Osmani', *Malumat* 7, no. 163 (15 December 1898): 859.
99. Ahmet Rasim, *İlk Büyük Muharrirlerden*, 24. This quote is also in Ebüzziya Tevfik, *Numune-i Edebiyat-ı Osmaniyye*, 214.

6

Family Matters: Oedipus, Tawfīq al-Ḥakīm and Ahmet Hamdi Tanpınar

Ahmet Hamdi Tanpınar (1901–62) believed that modernisation caused the Turks to experience a sense of guilt towards their ancestors and to suffer from a psychological complex: 'If I could dare, I would have claimed that we [Turks] are living the life of a man who suffers from a kind of Oedipal complex, that is, the complex of a man who unknowingly had killed his father, since the *Tanzimat*'.[1] This statement may at first suggest that the Turks started to experience this complex only after they had left behind the Ottoman past, 'their father', during modernisation and Westernisation. At the same time, as this chapter will show, the Turks had shown symptoms of a similar 'complex' also during the Ottoman period, according to Tanpınar. Like his Egyptian counterpart Tawfīq al-Ḥakīm (1898–1987), Tanpınar suggested that his national community could achieve cultural emancipation and overcome this complex once it turned westwards. Even if the Ottoman Empire's demise may have generated political and linguistic divisions in the Middle East, this chapter will demonstrate that Tanpınar and al-Ḥakīm, who shaped how critics have studied Turkish and Arabic literature, respectively, had similar visions of identity, culture and literature. By using Tanpınar's and al-Ḥakīm's shared engagement with Sophocles's (d. 406/5 BC) *Oedipus Rex* (c. 429–25 BC) as a point of departure, it will flesh out these similarities while revealing analogies between their works and the Greek tragedy.

Lorna Hardwick has described the appeal of *Oedipus Rex* for postcolonial writers: 'Sophocles' play, with its outsider/foreigner who is not and its mystery of self-discovery, is a rich field for exploring modern crises of identity and self-recognition – political and cultural as well as psychological'.[2] In a similar vein, the tragedy of Oedipus provides insights into the anxieties and hopes that one finds in critical and fictional writings by Tanpınar, who wrote on what it means to be a Turk, and al-Ḥakīm, who wrote on what it means to be an Egyptian and an Arab. Al-Ḥakīm and Tanpınar made numerous references to *Oedipus Rex* or the Oedipus complex in their writings. While Tanpınar wrote that the Turkish person suffered from a father complex, al-Ḥakīm did not argue that Egypt suffered from an Oedipus complex; however, he wrote an Arabic adaptation of *Oedipus Rex* and claimed that the play was appealing to the Egyptian mind.

King Oedipus remains unaware of his family lineage and confronts a tragic end once he learns about his family background. According to Sigmund Freud, '[t]he only reason why [Oedipus's] fate grips us is because it might also have been our own'.[3] The main character in al-Ḥakīm's *Return of the Spirit* (*ᶜAwdat al-rūḥ*, 1933), Muḥsin, and the main character in Tanpınar's *The Time Regulation Institute* (*Saatleri Ayarlama Enstitüsü*, first serialised in the newspaper *Yeni İstanbul* in 1954 and then published as book in 1961), Hayri İrdal, are 'tragic figures', too. They cannot fulfill their ambition to create a new culture that promises a sense of emancipation as they cannot escape from parent figures.[4] In both *The Time Regulation Institute* and *Return of the Spirit*, the Ottoman past that often finds embodiment in parent figures in Tanpınar's and al-Ḥakīm's works becomes a source of anxiety for the main characters. The past for Muḥsin and Hayri İrdal is like the past for Oedipus: a dark territory that can shatter one's plans and visions of self-identity.

Furthermore, Tanpınar and al-Ḥakīm often upheld nationalistic frameworks when they wrote about their culture and history; in other words, unlike Ziya Pasha (1829–80) or Hacı İbrahim (1826–88), Tanpınar and al-Ḥakīm did not describe Ottoman literature and culture as a multilingual reservoir that intertwined Arabic, Persian and Turkish to such an extent that they became inseparable. Tanpınar indeed wrote extensively on Arabic literature and the Arab mind in his critical writings, including his famous *On Dokuzuncu Asır Türk Edebiyatı Tarihi* (History of Nineteenth-Century Turkish Literature, 1949). However, unlike late Ottoman Turkish writings, his history defined Ottoman literature as Ottoman Turkish works that showed strong Arabic and Persian influences. Al-Ḥakīm did not discuss the Turkish literary heritage in his critical writings and depicted the Ottomans as Turkish invaders who have had no impact on Egypt's cultural formation.

Unlike Ziya Pasha and Jurjī Zaydān (1861–1914), both Tanpınar and al-Ḥakīm studied Arabic and Turkish literatures for understanding the 'soul', 'spirit' and 'psychology' of the Egyptian and Turkish subject. They believed that their national community's history would ultimately achieve emancipation as they Westernised without sacrificing their authenticity. Late Ottoman authors also emphasised that their communities needed to

Westernise; however, unlike most of these writers, Tanpınar and al-Ḥakīm believed that their national subject should Westernise adequately to maintain its 'spiritual' and 'psychological' health. Otherwise, their community could not achieve cultural emancipation.

Although both authors studied Ottoman literature and history within nationalist frameworks, their novels feature ethnically heterogeneous families who carry traces of the Ottoman past, hence undermining strictly nationalist visions. If Ottoman writings depicted Ottoman culture as a multilingual literary reservoir, this culture found an 'embodiment' as multiethnic families in *The Time Regulation Institute* and *Return of the Spirit*. Both Muḥsin and Hayri İrdal want to write works that express their nation's new spirit and pay homage to characters such as Halit Ayarcı and Saniyya, who stand for a new, modern society; however, they can never sublimate the parent figures and their multiethnic families from whom they seek emancipation. This chapter will thus undermine most typical readings of *Return of the Spirit* as the realisation of a nationalist vision and of *The Time Regulation Institute* as a satire on Turkish modernisation, by paying attention to those characters who have not received attention in earlier scholarship – the Tunisian Abdüsselam Bey in *The Time Regulation Institute* and the Turkish mother in *Return of the Spirit*. I argue that Muḥsin and Hayri İrdal seek a sense of emancipation by shifting the dynamics of the families in which they grew up; however, they often realise that their post-Ottoman societies share similar dynamics with the families with whom they associate a decrepit Ottoman past.

Oedipus Rex *and the Turkish Mother in Tawfiq al-Ḥakīm's* Return of the Spirit

Like Muḥsin, Tawfīq al-Ḥakīm had a Turkish mother and came from a prominent landowning family. Al-Ḥakīm went to France in 1925 to acquire a doctoral degree in law. During his time in Paris, he decided not to pursue his legal studies any further. Although al-Ḥakīm was not pleased with his education, he became acquainted with European culture there before he returned to Egypt in 1928. He wrote numerous novels, short stories, critical writings and plays. Al-Ḥakīm became a member of the Higher Council for Literature, Arts and Social Sciences in 1956 and the Egyptian Delegate to UNESCO in 1959, and he received the first State Prize in Literature in 1961.

Al-Ḥakīm described Egypt as a person with complex psychological features. On the one hand, he claimed that Egypt belonged to the Arab civilisation (*al-ḥaḍāra al-ᶜarabiyya*) because most Egyptians spoke Arabic and believed in Islam; on the other hand, he also emphasised that Egypt had distinct features that set it apart from the rest of the Arab world. He distinguished 'the spirit of Egypt' (*rūḥ Miṣr*) from the 'personality of Egypt' (*shakhṣiyyat Miṣr*).[5] According to al-Ḥakīm, the 'personality' consisted of various elements (*ᶜanāsir*) such as geography, history, politics and literature. Someone who wanted to understand Egypt's personality needed to study all these elements. However, the term 'spirit', so al-Ḥakīm noted, shared the same etymological root with the term 'smell' (*rāʾiḥa*).[6] Therefore, both spirit and smell shared similar characteristics; for example, one could not 'scientifically' observe them with a naked eye. Just as one cannot understand the smell of a rose by merely putting it under a microscope and dissecting it into different parts, one can never scientifically observe Egypt's spirit but merely 'smell' it. Al-Ḥakīm claimed to know Egypt because he, as a native of Egypt, had an intuitive understanding of it.[7]

According to al-Ḥakīm, Egypt had to prove to the rest of the world that it had a distinct personality to remain independent. The British claimed that Egypt was only a geographical region (*al-quṭr*) and not a deep-rooted civilisation; therefore, they believed that Egypt needed a foreign mandate. If the Egyptians could not lay out the Egyptian spirit's distinct features, imperial powers such as the British would find no qualms governing Egypt. Even if Egypt did not achieve full political sovereignty in 1919, its intellectual and civilisational revolution started then, so argued al-Ḥakīm.[8] To set free Egypt's spirit, one needed to separate it from other spirits that had corrupted it due to foreign invasions, including the Ottoman invasion.[9]

While al-Ḥakīm believed that Egypt had an unchanging essence and personality, he also claimed that Egypt needed to modernise and undergo important cultural changes. As he emphasised the need to resist imperialist powers, al-Ḥakīm believed that Egypt should Westernise without losing its authentic values. According to al-Ḥakīm, modern Arab thinkers should not repeat the mistakes of their medieval ancestors who had rejected essential components of Western civilisation, such as Greek drama, while they borrowed other elements, such as Platonic philosophy. They should borrow more comprehensively from Western civilisation. Al-Ḥakīm used the metaphor of clothes to emphasise that Arabic literature would not lose its true essence, even if it 'put on new clothes' – that is, even if it adopted Western styles and forms such as the tragedy and the novel.[10] Arabic literature had always retained its essence, even though it had sometimes changed its clothes.[11] By emphasising that Arabic literature was a deep-rooted literature that had 'always preserved its spirit',[12] he suggested that the new stylistic and thematic innovations which he had introduced to Arabic literature would not cause a significant rupture in its history.

Instead, he advocated a 'proper' Westernisation that would allow the Egyptians to borrow the technological advancements of the West while they also maintained their national essence. After all, he believed that the East would 'never have the respect of the West until it ha[d] some ideas of its own to offer'.[13]

Al-Ḥakīm thus felt no qualms about writing an Arabic adaptation of *Oedipus Rex* and other theatre plays while also emphasising the need to maintain one's authentic identity. Although al-Ḥakīm did not write about the Oedipal complex in his works, he wrote the first adaptation of *Oedipus Rex* in Arabic, beyond a translation, in 1949.[14] He emphasised that this version was an 'Islamic interpretation' of the play. While some thinkers may have believed that *Oedipus Rex* was foreign to Arab sensibilities, al-Ḥakīm argued that *Oedipus Rex* spoke to Arabs more so than to Europeans: 'All there is to the matter is that I am an Easterner, an Arab. I still retain some part of my original religious sense'.[15] Al-Ḥakīm suggested that he was more psychologically inclined than a European to appreciate and understand the play's main issues, such as the crucial role that divine forces played in people's lives.[16]

William M. Hutchins has argued that, according to al-Ḥakīm, *Oedipus Rex* captures the tension between 'the subjective reality of the heart'[17] – what al-Ḥakīm calls 'the fact' (*al-wāqi*ᶜ)[18] – and 'the objective reality of the intellect'[19] – what al-Ḥakīm calls 'the truth' (*al-ḥaqīqa*).[20] In other words, while Oedipus wants to believe that his past has no blemishes ('the subjective reality of the heart'), he ultimately has to confront the reality that he has killed his father and slept with his mother ('the objective reality of the intellect'). This tension between heart and intellect that lies at the core of *Oedipus Rex*, I propose, also characterises works by al-Ḥakīm and Tanpınar. Their critical writings imagine their national community as a subject whose essence has remained unchanged throughout the centuries and successfully left behind the Ottoman past; however, the main characters in their novels confront a past the traces of which undermine the desire to generate a new, authentic culture.

While his critical writings celebrate the emancipation of Egypt's spirit from foreign influences, including Ottoman invaders, al-Ḥakīm's famous novel, *Return of the Spirit*, features the main character Muḥsin who cannot realise his goal of becoming the eloquent tongue of his nation. Muḥsin feels a sense of submission to his beloved Saniyya and his Turkish mother.[21] Because his parents live in the countryside, Muḥsin shares an apartment with his poor relatives – his uncles Ḥanafī and ᶜAbduh, his aunt Zanūba and their cousin Salīm – and his childhood friend Mabrūk in the traditional quarter of al-Sayyida Zaynab in Cairo to pursue his studies. Later, Muḥsin, ᶜAbduh and Salīm all fall in love with Saniyya, the neighbour's daughter. However, Saniyya marries another man, the wealthy Muṣṭafā Bey. Muḥsin and his housemates feel disappointed when they learn about Saniyya's new marriage prospect; hence they participate in the 1919 revolution and as a result are imprisoned. With the intervention of Muḥsin's parents, they are transported to a relatively safe prison hospital.

Return of the Spirit provides almost no information on the historical events that preceded the 1919 revolution which culminated in Egypt's political sovereignty. The novel does not touch on the various economic, social and cultural shifts that prepared the ground for the 1919 revolution, including social protests across Egypt; instead, it suggests that a single political pioneer, Saᶜd Zaghlūl (1859–1927), suddenly awakened the true potential of Egyptians, which had stayed dormant for centuries. It reinforces the impression that the Ottoman past is a legacy that the Egyptians had entirely left behind.[22]

The only remnant from this Ottoman past is Muḥsin's Turkish mother. The novel suggests that Muḥsin's mother is the central dominating figure in the family, as she claims to civilise Muḥsin's entire family. For instance, she says to Muḥsin's father 'with pride, vanity and arrogance': 'So you see, I've civilized you and raised you, peasant, loafer'.[23] Even when she does not openly oppress Muḥsin, Muḥsin's mother often generates a sense of discomfort for Muḥsin, including physical discomfort: 'At last she began to examine [Muḥsin] from head to toe, inspecting him and touching him, as though conducting a limb-by-limb review' (174; 2: 11).

At the same time, *Return of the Spirit* also suggests that the Turkish mother has no severe impact on the other Egyptian characters. For example, Saniyya's mother describes Muḥsin's mother to Muḥsin in the following manner:

> By now she will have forgotten me. It goes back to the days when we were little girls. We were neighbors and grew up in the same area. All of us girls used to play together in front of their house. Your mother was Turkish, from a Turkish family. She was the youngest but was our leader. We feared and minded her. She was the daughter of a Turkish soldier with a blond mustache! Whatever game we played, she was the boss. We called her the queen and the sultan's daughter. She loved to set herself apart from us. If we wore red for the holiday, she wore green. And if we wore green, she wore red! Woe to us when she got angry! She used to say: 'Tomorrow, I am going to be extremely rich, and I'll buy you as my maids and slaves'. Oh, those days have passed. How sweet they were. (52; 1: 95)

Muḥsin's mother adopts a bossy attitude when she plays with the other children; at the same time, this quote suggests that the Turkish mother is no longer a frightening figure. The days when the Turkish mother threatened to enslave the Egyptians have now turned into a sweet memory.

Muḥsin claims to show no resemblance to his mother, and the Turkish mother even tells Muḥsin: 'You're just like them [the other Egyptians]! I mean, do you have any Turkish blood [*ibn turk*]?' (183; 2: 23).[24] She also '[feels] that her link to her son risked being hardly more than a legality' (213; 2: 71). Unlike the hierarchical space that characterises his parents' house, the apartment in which he lives with his poor relatives, so Muḥsin claims, seems to be unaffected by social hierarchies. Muḥsin experiences physical discomfort in the apartment in Cairo, yet he also enjoys a sense of equality that will come to characterise his nationalist vision. He yearns for an egalitarian camaraderie rather than a hierarchical family, as Egypt's spirit finally wakes up after centuries of dormancy: '[A]ll of them were sons of Egypt, with a single heart. By sunset that day Egypt had become a fiery mass' (325; 2: 242). Muḥsin wishes to break free from his Turkish mother as he, like other Egyptians, can affiliate himself with the motherland Egypt.

Like Muḥsin, the European characters believe that Egypt will soon achieve its true potential, as Monsieur Fournier believes that '[t]he Egypt that had slept for centuries rose to her feet in a single day. She had been waiting [. . .] for her beloved son, the symbol of her buried sorrows and hopes, to be born anew and this beloved was born again from the loins of the peasant' (324; 2: 240). Unlike Muḥsin, Mr Black and Monsieur Fournier make elaborate remarks about Egyptians. Mr Black describes the Egyptians as 'a deep-rooted civilization' and contrasts them with the 'arriviste people of Europe' (198; 2: 46). The Egyptian villagers have remained on the same soil for thousands of years and under the domination of two groups, the Bedouins and the Turks. Nevertheless, the Egyptians' essence has never been corrupted, despite centuries of conquest.

While the Turkish mother uses the term 'civilisation' quite often, the Europeans, known for claiming to perform a 'civilising mission' in their colonies, never use this term in the novel. Unlike Muḥsin's mother, who brags about how much she has civilised his father, both European characters tend to accept the superiority of the Egyptians: 'Deprive a European of schooling, and he'll be unspeakably ignorant. Europe's only power is in the intellect, that limited goddess we must flesh out with our will. The power of Egypt is in the heart, which is bottomless' (204; 2: 55). Muḥsin's mother acts submissively towards the European guests and wants to impress them with her 'Ottoman food' when they visit the family house (200; 2: 48). *Return of the Spirit* suggests that the Turkish mother feels subservient to the Europeans; in contrast, Egyptians never feel this sense of submission. Only the Turkish mother experiences the negative impacts of Western imperialism and colonialism – including a strong sense of self-doubt and humiliation – while other Egyptian characters never worry about these adverse effects as they envision a new, utopian and egalitarian future. *Return of the Spirit* thus suggests that, unlike the 'foreign' Turkish mother who immediately shows signs of weakness whenever she meets Europeans, the Egyptians whose spirit has remained merely dormant and yet still intact for centuries are not susceptible to Westernisation's negative consequences.

Literature plays a fundamental role in reinforcing Egypt's new communal vision. Muḥsin tells his friend '[w]ith youthful braggadocio': 'Tomorrow we'll be the eloquent tongue of the nation' (72; 1: 128). However, the desire to become an intellectual pioneer can undermine a sense of equality and camaraderie, for which he also yearns. Once he becomes a pioneer as an Egyptian writer who generates a new literature, Muḥsin may become like his Turkish mother, who also claims to 'civilise' people around her with her exquisite upbringing.

The hierarchies that existed among the different ethnic and linguistic communities in the Ottoman Empire did not dissipate even after the empire's demise; instead, these hierarchies continued to shape class and community dynamics in the modern Egyptian nation-state. Muḥsin feels substantial discomfort when his friends see his family's carriage. The carriage driver uses the term 'Bey', a Turkish term used for people of high socioeconomic status and calls Muḥsin 'Master Muḥsin Bey' (24; 1: 46). Muḥsin notes that he can never have the lifestyle of the villagers or his classmates, as they will always see him as 'Master Muḥsin Bey'. Muḥsin sees himself almost as a servant to his family's carriage rather than to his fellow Egyptians while describing their verdict on him: 'Muḥsin bowed his head in despair and walked towards the carriage as if to the gallows, as though he heard deep within him the echoes of an irreversible verdict proclaiming, "Muḥsin has left our pack forever!"' (25; 1: 47). Muḥsin feels disappointed whenever he wants to affiliate himself with his classmates, villagers and poor relatives: 'Muḥsin was a little embarrassed, for it appeared to him that, no matter who he was, he was still far from understanding the feelings of these people' (191; 2: 34–35). Muḥsin worries that he can never be like villagers and even asks himself: 'Or was he not of the same blood as these Egyptian farmers?' (193; 2: 38).

Muḥsin's love for Saniyya offers the possibility to break free from his family and to affiliate himself with the Egyptian nation. According to Jeff Shalan,

> Saniyya is more than a mere object of male desire. She is both a catalyst for the novel's humorous portrayal of the male characters and, more importantly, the one who generates the narrative's construction of, or movement towards, a national community, as well as Muḥsin's aspiration to be its voice. [. . .] But whether Saniyya's character can, in fact, support the symbolic weight of her role becomes, in turn, a crucial question for a novel whose powerful rhetorical appeal for national unity derives from an allegorical meaning deftly woven into the fabric of the story.[25]

Shalan has revealed both Saniyya's central role in forging a national consciousness and her inability to ensure a seamless transition into this consciousness. Therefore, *Return of the Spirit*, like *Oedipus Rex*, displays what al-Ḥakīm called the tension between heart and intellect. Muḥsin wants to believe that he has established complete independence from this past and believes that his love for Saniyya and literature will testify to a new future. When Muḥsin thinks that he received a letter from Saniyya, he believes that '[t]his letter [is] his entire past. His entire future [is] Saniyya' (216; 2: 77). Muḥsin also carries Saniyya's handkerchief, 'the way pious people carry the Holy Qur'an' (57; 1: 101). Saniyya's objects attain a fetish-like quality that seems to eradicate magically all traces of the Ottoman past.

Although Muḥsin believes that he will begin a new life thanks to Saniyya, 'the objective reality' is different. As Muḥsin becomes romantically attached to Saniyya, he also enjoys the privilege of his family lineage. When a servant in his family house calls Muḥsin 'Bey', Muḥsin reacts: 'The word bey rang in his ears strangely, although for once he didn't mind. He felt an unaccustomed pride and wished Saniyya could have been present to see and hear' (174; 2: 10). His love for Saniyya causes Muḥsin to take pride in his lineage: 'He felt a little ashamed of himself and found it odd that he was the son of parents like these, whom he did not resemble. He resolved to resemble them from now on' (178; 2: 15). The privileges that derive from his landowning family turn out to be too tempting to discard, as Muḥsin wants to impress Saniyya. After all, Muḥsin does not entirely let go of these privileges even when he lives with his poor relatives in Cairo. He can always go back to the luxurious family house in Damanhur whenever he wants. Thanks to his parents' interference, Muḥsin does not have to stay in a decrepit prison cell at the end of the novel but is instead transferred to a relatively comfortable hospital room.

Furthermore, Saniyya does not offer a sense of emancipation; in fact, both Saniyya and the Turkish mother evoke similar reactions in Muḥsin. When Muḥsin thinks about Saniyya, 'his heart [is] oppressed' (187; 2: 29). The following words capture Saniyya's impact on Muḥsin: 'He could scarcely breathe from joy. Happiness was strangling him. It had reached his throat. The joy would choke him if it didn't spill out' (229; 2: 96). Although Muḥsin may harbour different feelings for Saniyya and his mother, both characters generate a sense of discomfort and even oppression in Muḥsin's body. While Muḥsin aspires to emancipation, he often feels a sense of imprisonment, and indeed he is imprisoned at the end of the novel.

Muḥsin does not show any active effort to sublimate his desire for Saniyya. Saniyya ultimately gets married to Muṣṭafā. Only then can Muḥsin feel liberated from the demands of romantic love for Saniyya and ultimately join his comrades who fight for the nation. As Hutchins has put it, 'Muṣṭafā Bey's blond mustache and chestnut hair are not accidental details in *Return of the Spirit*. They suggest that he is partly of Turkish heritage – like Muḥsin's mother (and of course Muḥsin too, thanks to his mother)'.[26] Saniyya and Muṣṭafā are the only characters who get married and establish a family, revealing that the dynamics of the ethnically heterogeneous families from which Muḥsin tried to escape will not dissipate.

Although Muḥsin aspires to become a writer who expresses Egypt's authentic sentiments, he cannot become a prolific writer. Muḥsin never publishes his works, and the readers do not know the content of his writings. When Muḥsin understands that Saniyya will get married to Muṣṭafā, he gives all his fictional works to Saniyya as he leaves her:

> Muḥsin hesitated a little before departing. Finally, he didn't know why or in relation to what, he took from his pocket the sheaf of poems and prose and handed it to Saniyya. She took it in astonishment. He departed quickly and speedily descended the steps. Only God knew the secret feelings of this youth's heart at that hour. (305; 2: 211)

Readers will never know for sure whether Saniyya has read Muḥsin's works. 'Only God knew' the content of Muḥsin's writings that capture his 'secret feelings'. Muḥsin turns into a tragic figure who can never break free from his family's impact, his Turkish mother in particular, as readers cannot be assured by the end of the novel that Muḥsin would ever publish a work capturing Egypt's heart. As the next section will show, like Hayri İrdal in *The Time Regulation Institute*, he feels a perpetual sense of imprisonment.

The Oedipal Complex and the Tunisian 'Father' in Ahmet Hamdi Tanpınar's The Time Regulation Institute

Born in Istanbul in 1901, Tanpınar spent his childhood in different parts of the Ottoman Empire, such as Sinop, Siirt and Kirkuk, since his father served as judge and regent. He returned to Istanbul in 1918 to continue his higher education and took lessons from prominent literary figures, including Yahya Kemal (1884–1958), Mehmed Fuad Köprülü (1890–1966) and Cenab Şahabeddin (1870–1934). After working as a teacher in different schools across Turkey, he started to teach courses on aesthetics and mythology at the State Academy of Fine Arts in 1933. For the 100th anniversary of the *Tanzimat* Decree in 1839, Istanbul University established a chair on nineteenth-century Turkish literature, and Tanpınar was appointed as professor there. He composed works in different genres such as poetry, novel, short story, essay, criticism and history. He exhibited a deep engagement with different art forms, including sculpture and music. He also engaged with ancient Greek art and literature, as he translated into Turkish Euripides's (c. 480–c. 406 BC) *Alcestis* (438 BC), *Medea* (431 BC) and *Electra* (c. 418 BC), as well as Henri Lechat's (1862–1925) *La sculpture grecque* (Greek Sculpture, 1922).

Many conservative intellectuals have argued that Tanpınar castigated Turkey's Westernisation and called for a return to tradition. Indeed, as Nurdan Gürbilek has demonstrated, Tanpınar often used terms such as 'inner' and 'self' in his critical writings when he, for instance, called for a return to 'the wide, essential return to [Turks's] own reality'.[27] At the same time, as Gürbilek has also shown, Tanpınar believed that a complete return to tradition was not possible. Unlike Yahya Kemal, who glorified conquest and masculinity, Tanpınar wrote about loss and melancholy. As Nurdan Gürbilek has put it, '[e]ven if we may speak of a kind of conservatism in Tanpınar, it is less bound up with dead ancestors, illustrious grandfathers, martyrs swimming in blood and a censuring superego than with the dead mother, the lost Empire, the fabulous sultans of old always paired with mirrors and the impossible flow'.[28] Furthermore, as I will show, his literary history suggests that the 'inner self' about which Tanpınar wrote could not experience a sense of authenticity, even during the classical Ottoman period that witnessed the domination of Arabic and Persian heritage.

Tanpınar did not necessarily argue that modernisation caused the Turks to experience an uneasy relationship with tradition and hence to suffer from psychological complexes. Instead, his works suggest that the Turkish subject experienced something akin to an 'Oedipus complex', also during the Ottoman period that witnessed the domination of Arabic and Persian heritage, which prevented the Turks from experiencing a sense of authenticity and emancipation. As he argued in his literary history, *On Dokuzuncu Asır Türk Edebiyatı Tarihi*, once the Turks broke the chains of these heritages thanks to their recent Westernisation efforts, they would finally find their authentic voice.

On Dokuzuncu Asır Türk Edebiyatı Tarihi draws on various critics, such as Hippolyte Taine (1828–93), who called for analysing a text within its environment, and Ferdinand Brunetière (1849–1906), who studied the formation of genres. As Veli N. Yashin and E. Khayyat have already revealed and extensively discussed, Tanpınar also based himself on Orientalist philology.[29] The first section of his history examines *divan* (classical Ottoman) and folk poetry of the first half of the nineteenth century. In the section titled 'Tanzimat Seneleri' (The *Tanzimat* Years), he wrote about cultural and social developments during the *Tanzimat* era. Then, Tanpınar discussed the 'three pioneers of modernisation', Ahmet Cevdet Pasha (1822–95), Münif Pasha (1830–1910) and Şinasi (1826–71). Tanpınar devoted an entire section to the Young Ottomans. Another section titled 'Nevilerin Gelişmesi' (The Development of Genres), which examines genres such as newspaper, poem, theatre play, story and novel, which emerged during the late Ottoman period. He discussed all the authors who had played a vital role in the *Tanzimat* era, such as Ziya Pasha (1829–80), Namık Kemal (1840–88), Ahmet Midhat (1844–1912), Recaizade Mahmud Ekrem (1847–1914), Abdülhak Hamid Tarhan (1852–1937) and Muallim Naci (1849–93).

The main subject of Tanpınar's literary history is 'the Turkish person'. As Tanpınar wrote: '*History of Nineteenth-Century Turkish Literature*, before anything else, is about a crisis that the Turkish person started to suffer [in the nineteenth century]. The work is about the history of an inner order that slowly took shape around new horizons and values. We took care to depict this crisis, along with its social and historical causes, as much as the encounter between the old and the new at every instance'.[30] Tanpınar's work does not aim to merely provide a list of texts and authors from the nineteenth century; instead, like al-Ḥakīm, who wrote extensively about the Egyptian spirit as he wrote about Arabic literature, Tanpınar studied literature to understand the Turkish psyche.

At first sight, the title of Tanpınar's history, *On Dokuzuncu Asır Türk Edebiyatı Tarihi* (History of Nineteenth-Century Turkish Literature), suggests that the book is on Turkish literature only. At the same time, Tanpınar provided an extensive discussion of Arabic language and literature in the introduction to this history. The Turks had experienced a sense of belatedness even before the nineteenth century, because they belonged to the last circle of Islamic civilisation: 'Our old literature took shape as the last large creative circle of a shared civilisation that developed under the strong influence of Arabic and Persian literatures, which are not related to each other linguistically and which took shape in different installments during the same period'.[31] This sentence captures the influence paradigm that, as

The Ottoman Canon has shown, continues to shape the field of Ottoman Studies: just as the Turks were late in their Westernisation efforts, they were also late when they arrived in the circle of Islamic civilisation, as the Arab and Persian poets had already created important works of Islamic civilisation.

According to Tanpınar, unlike the Arab poets whose works captured their authentic sentiments and lived experience, the Ottoman poets wanted to show off their linguistic talent when they composed works in three languages; therefore, they failed to convey their authentic experience in their writings.[32] Tanpınar contrasted the purity of Arabic literature with Ottoman culture's heterogeneity. Unlike the Turks who struggled with three languages (Arabic, Persian and Turkish), the Arabs 'used only their own language'.[33] Arab poets thus had the opportunity to put into words whatever came to their mind, as both *al-Muᶜallaqāt* and Andalusian poetry expressed authentic experience. Arabs also had a particular advantage in prose because they used only their language and because Arabic prose had developed during the first years of the history of Islamic civilisation. Tanpınar believed that the Arabic *qaṣīda* had caused Ottoman authors to become preoccupied with linguistic craftsmanship; therefore, these authors had failed to express authentic sentiments.[34] According to him, an Ottoman poet who wrote in three languages fell apart by nature: 'One should not forget that those who composed poetry and prose often wrote in three languages. When language, which is described by Heidegger as "the house of thought", is multiplied in such a manner, human nature, of course, gets dispersed'.[35]

Although he believed that the Turkish subject remained under the strong influence of Arabic during the Ottoman period, Tanpınar complained in one of the letters he sent to his friend Tarık that the Turks did not know the Arabic-speaking communities well and never read books by Arab authors. In particular, the Turks had ignored 'the Arab nation after the murder of [Jean-Baptiste] Kléber in Egypt' in 1800.[36] Tanpınar claimed that, although Ottoman poets knew Arabic and Persian languages, they did not translate many Arabic and Persian works into Turkish. Thus, their society had almost no familiarity with Arabic and Persian works, resulting in a large gap between intellectuals and their society. The Turks should not make the same mistake as they turned westwards; in other words, Tanpınar claimed that the Turks should translate Western works into Turkish, in addition to learning Western languages.

Therefore, Tanpınar did not necessarily call for a return to tradition, and he often emphasised that the Turks needed to Westernise in a proper manner so that they could 'survive'; otherwise, they, like many other nations, would have to live under the hegemony of Western imperialism.[37] Tanpınar did not appreciate or agree with other poets and writers who called for a complete return to tradition or castigated Turkey's Westernisation efforts. For example, he described Mehmet Akif Ersoy (1873–1936) as a 'dry poet who follow[ed] the regulations of the Islamic tradition' (*kuru ehlisünnet şairi*) and believed that his poetry lacked the mystical Sufi tone that characterised much of the great religious poetry.[38]

Tanpınar also personified the *Tanzimat* as someone who had failed to Westernise properly.[39] According to Tanpınar, the *Tanzimat* did not know Europe well enough and was still too committed to the East; thus, the child born from the *Tanzimat* turned out to be a freak.[40] Europe laughed at the *Tanzimat* due to its clumsy character; however, it could not make fun of Turkey once Turkey learned how to Westernise properly during the first years of the Republic. Communities who wanted to civilise and Westernise needed to maintain their authenticity, because only '[t]hen foreign influences would be something natural for us. That is, [the Turks] would enter the global concert with [their] national identity intact'.[41] Tanpınar, like al-Ḥakīm, was resolute in this regard: 'We will become Europeanised. However, [we will do so] as the Turkish nation that resides in Asia Minor'.[42] Only then could the Turkish subject achieve the freedom of expressing its authentic voice.

While Tanpınar's critical works promise emancipation as the teleological end of the Turkish subject, *The Time Regulation Institute* reveals the impossibility behind this desire for emancipation and features a main character, Hayri İrdal, who always feels imprisoned. Although Tanpınar had intended to write his literary history in two volumes, he never wrote the second volume. E. Khayyat has argued that *The Time Regulation Institute* can be read as the second volume of Tanpınar's *On Dokuzuncu Asır Türk Edebiyatı Tarihi*. Building on Khayyat's work, I read Tanpınar's *The Time Regulation Institute* in conjunction with his literary history.[43] If the history describes a Turkish subject who aspires to emancipation, then the novel features a main character who can never escape from the influence of the Tunisian Abdüsselam Bey, described as a father-figure for Hayri İrdal. Therefore, like *Oedipus Rex*, Tanpınar's works also feature a clash between heart and intellect.

At the beginning of *The Time Regulation Institute*, Hayri İrdal tells his readers that the book we are reading is, in fact, his memoir of the institute and its founder, Halit Ayarcı. At the same time, the memoir provides extensive information on Hayri İrdal's early years, when he becomes interested in clocks after his uncle gives him a watch. He spends his time in the clock shop of Nuri Efendi, whose work significantly impacts

Hayri İrdal. Another person who plays a crucial role in Hayri İrdal's life is Abdüsselam Bey, who with his family lives in a big mansion in Hayri İrdal's district. As Abdüsselam Bey loses his family and fortune, he encourages Hayri İrdal to marry Emine, who also lives in Abdüsselam Bey's mansion. Abdüsselam Bey passes away after the War of Independence. After a feud between Hayri İrdal and Abdüsselam Bey's relatives about his inheritance, Hayri İrdal is deemed mentally unstable and hence taken to the psychoanalyst Dr Ramiz. After long sessions with Dr Ramiz, Hayri İrdal is released and frequents a coffeeshop. Hayri İrdal's first wife, Emine, passes away, and for a short while Hayri İrdal works for the Spiritualist Society. At the society, he meets Pakize, who becomes his second wife. After he is laid off from his job, Hayri İrdal meets Halit Ayarcı in the coffeeshop. He grabs Halit Ayarcı's attention by speaking about clocks and Nuri Efendi. Halit Ayarcı thus appoints Hayri İrdal to an important position at the Time Regulation Institute, aiming to synchronise all clocks and repair broken ones. Hayri İrdal also writes a book about a seventeenth-century figure that he fabricates, Ahmet the Timely Efendi, and then another book, the memoir or *The Time Regulation Institute* itself. In the end, Hayri İrdal wants to establish new apartments for workers at the institute. However, the workers rebel against this idea, and then the institute is abolished. Halit Ayarcı passes away in a traffic accident.

At first, Hayri İrdal seems to lack Muḥsin's literary ambition: 'I have never cared much for reading or writing; anyone who knows me can tell you that. Unless you count Jules Verne or the Nick Carter stories I read as a child, everything I know can be traced to *A Thousand and One Nights*, *A Parrot's Tale*, the armful of history books I've had occasion to pass my eyes over (always skipping the Arabic and Persian words) and the works of the philosopher Avicenna'.[44] Hayri İrdal has slight familiarity with the Ottoman reservoir that includes works such as Avicenna's writings and the Persian *A Parrot's Tale*; however, he also admits that he skips Arabic and Persian words when he reads old works. The few books that his father allowed him to read include 'works on Arabic grammar and syntax, such as *Emsile* and *Avamil*' (3–4; 7–8); hence, he was prevented from developing any deep engagement with the Ottoman cultural reservoir.

Although he claims to be a modest person without any significant achievements, Hayri İrdal, unlike Muḥsin, manages to publish books as he writes a memoir and a book on Ahmet the Timely Efendi, which is translated into eighteen languages. Likewise, while he claims not to be a cultural pioneer, Hayri İrdal also admits that he played a vital role for the Time Regulation Institute (7; 11). In one moment, Hayri İrdal claims that he has no strong ambitions: 'So I never was one for reading or writing'

(6; 9). Soon after, however, readers observe the extent of the ambition he has for composing *The Time Regulation Institute*: 'In fact I woke up at five o'clock – much earlier than usual – with this very task in mind. [. . .] So for better or worse I was left to make my own morning coffee, after which I ensconced myself in my armchair and began trying to imagine my life, sifting through all the things I would soon record – things that needed to be changed or embellished or omitted altogether' (6; 9–10).

Hayri İrdal reveals his agency as an author who decides what to include in and what to exclude from his memoir: 'In short, I have tried to arrange the events of my life into some semblance of order, bearing in mind the many strict rules of what we might call sincere writing: these are never as indispensable as when one is composing a memoir' (6; 10). Hayri İrdal emphasises that he wants to sound sincere when he writes this work, while also indicating that he does not write down whatever comes to his mind. Instead, he makes great efforts at organising his thoughts: 'A sincerity of this order – disinterested and unconditional – by its nature requires close scrutiny and constant filtering' (6; 10). Hayri İrdal acknowledges that hard work is necessary to generate a sense of sincerity that takes into account the reader's sentiments, since 'sincerity is not the work of one man alone' (6; 10).

Hayri İrdal's ultimate goal behind his hard work is to 'honor [. . .] the saintly man' (7; 10), Halit Ayarcı. Like Saniyya in *Return of the Spirit*, Halit Ayarcı promises to Hayri İrdal a new life that will help him break free from the past: 'I mentioned my life prior to meeting Halit Ayarcı. But can one really call it a life?' (8; 12). Hayri İrdal wants to believe that leaving behind the past should be as easy as changing clothes: 'A man who dons a new suit leaves his old self behind. How different it looks, as it recedes into the past!' (12; 16).

Like his memoir dedicated to a man who promises a new life, Hayri İrdal's composition of a book on Ahmet the Timely Efendi can be read as an attempt to escape from a haunting past. The need to march towards a new life necessitates leaving behind people like Abdüsselam Bey and fabricating people like Ahmet the Timely Efendi. After all, Ahmet the Timely Efendi becomes someone who addresses the needs of his era. Halit Ayarcı tells Hayri İrdal that a book on Ahmet the Timely Efendi demonstrates that the Turks have forbears who were 'both revolutionary and modern' (314; 305) and then tells him: 'If he had actually lived at the end of the seventeenth century, if he'd entertained the ideas we've attributed to him, well, then that would be a lie. He would be in the wrong age. He would have had to travel through time, which is, of course, impossible. In matters such as these, there is no set truth. It is a question of working with the century at hand and making him a man of his time. Our age needs Ahmet the Timely Efendi' (313; 303–4). The past should not be a source of psychological complexes; instead, it should be exploited, 'at the disposal of the present' (296; 287).

However, writing does not always promise emancipation from the fetters of the past because Hayri İrdal finds himself inadvertently writing about the Tunisian Abdüsselam Bey as he composes his memoir: 'Such matters are distant from the memoir I am writing. I am busy with my own chronicle. But to return to my earlier point, I was never quite able to escape the hold these friends had on me' (51; 54). Abdüsselam Bey is an 'Istanbul gentleman' who is 'a Tunisian aristocrat who indulged in an extravagant lifestyle in an enormous villa with a broad ochre facade' (35; 38). Hayri İrdal describes the complex and ethnically heterogeneous constitution of his family:

> Abdüsselam's first wife was a close relative of the bey of Tunis and a direct descendent of the Şerif line. His second wife was an elegant Circassian who had served in the Ottoman palace and was said to have once been intimate with Sultan Abdülhamid. The wife of one of Abdüsselam's many brothers was from the eminent Hidiv family, and the wife of another was the daughter of the warlord of a far-flung Caucasian tribe. (36; 38–39)[45]

Abdüsselam Bey's household is akin to Muḥsin's household, which, like many other prominent families of the Ottoman Empire, has members from different backgrounds, including descendants of the Sharif line and of the Egyptian khedive's family.

Just like Muḥsin who wants to leave behind his family, Hayri İrdal wants readers to believe that he can break free from the past and start a new life in a new house with different dynamics. After all, Abdüsselam Bey's fortune is declining. Hayri İrdal compares the fall of the Ottoman Empire with the demise of Abdüsselam Bey's family. Abdüsselam Bey has had a rich life until the declaration of the Second Constitution. Like Muḥsin, Abdüsselam Bey comes from a landowning family; however, he loses important lands after the 1908 Young Turk movement.[46] Ultimately, all his relatives leave him alone: 'Here was the man who had once lived in that enormous villa behind the Burmalı Mescit, amid a vast tribe of sons, grandchildren and relatives close and distant. Now he would die in the hands of two virtual strangers' (86; 86). Hayri İrdal becomes the only source of sustenance for Abdüsselam Bey. At the same time, Hayri İrdal does not want to remain associated with the head of a household whose fortunes are declining and whose family is falling apart.

Just as Muḥsin wants to cut all his ties to his Turkish mother, Hayri İrdal himself wants to cut all ties with the Tunisian Abdüsselam Bey. When he returns to Istanbul after his military service during World War I, Hayri İrdal learns that his father has passed away. He also wants to avoid confronting Abdüsselam Bey, so he 'change[s his] walking route, avoiding the direct road to the War Office, which [he] visited quite frequently in those days and taking the streets behind the Şehzade Mosque and Direklerarası instead' (80; 80). However, Abdüsselam Bey ultimately finds him and helps Hayri İrdal receive a job appointment that will lead to the succession of the events that drive the plot. Hayri İrdal's family 'surrender[s] [itself] to this miserable man because [Hayri İrdal lacks] the will to stand up to him' (89; 89).

Hayri İrdal marries Emine, his 'first wife, the mother of Zehra and Ahmet, [who] had grown up in [Abdüsselam Bey's] villa' (37; 39). The novel does not inform readers about Emine's background; however, by marrying and having children from someone who grew up in Abdüsselam Bey's house, Hayri İrdal most likely continues the ethnically heterogeneous lineage of Abdüsselam Bey. Furthermore, Abdüsselam Bey feels joy when Hayri İrdal's daughter is born and mistakenly gives her the name of his mother Zehra instead of Zahide (90; 89). Abdüsselam Bey even calls Zehra 'Mother' (90; 89), and Zehra calls Abdüsselam Bey 'her son' (92; 91).[47] As Abdüsselam Bey himself puts it, Hayri İrdal's family becomes akin to families with 'stories of incest as bizarre as any story ever told about the Egyptian pharaohs' (92; 92).

The psychoanalyst Dr Ramiz tells Hayri İrdal that Abdüsselam Bey serves as a father-figure: 'So, in a word, he was a father to you. And you wholeheartedly accepted him as such. You accepted him to such an extent that you even allowed the poor man to give your daughter his mother's name' (116; 114). He later declares: 'Yes. I have determined your illness. What you have is a typical case of a father complex' (112; 110). Dr Ramiz indicates that Hayri İrdal never liked his father and did not aim to take his father's place; therefore, he searched for new father-figures, such as Abdüsselam Bey. As a result, he could not declare independence. When Dr Ramiz emphasises that 'we all, both young and old, wrestle with this very condition' (118; 115), he suggests that all Turks share the same complex as Hayri İrdal. They can never leave behind the father-figures; hence, they can never enjoy a sense of emancipation.

Dr Ramiz wants Hayri İrdal to 'free [himself] from [his father] – which is to say, from this inferiority complex that [he] has inherited from him' (121; 118). After Abdüsselam Bey has passed away and his sessions with Dr Ramiz have come to an end, Dr Ramiz believes that

Hayri İrdal 'has conquered a true father complex' (132; 129). However, *The Time Regulation Institute* also suggests that Hayri İrdal can never fully sublimate Abdüsselam Bey. Instead of freeing himself from the father-figure, Hayri İrdal even becomes like Abdüsselam Bey: 'Without my quite knowing, I would on occasion even become Nuri Efendi or Abdüsselam Bey or, yes, even Seyit Lutfullah. [. . .] The moment I put on a suit sewn for me by one of those celebrated tailors, I can be no other than Abdüsselam Bey' (51; 53).

Özen Nergis Dolcerocca has argued that *The Time Regulation Institute* 'proposes nothing in the form of social change and it views all regulating, managing and calibrating systems – be they religious, the "authentic" culture of the Ottoman past or the modern-secular order – as essentially the same. They are all oppressive to the subject's inner temporal flow and to plural and incongruous temporalities'.[48] Although Hayri İrdal wants readers to think that his encounter with Halit Ayarcı has generated a complete rupture in his life, Hayri İrdal always feels a sense of imprisonment, both when he lives in Abdüsselam Bey's house and when he works for the Time Regulation Institute. Abdüsselam Bey's house has 'an uncanny way of trapping anyone who had the misfortune of being born there and many, it seems, who merely set foot inside' (35; 38). Hayri İrdal does not feel emancipated after he leaves Abdüsselam Bey's house, however. Whenever Hayri İrdal leaves the coffeehouse, he becomes 'a prisoner of [his] wandering and endlessly colluding mind' (151; 146). Dr Ramiz tells Hayri İrdal that he has 'imprisoned [himself] in a web of baseless fears and paranoia' (294; 285). Hayri İrdal describes himself as a puppet, 'with Halit Ayarcı pulling the strings' (343; 332), as Halit Ayarcı's eyes '[latch] onto [Hayri İrdal's eyes] like magnets' (222; 216). Halit Ayarcı describes Hayri İrdal as an 'an octopus, with [his] eight arms wrapped around the world' (360; 348). Imprisonment is Hayri İrdal's existential condition.

Derya Güler Aydın has drawn on Max Weber's theory of modernity and uses his concept of the 'iron cage' to demonstrate that the Time Regulation Institute carries the homogenising and oppressive characteristics of Western capitalist societies.[49] The establishment of the Time Regulation Institute signifies the rise of capitalism in Turkey, as work becomes the defining feature of one's identity. For example, Halit Ayarcı claims: 'We shall declare that man is first and foremost a creature who works and that work itself is time' (259; 251). Ultimately, work itself becomes a prison, as Hayri İrdal admits: 'Work makes us pure and beautiful; it is our bond with the outside world and makes us who we are. But work can also take possession of our souls. No matter how meaningless and absurd the job, we unwittingly become its prisoner' (376; 363).

The new life that Halit Ayarcı promises does not lead to emancipation but instead to people's commodification. Halit Ayarcı views people around him merely as 'objects occupying space' (196; 190) and 'sizes people up as if he might buy them' (195; 189). The novel's ending suggests that Abdüsselam Bey escapes from this commodification. Hayri İrdal notes during the celebration of the Time Regulation Institute: 'All the most important presences in my life – the Şerbetçibaşı Diamond, Seyit Lutfullah, Ahmet the Timely, the Blessed One and Nuri Efendi – rained down on me like confetti' (341; 330). At first, this sentence reinforces the impression that all people whom Hayri İrdal used to know become reduced to commodities. However, Hayri İrdal does not mention Abdüsselam Bey among the list of people who rain down on him like confetti. While many people from the past merely turn into the confetti that accommodate the Time Regulation Institute's new vision, Abdüsselam Bey distracts and even 'haunts' Hayri İrdal, who wants to compose a memoir that is supposed to be dedicated to Halit Ayarcı. Although Hayri İrdal avoids describing Abdüsselam Bey as a significant source of influence that shapes his life, Hayri İrdal cannot fully sublimate the Tunisian father-figure. Furthermore, as the novel's ending demonstrates, Halit Ayarcı cannot realise his vision of a new, modern society, as society's interest in the Time Regulation Institute wanes. Ultimately, Hayri İrdal and Halit Ayarci, like Muḥsin, need to come to terms with the fact that they cannot easily become pioneering figures for their community, as Halit Ayarcı declares: 'This institute is no longer mine! Now I'm just like everyone else here' (388; 376).

In certain instances, the novel suggests that, even though Hayri İrdal does not experience a sense of emancipation, his son, Ahmet, can break free from his father and establish a new future. Hayri İrdal observes: '[M]y son had not just overcome close family ties and the comforts that came with our new wealth and prosperity but that he had also taken on a far more difficult challenges: he had overcome himself' (380–81; 368). According to Hayri İrdal, '[p]erhaps to become his own person [. . .] [Ahmet] has no choice but to forget about [his father]' (381; 369), as Hayri İrdal also believes that '[e]very child breaks with his father' (382; 370). At the same time, he also observes that 'a part of [Hayri İrdal] still lives on in him' (52; 54). Ahmet wants to change his name when he learns that Hayri İrdal is writing *The Time Regulation Institute* because he worries that, if his father's memoir gets published, everyone will learn about his connection with Hayri İrdal and Abdüsselam Bey (140; 136). Ultimately, *The Time Regulation Institute* is published, and Ahmet cannot completely break free from his father. Furthermore, readers do not learn much about Ahmet's future; therefore, they cannot be certain whether Ahmet will achieve the emancipation that Hayri İrdal wanted for him, just as we do not know whether Muḥsin will produce works that express the authentic sentiments of his nation. Therefore, like *Return of the Spirit*, *The Time Regulation Institute* does not augur a future of emancipation; instead, it is the tragedy of Hayri İrdal, who cannot escape from an imperial family lineage shaping his fate.

Conclusion

In discussing their modernisation vision, Jale Parla has argued that *Tanzimat* writers did not aim to kill their fathers; instead, they wanted to revive them.[50] In other words, these writers did not view modernisation as a complete rupture from tradition; rather, they believed that their society should not discard tradition and instead achieve through modernisation and Westernisation the ideal social order that also characterised the 'golden age' – that is, the early modern Ottoman period. Tanpınar and al-Ḥakīm shared similar characteristics with those *nahḍa* and *Tanzimat* authors who considered themselves pioneers, or 'father-figures', who needed to guide their communities, as they laid out the personality traits of their national subjects and the ways to overcome their psychological complexes. At the same time, notwithstanding their paternalistic attitude, they also wanted to affiliate themselves with a young, dynamic nation-state that finally found its authentic voice as it broke free from the fetters of a linguistically and ethnically heterogenous Ottoman past. Their critical writings on literature, in particular, reinforce the narrative in which their communities' national spirit that for centuries remained dormant or subjected to strong foreign influences would finally achieve emancipation and authenticity. As al-Ḥakīm's and Tanpınar's critical writings promise a teleological story of emancipation, their novels also make manifest the desire to transition to a national community that experiences a sense of egalitarian camaraderie and a capitalist economy that undermines the power of established landowning families.

However, as Muḥsin and Hayri İrdal, like Oedipus, want to become pioneers, or 'philosopher-kings', of their communities, they also need to face 'the objective reality': both characters grew up in landowning families that enjoyed significant privileges during the Ottoman period and remained distant from much of their society. They thus confront family figures who sabotage their cultural vision for their nation-states. Neither Muḥsin nor Hayri İrdal can fully sublimate ethnically heterogeneous families who carry traces of the Ottoman past. The past can always turn into a source of anxiety sabotaging the attempts to overcome the sense of imprisonment that both characters feel.

Tanpınar and al-Ḥakīm lived at a time when their countries had recently achieved political sovereignty.[51] They both believed that this political sovereignty which came with the Ottoman Empire's demise did not necessarily mean that their communities had also attained cultural, spiritual, or intellectual sovereignty.[52] For example, al-Ḥakīm wrote that hegemonic powers not only conquered lands, but also minds.[53] These authors used terms such as spirit, self, or personality as they wrote about what it meant to be an Egyptian or a Turk. They studied literature to understand the psyche of their national subject. However, their novels feature traces of the Ottoman past, which sabotage the attempts to achieve the intellectual and spiritual emancipation that their critical writings promise.

Notes

1. Ahmet Hamdi Tanpınar, *Yaşadığım Gibi*, ed. Birol Emil (Istanbul: Dergâh Yayınları, 1996), 38.
2. Lorna Hardwick, 'Sophocles' *Oedipus* and Conflicts of Identity in Postcolonial Contexts', *Documenta* 22, no. 4 (2004): 377.
3. Sigmund Freud, *Interpreting Dreams* (London: Penguin Books, 2006), 276.
4. While I draw analogies between *Oedipus Rex* and Tanpınar's and al-Ḥakīm's writings, this chapter does not claim that Hayri İrdal and Muḥsin or Arabs and Turks, in general, suffer from an Oedipal complex. Furthermore, one cannot draw a perfect analogy between Oedipus and Muḥsin, or Oedipus and Hayri İrdal; for example, Muḥsin has an authoritative mother-figure, while Hayri İrdal struggles against Abdüsselam Bey, who is not his actual father. Instead, this chapter proposes that Tanpınar's and al-Ḥakīm's works share similar themes with the Greek play, such as one's inability to deny the past fully.
5. Tawfīq al-Ḥakīm, *Miṣr bayna ᶜahdayn* (Cairo: Maktabat Miṣr, n. d. [1983]), 11.
6. al-Ḥakīm, *Miṣr bayna ᶜahdayn*, 11. Al-Ḥakīm has been viewed as a pioneering literary figure throughout the Arab world. Jamīl Saᶜīd has written that many Iraqi writers preferred to read books by Egyptians rather than Iraqis, testifying to the impact of Egyptian literature on much of the Arab world in the early twentieth century. Jamīl Saᶜīd, *Naẓarāt fī al-tayyārāt al-adabiyya al-ḥadītha fī al-ᶜIrāq* (Cairo: Maᶜhad al-Dirāsāt al-ᶜArabiyya al-ᶜĀliyya, 1954), 7–8; quoted in Roger Allen, *The Arabic Novel: An Historical and Critical Introduction* (Syracuse: Syracuse University Press, 1982), 26.
7. Al-Ḥakīm also complained about Egypt's weak characteristics. For example, he believed that tolerance (*tasāmuḥ*) was one of the Egyptian personality's key traits since all religions and sects in Egypt lived together peacefully. At the same time, this tolerance generated a sense of lethargy as people accepted

their fate and made no effort to improve the socioeconomic condition of their society. Al-Ḥakīm, *Miṣr bayna ᶜahdayn*, 126–27.

8. al-Ḥakīm, *Miṣr bayna ᶜahdayn*, 14.
9. Ibid., 209. As Rasheed El-Enany has also pointed out, al-Ḥakīm in his earlier writings argued that it was incumbent upon art and literature to praise Egypt and the Arab world against a hegemonic Western civilisation, as Egyptian nationalism was in its nascent stage. In his later writings, al-Ḥakīm would warn the youth against yielding to the 'inferiority complex' that Muḥsin felt and using tradition as an excuse to isolate themselves from the world and resist change. Rasheed El-Enany, 'Tawfīq al-Ḥakīm and the West: A New Assessment of the Relationship', *British Journal of Middle Eastern Studies* 27, no. 2 (2000): 175.
10. Tawfīq al-Ḥakīm, *Fann al-adab* (Cairo: Maktabat Miṣr, n. d. [1952]), 12.
11. al-Ḥakīm, *Fann al-adab*, 27.
12. Ibid., 22. Another influential intellectual of the twentieth century, Ṭāhā Ḥusayn (1889–1973), called for a proper Westernisation that would not cause Egypt to lose its essence. Ḥusayn wanted Egypt to integrate into Europe to such an extent that it became a part of Europe, in terms of both outward appearance and essence (*ḥaqīqatan wa shaklan*). Ṭāhā Ḥusayn, *Mustaqbal al-thaqāfa fī Miṣr* (Cairo: Dār al-Maᶜārif, n. d. [1938]), 33. At the same time, Egyptians needed to attain not only 'exterior freedom' (*al-ḥurriya al-khārijiyya*) – that is, political independence – but also 'interior freedom' – that is, mental and psychological independence (*al-istiqlāl al-ᶜaqlī wa-l-nafsī*; Ḥusayn, *Mustaqbal*, 41). Like Ḥusayn, al-Ḥakīm also emphasised the importance of 'intellectual and mental sovereignty' in his writings.
13. El-Enany, 'Tawfīq al-Ḥakīm and the West', 173. As El-Enany has pointed out, al-Ḥakīm emphasised this point especially in his collection of essays, *ᶜAṣā al-Ḥakīm* (al-Ḥakīm's Walking-Stick, 1954). For a discussion of the concept of authenticity among modern Arab thinkers, see Harald Viersen, 'The Ethical Dialectic in al-Jabri's "Critique of Arab Reason"', in *Islam, State and Modernity: Mohammed Abed al-Jabri and the Future of the Arab World*, ed. Zaid Eyadat (New York: Palgrave Macmillan, 2018), 249–69.
14. Karen L. Carducci, 'Redeeming Jocasta: Tawfiq al-Hakim's "Eastern", "Arab" Reception of Sophocles' *Oedipus Tyrannus*', *Classical Receptions Journal* 11, no. 1 (2019): 107.
15. Tawfiq al-Hakim, *Plays, Prefaces and Postscripts of Tawfiq al-Hakim*, trans. William M. Hutchins (Washington, DC: Three Continental Press, 1981), 283; Tawfīq al-Ḥakīm, *al-Malik Ūdīb* (Cairo: Maktabat Miṣr, n. d. [1949]), 37–38. For al-Ḥakīm's engagement with *Oedipus Rex*, see also Ahmed Etman, 'The Greek Concept of Tragedy in Arab Culture: How to Deal with an Islamic *Oedipus*?' *Documenta* 22, no. 4 (2004): 281–99.
16. al-Hakim, *Plays*, 281; al-Ḥakīm, *al-Malik Ūdīb*, 33. Ahmed Etman and Karen L. Carducci have already pointed out significant differences between

Sophocles's *Oedipus Rex* and al-Ḥakīm's version of the play. For example, unlike the noble Oedipus in Sophocles's play, Oedipus, in al-Ḥakīm's version, does not solve the Riddle and later admits that he does not care whether Jocasta was his wife or his mother. Therefore, he does not express any strong discomfort with incest. In al-Ḥakīm's version, Oedipus speaks with his wife and children at the beginning of the play and expresses suspicion against the gods. He cares more about his family than society, hence meeting his tragic end. See Etman, 'The Greek Concept of Tragedy', 297, and Carducci, 'Redeeming Jocasta', 106.

17. William M. Hutchins, 'Introduction: A One-Man Egyptian Theater Tradition', in Tawfiq al-Hakim, *Plays, Prefaces and Postscripts of Tawfiq al-Hakim*, trans. W. M. Hutchins (Washington, DC: Three Continental Press, 1981), 7.
18. al-Hakim, *Plays*, 284; al-Ḥakīm, *al-Malik Ūdīb*, 42.
19. Hutchins, 'Introduction', 7.
20. al-Hakim, *Plays*, 284; al-Ḥakīm, *al-Malik Ūdīb*, 42.
21. The novel does not actually mention the name of the Turkish mother.
22. At the same time, al-Ḥakīm was not necessarily indifferent towards Turkey's political and cultural shifts. For example, he wrote about Mustafa Kemal Atatürk's (1881–1938) and İsmet İnönü's (1884–1973) diplomatic skills. Tawfīq al-Ḥakīm, *ᶜAwdat al-waᶜī* (Cairo: Maktabat Miṣr, n. d. [1974]), 62.
23. Tawfiq al-Hakim, *Return of the Spirit*, trans. William Maynard Hutchins (New York: Penguin, 2019), 201; Tawfīq al-Ḥakīm, *ᶜAwdat al-rūḥ* (Cairo: Maktabat al-Ādāb, n. d. [1933]), 2: 51.
24. The more literal translation of this sentence is: 'I mean, are you a son of a Turk?'
25. Jeff Shalan, 'Writing the Nation: The Emergence of Egypt in the Modern Arabic Novel', *Journal of Arabic Literature* 33, no. 3 (2002): 234.
26. William Maynard Hutchins, 'Introduction', in al-Hakim, *Return of the Spirit*, xxvii. Saniyya encourages Muṣṭafā to continue his family business and sell fabrics instead of working as a government bureaucrat in Cairo. Therefore, the novel's ending insinuates that Egypt needs ambitious merchants and a capitalist economy.
27. Nurdan Gürbilek, 'Dried Spring, Blind Mirror, Lost East: Ophelia, Water and Dreams', *Middle Eastern Literatures*, trans. Victoria Holbrook, 20, no. 2 (2017): 148.
28. Gürbilek, 'Dried Spring, Blind Mirror, Lost East', 146.
29. See Yashin 'The True Face of The Work', and E. Khayyat, *Istanbul 1940 and Global Modernity: The World According to Auerbach, Tanpınar and Edib* (Lanham: Lexington Books, 2019).
30. Tanpınar, *On Dokuzuncu Asır Türk Edebiyatı Tarihi*, 17.
31. Ibid., 23.
32. Ibid., 25–26.
33. Ibid., 51.
34. Ibid., 35.

35. Ibid., 25. Although the purity of Arabic literature contrasts with the heterogeneity and artificiality of Ottoman literature, Tanpınar also argued that both Arabic and Turkish literatures suffered from similar shortcomings, because they both belonged to Islamic civilisation. For example, Tanpınar wrote that Oriental tales such as *The Thousand and One Nights* and *maqāma* works were disconnected from reality (Tanpınar, *On Dokuzuncu Asır Türk Edebiyatı Tarihi*, 45–47).
36. Ahmet Hamdi Tanpınar, *Mektuplar*, ed. Zeynep Kerman (Ankara: Kültür Bakanlığı, 1974), 251–52. In his literary history, Tanpınar acknowledged that Egypt played a key role in Ottoman modernisation. Even the sultan himself wore a uniform 'in the Egyptian fashion'. The nineteenth century also witnessed an interest in fashion from 'Arabia and the South', although Turks had not accepted anything that came from the South and from Arabia before (Tanpınar, *On Dokuzuncu Asır Türk Edebiyatı Tarihi*, 83–84).
37. Ahmet Hamdi Tanpınar, *Edebiyat Üzerine Makaleler*, ed. Zeynep Kerman (Istanbul: Dergâh Yayınları, 1977), 87. Like al-Ḥakīm, Tanpınar often described East and West as two reified categories and laid out their 'psychological' features. For example, he believed that Easterners did not have tragedies because, while Eastern people accepted that life is full of coincidences, Western people viewed life as an exam. Ahmet Hamdi Tanpınar, *Mücevherlerin Sırrı: Derlenmemiş Yazılar, Anket ve Röportajlar: Deneme, Söyleşi*, ed. İlyas Dirin, Turgay Anar and Şaban Özdemir (Istanbul: Yapı Kredi Yayınları, 2002), 31–37.
38. Tanpınar, *Mücevherlerin Sırrı*, 154.
39. Tanpınar, *On Dokuzuncu Asır Türk Edebiyatı Tarihi*, 52.
40. Tanpınar, *Mücevherlerin Sırrı*, 35–37.
41. Ibid., 193.
42. Ahmet Hamdi Tanpınar, *Günlüklerin Işığında Tanpınar'la Başbaşa*, ed. İnci Enginün and Zeynep Kerman (Istanbul: Dergâh Yayınları, 2007), 265. Although scholars have described Westernisation as a key feature of *Tanzimat* literature, *Tanzimat* intellectuals did not completely cut ties with Islamic tradition. Tanpınar wrote that the increasing interest in the West also corresponded to an increasing interest in Islamic heritage among late Ottoman intellectuals. For example, Cevdet Pasha translated Ibn Khaldūn's (1332–1406) *Muqaddima* (1377) into Turkish (Tanpınar, *On Dokuzuncu Asır Türk Edebiyatı Tarihi*, 175).
43. Khayyat, *Istanbul 1940*, 76.
44. Ahmet Hamdi Tanpınar, *The Time Regulation Institute*, trans. Maureen Freely and Alexander Dawe (New York: Penguin, 2013), 3–4; Ahmet Hamdi Tanpınar, *Saatleri Ayarlama Enstitüsü* (Istanbul: Dergâh Yayınları, 2017), 7.
45. Later, Hayri İrdal also indicates that the slave of Abdüsselam's second wife came from Egypt (45; 47).
46. Another character whose origins can be traced to the Arab world is Seyit Lutfullah: 'Seyit Lutfullah had long since become a native of Istanbul and had

even forgotten his Arabic, but as with Abdüsselam Bey, the old Maghrebi of Tunisia, his ancient superstitions endured' (40–41; 43). The term 'even' here suggests that there were also Istanbullites who did not forget their Arabic. In the beginning of the novel, Hayri İrdal also mentions 'the Arab *kalfa*, Zeynep Hanım', who is one of the employees of the Clock Villa. He notes that Zeynep Hanım was hired since she, as a black woman, reminds Hayri İrdal of 'the old world' (6; 10).

47. The history of Egypt plays an important role in Hayri İrdal's life. Hayri İrdal's grandfather Tevkii Ahmet Efendi confronted many hardships during 'the Egyptian Affair' (the conflicts between the forces of the Ottoman Empire and those of Khedive Muḥammad ᶜAlī/Mehmed Ali between 1831 and 1841) and told his relatives that he would order a mosque's construction if this affair were resolved. Once the affair is resolved, he starts to plan the mosque's construction; however, this construction is never completed. Ultimately, Hayri İrdal has to take care of The Blessed One, a clock initially intended for this mosque (23–24; 26–27).
48. Özen Nergis Dolcerocca, '"Free Spirited Clocks": Modernism, Temporality and *The Time Regulation Institute*', *Middle Eastern Literatures* 20, no. 2 (2017): 181.
49. Derya Güler Aydın, 'Tanpınar'ın Saatleri Ayarlama Enstitüsü'nde Weber'in İzsürümü: Rasyonel ve İrrasyonel Değerler', *Bilig* 94 (2020): 29–50.
50. Jale Parla, *Babalar ve Oğullar: Tanzimat Romanının Epistemolojik Temelleri* (Istanbul: İletişim Yayınları, 2004), 20.
51. It is important to keep in mind that, although the United Kingdom recognised Egypt as a sovereign state in 1922, its impact on Egyptian domestic and economic policies continued until the 1952 Egyptian revolution.
52. Veli N. Yashin has already demonstrated that, as political sovereignty was fragile and under constant threat, Tanpınar affirmed a sense of sovereignty through his literary history that situated scattered works from the Ottoman past in a linear historical trajectory. See Yashin, '"The True Face of the Work"'.
53. al-Ḥakīm, *Fann al-adab*, 118.

Conclusion: Modernity, Ottoman Sa^{c}dī and Ottoman al-Mutanabbī

Şemseddin Sami (1850–1904) wanted his readers to learn other languages as they preserved the authenticity of their own language: 'If we speak Arabic, we should speak only Arabic; if we write in Persian, we should write only in Persian; if we speak French, we should speak only French; however, as we speak and write in Turkish, we should not use Arabic, Persian and French words in an unnecessary way. We should learn the languages of the world, but we should preserve our Turkish as Turkish'.[1] In a similar vein, Mayy Ziyāda (1886–1941) gave the following advice: 'Learn whatever language you want but strengthen your own language first. Learn the arts and sciences of other nations and acquaint yourself with their discoveries and culture, but remember to mention the culture, arts and sciences that your nation left behind'.[2] Both remarks show significant similarities. When Şemseddin Sami and Ziyāda used the term 'we' or 'you', they both referred to an autonomous national subject. On the one hand, this subject needed to protect the authenticity of its language; on the other hand, it was free to learn other literatures and languages of the world.

These remarks not only remind us that the formation of national identities and literatures took shape within a transnational context, but also provide key insights into current scholarly works that study translations and textual circulations in order to globalise Arabic and Turkish literary studies. Drawing on the rise of fields such as world literature and translation studies, these works have studied 'Arabic literature as world literature' or 'Turkish literature as world literature';[3] in other words, they have recontextualised Arabic or Turkish texts within global literary networks so as to move away from the nationalist frameworks that have shaped the study of Arabic and Turkish literatures. Reflecting more deeply on the formation of Arabic and Turkish literatures as categories of analysis in the late Ottoman period can also provide a new direction for this attempt to 'globalise' Arabic and Turkish literary studies. Future works that globalise Arabic and Turkish literatures may pay attention to diverse literary comparisons, such as the comparisons laid out in Chapter 2, which ultimately shaped how we conceptualise Arabic and Turkish literatures today.

Works from different linguistic traditions of the late Ottoman Empire have been analysed within the framework of different 'renaissance' movements – *rilindja* (Albanian modernity), *nahḍa* (Arab modernity), *haskala* (Jewish modernity), *zartonk* (Armenian modernity) and *Tanzimat* (Turkish modernity).[4] Ottoman Studies need to continue the endeavour of mapping out the empire's rich literary networks. As Ottoman literature cannot simply be studied as a part of Islamic Middle Eastern literatures, critics should also continue to study non-Islamicate literatures of the late Ottoman Empire, such as Armenian and Greek literatures. At the same time, it is also important to seek new paradigms, other than the nationalist framework. The late Ottoman literary landscape cannot be viewed as merely an amalgamation of disparate national traditions, such as Arabic, Turkish, Armenian and Greek. Such an approach can reinforce a one-to-one correspondence between one ethnic or religious community and a particular literary tradition. As a result, late Ottoman Greek literature can sometimes be studied as the possession of Greeks, or Judeo-Spanish literature as the possession of the Judeo-Spanish people. Thus, the original context in which texts emerge is valorised, causing critics to overlook the new afterlives that these texts may have adopted and other kinds of communities that such texts could have cultivated.

Recent endeavours to map out the late Ottoman Empire's literary networks do not have to preclude the questions of exclusion, canonisation and power hierarchies that characterised the Ottoman cultural landscape. Despite its multilingual character, the Ottoman literary canon I have 'accessed' in my close readings does not reflect the actual linguistic, religious and ethnic diversity of the empire's cultural landscape. *The Ottoman Canon* has studied works from Ahmet Midhat (1844–1912), Maᶜrūf al-Ruṣāfī (1875–1945) and Süleyman Nazif (1869–1927) in order to reveal the epistemological and material transformations that merely mapping out the empire's literary networks cannot reveal. As critics today are more drawn to the 'fluid' character of Ottoman translations and migrating texts within the empire, they can also pay attention to the 'solidification' of the canons that reinforced communal and cultural boundaries. Analysing how late Ottoman authors, such as Rūḥī al-Khālidī (1864–1913) and Namık Kemal (1840–88), generated the paradigms and concepts that shape the current scholarship on Arabic and Turkish literature can caution critics, in Haifa Saud Alfaisal's words, against 'rush[ing] into general periodic and/or conceptual formulas' in order to generate 'easily managed, packaged and marketed academic products (anthologies, readers and histories)'.[5]

Critics can thus situate literatures from different linguistic traditions such as Arabic and Armenian within a shared Ottoman cultural context, analysing both convergences and power hierarchies among them. A strong engagement with the imperial hierarchies and practices that have shaped the late Ottoman period can help critics overcome the tendency to posit a dichotomy between a tolerant and cosmopolitan Ottoman past and a homogenous and repressive nation-state. *The Ottoman Canon* has demonstrated that translations and travels also could contribute to the solidification of linguistic, literary and cultural boundaries. Authors such as Zaynab Fawwāz (1860?–1914), Jurjī Zaydān (1861–1914) and Maʿrūf al-Ruṣāfī translated or wrote about Ottoman Turkish works. At the same time, these authors did not merely 'transplant' but rather selectively transmitted what they read in or about Ottoman Turkish works to their Arabic audience. In contrast, both Hacı İbrahim (1826–88) and Ahmet Rasim (1864–1932) gave more references to Orientalist and pre-Ottoman Arabic works than to *nahḍa* Arabic writings from authors such as Zaydān, as they wrote about Arabic language and literature. Although authors such as Zaydān would describe their own time-period as the moment in which their Arab community experienced awakening and civilisational progress, Ahmet Rasim viewed Arabs as akin to 'grandparents' who had shown progress centuries ago, but not as people who lived in the Ottoman Empire and also experienced a sense of civilisational progress.

As my work has demonstrated, even when they engaged with Arabic works, writers such as Ziya Pasha or Namık Kemal did not claim that Arabic or Persian texts made them Arabised or Persianate. A Persian 'textual collective', as Mana Kia has argued, 'brought forth the [Persianate] self'.[6] In a similar vein, authors such as Ziya Pasha and Süleyman Nazif in their works suggested that a reservoir of Arabic, Persian and Turkish textual collectivities may have brought about an Ottoman self.

Attempts to study Arabic and Persian works within the comparative and global framework of Middle Eastern Studies examine how Arabic and Persian texts circulated to different parts of the world in order to create a cosmopolitan Arabophone or Persianate community.[7] These works have played a fundamental role in generating more bridges between Middle Eastern Studies and Comparative Literature. They also help critics study 'Arab literature as world literature' and 'Persian literature as world literature'. At the same time, as critics of Middle Eastern literatures study the cosmopolitan Arabic and Persianate communities that consume Arabic and Persian texts, they may sometimes assume that these texts belong to one particular canon only – the canon of Arabic literature or Persian literature. Thus, they risk overlooking diverse forms of communities, such as the Ottoman literati, who may also consume these texts and yet not necessarily identify with these cosmopolitan formations.

Therefore, as they study the Ottoman literati and its multilingual canon, critics can move beyond the current frameworks that investigate the classical Arabic heritage exclusively within the history of Arabic literature. Such an endeavour will ultimately undermine the current disciplinary divisions between classical and modern, as well as among Arabic, Turkish and Persian literatures in the study of Middle Eastern literatures. By fleshing out diverse reassessments of the Ottoman canon, my work calls for a rewriting of the history of not only modern Arabic and Turkish literatures, but also of the classical traditions with which these modern literatures engaged.

While critics can continue to analyse literary and cultural engagements with the West during the late Ottoman period, they can also pay attention to the refashionings of classical heritage. As Aria Fani and Kevin L. Schwartz have put it, 'in the late-nineteenth and early-twentieth centuries [...] Persianate pasts were being reassigned in endeavors that proved every bit as consequential and pressing as contending with new European intellectual currents and political entanglements'.[8] In a similar vein, my book sheds light on the reassessments of Persianate and Arabic pasts as constitutents of what is now studied as the 'literary modernity' of the Ottoman Empire. The current scholarship depicting the late Ottoman period as a moment of 'Westernisation' has often perpetuated the assumption that those who resisted against Westernisation and 'Western' forms such as the novel were 'traditional' writers. However, many 'traditional' and 'modern' authors depicted Arabic merely as a source of influence that Arabised Ottoman writers, rather than as streams filling an Ottoman literary reservoir in which Arabic works become 'Ottomanised'. Their works laid the foundation for the conceptualisation of Arabic literature as possession of the autonomous national Arab subject and of Turkish literature as possession of the autonomous national Turkish subject. Hacı İbrahim and Ahmet Rasim differed in their approach towards 'Western' forms such as novel and theatre play; however, both proponents of 'old literature' and 'new literature' had 'modern' views on Arabic works. In fact, the tendency among the proponents of 'old literature' to conceptualise the Ottoman language as Arabic language or Ottoman literature as Arabic literature may have prepared the ground for the conceptualisation of Ottoman literature as Turkish literature.

My book demonstrates that the earlier focus on a rupture between classical and modern traditions during the *Tanzimat* and *al-nahḍa* has habituated critics to think of Arabic and Turkish literatures as national literatures that have existed since time immemorial. If global modernity has generated a sense of loss, then the historiographical narrative that authors left behind the classical traditions when they entered modernity can be interpreted as an attempt to domesticate this loss, because it identifies with certitude what was left behind. Yet, no historical narrative or archival documentation can domesticate this loss, just as a return to an 'unadulterated tradition' is not possible. Rather, classical works 'haunt' modern texts, making attempts to assign texts to fixed time-periods and to maintain the current institutional distinctions between classical and modern or Arabic and Turkish literatures extremely difficult, if not futile. However, scholars in the fields of Ottoman Studies and Middle Eastern literatures have often adopted the methodological inclinations of the disciplines of philology and history. As a result, they have often tended to overlook the diverse, and sometimes even contradictory meanings that texts attained within different contexts and the various communities that they cultivated. Rather, the texts they have studied were often solely assigned to and almost exclusively studied within their source culture or original context. Listing these texts in a linear, chronological order even generated a sense of mastery and ultimately domesticated loss.

Due to its focus on canonised writers in the fields of Arabic and Turkish literatures, *The Ottoman Canon* has paid attention to writings and authors from a few urban centres that have received the most attention in these fields – that is, Cairo, Beirut and Istanbul. At the same time, future research may focus on areas that have not received much attention in the study of Arabic and Turkish literary modernities. The chapter on Maᶜrūf al-Ruṣāfī and the Ottoman Iraqi provinces constitutes one example of how shifting the focus away from these urban centres can provide new perspectives on modernity movements in the Middle East. While my book focuses mainly on Istanbul, Cairo and the Levant as it examines canonisation and academic divisions, future research may also investigate texts related to the Maghreb, such as the works by ᶜAbd al-Qādir al-Jazāᵓirī (1808?–83) and Khayr al-Dīn al-Tūnisī/Tunuslu Hayreddin Pasha (1820–90), not only to reassess Maghrebi cultural production, but also to reshape our understanding of Arabic and Turkish literary modernities.[9]

The comparative textual analysis of this study can serve as a starting point for future research examining the reconfigurations of heritage in late Ottoman works during a time of massive cultural and political upheaveals. Many Arab and Arabophone writers, such as ᶜAbd al-Qādir al-Jazāᵓirī, Muḥammad al-Muwayliḥī (1858–1930), Jurjī Zaydān, Rūḥī al-Khālidī and Aḥmad Shawqī (1868–1932), engaged with political and cultural developments in the Ottoman Empire. These authors advocated 'Ottomanist' views when they wrote that the Ottoman state had to remain strong to protect its subjects against Western imperialism. As these authors engaged with the political and literary developments of the Ottoman Empire, they could also be seen as key contributors to the *nahḍa* project that envisioned a bounded and modern Arab subject. A key aspect of this project was to view works such as Kaᶜb ibn Zuhayr's (d. c. 646/47) 'Bānat Suᶜād' as part of a classical heritage that served as pedestal for the construction of this subject. Therefore, their numerous essays on Arabic literature and poets such as al-Mutanabbī (d. 965) and al-Maᶜarrī (973–1057) not only displayed their comprehensive erudition in the Arabic literary tradition, but also situated poets such as al-Mutanabbī within an Arabic *turāth* that could serve as such a pedestal.

As these authors situated poets like Kaᶜb ibn Zuhayr within a lineage of the Arabic *turāth*, late Ottoman authors such as Süleyman Nazif emphasised familial bonds between Kaᶜb ibn Zuhayr and Fuzuli in order to reinforce their vision of the Ottoman literary reservoir. 'Bānat Suᶜād' constituted a key work of the Ottoman canon that generated a sense of imaginary unity for the Ottoman literati. Even when late Ottoman literature has been assumed to undergo vast shifts under the influence of French literature, many late Ottoman works, like *Firak-ı Irak* itself, frequently made references to pre-Ottoman Arabic writings. In fact, late Ottoman Turkish writings quote much more extensively from pre-Ottoman Arabic poems such as 'Bānat Suᶜād' than from 'Ottoman Arabic texts' – that is, Arabic texts written during the Ottoman period. The earlier scholarship has not paid sufficient attention to Ottoman Arabic works, because it has viewed the time-period between the thirteenth and nineteenth centuries as an age of decadence for the Arab world.[10] It is fundamental to conduct more scholarship on Ottoman Arabic texts; at the same time, this chapter points to another possible direction for Arabic Studies: in addition to studying Ottoman Arabic literature, critics can also look at the new receptions that pre-Ottoman Arabic texts, such as Kaᶜb ibn Zuhayr's 'Bānat Suᶜād', experienced in the Ottoman context.

The Ottoman literati's imperialistic vision was exclusionist. After all, almost all members of these literati were men. Furthermore, their circle did not include authors who wrote in Greek and Armenian; it did not even include *nahḍa* authors. While pointing out the numerous hiearchies and exclusions that this imperialistic vision generated, critics can also flesh out this vision to move beyond the current ways in which we categorise texts such as Kaᶜb ibn Zuhayr's 'Bānat Suᶜād' or Saᶜdī's (c. 1213–91/92) *Būstān*. For example, Süleyman Nazif's *Firak-ı Irak* reminds us that Kaᶜb ibn Zuhayr and al-Mutanabbī can inhabit many worlds: if Maᶜrūf al-Ruṣāfī wrote about an 'Arab Kaᶜb ibn Zuhayr' and an 'Arab al-Mutanabbī', Süleyman Nazif described an 'Ottoman Kaᶜb ibn Zuhayr' and an 'Ottoman al-Mutanabbī'. Likewise, Ziya Pasha suggested that an 'Ottoman Saᶜdī' took repose in the Ottoman tavern, although this Saᶜdī has not received much attention in the scholarship on Persian literature.

Ultimately, studying the construction of Arabic and Turkish literatures sheds new light on the history of literature itself. According to Jeffrey Sacks, even though literature is a Latin word and has a Latin 'origin', it is not necessarily Latin. Literature was not 'invented' in Europe as a stable object and then became 'adapted' or 'appropriated' in non-Western contexts:

> For it is the translation of literature and its rendering according to diverse and global languages that gives it to be what it is. Literature, that most Latin of words, is already and from the very beginning, susceptible to translation and it may therefore be said to be itself only insofar as its Latin provenance is touched upon in advance by those idioms into which it will have been translated. If literature may be said to have a beginning, then, it begins as translation, among its ruins and remains.[11]

Literature's 'translations' in the late Ottoman context have made literature what it is today. Literature, then, is not merely borrowed from the West; rather, it takes shape as it is translated, reiterated and reused in Arabic and Turkish works.

The past few decades have witnessed a rise in scholarship studying non-Muslim and women authors of the Ottoman Empire in order to shed light on texts that have been excluded from canons. My book demonstrates that literature was conceptualised as a possesssion that communities needed to own. Such a conceptualisation often served to overcome the sense of 'fatherlessness' from which many late Ottoman authors suffered. Yet, the desire to 'possess' a literature perpetuates exclusionist practices and reinforces the current institutional divisions that cause critics to overlook the diverse 'imaginary packagings' in which texts can appear. In addition to studying more women, non-Muslim and non-Western authors, Comparative Literature can reflect on the many exclusions that the institutionalisation of literature has generated.

While much of the earlier scholarship has already demonstrated that many Ottoman writers engaged with the Arabic, Persian and Turkish *languages*, I have emphasised that these writers also engaged with specific *poets and texts* of the Arabic and Persian traditions in order to move beyond the current institutional divisions that shape Middle Eastern Studies. These traditions have often been studied as sources of influence rather than as streams flowing into the Ottoman literary reservoir; however, writers such as Ziya Pasha and Süleyman Nazif did not claim that Persian or Arabic texts made the Ottoman literati Persianate or Arabised. Furthermore, the current scholarship has mapped out the diverse linguistic traditions that circulated within the late Ottoman Empire, such as the Armenian, Greek and Judeo-Spanish traditions; it has thus overcome the previous nationalistic framework that has ignored the diverse linguistic traditions of the empire. *The Ottoman Canon* demonstrates that the Ottoman cultural vision that shaped authors such as Süleyman Nazif included works written outside the Ottoman territories and even before the establishment of the empire, such as Kaᶜb ibn Zuhayr's 'Bānat Suᶜād'. It has called for paying attention to the 'new life' or 'afterlife' that Kaᶜb ibn Zuhayr's and al-Mutanabbī's works adopted in the Ottoman context. Ultimately, *The Ottoman Canon* emphasises the need to flesh out the Ottoman canon's multilingual character for generating a new literary history that can rethink and sometimes even move beyond the categories that many critics take for granted, such as 'Ottoman literature' and 'classical Arabic literature'.

Notes

1. Şemsettin Sami, *Süreli Yayınlarda Çıkmış Dil ve Edebiyat Yazıları: İnceleme–Metin*, ed. Yüksel Topaloğlu (Istanbul: Ötüken, 2012), 354.
2. Mayy Ziyāda, 'al-Gharāᵓiz al-saykūlūjiyya al-thalāth', *al-Muqtaṭaf* 68 (April 1926): 394; translation in Khaldi, *Egypt Awakening in the Early Twentieth Century*, 15.
3. For recent examples, see Burcu Alkan and Çimen Günay-Erkol (eds), *Turkish Literature as World Literature* (New York: Bloomsbury, 2021), and Sarah R. Bin Tyeer and Claire Gallien, eds, *Islam and New Directions in World Literature* (Edinburgh: Edinburgh University Press, 2022).
4. Isa Blumi, *Reinstating the Ottomans: Alternative Balkan Modernities, 1800–1912* (New York: Palgrave Macmillan, 2011), 178. As Blumi has put it, 'the criteria for acknowledging what constituted a historical force have been established by the paradigm of the nation-state' (178).
5. Alfaisal, 'The Politics of Literary Value in Early Modernist Arabic Comparative Literary Criticism', 277.
6. Kia, *Persianate Selves*, 22.
7. For recent examples, see Ronit Ricci, *Islam Translated: Literature, Conversion and the Arabic Cosmopolis of South and Southeast Asia* (Chicago: University of Chicago Press, 2011), and Kia, *Persianate Selves*.

8. Aria Fani and Kevin L. Schwartz, 'Persianate Pasts; National Presents: Persian Literary and Cultural Production in the Twentieth Century', *Iranian Studies* 55, no. 3 (2022): 607.
9. For example, one could analyse the works that ᶜAbd al-Qādir al-Jazāʾirī wrote when he lived in different parts of the Ottoman Empire, such as Bursa and Damascus. For his time in the Ottoman Empire, see Ramazan Muslu, *Emir Abdülkādir El-Cezâirî ve Tasavvufî Görüşleri* (Istanbul: İnsan Yayınları, 2011), 61–95. For more on his life in Damascus, see ᶜAshrātī Sulaymān, *al-Amīr ᶜAbd al-Qādir fī bilād al-mashriq* (Algiers: Dār al-Quds al-ᶜArabī li-l-Nashr wa-l-Tawzīᶜ, 2011). For a recent work on Khayr al-Dīn al-Tūnisī, see Peter Hill and Johann Strauss, 'Khayr al-Din al-Tunisi's *Muqaddima* to *Aqwam al-masalik fi maᶜrifat ahwal al-mamalik* (*The Surest Path to Knowing the Conditions of Kingdoms*), in Arabic, French and Ottoman Turkish', in *Ottoman Translations: Circulating Texts from Bombay to Paris*, ed. Marilyn Booth and Claire Savina (Edinburgh: Edinburgh University Press, 2023), 121–89. For an analysis of Khayr al-Dīn al-Tūnisī's works within a Mediterranean framework, see Clancy-Smith, *Mediterraneans*, 315–41.
10. For a more comprehensive discussion of this scholarship, see Wagner (ed.), *A Handbook and Reader of Ottoman Arabic*.
11. Jeffrey Sacks, 'Latinity', *CR: The New Centennial Review* 9, no. 3 (2009): 253.

References

ᶜAbd al-Raḥīm, F. *Muᶜjam al-dakhīl fī al-lugha al-ᶜarabiyya al-ḥadītha wa lahjātuhā*. Damascus: Dār al-Qalam, 2011.

Abdürrahman Fehmi. *Medreset ül-Arap*. Istanbul: Matbaa-i Ebüzziya, AH 1304 [1886/87].

Adıvar, Halide Edib. *Memoirs of Halidé Edib. 1926. New Introduction by Hülya Adak*. Piscataway: Gorgias Press, 2004.

Aḥmad, ᶜAbd Allāh ᶜAbd al-Muṭṭalib. *Al-Muwayliḥī al-Ṣaghīr: ḥayātuh wa adabuh*. [Cairo]: al-Hayʾa al-Miṣriyya al-ᶜĀmma li-l-Kitāb, 1985.

Ahmedani, Usman and Dženita Karić. 'Finding the Lost Andalusia: Reading Abdülhak Hamid Tarhan's *Tarık or the Conquest of al-Andalus* in its Multiple Renderings'. In *Ottoman Translations: Circulating Texts from Bombay to Paris*, edited by Marilyn Booth and Claire Savina, 190–224. Edinburgh: Edinburgh University Press, 2023.

Ahmed Vefik Paşa. 'Lehce-i Osmanî Mukaddimesi'. In *Yeni Türk Edebiyatı Antolojisi III*, edited by Mehmet Kaplan, İnci Enginün, Birol Emil and Zeynep Kerman, 3: 3–4. Istanbul: Marmara Üniversitesi Yayınevi, 1994.

Ahmet Midhat. *Ahbar-ı Asara Tamim-i Enzar*. Istanbul: AH 1307 [1899/1900].

——. *Çengi; Kafkas; Süleyman Muslî*. Ankara: Türk Dil Kurumu, 2000.

——. *Hasan Mellah yahud Sır İçinde Esrar*. Istanbul: Şark Matbaası, AH 1291 [1874/75].

——. 'Hikâye Tasvir ve Tahriri'. In *Yeni Türk Edebiyatı Antolojisi III*, edited by Mehmet Kaplan, İnci Enginün, Birol Emil and Zeynep Kerman, 3: 53–57. Istanbul: Marmara Üniversitesi Yayınevi, 1994.

——. 'Ölüm Allah'ın Emri'. In *Letaif-i Rivayat*. Istanbul: Kırk Anbar Matbaası, AH 1290 [1873/74].

——. 'Romancı ve Hayat'. In *Yeni Türk Edebiyatı Antolojisi III*, edited by Mehmet Kaplan, İnci Enginün, Birol Emil and Zeynep Kerman, 3: 63–69. Istanbul: Marmara Üniversitesi Yayınevi, 1994.

Ahmet Rasim. *Arapların Medeniyet-i Terakkiyesi.* Istanbul: Şirket-i Mürettibiyye Matbaası, AH 1304 [1886/87].
—. *İki Hatırat, Üç Şahsiyet: Said Paşa.* Istanbul: Matbaa-i Hayriyye ve Şürekası, 1916/17.
—. *İlk Büyük Muharrirlerden Şinasi.* Istanbul: Yeni Matbaa, 1927.
—. *Matbuat Hatıralarından: Muharrir, Şair, Edib.* Istanbul: Kanaat Kütüphane ve Matbaası, 1924.
Aksoy, Musa. *Moderniteye Karşı Geleneğin Savaşçısı: Hacı İbrahim Efendi.* Ankara: Akçağ, 2005.
Alfaisal, Haifa Saud. 'Liberty and the Literary: Coloniality and Nahdawist Comparative Criticism of Rūḥī al-Khālidī's *History of the Science of Literature with the Franks, the Arabs and Victor Hugo* (1904)'. *Modern Language Quarterly* 77, no. 4 (2016): 523–46.
—. 'The Politics of Literary Value in Early Modernist Arabic Comparative Literary Criticism'. *Journal of Arabic Literature* 50, no. 3–4 (2019): 251–77.
Alkan, Burcu and Çimen Günay-Erkol, eds. *Turkish Literature as World Literature.* New York: Bloomsbury, 2021.
Allan, Michael. *In the Shadow of World Literature: Sites of Reading in Colonial Egypt.* Princeton: Princeton University Press, 2016.
Allen, Roger. '*Hadith ᶜIsa Ibn Hisham* by Muhammad Al-Muwailihī'. *Journal of Arabic Literature* 1, no. 1 (1970): 88–108.
—. *The Arabic Novel: An Historical and Critical Introduction.* Syracuse: Syracuse University Press, 1982.
'Almanya İmparator ve İmparatoriçesi Hazaratanın Hazret-i Ömer (r. d.) Cami Havlisinde Duruşları'. *Malumat* 7, no. 160 (24 November 1898): 796.
'Almanya İmparator ve İmparatoriçesi Hazaratanın Hereke Fabrika-i Hümayun Köşkü Kapusunda'. *Malumat* 7, no. 159 (17 November 1898): 780.
'Almanya İmparator ve İmparatoriçesi Hazaratanın Kadim Mescid-i Aksa'dan Çıkışları'. *Malumat* 7, no. 160 (24 November 1898): 800.
'Almanya İmparator ve İmparatoriçesi Hazaratanın Kudüs Şimendöferine Rükubları'. *Malumat* 7, no. 163 (15 December 1898): 869.
Altuğ, Fatih. 'Namık Kemal'in Edebiyat Eleştirisinde Modernlik ve Öznellik'. Unpubl. PhD dissertation, Boğaziçi University, 2007.
Andrews, Walter G. 'Starting Over Again: Some Suggestions for Rethinking Ottoman Divan Poetry in the Context of Translation/Transmission'. In *Translations: (Re)shaping of Literature and Culture*, edited by Saliha Paker, 15–40. Istanbul: Boğaziçi University Press, 2002.
Arslan, C. Ceyhun. 'Kaᶜb ibn Zuhayr Weeps for Sultan Murad IV: Baghdad, Heritage and the Ottoman Empire in Maᶜrūf al-Ruṣāfī's Poetry'. In *The Routledge Handbook of Arabic Poetry*, edited by Suzanne Pinckney Stetkevych and Huda J. Fakhreddine, 201–18. London: Routledge, 2024.
Ayalon, Ami. *The Arabic Print Revolution: Cultural Production and Mass Readership.* Cambridge: Cambridge University Press, 2016.

References

Ayyıldız, Erol. *Arapça bir Rü'ya Fantezisi, Tercemesi ve Namık Kemal'in 'Rü'ya'sı ile Mukayesesi*. Bursa: Uludağ Üniversitesi İlahiyat Fakültesi, n. d.

——. *Irak Şiirinde Yeni Türk Edebiyatı Tesiri*. Bursa: Uludağ Üniversitesi İlahiyat Fakültesi, n. d.

Badawi, M. M. *A Short History of Modern Arabic Literature*. Oxford: Clarendon Press, 1993.

Baker, Patricia L. 'The Fez in Turkey: A Symbol of Modernization?' *Costume* 20, no. 1 (1986): 72–85.

Balaÿ, Christophe. 'Diasporadaki Fars Edebiyatı: İstanbul 1865–1895'. Translated by Çiğdem Kurt. In *Tanzimat ve Edebiyat: Osmanlı İstanbulu'nda Modern Edebi Kültür*, edited by Fatih Altuğ and Mehmet Fatih Uslu, 267–78. Istanbul: Türkiye İş Bankası Kültür Yayınları, 2014.

Bashkin, Orit. '"Religious Hatred Shall Disappear from the Land": Iraqi Jews as Ottoman Subjects, 1864–1913'. *International Journal of Contemporary Iraqi Studies* 4, no. 3 (2010): 305–23.

Baydas, Khalil. 'Stages for the Mind'. Introduced and translated by Spencer Scoville. In *The Arab Renaissance: A Bilingual Anthology of the* Nahda, edited by Tarek El-Ariss, 206–16. New York: The Modern Language Association of America, 2018.

Beecroft, Alexander. *An Ecology of World Literature: From Antiquity to the Present Day*. Brooklyn: Verso, 2015.

Behdad, Ali. *Belated Travelers: Orientalism in the Age of Colonial Dissolution*. Durham, NC: Duke University Press, 1994.

Ben Ismail, Youssef. 'A History of the Ottoman Fez before Mahmud II (c. 1600–1800)'. *Muqarnas* 38, no. 1 (2021): 155–83.

Benigni, Elisabetta. '"Metempsychosis" and "Marvelous Affinities": Re-Imagining the Past in the *Ilyāḏah* by Sulaymān al-Bustānī (1904) and in the *Divano di ᶜOmar ben al-Fared* by Pietro Valerga (1874)'. *Oriente Moderno* 101 (2021): 275–98.

Bernheimer, Charles, ed. *Comparative Literature in the Age of Multiculturalism*. Baltimore: Johns Hopkins University Press, 1995.

Bilgegil, M. Kaya. *Harâbât Karşısında Nâmık Kemâl*. Erzurum: Salkımsöğüt Yayınevi, 2014.

——. *M. Kaya Bilgegil'in Makaleleri*. Edited by Zöhre Bilgegil. Ankara: Kültür Bakanlığı, 1993.

——. *Ziyâ Paşa Üzerinde bir Araştırma*. Istanbul: Atatürk Üniversitesi Basımevi, 1970.

Bin Tyeer, Sarah R. and Claire Gallien, eds. *Islam and New Directions in World Literature*. Edinburgh: Edinburgh University Press, 2022.

Blumi, Isa. *Reinstating the Ottomans: Alternative Balkan Modernities, 1800–1912*. New York: Palgrave Macmillan, 2011.

Booth, Marilyn. *Classes of Ladies of Cloistered Spaces: Writing Feminist History through Biography in fin-de-siècle Egypt*. Edinburgh: Edinburgh University Press, 2015.

——, ed. *Migrating Texts: Circulating Translations around the Ottoman Mediterranean*. Edinburgh: Edinburgh University Press, 2019.

Booth, Marilyn and A. Holly Shissler, 'Fatma Aliye's *Nisvan-ı İslam*: Istanbul, Beirut, Cairo, Paris, 1891–6'. In *Ottoman Translations: Circulating Texts from Bombay to Paris*, edited by Marilyn Booth and Claire Savina, 327–88. Edinburgh: Edinburgh University Press, 2023.

Booth, Marilyn and Claire Savina, eds. *Ottoman Translations: Circulating Texts from Bombay to Paris*. Edinburgh: Edinburgh University Press, 2023.

Boqvist, Marianne. 'Visualising the Ottoman Presence in Damascus: Interpreting 16th Century Building Complexes'. In *Istanbul as Seen from a Distance: Centre and Provinces in the Ottoman Empire*, edited by Elisabeth Özdalga, M. Sait Özervarlı and Feryal Tansuğ, 121–38. Istanbul: Swedish Research Institute in Istanbul, 2011.

Bozarslan, Hamit. 'The Ottomanism of the Non-Turkish Groups: The Arabs and the Kurds after 1908'. *Die Welt des Islams* 56, no. 3–4 (2016): 317–35.

Bradley, Mark. 'Introduction'. In *Classics and Imperialism in the British Empire*, edited by Mark Bradley, 1–26. New York: Oxford University Press, 2010.

Brockelmann, Carl. *Geschichte der arabischen Litteratur*. Leipzig: C. F. Amelangs Verlag, 1909.

Camoglu, Arif. 'Inter-Imperial Dimensions of Turkish Literary Modernity'. *MFS Modern Fiction Studies* 64, no. 3 (2018): 431–57.

Carducci, Karen L. 'Redeeming Jocasta: Tawfiq al-Hakim's "Eastern", "Arab" Reception of Sophocles' *Oedipus Tyrannus*'. *Classical Receptions Journal* 11, no. 1 (2019): 100–16.

Cooppan, Vilashini. 'The Ethics of World Literature: Reading Others, Reading Otherwise'. In *Teaching World Literature*, edited by David Damrosch, 34–43. New York: The Modern Language Association of America, 2009.

Cenab Şahabeddin. *Hac Yolunda*. Istanbul: Matbaa-i Ahmet İhsan, 1909.

Cenap Şahabettin. *Âfâk-ı Irak: Kızıldeniz'den Bağdat'a Hatıralar*, edited by Bülent Yorulmaz. Istanbul: Dergâh Yayınları, 2002.

'Cevab'. *Malumat* 8. no 169 (26 January 1899): 970–71.

Chambers, Iain. *Mediterranean Crossings: The Politics of an Interrupted Modernity*. Durham, NC: Duke University Press, 2008.

Chow, Rey. 'In the Name of Comparative Literature'. In *Comparative Literature in the Age of Multiculturalism*, edited by Charles Bernheimer, 107–16. Baltimore: Johns Hopkins University Press, 1995.

Clancy-Smith, Julia A. *Mediterraneans: North Africa and Europe in an Age of Migration, c. 1800–1900*. Berkeley: University of California Press, 2011.

Csirkés, Ferenc. 'Turkish/Turkic Books of Poetry, Turkish and Persian Lexicography: The Politics of Language under Bayezid II'. In *Treasures of Knowledge: An Inventory of the Ottoman Palace Library (1502/3–1503/4)*, edited by Gülru Necipoğlu, Cemal Kafadar and Cornell H. Fleischer, 673–733. Leiden: Brill, 2019.

Çelik, Zeynep, ed. *Avrupa Şark'ı Bilmez: Eleştirel Bir Söylem (1872–1932)*. Istanbul: Koç Üniversitesi Yayınları, 2020.

Çetinsaya, Gökhan. *The Ottoman Administration of Iraq, 1890–1908*. Abingdon: Routledge, 2017.

Dağlar, Abdülkadir. 'Klâsik Türk Edebiyatı Şerh Geleneği ve Hacı İbrâhim Efendi'nin Şerh-i Belâgat'ına Dâir'. *Turkish Studies* 2, no. 2 (2007): 161–78.

Ḍayf, Shawqī. *Al-Adab al-ᶜarabī al-muᶜāṣir*. Cairo: Dār al-Maᶜārif, 1957.

Deringil, Selim. '"They Live in a State of Nomadism and Savagery": The Late Ottoman Empire and the Post-Colonial Debate'. *Comparative Studies in Society and History* 45, no. 2 (2003): 311–42.

Deuchar, Hannah Scott and Bridget Gill. '"Pour Our Treasures into Foreign Laps": The Translation of *Othello* into Arabic and Ottoman Turkish'. In *Ottoman Translations: Circulating Texts from Bombay to Paris*, edited by Marilyn Booth and Claire Savina, 69–98. Edinburgh: Edinburgh University Press, 2023.

Develi, Hayati. *Osmanlı'nın Dili*. Istanbul: 3F Yayınevi, 2006.

DeYoung, Terri. *Mahmud Sami Al-Barudi: Reconfiguring Society and the Self*. Syracuse: Syracuse University Press, 2015.

Di Leo, Jeffrey R. *On Anthologies: Politics and Pedagogy*. Lincoln: University of Nebraska Press, 2004.

[Dilmen], İbrahim Necmi. *Tarih-i Edebiyat Dersleri*. Istanbul: Matbaa-i Amire, 1922.

Dizdaroğlu, Hikmet, Nurullah Ataç and Sami N. Özerdim. *Ataç: Ataç Üzerine, Söyleşiler, Nurullah Ataç Bibliyografyası*. Ankara: Ankara Üniversitesi Basımevi, 1962.

Dolcerocca, Özen Nergis. '"Free Spirited Clocks": Modernism, Temporality and *The Time Regulation Institute*'. *Middle Eastern Literatures* 20, no. 2 (2017): 177–97.

Duff, David. *Modern Genre Theory*. London: Routledge, 2000.

Dupont, Anne-Laure. *Ǧurǧī Zaydān, 1861–1914: écrivain réformiste et témoin de la renaissance arabe*. Damascus: Institut Français du Proche-Orient, 2006.

Ebüzziya Tevfik. *Merhum Namık Kemal Bey*. Istanbul, AH 1327 [1909/10].

——. *Numune-i Edebiyat-ı Osmaniyye*. Istanbul: Matbaa-i Ebüzziya, AH 1307 [1889/90].

——. *Yeni Osmanlılar Tarihi*. Istanbul: Kervan, 1973–74.

El-Ariss, Tarek. *Leaks, Hacks and Scandals: Arab Culture in the Digital Age*. Princeton: Princeton University Press, 2019.

——. 'Let There Be *Nahdah*'. *Cambridge Journal of Postcolonial Literary Inquiry* 2, no. 2 (2015): 260–66.

——, ed. *The Arab Renaissance: A Bilingual Anthology of the* Nahda. New York: The Modern Language Association of America, 2018.

El-Enany, Rasheed. 'Tawfīq al-Ḥakīm and the West: A New Assessment of the Relationship'. *British Journal of Middle Eastern Studies* 27, no. 2 (2000): 165–75.

Elinson, Alexander E. *Looking Back at al-Andalus: The Poetics of Loss and Nostalgia in Medieval Arabic and Hebrew Literature*. Boston: Brill, 2009.

Ersoy, Ahmet A. 'Ottomans and the Kodak Galaxy: Archiving Everyday Life and Historical Space in Ottoman Illustrated Journals'. *History of Photography* 40, no. 3 (2016): 330–57.

[Ertaylan], İsmail Hikmet. *Türk Edebiyatı Tarihi I–IV.* Ankara: Türk Tarih Kurumu Basımevi, 2011.

——. *Ziya Paşa: Hayatı ve Eserleri*. Istanbul: Kanaat Kütüphanesi, 1932.

Ertürk, Nergis. *Grammatology and Literary Modernity in Turkey*. Oxford: Oxford University Press, 2013.

——. 'An Uncanny Turkic: İsmail Gasprinskii's Language Lesson'. *Middle Eastern Literatures* 19, no. 1 (2016): 34–55.

Esen, Nüket. *Hikâye Anlatan Adam: Ahmet Mithat*. Istanbul: İletişim, 2014.

Etman, Ahmed. 'The Greek Concept of Tragedy in Arab Culture. How to Deal with an Islamic *Oedipus*?' *Documenta* 22, no. 4 (2004): 281–99.

Evered, Emine Ö. *Empire and Education under the Ottomans: Politics, Reform and Resistance from the Tanzimat to the Young Turks*. London: I. B. Tauris, 2012.

Faik, Esad and Ali Sedad. 'Aynen Varakadır'. *Ceride-i Havadis* 4893 (4 March 1882): 3.

Fani, Aria and Kevin L. Schwartz. 'Persianate Pasts; National Presents: Persian Literary and Cultural Production in the Twentieth Century'. *Iranian Studies* 55, no. 3 (2022): 605–9.

Fawwāz, Zaynab. *al-Durr al-manthūr fī ṭabaqāt rabbāt al-khudūr.* Bulaq: al-Matbaᶜa al-Kubrā al-Amiriyya, AH 1312 [1894/95].

Fazlıoğlu, İhsan. 'Osmanlı Döneminde "Bilim" Alanında Türkçe Telif ve Tercüme Eserlerinin Türkçe Oluş Nedenleri ve Bu Eserlerin Dil Bilincinin Oluşmasındaki Yeri ve Önemi'. *Kutadgubilig* 3 (2003): 87–106.

Fazlıoğlu, Şükran. *Arap Romanında Türkler*. Istanbul: Küre Yayınları, 2006.

Feldman, Walter. 'The Indian Style and the Ottoman Literary Canon'. *International Journal of Persian Literature* 3 (2018): 3–38.

'Fez or Tarbush'. *Textile Research Centre Leiden*. https://trc-leiden.nl/trc-digital-exhibition/index.php/from-kaftan-to-kippa/item/54-fez-and-tarbush.

Findley, Carter V. *Turkey, Islam, Nationalism and Modernity: A History, 1789–2007*. New Haven: Yale University Press, 2010.

Fortna, Benjamin C. *Learning to Read in the Late Ottoman Empire and the Early Turkish Republic.* London: Palgrave Macmillan, 2011.

Freud, Sigmund. *Interpreting Dreams*. London: Penguin Books, 2006.

'Galatat'. *Malumat* 7, no. 157 (3 November 1898): 740–43.

Ghraowi, Ghayde and Hacı Osman Gündüz (Ozzy), eds. 'The Ascendant Field: Critical Engagements with Ottoman Arabic Literature'. *Philological Encounters* 7, no. 3–4 (2022).

Gibb, E. J. W. *A History of Ottoman Poetry*. England: Luzac & co., 1900–9.

Goethe, Johann Wolfgang von. *Briefe*: *mit Einleitungen und Erläuterungen*. Edited by Philipp Stein. Berlin: Otto Eisner, 1905.

——. *West-östlicher Divan*. Leipzig: Insel, 1912.

Gould, Rebecca. 'Inimitability versus Translatability: The Structure of Literary Meaning in Arabo-Persian Poetics'. *Translator* 19, no. 1 (2013): 81–104.

Göçgün, Önder. *Ziya Paşa*. Izmir: Kültür ve Turizm Bakanlığı, 1987.

Greene, Annie. 'Burying a Rabbi in Baghdad: The Limits of Ottomanism for Ottoman-Iraqi Jews in the Late Nineteenth Century'. *Journal of Jewish Identities* 12, no. 2 (2019): 97–123.

Guillory, John. *Cultural Capital: The Problem of Literary Canon Formation*. Chicago: University of Chicago Press, 1993.

Guth, Stephan. *Brückenschläge: eine integrierte 'turkoarabische' Romangeschichte (Mitte 19. bis Mitte 20. Jahrhundert)*. Wiesbaden: Reichert Verlag, 2003.

—. 'From Water-Carrying Camels to Modern Story-Tellers, or How "*riwāya*" Came to Mean [Novel]: A History of an Encounter of Concepts'. In *Borders and Beyond: Crossings and Transitions in Modern Arabic Literature*, edited by Kerstin Eksell and Stephan Guth, 147–79. Wiesbaden: Harrassowitz Verlag, 2011.

Güler Aydın, Derya. 'Tanpınar'ın Saatleri Ayarlama Enstitüsü'nde Weber'in İzsürümü: Rasyonel ve İrrasyonel Değerler'. *Bilig* 94 (2020): 29–50.

Gürbilek, Nurdan. 'Dried Spring, Blind Mirror, Lost East: Ophelia, Water and Dreams'. Translated by Victoria Holbrook. *Middle Eastern Literatures* 20, no. 2 (2017): 133–61.

Haarmann, Ulrich W. 'Ideology and History, Identity and Alterity: The Arab Image of the Turk from the ᶜAbbasids to Modern Egypt'. *International Journal of Middle East Studies* 20, no. 2 (1988): 175–96.

Hacı İbrahim. 'Bakiye-i İbret'. *Tercüman-ı Hakikat* 1257 (23 August 1882): 3.

—. 'Bahs ü Münazaradan Husule Gelen Netayic'. *Tercüman-ı Hakikat* 1113 (3 March 1882): 2–3.

—. 'Mevadd-ı Fenniyye: Tercüman-ı Hakikat'in 1115 Numaralı Nüshasına Belagat-ı Osmaniyye Mübahasesine Dair Münderic Olan Makale Üzerine Mütalaa', *Tercüman-ı Hakikat* 1121 (13 March 1882): 3.

—. 'Mevadd-ı Fenniyye'. *Tercüman-ı Hakikat* 1136 (30 March 1882): 3–4.

—. 'Mevadd-ı Fenniyye: Belagat-ı Osmaniyye. İbrahim ve Abdülrahman Efendiler'e Mukabele'. *Tercüman-ı Hakikat* 1115 (6 March 1882): 3.

—. 'Mülahazat'. *Tercüman-ı Hakikat* 1293 (4 October 1882): 3.

—. 'Rusuhi, Ali Raif Efendi'ye Cevab'. *Saadet* 338 (18 April 1886).

—. 'Saadetlü el-Hac İbrahim Efendi Hazretleri Tarafından Bu Kere Dahi Tevarüd Eden Varakadır'. *Vakit* 8, no. 2514 (4 November 1882): 3.

—. 'Saadetlü el-Hac İbrahim Efendi Hazretlerinden Mevrud Varakadır'. *Tarık* 5, no. 1525 (25 August 1888): 3.

—. 'Saadetlü el-Hac İbrahim Efendi Hazretlerinin Varakalarından'. *Tarık* 5, no. 1200 (9 September 1888): 3.

—. 'Saadetlü el-Hac İbrahim Efendi Hazretlerinin Bu Kere Dahi İrsal Buyurmuş Oldukları Varakadır'. *Vakit* 8, no. 2510 (31 October 1882): 3.

—. 'Saadetlü el-Hac İbrahim Efendi Hazretlerinin Varakalarında Beyan Olunan Ruzname-i İmtihandan Ma Bad'. *Tarık* 5, no. 1650 (29 October 1888): 3.

——. 'Saadetlü el-Hac İbrahim Efendi Hazretlerinin Varakalarından Ma Bad'. *Tarık* 7, no 1200 (9 September 1888): 3.
——. 'Saadetlü el-Hac İbrahim Efendi Hazretlerinden Varid Olan Varakadır'. *Tarık* 5, no. 1594 (3 September 1888): 3.
——. 'Tercüman-ı Hakikat'ın 1305 Numaralı Nüshasındaki İtirazata Cevab'. *Vakit* 8, no. 2501 (21 October 1882): 3.
——. 'Teşekkür ve Temenni'. *Tercüman-ı Hakikat* 1146 (12 April 1882): 2.
al-Ḥakīm, Tawfīq. *ᶜAwdat al-rūḥ*. Cairo: Maktabat al-Ādāb, n. d. [1933].
——. *ᶜAwdat al-waᶜī*. Cairo: Maktabat Miṣr, n. d. [1974].
——. *Fann al-adab*. Cairo: Maktabat Miṣr, n. d. [1952].
——. *Al-Malik Ūdīb*. Cairo: Maktabat Miṣr, n. d. [1949].
——. *Miṣr bayna ᶜahdayn*. Cairo: Maktabat Miṣr, n. d. [1983].
——. *Plays, Prefaces and Postscripts of Tawfiq al-Hakim*. Washington, DC: Three Continents Press, 1981.
——. *Return of the Spirit*. Translated by William Maynard Hutchins. New York: Penguin, 2019.
'Haleb Kalesi'nden Kışla-i Hümayun'e Doğru Bir Manzara'. *Malumat* 8, no. 178 (6 April 1899): 1159.
Ḥarb, Muḥammad. *Riḥlat Jurjī Zaydān ilā al-Āstāna ᶜām 1909*. Cairo: Dār al-Hilāl, 2004.
Hardwick, Lorna. 'Sophocles' *Oedipus* and Conflicts of Identity in Post-Colonial Context'. *Documenta* 22, no. 4 (2004): 376–87.
Hatem, Mervat F. *Literature, Gender and Nation-Building in the Nineteenth-Century Egypt: The Life and Works of ᶜAᵓisha Taymur*. New York: Palgrave Macmillan, 2011.
Havemann, Axel. 'Between Ottoman Loyalty and Arab "Independence": Muḥammad Kurd ᶜAlī, Ǧirǧī Zaydān and Šakīb Arslān'. *Quaderni Di Studi Arabi* 5/6 (1987): 347–56.
Havlioğlu, Didem. *Mihrî Hatun: Performance, Gender-Bending and Subversion in Ottoman Intellectual History*. New York: Syracuse University Press, 2017.
Haleb'den: Refet. 'Şemmet ül-Edeb'. *Malumat* 7, no. 161 (1 December 1898): 823.
Hill, Peter and Johann Strauss. 'Khayr al-Din al-Tunisi's *Muqaddima* to *Aqwam al-masalik fi maᶜrifat ahwal al-mamalik* (*The Surest Path to Knowing the Conditions of Kingdoms*) in Arabic, French and Ottoman Turkish'. In *Ottoman Translations: Circulating Texts from Bombay to Paris*, edited by Marilyn Booth and Claire Savina, 121–89. Edinburgh: Edinburgh University Press, 2023.
Hodgkin, Samuel. 'Classical Persian Canons of the Revolutionary Press: Abū al-Qāsim Lāhūtī's Circles in Istanbul and Moscow'. In *Persian Literature and Modernity: Production and Reception*, edited by Hamid Rezaei Yazdi and Arshavez Mozafari, 185–212. London: Routledge, 2019.
Holbrook, Victoria Rowe. *The Unreadable Shores of Love: Turkish Modernity and Mystic Romance*. Austin: University of Texas Press, 1994.
Holt, Elizabeth M. *Fictitious Capital: Silk, Cotton and the Rise of the Arabic Novel*. New York: Fordham University Press, 2017.

——. 'From Gardens of Knowledge to Ezbekiyya after Midnight: The Novel and the Arabic Press from Beirut to Cairo, 1870–1892'. *Middle Eastern Literatures* 16, no. 3 (2013): 232–48.

Ḥusayn, Ṭāhā. *Mustaqbal al-thaqāfa fī Miṣr*. Cairo: Dār al-Maᶜārif, n. d. [1938].

Hämeen-Anttila, Jaakko. *Maqama: A History of a Genre*. Wiesbaden: Harrassowitz Verlag, 2002.

al-Imām ᶜAlī. *Dīwān Amīr al-Muʾminīn al-Imām ᶜAlī bin Abī Ṭālib raḍiya Allāh ᶜanhu wa karrama Allāh wajhah*. Edited by ᶜAbd al-ᶜAzīz al-Karam. N. p., 1988.

d'Istria, Dora. *La Poésie des Ottomans*. Paris: Maisonneuve, 1877.

ᶜIzz al-Dīn, Yūsuf. *al-Ruṣāfī yarwī sīrat ḥayātih: sijill li-l-ḥayā al-ijtimāᶜiyya wa-l-siyāsiyya wa-l-fikriyya bi-kull jarāʾa wa-ṣarāḥa*. Damascus: Manshūrāt al-Madā, 2004.

İbrahim Avni. 'Saadetlü el-Hac İbrahim Efendi Hazretlerinin Varakalarında Beyan Olunan Ruzname-i İmtihandan Ma Bad'. *Tarık* 5, no. 1251 (30 October 1888): 3.

'İbrahim Efendi Hazretlerine Mukabele', *Tercüman-ı Hakikat* 1130 (23 March 1886): 3.

İhsanoğlu, Ekmeleddin. *Darülfünun: Osmanlı'da Kültürel Modernleşmenin Odağı*. Istanbul: IRCICA, 2010.

——. *The Turks in Egypt and Their Cultural Legacy: An Analytical Study of the Turkish Printed Patrimony in Egypt from the Time of Muhammad 'Ali with Annotated Bibliographies*. Translated by Humphrey Davies. New York: The American University in Cairo Press, 2012.

İnal, Mahmud Kemal, ed. *Son Asır Türk Şairleri*. Istanbul: Milli Eğitim Basımevi, 1970.

'İmparator ve İmparatoriçe Hazaratanın Protestan Kilisesini Ziyaretleri'. *Malumat* 7, no. 163 (15 December 1898): 868.

İsmail Hakkı. *Muallim Naci Efendi*. Istanbul: Nişan Berberyan Matbaası, AH 1311 [1893/94].

İsmail Zühdü. 'Muhbir-i Mahsusamızın Mektupları 2 (Kudüs Hatıratı)'. *İkdam* 5, no. 1553 (5 November 1898): 1.

İyişenyürek, Orhan. 'Köprülüzâde Abdullah Paşa ve El Yazısı Divanının Muhtevası'. *Cumhuriyet İlahiyat Dergisi* 26, no. 1 (2022): 23–44.

Jabbari, Alexander. 'From Persianate Cosmopolis to Persianate Modernity: Translating from Urdu to Persian in Twentieth-Century Iran and Afghanistan'. *Iranian Studies* 55, no. 3 (2022): 611–30.

——. 'The Making of Modernity in Persianate Literary History'. *Comparative Studies of South Asia, Africa and the Middle East* 36, no. 3 (2016): 418–34.

Jacob, Wilson Chacko. *Working Out Egypt: Effendi Masculinity and Subject Formation in Colonial Modernity, 1870–1940*. Durham, NC: Duke University Press, 2011.

Jauss, Hans Robert. 'Theory of Genres and Medieval Literature'. In *Modern Genre Theory*, edited by David Duff, 127–47. New York: Routledge, 2000.

Johnson, Rebecca C. *Stranger Fictions: A History of the Novel in Arabic Translation*. Ithaca: Cornell University Press, 2021.
Joyce, James. *A Portrait of the Artist as a Young Man*. Trans. Jeri Johnson. New York: Oxford University Press, 2008.
Jusdanis, Gregory. *Belated Modernity and Aesthetic Culture: Inventing National Literature*. Minneapolis: University of Minnesota Press, 1991.
Kadhim, Hussein N. *The Poetics of Anti-Colonialism in the Arabic* Qaṣīdah. Boston: Brill, 2004.
Kaplan, Mehmet, İnci Enginün and Birol Emil, eds. *Yeni Türk Edebiyati Antolojisi I*. Istanbul: Marmara Üniversitesi Yayınevi, 1988.
Kaplan, Mehmet, İnci Enginün and Birol Emil, eds. *Yeni Türk Edebiyati Antolojisi II*. Istanbul: Marmara Üniversitesi Yayınevi, 1993.
Kaplan, Mehmet, İnci Enginün, Birol Emil and Zeynep Kerman, eds. *Yeni Türk Edebiyati Antolojisi III*. Istanbul: Marmara Üniversitesi Yayınevi, 1994.
Karacagil, Ö. Kürşad. 'II. Wilhelm'in Osmanlı İmparatorluğu'nu Ziyareti ve Mihmandarı Mehmed Şakir Paşa'nın Günlüğü (1898)'. *Türkiyat Mecmuası* 24, no. 2 (2014): 73–97.
Karakoç, Kani İrfan. 'Ulus-devletleşme Süreci ve "'Türk' Edebiyatı"nın İnşası (1923–1950)'. Unpubl. PhD dissertation, İhsan Doğramacı Bilkent University, 2012.
Kern, Karen M. *Imperial Citizen: Marriage and Citizenship in the Ottoman Frontier Provinces of Iraq*. Syracuse: Syracuse University Press, 2011.
Khaldi, Boutheina. *Egypt Awakening in the Early Twentieth Century: Mayy Ziyādah's Intellectual Circles*. New York: Palgrave Macmillan, 2012.
al-Khālidī, Rūḥī. *Tārīkh ᶜilm al-adab ᶜinda al-Ifranj wa-l-ᶜArab wa-Fīktūr Hūkū*. Damascus: Ittiḥād al-Kuttāb wa-l-Ṣuḥufiyyīn al-Filasṭīniyyīn, 1984.
Al-Khateeb, H. 'Rūḥī al-Khālidī: A Pioneer of Comparative Literature in Arabic'. *Journal of Arabic Literature* 18, no. 1 (1987): 81–87.
al-Khatīb, Ḥ. *Rūḥī al-Khālidī: rāᵓid al-adab al-ᶜarabī al-muqāran*. Amman: Dār al-Karmal, 1985.
Khayyat, E. 'Bastards and Arabs'. In *Handbook and Reader of Ottoman Arabic*, edited by Esther-Miriam Wagner, 87–140. Cambridge: Open Book Publishers, 2021.
——. *Istanbul 1940 and Global Modernity: The World According to Auerbach, Tanpınar and Edib*. Lanham: Lexington Books, 2019.
Khuri-Makdisi, Ilham and Yorgos Dedes. 'Translating Qasim Amin's Arabic *Tahrir al-marᵓa* (1899) into Ottoman Turkish'. In *Ottoman Translations: Circulating Texts from Bombay to Paris*, edited by Marilyn Booth and Claire Savina, 227–85. Edinburgh: Edinburgh University Press, 2023.
Kia, Mana. *Persianate Selves: Memories of Place and Origin before Nationalism*. Palo Alto: Stanford University Press, 2020.
Kim, Sooyong and Orit Bashkin. 'Revisiting Multilingualism in the Ottoman Empire'. *Review of Middle East Studies* 55, no. 1 (2021): 130–45.
Kim, Sooyong. *The Last of an Age: The Making and Unmaking of a Sixteenth-Century Ottoman Poet*. London: Routledge, 2018.

——. 'The Poet Nefʿī, Fresh Persian Verse and Ottoman Freshness'. *Iranian Studies* 55, no. 2 (2022): 551–73.

Köker, Neveser. 'Inconvertible Romance: Piety, Community and the Politically Disruptive Force of Love in *Akabi Hikayesi*'. In *Ottoman Culture and the Project of Modernity: Reform and Translation in the Tanzimat Novel*, edited by Monica M. Ringer and Etienne E. Charrière, 133–46. London: I. B. Tauris, 2020.

Köprülü, Mehmed Fuat and Şehabeddin Süleyman. *Malumat-ı Edebiyye*. Istanbul: Kanaat Matbaası, 1914/15.

Köroğlu, Erol. 'Tanpınar'a Göre Ahmet Midhat: Esere Hayattan Girmek yahut Eseri Hayatla Yargılamak'. In *Merhaba Ey Muharrir!: Ahmet Mithat Üzerine Eleştirel Yazılar*, edited by Nüket Esen and Erol Köroğlu, 329–38. Istanbul: Boğaziçi Üniversitesi Yayınevi, 2006.

Kramnick, Jonathan Brody. *Making the English Canon: Print-Capitalism and the Cultural Past, 1700–1770*. Cambridge: Cambridge University Press, 1998.

'Kudüs-ü Şerif Manazarından Jeriko Şehriyle Bahr-ı Lut'. *Malumat* 7, no. 168 (19 December 1898): 168.

Kuntay, Mithat Cemal. *Namık Kemal: Devrinin İnsanları ve Olayları Arasında*. Istanbul: Milli Eğitim Basımevi, 1949.

Kuru, Selim. 'Early, Yet Already Late: Literary Musings on Historical Questions'. *Journal of the Ottoman and Turkish Studies Association* 7, no. 1 (2020): 55–57.

Le Bon, Gustave. *Avrupa Harbinden Alınan Psikolociyai* [Psikolojik] *Dersler*. Translated by Abdullah Cevdet. Istanbul: Kanaat Matbaası, 1918.

——. *La Civilisation des Arabes*. Paris: Librairie de Firmin-Didot et Cie, 1884.

——. *Ruh ül-cemaat*. Translated by Mehmed Fuad Köprülü and Sadreddin Celal. Istanbul: Uhuvvet Matbaası, AH 1327 [1909/10].

——. *Ruh-ı Siyaset ve Müdafaa-i İctimaiyye*. Translated by Mehmet Fuad Köprülü. Istanbul: Ahmet İhsan ve Şürekası Matbaacılık Osmanlı Şirketi, 1910.

Levend, Agah Sırrı. *Ahmet Rasim*. Ankara: Ankara Üniversitesi Basımevi, 1965.

Levy, Lital. 'The *Nahḍa* and the *Haskala*: A Comparative Reading of "Revival" and "Reform"'. *Middle Eastern Literatures* 16, no. 3 (2013): 300–16.

'Lisan-ı Osmani'. *Malumat* 7, no. 162 (8 December 1898): 839.

'Lisan-ı Osmani'. *Malumat* 7, no. 163 (15 December 1898): 859.

Liu, Lydia H. *Translingual Practice: Literature, National Culture and Translated Modernity – China, 1900–1937*. Palo Alto: Stanford University Press, 1995.

Lornejad, Siavash and Ali Doostzadeh. *On the Modern Politicization of the Persian Poet Nezami Ganjavi*. Yerevan: Caucasian Centre for Iranian Studies, 2012.

Lustig, Darrah. 'The Task of the Survivor in Ruth Klüger's "weiter leben" (1992) and "Still Alive" (2001)'. *Studia austriaca*, 21 (2013): 29–50.

Makdisi, Ussama. 'Ottoman Orientalism'. *The American Historical Review* 107, no. 3 (2002): 768–96.

Manjak bin Muḥammad Bāshā. *Hādhā dīwān al-Amīr Manjak Ibn al-Marḥūm Muḥammad Bāshā*. Damascus: al-Maṭbaʿa al-Ḥifniyya, AH 1301 [1883/84].

Marcus, Sharon. *Between Women: Friendship, Desire and Marriage in Victorian England*. Princeton: Princeton University Press, 2007.
Mardin, Şerif. *The Genesis of Young Ottoman Thought: A Study in the Modernization of Turkish Political Ideas*. Syracuse: Syracuse University Press, 2000.
Markiewicz, Christopher. 'Books on the Secretarial Arts and Literary Prose'. In *Treasures of Knowledge: An Inventory of the Ottoman Palace Library (1502/3–1503/4)*, edited by Gülru Necipoğlu, Cemal Kafadar and Cornell H. Fleischer, 1: 657–72. Leiden: Brill, 2019.
Masters, Bruce. *The Arabs of the Ottoman Empire, 1516–1918: A Social and Cultural History*. New York: Cambridge University Press, 2013.
Mattar, Karim. *Specters of World Literature: Orientalism, Modernity and the Novel in the Middle East*. Edinburgh: Edinburgh University Press, 2020.
Melas, Natalie. *All the Difference in the World: Postcoloniality and the Ends of Comparison*. Palo Alto: Stanford University Press, 2007.
Mestyan, Adam. *Arab Patriotism: The Ideology and Culture of Power in Late Ottoman Egypt*. Princeton: Princeton University Press, 2017.
al-Miṣrī, Ḥusayn Mujīb. *Bayna al-adab al-ᶜarabī wa-l-turkī: dirāsa fī al-adab al-islāmī al-muqāran*. Cairo: al-Dār al-Thaqāfiyya li-l-Nashr, 2003.
Mizancı Murat. *Turfanda mı yoksa Turfa mı*. Istanbul: Mahmud Bey Matbaası, AH 1308 [1890/91].
Motika, Raoul and Christoph Herzog. 'Orientalism *Alla Turca*: Late 19th/Early 20th Century Ottoman Voyages into the Muslim "Outback"'. *Die Welt des Islams* 40, no. 2 (2000): 139–95.
Morna, Berna. *Türk Romanına Eleştirel Bir Bakış 1: Ahmet Mithat'tan Ahmet Hamdi Tanpınar'a*. Istanbul: İletişim Yayınları, 2004.
Mufti, Aamir R. *Forget English!: Orientalisms and World Literatures*. Cambridge: Harvard University Press, 2016.
'Muḥammad Nāmiq Kamāl Bek'. *Al-Hilāl* 5, no. 5 (1896): 162–67.
al-Musawi, Muhsin J. *The Medieval Islamic Republic of Letters: Arabic Knowledge Construction*. Notre Dame: University of Notre Dame Press, 2015.
Muslu, Ramazan. *Emir Abdülkādir El-Cezâirî ve Tasavvufî Görüşleri*. Istanbul: İnsan Yayınları, 2011.
al-Mutanabbī, Abū al-Ṭayyib. *Dīwān al-Mutanabbī*. Beirut: Dār Bayrūt, 1983.
al-Muwayliḥī, Ibrāhīm. *Mā hunālika*. Cairo: Maṭbaᶜat al-Muqaṭṭam, 1896.
——. *Spies, Scandals and Sultans: Istanbul in the Twilight of the Ottoman Empire*. Translated by Roger Allen. Lanham: Rowman & Littlefield Publishers, 2008.
al-Muwayliḥī, Muḥammad. *What ᶜĪsā ibn Hishām Told Us, or, A Period of Time*. Edited and translated by Roger Allen. New York: New York University Press, 2015.
'Mülahazat'. *Malumat* 7, no. 165 (29 December 1898): 901.
al-Nahrawali, Qutb al-Din. *Journey to the Sublime Porte: The Arabic Memoir of a Sharifian Agent's Diplomatic Mission to the Ottoman Imperial Court in the Era of Süleyman the Magnificent*. Translated by Richard Blackburn. Beirut: Ergon Verlag Würzburg in Kommission, 2015.

Namık Kemal. *Doğumunun Yüzellinci Yılında Namık Kemal*. Ankara: Atatürk Kültür Merkezi, 1993.

——. *Külliyat-ı Kemal. Birinci Tertib. 3. Makalat-ı Siyasiyye ve Edebiyye*. Istanbul: Selanik Matbaası, n. d.

——. *Mukaddime-i Celal*. Istanbul: Matbaa-i Ebüzziya, AH 1309 [1891/92].

——. *Namık Kemal'in Talim-i Edebiyat Üzerine Bir Risalesi*. Edited by Necmettin Halil Onan. Ankara: Milli Eğitim Basımevi, 1950.

——. *Rüya ve Magosa Mektubu*. Cairo: Matbaa-i İctihad, 1908.

——. *Tahrib-i Harabat*. Istanbul: Matbaa-i Ebüzziya, AH 1303 [1885/86].

——. 'Kemal Bey'in Bir Makalesi'. *Şark*. Edited by Mustafa Reşid. 1, no. 5 (AH 1298 [1880/81]): 97–101.

Niyazioğlu, Aslı. *Dreams and Lives in Ottoman Istanbul: A Seventeenth Century Biographer's Perspective*. New York: Routledge, 2017.

Noorani, Yaseen. 'Translating World Literature into Arabic and Arabic into World Literature: Sulayman al-Bustani's *al-Ilyadha* and Ruhi al-Khalidi's Arabic Rendition of Victor Hugo'. In *Migrating Texts: Circulating Translations around the Ottoman Mediterranean*, edited by Marilyn Booth, 236–65. Edinburgh: Edinburgh University Press, 2019.

Novillo-Corvalán, Patricia. 'Joyce's and Borges's Afterlives of Shakespeare'. *Comparative Literature* 60, no. 3 (2008): 207–27.

Ouyang, Wen-chin. *Poetics of Love in the Arabic Novel: Nation-State, Modernity and Tradition*. Edinburgh: Edinburgh University Press, 2012.

Özdalga, Elisabeth, M. Sait Özervarlı and Feryal Tansuğ, eds. *Istanbul as Seen from a Distance: Centre and Provinces in the Ottoman Empire*. Istanbul: Swedish Research Institute in Istanbul, 2011.

Özgül, M. Kayahan. *Dîvân Yolu'ndan Pera'ya Selâmetle: Modern Türk Şiirine Doğru*. Ankara: Hece Yayınları, 2006.

——. *Kemâl'le İhtimal yahut Nâmık Kemâl'in Şiirine Tersten Bakmak*. Istanbul: Dergâh Yayınları, 2014.

Paker, Saliha. 'On the Poetic Practices of "a Singularly Uninventive People" and the Anxiety of Imitation: A Critical Re-Appraisal in Terms of Translation, Creative Mediation and "Originality"'. In *Tradition, Tension and Translation in Turkey*, edited by John Milton, Saliha Paker and Şehnaz Tahir Gürçağlar, 27–52. Amsterdam: John Benjamins Publishing Company, 2015.

——. 'Translation as Terceme and Nazire: Culture-Bound Concepts and Their Implications for a Conceptual Framework for Research on Ottoman Translational History'. In *Crosscultural Transgressions: Research Models in Translation Studies II: Historical and Ideological Issues*, edited by Theo Hermans, 120–43. Northampton: St Jerome Pub, 2002.

——. 'Turkish Tradition'. In *Routledge Encyclopedia of Translation Studies*, edited by Mona Baker, 571–82. New York: Routledge, 2001.

Pala, İskender. *Ansiklopedik Divân Şiiri Sözlüğü*. Ankara: Akçağ Basım, 1990.

Pamuk, Şevket. *Uneven Centuries: Economic Development of Turkey since 1820*. Princeton: Princeton University Press, 2018.

Parla, Jale. *Babalar ve Oğullar: Tanzimat Romanının Epistemolojik Temelleri.* Istanbul: İletişim Yayınları, 2004.
Parlatır, İsmail. 'Rüya'nın Fikir Örgüsü'. In *Doğumunun Yüzellinci Yılında Namık Kemal*, 59–66. Ankara: Atatürk Kültür Merkezi Yayınları, 1993.
Philipp, Thomas. *Jurji Zaidan and the Foundations of Arab Nationalism: A Study.* Syracuse: Syracuse University Press, 2014.
——. 'Jurji Zaidan and the Ottoman Revolution: Between Arab Nationalism and Ottomanism, 1908–1914'. In *Jurji Zaidan: Contributions to Modern Arab Thought and Literature*, edited by George C. Zaidan and Thomas Philipp, 145–63. Bethesda: Zaidan Foundation, 2013.
Pratt, Mary Louise. *Imperial Eyes: Travel Writing and Transculturation.* New York: Routledge, 2003.
Pormann, Peter E. 'The Arab "Cultural Awakening (*Nahḍa*)", 1870–1950 and the Classical Tradition'. *International Journal of the Classical Tradition* 13, no. 1 (2006): 3–20.
al-Qaysi, Abdul Wahhab Abbas. 'The Impact of Modernization on Iraqi Society during the Ottoman Era: A Study of Intellectual Development in Iraq, 1869–1917'. Unpubl. PhD dissertation, University of Michigan, 1958.
Quataert, Donald. 'Clothing Laws, State and Society in the Ottoman Empire, 1720–1829'. *International Journal of Middle East Studies* 29, no. 3 (1997): 403–25.
Qutbuddin, Tahera. 'Books on Arabic Philology and Literature: A Teaching Collection Focused on Religious Learning and the State Chancery'. In *Treasures of Knowledge: An Inventory of the Ottoman Palace Library (1502/3–1503/4)*, edited by Gülru Necipoğlu, Cemal Kafadar and Cornell H. Fleischer, 1: 607–34. Leiden: Brill, 2019.
al-Rashūdī, ᶜAbd al-Ḥamīd. *Al-Ruṣāfī: ḥayātuh–āthāruh–shiᶜruh.* Beirut: Manshūrāt al-Jamal, 2012.
——. *Dhikrā al-Ruṣāfī.* Baghdad: Maktabat al-Zawrāʾ, 1950.
Rastegar, Kamran. 'Literary Modernity between Arabic and Persian Prose: Jurji Zaydan's Riwayat in Persian Translation'. *Comparative Critical Studies* 4, no. 3 (2007): 359–78.
——. *Literary Modernity between the Middle East and Europe: Textual Transactions in Nineteenth-Century Arabic, English and Persian Literatures.* New York: Routledge, 2007.
Recaizade Mahmud Ekrem. 'Mevadd-ı Fenniyye: Arz-ı Mazeret ve Beyan-ı Nedamet'. *Tercüman-ı Hakikat* 1304 (17 October 1882): 2–3.
——. *Talim-i Edebiyat.* Istanbul: Mihran Matbaası, AH 1299 [1881/82].
'Resimlerimiz'. *Malumat* 8, no. 175 (16 March 1899): 1110–11.
Ricci, Ronit. *Islam Translated: Literature, Conversion and the Arabic Cosmopolis of South and Southeast Asia.* Chicago: University of Chicago Press, 2011.
Ringer, Monica M. and Etienne Charrière, eds. *Ottoman Culture and the Project of Modernity: Reform and Translation in the Tanzimat Novel.* New York: I. B. Tauris, 2020.

Roper, Geoffrey. 'Aḥmad Fāris Al-Shidyāq and the Libraries of Europe and the Ottoman Empire'. *Libraries & Culture* 33, no. 3 (1998): 233–48.

Ross, Trevor. *The Making of the English Literary Canon: From the Middle Ages to the Late Eighteenth Century*. Montreal and Kingston: McGill-Queen's University Press, 1998.

al-Rūṣafī, Maᶜrūf. *Āthāruhu fī al-naqd wa-l-adab*, 3 vols. Edited by Dāwūd Sallūm, ᶜĀdil Kuttāb Naṣīf al-ᶜAzzāwī and ᶜAbd al-Ḥamīd al-Rashūd. Beirut: Manshūrāt al-Jamal, 2014.

——. 'Dafᶜ al-hujna fī irtiḍākh al-lukna'. In *Āthāruhu fī al-naqd wa-l-adab*, edited by Dāwūd Sallūm, ᶜĀdil Kuttāb Naṣīf al-ᶜAzzāwī and 'Abd al-Ḥamīd al-Rashūdī, 2: 145–99. Beirut: Manshūrāt al-Jamal, 2014.

——. *Dīwān al-Ruṣāfī*. Beirut: Maṭbaᶜat Dār al-Maᶜraḍ, 1931.

——. *Dīwān al-Ruṣāfī*. Edited by Muṣṭafā ᶜAlī. Baghdad: Manshūrāt Wizārat al-Iᶜlām fī al-Jumhūriyya al-ᶜIrāqiyya, 1972–77.

——. *Dīwān al-Ruṣāfī*. Edited by Muṣṭafā al-Saqqā. Cairo: Dār al-Fikr al-ᶜArabī, 1953.

——. *Al-Risāla al-ᶜirāqiyya fī al-siyāsa wa-l-dīn wa-l-ijtimāᶜ, yalīhi Kāmil al-Jādirjī fī ḥiwār maᶜa al-Ruṣāfī*. Beirut: Manshūrāt al-Jamal, 2012.

——. 'al-Ruʾyā fī baḥth al-ḥurriya'. In *Āthāruhu fī al-naqd wa-l-adab*, edited by Dāwūd Sallūm, ᶜĀdil Kuttāb Naṣīf al-ᶜAzzāwī and ᶜAbd al-Ḥamīd al-Rashūdī, 3: 620–42. Beirut: Manshūrāt al-Jamal, 2014.

Ruşen Eşref. *Diyorlar ki*. Istanbul: Kanaat Matbaası, 1918.

Sacks, Jeffrey. *Iterations of Loss: Mutilation and Aesthetic Form, Al-Shidyaq to Darwish*. New York: Fordham University Press, 2015.

——. 'Latinity'. *CR: The New Centennial Review* 9, no. 3 (2009): 251–86.

Ṣāʾib Tabrīzī. *Dīvān-i Ṣāʾib Tabrīzī*. Tehran: Shirkat-i Intishārāt-i ᶜIlmī va Farhangī, 1992.

Saᶜīd, Jamīl. *Naẓarāt fī al-tayyārāt al-adabiyya al-ḥadītha fī al-ᶜIrāq*. Cairo: Maᶜhad al-Dirāsāt al-ᶜArabiyya al-ᶜĀliyya, 1954.

Sālim, Muḥammad Ḥāmid. 'Rithāʾ al-mudun bayna al-shāᶜir al-turkī Sulaymān Naẓīf wa-l-ᶜirāqī Maᶜrūf al-Ruṣāfī: "Baghdād" Numūdhajan'. *Majallat al-Dirāsāt al-Sharqiyya* 57 (2016): 441–523.

Sanni, Amidu. 'The Discourse on Laḥn in Arabic Philological and Literary Traditions'. *Middle Eastern Literatures* 13, no. 1 (2010): 1–19.

Sarıtaş, İbrahim. 'Alman İmparatorluğu'nun Türk Dünyasına Yönelik Propaganda Faaliyetleri: Arkeolog Max Freiherr von Oppenheim ve Doğu Haber Ajansı'. *Bilig* 91 (2019): 113–35.

Selim, Samah. 'The Narrative Craft: Realism and Fiction in the Arabic Canon'. *Edebiyat: Journal of Middle Eastern Literatures* 14, no. 1–2 (2003): 109–28.

——. 'Translation, Popular Fiction and the Nahdah in Egypt'. In *Other Renaissances: A New Approach to World Literature*, edited by Brenda Deen Schildgen, Gang Zhou and Sander L. Gilman, 35–58. New York: Palgrave Macmillan: 2006.

Semenderî, Mehnâz and Esedullâh Vâhid. 'Ḥayāt-i adabī-yi Żiyā Pāshā va zabān-i fārsī'. *Nüsha: Şarkiyat Araştırmaları Dergisi* 16, no. 42(2016): 55–68.
Shalan, Jeff. 'Writing the Nation: The Emergence of Egypt in the Modern Arabic Novel'. *Journal of Arabic Literature* 33, no. 3 (2002): 211–47.
Sharārah, ᶜAbd al-Laṭīf. *al-Ruṣāfī: Dirāsa taḥliliyya*. Beirut: Dār Ṣādir, 1960.
al-Shayyāl, Jamāl al-Dīn. *Tārīkh al-tarjama wa-l-ḥaraka al-thaqāfiyya fī ᶜaṣr Muḥammad ᶜAlī*. Cairo: Dār al-Fikr al-ᶜArabī, 1951.
Sheehi, Stephen. *The Arab Imago: A Social History of Portrait Photography, 1860–1910*. Princeton: Princeton University Press, 2016.
——. 'Towards a Critical Theory of *al-Nahḍah*: Epistemology, Ideology and Capital'. *Journal of Arabic Literature* 43, no. 2–3 (2012): 269–98.
Shāfiᶜī, Muḥammad ibn Idrīs. *Dīwān al-Shāfiᶜī*. Edited by Muḥammad ᶜAbd al-Munᶜim Khafājī. Cairo: Maktabat al-Kulliyāt al-Azhariyya, 1985.
Siddiq, Muhammad. *Arab Culture and the Novel: Gender, Identity and Agency in Egyptian Fiction*. New York: Routledge, 2007.
Snir, Reuven. 'Arabic Journalism as a Vehicle for Enlightenment: Iraqi Jews in the Arabic Press During the Nineteenth and Twentieth Centuries'. *Journal of Modern Jewish Studies* 6, no. 3 (2007): 219–37.
——. '"If I Forget Thee, O Baghdad": The Demise of Arab-Jewish Identity and Culture'. *Asian and African Studies* 30, no. 1 (2021): 173–88.
——. *Modern Arabic Literature: A Theoretical Framework*. Edinburgh: Edinburgh University Press, 2017.
Somay, Bülent. *The Psychopolitics of the Oriental Father: Between Omnipotence and Emasculation*. New York: Palgrave Macmillan, 2014.
Stetkevych, Suzanne Pinckney. *The Mantle Odes: Arabic Praise Poems to the Prophet Muḥammad*. Bloomington: Indiana University Press, 2010.
Strauss, Johann. *The Egyptian Connection in Nineteenth-Century Ottoman Literary and Intellectual History*. Beirut: Orient-Institut der Deutschen Morgenländischen Gesellschaft, 2000.
'Sual'. *Malumat* 7, no. 164 (22 December 1898): 887.
Sulaymān, ᶜAshrātī. *Al-Amīr ᶜAbd al-Qādir fī Bilād al-Mashriq*. Algiers: Dār al-Quds al-ᶜArabī li-l-Nashr wa-l-Tawzīᶜ, 2011.
Suleiman, Yasir. *The Arabic Language and National Identity: A Study in Ideology*. Edinburgh: Edinburgh University Press, 2003.
'Suriye'ye Vuku Seyahatleri Hasebiyle "Hohenzollern" Yatıyla Birlikte Beyrut Taraflarına Gitmek Üzere Köprüden Huruc Eden "İclaliyye" Zırhlı-i Hümayunun Resmini de Bu Nüshamızda Dercediyoruz'. *Malumat* 7, no. 168 (19 December 1898): 960.
Süleyman Nazif. *Firak-ı Irak*. Istanbul: Mahmud Bey Matbaası, 1918.
——. *İki Dost*. Istanbul: Kanaat Kütüphanesi, 1925.
'Şam'da Sultan-ı Selim Cami-i Şerifi'. *Malumat* 8, no. 173 (18 February 1899): 1076.
Şehabeddin Süleyman. *Tarih-i Edebiyat-ı Osmaniyye*. Istanbul: Sancakyan Matbaası, 1912.

Şemseddin Sami. *Kamus-ı Türki*. Istanbul: Ahmet Cevdet Matbaası, 1900.
——. *Lisan*. Istanbul: Mihran Matbaası, 1885.
——. 'Şiir ve Edebiyattaki Teceddüd-i Ahîrimiz'. In *Yeni Türk Edebiyatı Antolojisi III*, edited by Mehmet Kaplan, İnci Enginün, Birol Emil and Zeynep Kerman, 3: 318–23. Istanbul: Marmara Üniversitesi Yayınevi, 1994.
Şemsettin Sami. *Süreli Yayınlarda Çıkmış Dil ve Edebiyat Yazıları: İnceleme–Metin*. Edited by Yüksel Topaloğlu. Istanbul: Ötüken, 2012.
'Şevketlü Padişahımız Gazi Büyük Abdülhamid Han-ı Sani Efendimiz Hazretleri ve Almanya İmparatoru Haşmetlü İkinci Wilhelm Hazretleri'. *Malumat* 7, no. 155 (20 October 1898): 705–6.
Tageldin, Shaden M. *Disarming Words: Empire and the Seductions of Translation in Egypt*. Berkeley: University of California Press, 2011.
——. 'One Comparative Literature?: "Birth" of a Discipline in French-Egyptian Translation, 1810–1834'. *Comparative Literature Studies* 47, no. 4 (2010): 411–45.
Tahsin Paşa. *Abdülhamid: Yıldız Hatıraları*. Istanbul: M. A. Halit Kitaphanesi, 1931.
al-Ṭahṭāwī, Rifāᶜa Rāfiᶜ. 'Takhlīṣ al-ibrīz fī talkhīṣ Bārīz aw al-dīwān al-nafīs bi-Īwān Bārīs'. In *al-Aᶜmāl al-kāmila li-Rifāᶜa Rāfiᶜ al-Ṭahṭāwī*. Edited by Muḥammad ᶜAmāra, 13–305. Cairo: Dār al-Shurūq, 2010.
Tanpınar, Ahmet Hamdi. *Edebiyat Üzerine Makaleler*. Edited by Zeynep Kerman. Istanbul: Dergâh Yayınları, 1977.
——. *Günlüklerin Işığında Tanpınar'la Başbaşa*. Edited by İnci Enginün and Zeynep Kerman. Istanbul: Dergâh Yayınları, 2007.
——. *Mektuplar*. Ankara: Kültür Bakanlığı, 1974.
——. *Mücevherlerin Sırrı: Derlenmemiş Yazılar, Anket ve Röportajlar: Deneme, Söyleşi*. Edited by İlyas Dirin, Turgay Anar and Şaban Özdemir. Istanbul: Yapı Kredi Yayınları, 2002.
——. *On Dokuzuncu Asır Türk Edebiyatı Tarihi*. Istanbul: Dergâh Yayınları, 2018.
——. *Saatleri Ayarlama Enstitüsü*. Istanbul: Dergâh Yayınları, 2017.
——. *The Time Regulation Institute*. New York: Penguin, 2013.
——. *Yaşadığım Gibi*. Edited by Birol Emil. Istanbul: Dergâh Yayınları, 1996.
Taşdelen, Esra. 'Literature as a Mirror of History: A Comparative Study of the Historical Fictions of Ahmet Hikmet Müftüoğlu (1870–1927) and Jurjī Zaydān (1861–1914)'. Unpubl. PhD dissertation, University of Chicago, 2014.
et-Tehtavi, Rifaa. *Tercüme-i Rıhlet-i Rifaa*. Translated by Rüstem Besim. Cairo: Matbaa-i Sahib es-Saadet el-Ebediyye, AH 1255 [1839/40].
'Terakkiyat-ı Ciddiye Muhibbanına Müjde!' *Malumat* 174, no. 8 (6 March 1899): 1081–82.
Tevfik Fikret. *Rübâb-ı Şikeste ve Tevfik Fikret'in Bütün Diğer Eserleri*. Edited by Fahri Uzun. Istanbul: İnkilâp Kitabevi, 1985.
——. *Rübab-ı Şikeste*. Istanbul: Tanin Matbaası, 1910/11.
al-Tikriti, Nabil. 'Ottoman Iraq', *The Journal of the Historical Society* 7, no. 2 (2007): 201–11.

Tızlak, Fahrettin. 'Hatt-ı Hümayunlar Işığında III. Selim Dönemi'nde İstanbul'da Fırınların ve Ekmeklerin Tebdil-i Kıyafetle Denetimi'. *Cedrus* 3 (2015): 337–50.

Todorov, Tzvetan. 'The Origin of Genres'. In *Modern Genre Theory*, edited by David Duff, 193–209. New York: Routledge, 2000.

Tuğluk, Abdulhakim. 'Ebüzziya Tevfik'in "Merhûm Nâmık Kemâl Bey" Adlı Eseri (İnceleme-Metin)'. *Türkiyat Mecmuası* 28, no. 1 (2018): 179–99.

Turan, Namık Sinan. '16. Yüzyıldan 19. Yüzyıl Sonuna Dek Osmanlı Devletine Gayri Müslimlerin Kılık Kıyafetlerine Dair Düzenlemeler'. *Ankara Üniversitesi SBF Dergisi* 60, no. 4 (2005): 239–67.

Tzoreff, Avi-ram. 'Acknowledging Loss, Materializing Language: Translation and Hermeneutics of Gaps in Nineteenth Century Baghdad'. *Middle Eastern Studies* 59, no. 1 (2023): 1–21.

Uslu, Mehmet Fatih and Fatih Altuğ, eds. *Tanzimat ve Edebiyat: Osmanlı Istanbulu'nda Modern Edebi Kültür*. Istanbul: Türkiye İş Bankası Kültür Yayınları, 2014.

Viersen, Harald. 'The Ethical Dialectic in al-Jabri's "Critique of Arab Reason"'. In *Islam, State and Modernity: Mohammed Abed al-Jabri and the Future of the Arab World*, edited by Zaid Eyadat. New York: Palgrave Macmillan, 2018.

Wagner, Esther-Miriam, ed. *A Handbook and Reader of Ottoman* Arabic. Cambridge: Open Book Publishers, 2021.

al-Warrāq, Maḥmūd. *Dīwān Maḥmūd al-Warrāq: shāᶜir al-ḥikma wa-l-mawᶜiẓa*. Ajman: Muᵓassasat al-Funūn, 1991.

Wick, Alexis. *The Red Sea: In Search of Lost Space*. Oakland: University of California Press, 2016.

Yağlı, Ali. 'Une étude comparative entre *Le Comte de Monte-Cristo* d'Alexandre Dumas Père et *Denizci Hasan* (Hasan le Marin) d'Ahmet Mithat Efendi'. *RumeliDE Dil ve Edebiyat Araştırmaları Dergisi* 18 (2020): 457–69.

Yamini-Hamedani, Azadeh. 'Foundational Metaphors: Goethe's World Literature; Posnett's Comparative Literature'. In *Foundational Texts of World Literature*, edited by Dominique Jullien, 155–64. New York: Peter Lang, 2011.

Yashin, Veli N. '"The True Face of the Work": Sovereignty and Literary Form in Literary Historiography'. *Middle Eastern Literatures* 20, no. 2 (2017): 162–76.

Yessayan, Zabel. *In the Ruins: The 1909 Massacres of Armenians in Adana, Turkey*. Translated by G. M. Goshgarian. Boston: AIWA Press, 2016.

Zaidan, George C. and Thomas Philipp, eds. *Jurji Zaidan: Contributions to Modern Arab Thought and Literature*. Bethesda: Zaidan Foundation, 2013.

Zaydān, Jurjī. 'Aḥmad Midḥat: al-Kātib al-turkī al-shahīr'. *Al-Hilāl* 21, no. 6 (1913): 355–57.

——. 'Ājāl al-duwal aw iᶜmārahā qadīman wa ḥadīthan'. *al-Hilāl* 21, no. 8 (1913): 451–66.

——. *The Autobiography of Jurji Zaidan: Including Four Letters to His Son*. Washington, DC: Three Continents Press, 1990.

——. 'al-Astāna al-ᶜaliyya'. *al-Hilal* 18, no. 1 (1909): 3–38.

——. 'al-Astāna al-ᶜaliyya'. *al-Hilāl* 18, no. 2 (1909): 67–107.
——. 'al-Astāna al-ᶜaliyya'. *al-Hilāl* 18, no. 3 (1909): 131–65.
——. *al-Ḥajjāj bin Yūsuf*. Cairo: Maṭbaᶜat al-Hilāl, 1902.
——. *Tarājim mashāhīr al-sharq fī al-qarn al-tāsiᶜ ᶜashr*. Beirut: Manshūrāt Dār Maktabat al-Ḥayāh, n. d. [1902–3].
——. *Tārīkh ādāb al-lugha al-ᶜarabiyya*. Beirut: Dār al-Fikr, 2011.
——. *Tārīkh al-tamaddun al-islāmī*. Cairo: Maṭbaᶜat al-Hilāl, 1902.
Zeki. 'Muktetafat'. *Malumat* 7, no. 160 (24 November 1898): 801–2.
——. 'Muktetafat'. *Malumat* 7, no. 164 (22 December 1898): 883.
——. 'Muktetafat'. *Malumat* 8, no. 171 (16 February 1899): 1018–19.
Zeydan, Corci. *Medeniyet-i İslamiyye Tarihi*. Translated by Zeki Megamiz. Istanbul: İkdam Matbaası, 1912/13.
Ziya Paşa. *Harabat*. Istanbul: Matbaa-i Amire, AH 1291–92 [1874/75–75/76].
——. *Mukaddime-i Harabat*. Istanbul: Matbaa-i Ebüzziya, AH 1311 [1893/94].
——. 'Şiir ve İnşa'. *Hürriyet* 11 (7 September 1868): 4–7.
Ziyāda, Mayy. 'al-Gharāʾiz al-saykūlūjiyya al-thalāth'. *Al-Muqtaṭaf* 68 (April 1926): 385–94.

Index

Note: authors with surnames in square brackets are filed under the first letter of that surname

Abū Tammām, 42, 56, 148
adab, 10–11
afterlife concept, 5, 6
Ahmed Çelebi, 1–2, 8, 38
Ahmet Cevdet Pasha, 73, 121
Ahmet Midhat, 3, 19, 62, 78n, 146, 147, 155, 181, 197
  Ahbar-ı Asara Tamim-i Enzar, 101
  criticism of, 109
  and deterritorialisation, 85
  disguising texts, 103–4
  Hasan Mellah, 19–20, 84–6, 87–92, 104–7
  'Ölüm Allah'ın Emri', 106
  prose works, 105
  'Romancı ve Hayat', 105
  'true form' of the novel, 101
Ahmet Rasim, 21, 145, 146, 154–64, 198, 199
  Arapların Terrakkiyat-ı Medeniyyesi, 160–1
  İlk Büyük Muharrirlerden Şinasi, 162–3
  iltikat, 160
  and the 'new literature', 155
  photos, 21, 156
  and taverns, 155
  visit to Syria, 154–7
Ahmet Vefik Pasha, 100
Aksoy, Musa, 149
Alfaisal, Haifa Saud, 70, 197–8
Allan, Michael, 11, 58
Altuğ, Fatih, 72
Amīn, Qāsim, 127
Andalusian literature, 39, 40, 41, 42, 45–6, 47, 70, 182
Andrews, Walter G., 106
Anvarī, 40, 134
Arabic canon, 7
Arabic language, 122–3
  in al-Ruṣāfī's writings, 122–5, 127–8
  boundaries with Turkish language, 119, 123, 124, 127–8, 129
  classical Arabic, 137
  translations between Arabic and Turkish, 126–8, 129–31
  view of Ottoman language as Arabic, 149–50
  words, 122–28
Arabic literature, 2, 10–11, 16–17, 36, 37–8, 56, 126
  Arabic poetry in *Harabat*, 38–40, 41–2, 45–6
  and the classics debate, 65–75
  clothes metaphor, 173
  construction of, 202
  equivalence with Turkish literature, 57, 58, 60, 63
  first Arabic novel, 109–10
  and French literature, 57
  and global capitalism, 100

influence on Ottoman culture, 21, 72–3, 157–8
Iraq and the Arabic literary modernity, 119–22
literature as a matter of debts and transactions, 154–64
and Middle Eastern Studies, 198–9
as national literature, 6, 20, 64, 75n, 110, 199–200
non-Ottoman Arabic texts, 9
Ottoman literature as Arabic literature, 150
similarities with Turkish literature, 15
as springs (*menba*), 18
as works of distant ancestors, 3
as world literature, 196–7, 198–9
Asmai, 127
Ataç, Nurullah, 126
Atatürk, Mustafa Kemal, 95
Atufi, 39–40, 41
authenticity, 22, 116n, 171–2, 180, 183, 190, 196
Ayyıldız, Erol, 128–9, 131, 132

Badawi, Muhammad, 126
Baghdad, 16, 17, 30, 119, 120, 131, 132–3, 134, 135, 136, 139–40n
Baki, 34
al-Bārūdī, Maḥmūd Sāmī, 65–6
Bashkin, Orit, 4
Baydas, Khalīl, 101
Beecroft, Alexander, 57
Behdad, Ali, 162
Beirut, 16, 17, 59, 136, 200
Bilgegil, M. Kaya, 11, 29
Boileau, 70
Boqvist, Marianne, 29
Boucher, Richard, 66
Bradley, Mark, 73
Brockelmann, Carl, 158

Cairo, 59–60, 92, 93, 108, 174, 176, 178, 200
Camoglu, Arif, 9
Cenab Şahabeddin, 5, 16, 120
Ceride-i Havadis, 150
Çetinsaya, Gökhan, 120
Charrière, Etienne E., 14
Chow, Rey, 31
Clancy-Smith, Julia A., 87
classics/classical, 19, 56, 58–9, 110
and Arabic literature, 65–75
definition of, 66–7
and Orientalism, 74
refashioning, 199–200
Zaydān's use of the term, 67–8
close reading, 13, 14–15
Comparative Literature, 5, 56–7, 63, 68–9, 71, 198, 202
Csirkés, Ferenc, 41

Damascus, 29–30, 41
darülfünun, 44
Dedalus, Stephen, 103
Dedes, Yorgos, 127
Deringil, Selim, 17, 120
deterritorialisation, 85, 90, 92, 99, 103, 104, 107–8
Di Leo, Jeffrey, 30
dictionaries, 83, 94, 125
[Dilmen], İbrahim Necmi, 37
disguise and camouflage, 20, 83–117
clothing as disguise, 89, 91, 93, 94–6, 109
gender and religious difference in Ahmet Midhat's *Hasan Mellah*, 87–92
and identity, 87, 88–9
imagery of, 85
and mobility, 107–8
people in disguise, 86–100
tabdīl/tebdil, 93–4, 103
taming the ghost in al-Muwayliḥī's *What ʿĪsā ibn Hishām Told Us*, 92–100
texts in disguise, 100–10
displacement, 20, 45, 47, 84, 85, 86, 93, 100, 104, 109
d'Istria, Dora, 74, 158
divan poetry, 46–7, 181
Diyorlar ki, 5
Dolcerocca, Özen Nergis, 188
dream genre, 131
dress regulations, 86–7, 94–5
Dumas, Alexandre, 106
Dupont, Anne-Laure, 57, 59, 158

Ebussuud Efendi, 1
Ebüzziya Tevfik, 31, 32, 34, 63, 163–4
  Merhum Namık Kemal Bey, 62
edeb, 11
edebiyat, 11
Egypt, 11, 124, 171
  in al-Ḥakīm's writings, 172–9
  personality and spirit of, 173
  and Westernisation, 173
El-Ariss, Tarek, 12
[Eldem], İsmail Hakkı, 19, 56, 66, 73, 75n
Elinson, Alexander E., 45
Eliot, T. S., 66
Ersoy, Ahmet A., 157
Ersoy, Mehmet Akif, 183
[Ertaylan], İsmail Hikmet, 37
Ertürk, Nergis, 59, 85, 108
Evered, Emine Ö., 120
Evliya Çelebi, *Seyahatname,* 4

Fakhr-i Dāʿī, 158
families
  in al-Ḥakīm *Return of the Spirit*, 172–9
  in Tanpınar *The Time Regulation Institute*, 179–90
Fani, Aria, 199
al-Farazdaq, 48, 66
Fatma Aliye, 63–4
Fatma Fahrünnisa, 10
Fawwāz, Zaynab, 63–4, 102, 198
Fazlıoğlu, İhsan, 128
Fazlıoğlu, Şükran, 17, 60
Feldman, Walter, 11
fez *see* tarboosh (fez)
Firdavsī, 6, 32, 40
Fortna, Benjamin C., 59
Freud, Sigmund, 171
Fuzuli, 40, 119, 132, 133–5, 137, 201

garden imagery, 100
Gasprinskii, İsmail, 85
Ghraowi, Ghayde, 8–9
Gibb, Elias John Wilkinson, 158
Goethe, Johann Wolfgang von, 48
grammar, 68, 83, 124, 125–6, 127
Greene, Annie, 32–3
Guillory, John, 7, 35
Güler Aydın, Derya, 188
Gülhane Decree 1839, 47
Gündüz, Hacı Osman (Ozzy), 8–9
Gürbilek, Nurdan, 180
Guth, Stephan, 102

Haarmann, Ulrich W., 17
Hacı İbrahim, 21, 145–69, 157, 162, 171, 198, 199
  and al-Mutanabbī, 146–54
  Imruʾ al-Qays, discussion of, 148–9
  comparing Arabic poetry to diet, 147–8
  life details, 147
  and Orientalist scholarship, 152–3
  as a supporter of the 'old literature', 146
  view of Ottoman language as Arabic, 149–50
  view that Ottomans should learn Arabic, 153
hafid, 49
al-Ḥakīm, Tawfīq, 3, 9, 22, 68
  adaptation of *Oedipus Rex*, 173, 192–3n
  belief in Oedipal complex, 170–1, 172–9
  Return of the Spirit, 171, 172–9
  and Westernisation, 171–2, 173–4
Halide Edib, 4–5, 10, 16
al-Hamadānī, Badīʿ al-Zamān, 107
Harabat see Ziya Pasha
Hardwick, Lorna, 170
al-Ḥarīrī, *Maqāmāt*, 1, 21–2, 107, 151, 163
Ḥassān ibn Thābit, 119, 133–4, 135
Hatem, Mervat F., 11
Havlioğlu, Didem, 7, 15
al-Hilāl, 18–19, 58, 60, 62, 64, 103
historical methodology/history, 10, 13–17, 162
Hodgkin, Samuel, 6
Holbrook, Victoria Rowe, 2, 5–6
Holt, Elizabeth M., 100
homeland, 60–1, 66, 87, 122, 132, 134–5, 136
Hovsep Vartan Pasha, 92
Hürriyet, 33
Hutchins, William M., 173, 179

Ibn Abī Sulmā, Zuhayr, 149, 153–4
Ibn al-ʿArabī, 29, 30
Ibn al-Fāriḍ, 38, 39–40, 42

Ibn al-Rūmī, 40, 42, 66
İbrahim Avni, 151
Ibrāhīm, Ḥāfiẓ, 136
İkdam, 121, 156
iltikat, 160
imperialism, 9, 15, 57, 135, 177, 182–3, 201
Imruʾ al-Qays, 21, 61, 99, 146, 148–9, 153–4
influence paradigm, 2, 3–4, 181–2
interculture concept, 6, 7
Iraq, 118, 200
  and the Arabic literary modernity, 119–22
  Jews, 139–40n
  Ottoman defeat in Iraq, 20–1, 119, 131–3, 134–8
  Ottoman policies, 120–1
Islahat Decree 1856, 47, 90
Istanbul, 17, 64, 66, 99, 118, 121–2, 129, 136, 147, 158, 180

Jabbari, Alexander, 3
Jacob, Wilson Chacko, 95
Jago, Thomas S., 29–30
al-Jāḥiẓ, 42, 66, 92
Jarīr, 40
Jauss, Hans Robert, 104
al-Jazāʾirī, ʿAbd al-Qādir, 200, 204n
Johnson, Rebecca C., 69
Joyce, James, 103

Kaʿb ibn Zuhayr, 6, 23, 41, 70, 118, 119, 133–5, 137, 157, 201–2, 203
Kadhim, Hussein N., 136, 137
Khaldi, Boutheina, 9
al-Khālidī, Rūḥī, 19, 63, 64, 66, 68–70, 72, 197, 200
Al-Khateeb, H., 69
Khayyat, E., 38, 181, 183
Khuri-Makdisi, Ilham, 127
Kia, Mana, 198
Kim, Sooyong, 4, 7, 15
Köker, Neveser, 92
Köprülü, Mehmed Fuad, 2, 73, 158
Köprülüzade Abdullah Pasha, 6, 43
Köroğlu, Erol, 109
Kuru, Selim, 13, 14, 15

laḥn, 123
Lamartine, Alphonse de, 48, 72
Le Bon, Gustave, *La Civilisation des Arabes*, 21, 146, 157–61
linguistic traditions, 10, 11–12, 16, 18, 31, 35–7, 182, 196, 197–8, 203
literary modernity, 20, 24n
  and *Harabat*, 44–50
  literature as a matter of debts and transactions, 154–64
  literature as possession, 161–2
  and the Ottoman canon, 3–13
literary networks, 10, 196, 197

al-Maʿarrī, 39, 61, 122, 201
Makdisi, Ussama, 17
Malumat, 21, 145, 146, 150, 151–2, 154, 163–4
  'Muktetafat' section, 155–6, 157
  photos, 21, 146, 156–7
  'Şemmet ül-Edeb' section, 156
maqāma, 86, 102, 103, 104, 106, 107, 109
Marcus, Sharon, 13
Markiewicz, Christopher, 2
Mattar, Karim, 11, 74, 96
Megamiz, Zeki, 121, 127, 156
Midhat Pasha, 120
Mihri Hatun, 7
Misailidis, Evangelinos, 10
Miṣbāḥ al-sharq, 66, 92, 105, 107, 109
Mizancı Murat, 101
Molière, 48, 70
mosques, 42–4
al-Muʿallaqāt, 6, 22, 35, 41, 63, 182
Muallim Naci Efendi, 69, 181
Mufti, Aamir R., 74
Murad III, Sultan, 43
Murad IV, Sultan, 134
al-Musawi, Muhsin J., 58
Mustafa Fazıl/Muṣṭafā Fāḍil Pasha, 33
Mustafa Reşid Pasha, 62
al-Mutanabbī, 1, 2, 3, 5–6, 8, 21, 38, 39, 42, 56, 61–2, 63, 73–4, 99, 122, 132, 134, 135, 155, 156, 201, 202, 203
  as an Ottoman poet, 119
  poetry described as iron chickpeas, 146–54

al-Muwayliḥī, Ibrāhīm, 17, 92, 99, 114n
Mā hunālika (*Spies, Scandals and Sultans*), 99
al-Muwayliḥī, Muḥammad, 5, 8, 66, 109, 200–1
What ᶜĪsa ibn Hishām Told Us, 19–20, 85–6, 92–100, 102, 104, 105, 106, 107–8

al-nahḍa, 12, 13, 15–16, 17, 57, 72, 126, 201
Jurjī Zaydān and the Turkish *nahḍa*, 59–65
al-Nahrawālī, Quṭb al-Dīn, 1–2, 38
Namık Kemal, 5, 18–19, 30, 31, 44, 58, 74, 77n, 100–1, 103, 118, 121, 181, 197, 198
article in *al-Hilāl*, 62–4
criticism of dictionaries, 83, 94
criticism of Ziya Pasha, 70–2
İntibah, 61
as pioneer of modern Turkish literature, 60–1, 62–3, 64, 69, 74
Rüya, 20, 119, 126, 127, 128, 129–31
similarities with French writers, 69–70
Tahrib-i Harabat, 70–2
Vatan yahut Silistre, 87
nazire, 86, 105–7, 109
Nedim, 34
Nefi, 4, 6, 21, 40, 48, 71, 72, 119, 133–5
newspapers, 33, 46, 100, 108, 125, 139
Nigar Hanım, 5
Niyazioğlu, Aslı, 131
Niẓāmī, 42
non-Muslim authors, 202
Noorani, Yaseen, 11, 70
novel genre, 19–20, 83–117
first Arabic novel, 109–10
gender and religious difference in Ahmet Midhat's *Hasan Mellah*, 87–92
and global capitalism, 100, 104, 108
historical novels, 60, 101, 103
maqāma genre, 107–8, 109
people in disguise, 86–100
riwāya, 102
taming the ghost in al-Muwayliḥī's *What ᶜĪsā ibn Hishām Told Us*, 92–100
texts in disguise, 100–10
true form of, 101

ocean metaphor, 18, 31, 48, 49, 65, 72
and the formation of canons, 32–44
Oedipal complex, 22
in al-Ḥakīm *Return of the Spirit*, 172–9
in Tanpınar *The Time Regulation Institute*, 179–90
Orientalism, 74, 152–3, 157–8, 162, 181
Ottoman canon, 1–2
definition and scholarship, 7
deracination of, 8, 35
and the empire's cultural landscape, 197–8
as an imaginary construct, 7–8, 11, 14
and literary modernity, 3–13, 16
and non-Ottoman Arabic texts, 9
reassessment of, 6, 11, 74
as a reservoir, 6, 10, 12, 18–20, 30, 31, 46, 74, 109
women, exclusion of, 9
Ottoman Empire, 15, 16, 17, 131, 200–1
defeat in Iraq, 20–1, 119, 131–3, 134–8
Iraqi policies, 120–1
reforms and changes, 47, 59, 74–5, 84, 90, 104–5
Turkification, 60
Ottoman identity, 2, 83, 90, 92, 95, 135
Ottoman language, 124–6, 128, 148
view of Ottoman language as Arabic, 149–50
Ottoman literati, 4, 6–7, 8, 15, 17, 32, 41, 128, 199, 201–2
Ottoman/Turkish literature, 8, 10–11
Arabic literature, influence of, 21, 72–3, 74, 145–6
boundaries between 'old literature' and 'new literature', 4–5, 15, 21, 145–6
construction of, 202
described as Arabic literature, 150
equivalence with Arabic literature, 57, 58, 60, 63

literature as a matter of debts and transactions, 154–64
as a mirror-image, 19, 58, 60, 63, 73
and Namık Kemal, 60–4
as national literature, 6, 20, 64, 75n, 110, 199–200
as 'our literature', 56
Persian literature, influence of, 73
as a precursor of modern Turkish literature, 12
sense of displacement, 20, 45, 47, 84, 92, 100, 104, 109
similarities between Ottoman and French writers, 69–70
similarities with Arabic literature, 15
as world literature, 23, 85, 196–7
Ottomanism, 32–3, 59, 95
Ouyang, Wen-chin, 107
Özgül, M. Kayahan, 60–1

Paker, Saliha, 2, 6, 126
Pamuk, Şevket, 84, 90
Parla, Jale, 190
Persianate, 2, 3, 4, 6, 40, 198–9, 203
Persian canon, 6, 7
Persian literature, 2, 3, 4, 16–17, 36, 37–8, 56, 61
influence on Ottoman literature, 73
Kerem and Aslı, 106, 107
Persian poetry in *Harabat*, 40–1
as springs (*menba*), 18
as world literature, 198–9
philology, 2, 5–6, 200
photography, 21, 146, 156–7, 158
poetry, 1, 2, 3, 4, 18
and abominable issues, 147, 148–9
Andalusian poems, 39, 40, 41, 42, 45–6, 47, 182
Arabic and Persian influence on Ottoman poetry, 34–5, 36, 37, 37–8, 56, 74
Arabic poetry in *Harabat*, 38–40, 41–2, 45–6
divan poetry, 46–7, 181
folk poetry, 34, 181
Harabat, 29–54
imitation, 34
Muʿallaqāt poems, 41
nazire poems, 86, 105–7, 109
Persian poetry in *Harabat*, 40–1
poet-translators, 6–7
Pratt, Mary Louise, 16
profit, 159–60
Pym, Anthony, 6

Quataert, Donald, 95
Qur'an, 41, 123, 133–4, 135, 160
Qutbuddin, Tahera, 7, 39, 40

Racine, Jean, 48, 70, 72
Rastegar, Kamran, 108
al-Rayḥānī, Amīn, 118
Recaizade Mahmud Ekrem, 109, 129, 145, 147, 149, 181
Ringer, Monica M., 14
Rıza Tevfik, 5
Roper, Geoffrey, 66
Ross, Trevor, 8
al-Rundī, Abū al-Baqāʾ, 45–6
al-Ruṣāfī, Maʿrūf, 9, 20–1, 63, 93–4, 118–44, 197, 198, 200, 202
al-Ruʾyā fī baḥth al-ḥurriya, 119, 127, 129–31
'Baʿda al- Nuzūḥ', 136
complaints about 'commoners', 125, 128
Dafʿ al-hujna fī irtiḍākh al-lukna, 118–19, 123, 124–5, 127, 128, 130
Iraq and the Arabic literary modernity, 119–22
life details, 121–2
'Nuwāḥ Dijla', 119, 128, 131–2, 135–6, 137–8
and the Ottoman language, 124–6, 128
translation, social reform and anxieties about a new language, 122–8
as a translator, 119, 128, 129–31
writings on the Arabic language, 122–5, 127–8
Rüstem Besim, 126–7

Ṣāʾib Tabrīzī, 40–1
Sacks, Jeffrey, 90, 103, 110, 202
Sālim, Muḥammad Ḥāmid, 132
Sami Paşazade Sezai, 5
Sanāʾī, 48, 71–2

Sanni, Amidu, 123
Şark, 61
Schwartz, Kevin L., 199
Şehabeddin Süleyman, 37, 73
self, sense of, 11, 34, 48, 85, 87, 90, 102–3, 170, 180, 191, 198
Selim I, Sultan, 29, 40, 43, 44
Selim, Samah, 102–3
Şemseddin Sami, 87, 101, 110, 125–6, 196
Servet-i Fünun, 151–2
Shalan, Jeff, 177–8
al-Shanfarā, 39, 41
al-Shayyāl, Jamāl al-Dīn, 126
Sheehi, Stephen, 74–5, 84, 109
al-Shidyāq, Aḥmad Fāris, 66
Siddiq, Muhammad, 104
Şinasi, 21, 37, 162–4, 181
solecisms, 123, 128, 129, 130
Somay, Bülent, 95, 162
Sophocles, *Oedipus Rex*, 22, 170–1, 173, 192–3n
sovereignty, 4, 159, 191
spring metaphor, 18, 37–8
Strauss, Johann, 46
Suleiman, Yasir, 122
Süleyman I, Sultan, 43, 44, 70
Süleyman Nazif, 9, 20–1, 29, 44, 118, 122, 128, 137, 197, 198, 203
 'Dicle ve Ben', 131–2, 133
 Firak-ı Irak, 119, 132, 133, 135, 138, 201–2
 'Fuzuli-i Bağdadi'den Nefı-i Erzurumi'ye', 133–5
Syria, 21, 29–30, 120, 146, 154–7

Tageldin, Shaden M., 11, 56–7, 72
Tahsin Pasha, 120
al-Ṭahṭāwī, Rifā῾a Rāfi῾, 57, 121, 126
Tanpınar, Ahmet Hamdi, 22, 37–8, 49, 67, 73
 belief in Oedipal complex and the Turks, 170–1
 On Dokuzuncu Asır Türk Edebiyatı Tarihi, 171, 180–3
 life details, 179–80
 The Time Regulation Institute, 171, 172, 179–90
 views on Arabic literature, 12–13, 22, 37–8, 171–2, 180–3
 and Westernisation, 171–2, 180, 182–3
Tanzimat, 12–13, 21, 63, 64, 84, 90, 126, 161, 181, 183, 190
tarboosh (fez), 19, 83, 93, 94–8, 109, 118
Tarhan, Abdülhak Hamid, 163, 181
Tarık, 150, 151
Tasvir-i Efkar, 62
tavern imagery, 42–3, 44, 46, 70–1, 135, 155
Tercüman-ı Hakikat, 147, 148, 149–50, 153
Tevfik Fikret, 129
textual circulations, 15–16
textual communities, 41
theatre plays, 72, 102, 105
The Thousand and One Nights, 19, 85, 86, 104, 107, 108
Tigris, River, 20, 119, 132, 133, 134, 135–8
Todorov, Tzvetan, 104
tradition, 2, 3, 4, 5, 6–7, 8, 12, 14, 18, 31, 35, 38, 41, 46, 47–8, 71, 96, 100, 101, 110, 157, 162–3, 190, 197, 199–200, 202–3
 Islamic tradition, 131, 183
 Ottoman cosmopolitan tradition, 72
 return to tradition, 180, 182–3
 Roman and Greek traditions, 73
translations, 20, 23, 57, 69, 72, 74, 94, 106, 119, 146, 198, 202
 ability to translate, 151–2
 boundaries, establishing, 119, 123, 162, 198
 al-Ruṣāfī's translations, 129–31
 between Arabic and Turkish, 126–8, 129–31
travel, 4, 5, 15–16, 64, 85, 89, 107, 120, 154–7, 198
Tuğluk, Abdulhakim, 62
turāth, 16, 65, 128, 137, 201
turban (*al-῾imāma*), 97–8, 118
Turkish language
 boundaries with Arabic language, 119, 123, 124, 127–8, 129

language of science, 128
translations between Arabic and Turkish, 126–8, 129–31
Turkish literature *see* Ottoman/Turkish literature

ümm, 49
[Ünaydın], Ruşen Eşref, 5
ᶜUrfī, 40, 134
[Uşaklıgil], Halid Ziya, 5, 37

Wagner, Esther-Miriam, 8
Weber, Max, 188
Westernisation, 33–4, 37, 47–8, 171–2, 173–4, 180, 182–3, 190, 199
Wick, Alexis, 13
women, 9, 63–4, 202
as characters, 129–31, 133

Yamini-Hamedani, Azadeh, 48
Yashin, Veli N., 12, 72, 181
Yessayan, Zabel, 95
Young Ottomans, 32–4, 44, 46, 51n, 181
Young Turk Revolution, 64

Zati, 7
Zaydān, Jurjī, 18–19, 56–82, 75n, 95, 100, 171, 198, 200–1
al-ᶜAbbāsa ukht al-Rashīd, 87
al-Alfāẓ al-ᶜarabiyya wa-l-falsafa al-lughawiyya, 154
Arabic literature and the classics debate, 65–75
as a comparatist, 68–9
compared with Fawwāz, 63–4
disguising texts, 103–4
distinctions between Arabs and Turks, 60
life details, 59–60
and Namık Kemal, 62–5, 103
Tārīkh ādāb al-lugha al-ᶜarabiyya, 58, 60, 64–5, 66, 67, 68, 154
Tārīkh ādāb al-lugha al-turkiyya, 64–5
translations of works into Turkish, 127
and the Turkish *nahḍa*, 59–65
use of ‘classics’ as a term, 67–8
vision of Arab cultural nationalism, 57–8
Ziya Pasha, 3, 9, 10, 18, 29–55, 65, 69–70, 124, 135, 171, 181, 198, 202, 203
Arabic poetry in *Harabat*, 38–40, 41–2, 45–6
compared with Goethe, 48
controversy/criticism about *Harabat*, 69, 70–2
Harabat introduction, 30–1, 35–7, 41–2, 44, 49, 56
hardships and ill health, 44–5
modernity and *Harabat*, 44–50
and mysticism, 35, 37
Ottoman ocean and the formation of canons, 32–44
Persian poetry in *Harabat*, 40–1
reason for the *Harabat* title, 42–3
‘Şiir ve İnşa’, 34–5, 36, 46
similarities with French writers, 69–70
Syrian governor, 29–30
Terci-i Bend, 45, 54n
Terkib-i Bend, 45, 54n
world communities in *Harabat*, 48–9
Ziyāda, Mayy, 9, 196

EU representative:
Easy Access System Europe
Mustamäe tee 50, 10621 Tallinn, Estonia
Gpsr.requests@easproject.com

www.ingramcontent.com/pod-product-compliance
Lightning Source LLC
Chambersburg PA
CBHW070346240426
43671CB00013BA/2416
* 9 7 8 1 3 9 9 5 2 5 8 3 1 *